The Gender

Key psychoanalytic papers on the subject of femininity and masculinity from the very different British, French and American perspectives are brought together in this book for the first time. Indeed, three of the French papers had not been translated into English before. An introductory discussion of important theoretical differences, in particular of the conception of the unconscious and psychic development, enables the reader to overcome the barriers of international dialogue and really to engage with the arguments. The papers are gathered around the central issue of the interplay of body and psyche in psychoanalysis and by examining this interplay Dana Breen offers a way forward in the understanding of femininity. At the same time she shows how the outspoken controversy over femininity has masked a more silent revolution in the understanding of masculinity.

The Gender Conundrum is divided into four sections; the Oedipus complex; the phallic question; the representation of the body; and bisexuality. Papers included are by: M. Aisenstein, D. Bernstein, P. Blos, D. Braunschweig and M. Fain, R. Britton, J. Chasseguet-Smirgel, A. Gibeault, W.H. Gillespie, M. Glasser, R.R. Greenson, M.E. Laufer, A. Limentani, J. McDougall and M. Montrelay.

Offering an international perspective, with introductions of exemplary clarity, this collection of seminal papers fills a considerable gap in the literature and provides a classic reference text for psychoanalysis and gender studies.

Dana Breen is a Training Psychoanalyst in private practice and is actively involved in the training organization of the British Institute of Psycho-Analysis. She is Book Review Editor of the *International Journal of Psycho-Analysis*. She was formerly a research fellow at the University of Sussex.

The New Library of Psychoanalysis was launched in 1987 in association with the Institute of Psycho-Analysis, London. Its purpose is to facilitate a greater and more widespread appreciation of what psychoanalysis is really about and to provide a forum for increasing mutual understanding between psychoanalysts and those working in other disciplines such as history, linguistics, literature, medicine, philosophy, psychology, and the social sciences. It is intended that the titles selected for publication in the series should deepen and develop psychoanalytic thinking and technique, contribute to psychoanalysis from outside or contribute to other disciplines from a psychoanalytical perspective.

The Institute, together with the British Psycho-Analytical Society, runs a low-fee psychoanalytic clinic, organizes lectures and scientific events concerned with psychoanalysis, publishes the *International Journal of Psycho-Analysis*, and runs the only training course in the UK in psychoanalysis leading to membership of the International Psychoanalytical Association – the body which preserves internationally agreed standards of training, of professional entry, and of professional ethics and practice for psychoanalysis as initiated and developed by Sigmund Freud. Distinguished members of the Institute have included Michael Balint, Wilfred Bion, Ronald Fairbairn, Anna Freud, Ernest Jones, Melanie Klein, John Rickman, and Donald Winnicott.

Volumes 1–11 in the series have been prepared under the general editorship of David Tuckett, with Ronald Britton and Eglé Laufer as associate editors. Subsequent volumes are under the general editorship of Elizabeth Bott Spillius, with, from Volume 17, Donald Campbell, Michael Parsons, Rosine Jozef Perelberg and David Taylor as associate editors.

IN THE SAME SERIES

NEW LIBRARY OF PSYCHOANALYSIS
18

General editor: Elizabeth Bott Spillius

The Gender Conundrum

Contemporary Psychoanalytic Perspectives on Femininity and Masculinity

Edited and introduced by
DANA BREEN

LONDON AND NEW YORK

First published in 1993
by Routledge
11 New Fetter Lane, London EC4P 4EE

Simultaneously published in the USA and Canada
by Routledge
29 West 35th Street, New York, NY 10001

Reprinted in 1997

© 1993 General introduction and introductions to parts Dana Breen; Individual
chapters the authors or their estates

Phototypeset in 11pt Bembo by
Mews Photosetting, Beckenham, Kent
Printed and bound in Great Britain by
Mackays of Chatham PLC, Chatham, Kent

All rights reserved. No part of this book may be reprinted or reproduced or utilized in
any form or by any electronic, mechanical, or other means, now known or hereafter
invented, including photocopying and recording, or in any information storage or
retrieval system, without permission in writing from the publishers.

British Library Cataloguing in Publication Data
A catalogue record for this book is available from the British Library.

Library of Congress Cataloguing in Publication Data
The Gender conundrum : psychoanalytic perspectives on femininity and
masculinity / edited by Dana Breen.
p.   cm. – (New library of psychoanalysis : 18)
1. Sex differences (Psychology) 2. Femininity (Psychology)
3. Masculinity (Psychology) 4. Psychoanalysis. I. Breen, Dana.
II. Series.
BF175.5.S49G46   1993
155.3′3–dc20   92–37650
ISBN 0–415–09163–2
0–415–09164–0 (pbk)

Contents

Contents

Acknowledgements

I wish to thank David Tuckett, who invited me to work on this book when he was general editor of the series. It gave me the impetus to develop my ideas. Elizabeth Bott Spillius took over the series and I am grateful for the generous time and encouragement she gave me throughout the numerous drafts. I also want to thank Juliet Mitchell Rossdale, Susan Lipshitz Phillips and Steven Ablon for their useful comments and Thomas Elsaesser for his help with the German nuances of Freud's text.

I want to thank Jill Duncan for her patience with my unending requests for obscure books and papers.

I am grateful to my husband Ian and my daughter Sasha and my son Noah who, as always, have been supportive of my work and to Noah for helping to reorganize my bibliography.

I would also like to thank the following for their kind permission to reproduce copyright material: *The International Journal of Psycho-Analysis* for 'Freud and female sexuality' vol. 57 (1976), J. Chasseguet-Smirgel; 'Concepts of vaginal orgasm', vol. 50 (1969), W.H. Gillespie; 'Female genital anxieties, conflicts and typical mastery modes', vol. 71 (1990), D. Bernstein; '"The weak spot", some observations on male sexuality', vol. 50 (1985), M. Glasser; 'The dead father: on early psychic trauma and its relation to disturbance in sexual identity and in creative activity', vol. 70 (1989), J. McDougall; and 'Dis-identifying from mother: its special import-ance for the boy', vol. 49 (1968), R. Greenson; *The Journal of the American Psychoanalytic Association* for 'Son and father', vol. 32 (1984), P. Blos; *The Psychoanalytic Study of the Child* for 'The female Oedipus complex and the relationship to the body', vol. 41 (1988), M.E. Laufer; *Les Cahiers du Centre de Psychoanalyse et de Psychothérapie* for 'Du Feminin et du Masculin', *Cahiers* no. 16–17 (1988), A. Gibeault, and 'Notes cliniques sur une identification à la petite fille', *Cahiers* no. 8 (1984) M. Aisenstein;

Karnac and the Melanie Klein Trust for 'The missing link: parental sexuality', R. Britton in *The Oedipus Complex Today, Clinical Implications* (1989); Payot for 'L'ombre phallique' in *Eros et Thanatos* (1971), D. Braunschweig and M. Fain; Editions de Minuit for 'Recherches sur la féminité' (1978); M. Montrelay and Parveen Adams for her translation of the paper, and *Psichiatria e Psicoterapia Analitica* for 'To the limits of heterosexuality: the vagina-man', vol. 2 (1984), A. Limentani. I want to thank Rachel Bowlby for her translation of 'The phallic shadow', 'On the feminine and the masculine: afterthoughts on Jacqueline Cosnier's book, *Destins de la féminité*' and 'Clinical notes on the identification with the little girl'.

Above all, I am indebted to all the authors for allowing me to reprint their papers.

General introduction

It is important to understand clearly that the concepts of 'masculine' and 'feminine', whose meaning seems so unambiguous to ordinary people, are amongst the most confused that occur in science.

(Freud, *Three Essays on Sexuality*,
1905 footnote, 1915, SE 7, p. 219)

I am accustoming myself to regarding every sexual act as a process in which four individuals are involved.

(Freud, Letters, 1899, J. Masson (ed.))

It is part of the complexity of Freud's work that his theory has been seen by some as ascribing an inescapable biological destiny to man and woman, while others have understood him to uphold the revolutionary belief that, psychologically speaking, we are not born man or woman, and that masculinity and femininity are constructed over a period of time and are relatively independent of biological sex.

I believe that this duality is there in Freud's work not because he was confused or changed his mind or developed his ideas, but because an inherent tension exists at the heart of the matter, which is why this opposition is not going away and why the debate is still alive half a century after his death.

It is in relation to women that the disjunction between biology and psychology is greatest in Freudian theory, and the debate on female sexuality therefore comes to embody that tension. There has been an attempt to resolve the 'mystery' of woman by grounding female sexuality in a biological perspective or, on the contrary, by pulling it right out of this and into a linguistic approach. I believe that the way forward is to make positive use of this very tension and duality, which philosophers refer to as 'essence' and 'existence'.

1

This Introduction will be largely guided by my argument of this general thesis while some other aspects of the subject, as well as some of the historical details, are left to the introductions to the individual parts of the book. For the sake of simplicity only, I have decided to deal with men and women separately, although the issues are intimately linked.

Cultural traditions have influenced perspectives, with the Anglo-Saxon tradition being more empirical and developmental and more tied to a biological perspective, and French culture opting for a more philosophical approach. While French psychoanalysis has developed within the intelligentsia of academia, with its rich cross-fertilization of disciplines and its brilliance at grasping the theoretical issues, British psychoanalysis has maintained a very British suspiciousness of 'intellectuality' and an insularity which has enabled it to develop a finesse for clinical and technical understanding. In the United States, the cultural *ambiance* has been different. Psychoanalysis there has gone in two opposite directions: a biological direction, fostered by the fact that psychoanalysis has been a branch of medicine (while in Europe psychoanalysis was largely frowned upon until recently in medical circles); and a social direction, encouraged by the vast possibilities for social psychological and developmental studies in the universities and promoted by the American ideals of social equality and social adjustment, sometimes at the expense of the concept of the unconscious.

Discourse across cultural barriers is difficult, if not impossible, when the differences in premises, theories and concepts are not understood, and I will discuss some important differences later on in this Introduction.

Mainly about women

Bifocality in Freud's understanding of femininity

For Freud, masculinity and femininity are formed from the moment of recognition of genital difference. It is more than just the perception of the difference, it is the fact that the perception suddenly takes on meaning. The meaning for the boy is that the penis can be absent and therefore that his can be lost; the meaning for the girl is that she has something missing. The threat of loss for the boy is linked to the prohibition of incest. For the girl there is no threat since she has nothing to lose. Hence the recognition of genital difference engenders a differential development in boy and girl. The 'castration complex' refers to the whole constellation of mental processes surrounding this recognition which initiates the distinction between the sexes. For the girl Freud prefers to use the concept of 'penis envy' since she need not fear castration. It is this envy which will turn her away from her mother, whom she makes responsible for her lack, and towards her father in her search for what she lacks; hence it initiates her Oedipus complex.

But masculine and feminine for Freud are not simply a reference to the development of boy and girl. They refer to the way in which *each individual* deals with that recognition of difference. If a girl maintains the phantasy belief that she possesses a penis (thanks to the ego's capacity to split), then her development will be masculine and not feminine (the 'masculinity complex'). A boy's development will be feminine if his fear of castration is so great that he 'renounces' his penis in phantasy. This has not always been clearly understood and has lead to confusions and misrepresentations. What Freud describes as 'feminine' has often been taken to mean 'characteristic of women', which is not so. A case in point is his notion of 'feminine masochism', which he specifically discusses in relation to men.

Freud's theory disputes the naturalness of the heterosexual drive.

> It would be a solution of ideal simplicity if we could suppose that from a particular age onwards the elementary influence of the mutual attraction between the sexes makes itself felt and impels the small woman towards men, while the same law allows the boy to continue with his mother.
>
> (Freud 1933: 119)

This is clearest in the case of the girl for whom heterosexuality is described as the end result of a long psychological process, not a biological one. Her heterosexuality only develops after a homosexual phase, in the wake of disappointment.

Freud's theory has been seen by some as describing an inescapable biological destiny to man. In fact the bedrock Freud describes is more anatomical than biological. It is anatomy which determines the cataclysm which initiates the psychological reorganization shaping masculinity and femininity. Anatomy is a given, and each sex has to grapple with the particular significance it has in their case. What is not given is what each individual makes of this anatomy. And what each individual makes of his or her anatomy will influence the course of his or her psychosexuality, his or her choice of object as homosexual or heterosexual (and this can be even more complicated in that the object may be of one anatomical sex but treated as if of the other sex). For Freud there is no natural sexuality, it is always psychosexuality, always a construction relatively independent of biology. If 'anatomy is destiny', it means that sexual difference has inevitably to be reckoned with. The anatomical difference, not in itself

3

but through the meaning it takes on, will shape object relations. The objection which has been voiced has come not so much from the fact that anatomy is destiny as such — there is no objection to this destiny in men — but because of Freud's suggestion that the female anatomy signifies a lack to her, that the experience of lack is her destiny. This has been interpreted as meaning that women are lacking.

Biology does have a role in the Freudian model of development through the phylogenetic unfolding of organizations (oral, anal, phallic). There is also a certain determinism in the inevitable advent of the Oedipus complex. His use of the myth of Oedipus conveys the inescapability of this drama, the fact that it transcends individual experience. Oedipus is responding to a force greater than himself. 'It was Apollo! He brought this pain, this suffering to me. But it was my own hand that struck the blow. Not his' (Sophocles). Freud writes, 'these wishes, repugnant to morality, which have been forced upon us by *Nature*' (Freud 1900; italics mine). In Freud's account it is only for the boy that there is a 'natural' phylogenetically determined entry into the structure of interpersonal relationships he calls the Oedipus complex, even if it is the prohibition of incest more than his 'natural' wishes which mark his masculine development. In the case of the girl, a dual perspective is clearest: her body is her destiny, but her psychosexuality does not simply parallel her biological destiny.

Freud often cautioned against the assumed meaning of the concepts of masculine and feminine which he thought were 'amongst the most confused that occur in science'. In particular, he warned against equating active with masculine and passive with feminine: 'the contrast between the sexes fades away into one between activity and passivity, in which we far too readily identify activity with maleness and passivity with femaleness' (Freud 1930: 106). He also writes that

> psycho-analysis cannot elucidate the intrinsic nature of what in conventional or in biological phraseology is termed 'masculine' and 'feminine': it simply takes over the two concepts and makes them the foundation of its work. When we attempt to reduce them further, we find masculinity vanishing into activity and femininity into passivity, and that does not tell us enough.
>
> (Freud 1920: 171)

The German verb *Verblassen* in the first quotation and *Verflüchtigen* in the second (translated as 'fades away' and 'vanishes') more clearly than the English translation conveys the idea that as one tries to grasp the nature of masculinity and femininity, one finds that it gets out of focus, that one cannot grasp it. We can assume that Freud is making a point here about the nature of the connection between the biological and the

4

psychological, that while the biological differences can be easily grasped, as one looks from the point of view of psychoanalysis one can no longer grasp them, but yet they are not unrelated images either. The moment of 'evaporation' (*Verflüchtigen*) is the moment when the two perspectives are out of focus because they do not completely overlap. This out-of-focusness most clearly for me expresses the duality in Freud's position; body and mind are connected, but not completely, and the disjunction between them is difficult to grasp. A concept which is equally imbued with this bifocal vision and elusive to the grasp is Freud's notion of bisexuality. It is a biological concept on the one hand ('human nature is inherently bisexual'), while he also considers bisexuality in terms of identification or Oedipal positions. Women he considers to be more bisexual then men because of the initial homosexual phase of attachment.

The early debate over the place of the biological in femininity

The controversy over the subject of female sexuality which broke out in the 1920s following Freud's paper on the 'Anatomical distinction between the sexes' (1925) and which continues implicitly or explicitly to this day, rests on this relationship of mind and body. For Freud's opponents – Horney, Klein and Jones – there is a biological drive which propels the girl in a heterosexual direction and her female anatomy is known to her in its positive aspects rather than experienced simply as a lack; penis envy expresses the desire to take the penis into herself in a feminine way or else it is a secondary defence against femininity or the result of interpersonal frustrations. Mind and body are hence, for them, very closely connected, unless psychopathological reactions intervene.

Prompted by women analysts,[1] Freud's researches into the 'dark continent' led him to discover the fundamental importance of the girl's early relationship to her mother, a phase of such importance that he compared it to the discovery of a hidden civilization, the discovery of which transformed the understanding of analytic discourse. While Van Ophuijsen, writing in 1917 before the discovery of that early phase, was able to write confidently

> it will be agreed that there can be no misunderstanding about this statement of hers [this woman patient]: 'Often when I am restless and don't know what to do with myself I have a feeling that I would like to ask my mother to give me something that she cannot give me'.
>
> (1924: 40)

the discovery and exploration of the early relationship to the mother led to a more complex picture where it is far more than the wish to be given a penis which the girl craves from her mother. By 1940 it had long been generally accepted that 'the girl traverses a long and complicated route before entering the Oedipus complex. Indeed during the examination of the pre-Oedipal phenomena we become uncertain as to the comparative importance of pre-Oedipal and Oedipal phenomena in feminine development' (Brunswick 1940: 233). Freud's choice of imagery – the discovery of the Minoan-Mycenaean civilization hidden behind the Greek one – must attest to how much this phase came as a surprise but especially how he felt it had an all-encompassing logic of its own. Nevertheless, he had already stated that the little girl started off as a little man in her strivings towards her mother; what he now adds and which comes as a surprise is how important, long-lasting and complex this early relationship is and how fundamental it is to the understanding of female sexuality. What comes as a surprise is that the 'homosexual' relationship for the girl is of such structuring importance and distinct from, though connected to, the subsequent heterosexual relationship. However, this discovery of the importance of the early phase of the girl's attachment to the mother in no way changed Freud's view on the formation of femininity.

Psychoanalysts on both sides of the controversy accepted the importance of this early phase and their work developed its understanding. What differed was whether this phase was to be seen as essentially a feminine or a masculine phase, whether the girl's sexuality at this time was thought to be receptive or phallic, whether her psychosexuality follows her biological reality. This is not questioned for the boy, since psychosexual and biological tally.

Helene Deutsch, Lampl-de Groot and Marie Bonaparte took up Freud's view, but sometimes the subtlety of his position was lost. Whereas he was mainly following the consequences of the recognition of sexual difference on psychosexual development in men and women, they looked for set characteristics in women and a set notion of femininity. Lampl-de Groot, for instance, writes (1933):

> The purely feminine orientation of the woman to the man leaves no place for activity. Feminine love is passive, a narcissistic process the purely feminine woman does not love, she lets herself be loved. [. . .] It is well known that many women also retain some of this activity in their relations to men and love them with real object love, that is, with 'masculinity'.
>
> (Lampl-de Groot 1985: 27–8)

Similarly, while Freud described 'feminine masochism' in both men and women, referring to a particular phantasy of the child in relation to the father, these authors speak of masochism as a characteristic of female sexuality. For Deutsch, the active libido linked with the clitoris is transformed into masochism and the wish to be castrated by the father, with childbirth as the ultimate gratification of the erotic instinct and the acme of masochistic pleasure. Bonaparte states that coitus itself is a masochistic pleasure (1953).

It did Freud a disservice that these ideas have often been taken to be his ideas. In fact, Freud's theory is one which is concerned more with movement (development of object relationships and defensive manoeuvres) than categorizations. While Freud was grappling with the out-of-focusness of femininity and masculinity, and with their vicissitudes following the discovery of sexual difference, other psychoanalysts were now concerned with the female character. Juliet Mitchell, in Mitchell and Rose (1982) points out that when the 'Freud–Jones' controversy began, whatever the position, 'the issue subtly shifts from what distinguishes the sexes to what has each sex got of value that belongs to it alone', and therefore there is an inevitable return to the biological explanation, from which Freud had deliberately departed.

Freud's last paper devoted to femininity, Lecture 33 in *New Introductory Lectures* (1933) nevertheless clearly encompasses again the bifocality in his thinking. He states on the one hand that 'psychoanalysis does not try to describe what a woman is ... but sets about enquiring how she comes into being'. On the other hand, he explains the masculinity complex in girls by referring to the constitutionally greater activity of men and wave of passivity of women:

> We can only suppose that it is a constitutional factor, a greater amount of activity, such as is ordinarily characteristic of a male. However that may be, the essence of this process is that at this point in development the wave of passivity is avoided which opens the way to the turn towards femininity.
>
> (Freud 1933: 130)

The study of pre-Oedipal phenomena by psychoanalysts on both sides of the controversy did, however, further the understanding of women, in particular the role of oral (Deutsch 1946; Sachs 1929; Brierley 1936) and anal (Pfeiffer 1972; Brierley 1936) components, and the central importance of maternity in the psychology of women (Deutsch 1946).

The widening gap between perspectives after the 1960s

Interest in female sexuality took a back seat from the mid-1930s for a few decades; maybe the debate had reached a stalemate and could go no further at this point; maybe a preoccupation with world events took people's minds in other directions, to aggression and the death instinct. Certainly it was a *Zeitgeist* which brought it back to the surface in the 1960s along with the general questioning of social structures and prejudices in society at large and with the spread of the feminist movement. This movement had an impact on the standing of psychoanalysis itself, though not operating in a uniform direction. While American culture had long before eagerly adopted psychoanalysis, something Freud had been suspicious of ('they don't realize that I am bringing them the plague'), now American feminists turned against psychoanalysis, because they believed it condoned social structures and described women as inferior. Quite the opposite occurred in France, where French culture had been staunchly anti-psychoanalytic until the May 1968 revolution (except in certain circles; in particular, the group of surrealists to which Lacan associated himself); people suddenly, feminists and Marxists included, turned to psychoanalysis – via Lacan's interpretation of Freud – for the answers to their questions. The bifocality of Freud's theory had been split again, with the Americans taking up the determining effect of anatomy, the French, in a large part, concentrating on the independence of the psychological construction of femininity from the biological path. Some American feminists – Chodorow (1989), Jean Baker Miller (1976), Dinnerstein (1976) – later turned back to psychoanalysis in the 1970s, in this case to a social interpretation of Freud, in what is referred to as 'psychoanalytic feminism'.

Within France a split also occurred, with only some psychoanalysts espousing Lacan's ideas. The crux of Lacan's interpretation of Freud and questioning of psychoanalytic developments revolved around the place of the body and biology in psychoanalysis, and femininity was again an important area of debate since it is always woman who comes to embody that question, since it is female sexuality which for Freud departs from the straight biological path.

British psychoanalysts, and in particular Kleinians, were alone in never really regaining much of an interest in the subject in the 1960s or after. Klein herself last wrote about femininity in 1945 and showed no interest in the subject after that. Her description of an early femininity and natural heterosexual drive and of the essentially defensive nature of penis envy and the phallic phase, though not held by all, is not openly challenged either, within the British Society. I believe that this is because the interest of many psychoanalysts (in particular Kleinian) in the British Society has shifted away from sexuality to separation anxiety and the states and defences this anxiety leads to. Nevertheless, there are some important papers written on the subject after the 1960s by British psychoanalysts and it is noteworthy that they are all non-Kleinian: Gillespie (1969),

Balint (1973), Burgner and Edgcumbe (1975), Mitchell in Mitchell and Rose (1982), Laufer (1982, 1986).[2]

The returning interest in female sexuality in France and the United States is reflected in the publication of a number of important books and papers in the sixties and early seventies: *Chasseguet-Smirgel*'s collection, *Recherches psychoanalytiques nouvelles sur la sexualité feminine* was published in France in 1964 and in the English language in 1970; *Sherfey*'s lengthy paper on female sexuality, based on the work of Masters and Johnston, was published in 1966 in the *Journal of the American Psychoanalytical Association* followed by a number of discussion papers. *Lacan* presented a paper on femininity, 'Guiding remarks for a congress on feminine sexuality', at a Congress on Feminine Sexuality in 1960. In 1976 the American Psychoanalytic Association devoted to female sexuality a special supplement edited by *Harold Blum*.

In France the old debate of the 1920s was being revived in a new register. Both sides claimed their faithfulness to Freud, Chasseguet-Smirgel wishing to 're-examine the theories of female sexuality using the Freudian approach to the unconscious', Lacan claiming a 'return to Freud'. The discussion was more sophisticated and elaborated, but the main underlying dimension of the earlier controversy remained present with the authors of the Chasseguet-Smirgel book assuming an early awareness of the male and female genital organs 'virtually from the beginning', while Lacan's work rested on the theory of phallic monism.

Chasseguet-Smirgel suggested that the theoretical differences of the early debate had been left behind or minimized in order not to disrupt the psychoanalytic movement while it was still becoming established and that the time at which this attitude was important had now gone. 'The vitality of any doctrine depends on the possibility of rethinking certain aspects without disrupting the whole structure' (1981: 3). The key concepts from the early debate are re-examined throughout the papers in her book. Penis envy, the cornerstone of the debate, is understood by all the authors of this collection not as primary and the initiator of femininity, as it was for Freud, but as a defence, and a number of different defensive functions are suggested: the wish for a penis as a protection from a dangerous penis (Luquet-Parat) and as a protection from the all-controlling anal mother or the devouring oral mother (McDougall, Chasseguet-Smirgel), and penis envy as a disguise against rivalry with women or unfulfilled desire in relation to the mother (McDougall, Torok). The wish for a penis is also seen as expressing the wish to repair the mother and remain the object of her desire (McDougall).

Narcissism and masochism are considered from the point of view of object relations. Grunberger gives a different origin to the importance of narcissism in feminine development, which Freud and Lampl-de Groot attributed to compensation for the lack of a penis. He explains it from the point of view of the mother–daughter relationship, which he believes to be particularly frustrating for the girl because the mother is only a substitute for a truly adequate sexual object. Female narcissism is the attempt to make up for the maternal deficiency. Because of this deficiency, Grunberger writes, the girl will also immediately and blindly choose her father as ego-ideal and libidinal object. The construction of an ideal image of the father while she despises the pre-genital satisfactions provided by the mother explains, he believes, the peculiar survival of her manifest Oedipal attachment and her tendency to dichotomize between an ideal Oedipal love and the pre-Oedipal attachment which is opposed to it.

If the vagina is not known by little girls, Chasseguet-Smirgel suggests, it is because of an 'incorporation-guilt' which forbids the erotic cathexis of the vagina and restricts pleasure to the clitoris only. She suggests that a split occurs at the time of the change of object so that the aggressive instincts in relation to the father will be repressed and counter-cathected, resulting in a 'specifically feminine form of guilt attached to the anal-sadistic component of sexuality' (1981: 97). In particular, guilt is connected with the 'basically feminine wish to incorporate the paternal penis, which invariably includes the anal-sadistic instinctual components' (1981: 102). This repression will have consequences for women's psychosexual development and will interfere with achievement in fields that take on an unconscious phallic significance. Female masochism is linked to this guilt.

In the renewed debate of the 1960s it is only *Lacan* and his followers who go back to the 'Freud' side of the Freud–Jones debate on female sexuality, to phallic monism and the central place given to castration. His concern is to pursue that aspect of Freud's thinking which wants to keep psychoanalysis separate from biology. His is a total theoretical model within which both masculinity and femininity take their place; his views on femininity can only be understood within an understanding of this model. Lacan says that he is returning to the Freud of *The Interpretation of Dreams* and *The Psychopathology of Everyday Life*, the Freud of the 'talking cure', which means a return to language as central in psychoanalysis. This, in fact, also means a return to the Freud of the period before his discovery of the importance of pre-Oedipal phenomena. For his understanding of femininity he goes back to *Some Psychical Consequences of the Anatomical Distinction Between the Sexes*. Lacan's innovation is to make use of structural linguistics (in particular, Ferdinand de Saussure's work) for a re-reading of the texts, and in this sense it is as much a 'reinvention of Freud' (Turkle) as a return to Freud. He suggests that 'the unconscious is structured as a language' with its different laws governing it, and moreover that the unconscious is intimately connected with language and with the father as representative of the moment of rupture of the union between mother and child, the moment of 'entry into culture' through language, through the third person. The father introduces the law of the language system, and it is then that the child becomes a subject. The 'law of the phallus' is not a reference to an anatomical organ or a particular person but a metaphor which signifies the separation of human beings from their object of desire. It refers to a lack in *both* girl and boy.

Lacan thought it was a misunderstanding of Freud to look for the subject's truth beyond language, and this is what makes his perspective different from the others. Ferdinand de Saussure suggested that the study of language could not be done purely from a 'diachronic' — that is, from a historical — point of view, but necessitated a 'synchronic' approach — that is, a structural, ahistorical approach which looks for internal laws and which will bring to light some radically new properties of language. Lacan applied this structuralist approach to the field of psychoanalysis.

What concerns us here is that in placing his perspective firmly within a linguistic point of view, Lacan was removing it both from the genetic historical perspective and from a biological approach. Hence, for him, psychoanalytically speaking, the body does not count, and human psychology is constituted by language. Lacan is taking to its extreme that aspect of Freud's work which upholds that masculinity and femininity are independent of biological reality, that they are constructed from the moment of recognition of sexual difference. For him, because there is no reality outside language, not only does he discard the role of the body but he also discards the role of early phenomena.[3] Lacan's return to Freud is a return to that Freud who wants to keep psychoanalysis separate from biology and within the area of mental representation, and for whom there is no such thing as a pre-given male or female subject. Lacan wanted to re-orientate psychoanalysis to the study of how the human subject is constructed and how this happens within the terms of language — that is, from a logic which comes from outside the individual.

Lacan questions the assumption of a natural heterosexual drive and puts forward the idea that a being conceptualizes itself from the position of the Other. For him there is no essence of femininity or masculinity, and an account of masculine and feminine sexuality can only be within the terms of language. The unconscious severs the subject from any unmediated relation to the body; that is, for the human subject enmeshed in the linguistic system, there is no one-to-one relationship between the body and the construction of the self as masculine or feminine. The 'feminine' does not exist as an entity in itself but only as a division in language; feminine is always opposed to masculine and in the linguistic system 'feminine' refers to the negative pole, to 'lack' and to 'the Other'. Feminine mystery is no longer understood as Freud's own difficulties with femininity, as some have suggested, but is part of the feminine. The question of 'feminine mystery' comes to be embodied in the woman through the question: 'What does a woman want?' Castration refers to the symbolic representation of lack, since there is nothing missing in reality. Jacqueline Rose, in Mitchell and Rose (1982) warns that psychoanalysis does not produce that definition (of feminine as lack) but only gives an account of how that definition comes to be. This is a warning against confusing the purpose of the theory with what the theory is describing.

Indeed, Freud's notion of the role of 'penis envy' in femininity has been taken as denigrating to women and as if he were claiming by it their *actual* inferiority. It is not Lacan's (or Freud's) theory which is phallocentric, but what they have brought to light is the phallocentrism in linguistic structures and hence in the construction of masculinity and femininity which the child takes on when he becomes a subject through becoming a speaking being. I would say that if phallocentrism exists, it is more in stopping short of looking for a specific feminine experience than in describing the role of the experience of lack in the feminine unconscious.

By separating psychoanalysis radically from biology through the adoption of a linguistic approach, Lacan's theory simplifies the bifocality Freud thought was difficult to grasp (even if Lacan's *writing* is difficult to grasp), but in so doing something gets lost. I will come back to this later.

In the United States psychoanalysis took the opposite direction, with the body taking centre stage. *Masters and Johnson* made a physiological study of the female orgasm in an attempt finally to resolve the feminine mystery, and *Mary Jane Sherfey* gave the findings psychoanalytic backing. Masters and Johnson found that the clitoris is always involved in orgasm, whatever the source of stimulation and that 'the female's physiologic responses to effective sexual stimulation . . . develop with consistency regardless of the source of the psychic or physical sexual stimulation' (quoted in Sherfey 1966: 254). Sherfey suggested a revision of Freudian theory in the the light of the findings, in particular his clitoral–vaginal transfer theory, because 'it is a physical impossibility to separate the clitoral from the vaginal orgasm as demanded by psychoanalytic theory' (1966: 78). She suggested a revision of concepts using the findings of modern embryology which show that in the first weeks all embryos are morphologically female. She also suggested from the work of Masters and Johnson on the female's capacity for multiple orgasms, each creating more tension, that 'the human female is sexually insatiable in the presence of the highest degrees of sexual satiation and it is only culture which restricts her behaviour'.

Sherfey's work takes no account of unconscious meanings and representations (or even conscious psychological reactions) and as such has been criticized (Kestenberg 1968; Keiser 1968). It has also been criticized for ignoring the role of adult integration as an end result of progressive development (Kestenberg 1968; Benedek 1968).

> It is clear from the Masters–Johnson data that female orgasm, as defined by them, depends on previous training . . . . The inaccessibility of the vagina in childhood permits only limited priming of this organ, while the external genitalia are more intensely libidinized until the onset of menses. Freud's transfer theory is based on these considerations.
>
> (Judith Kestenberg 1968: 419)

Even the physiological conclusions are found inadequate:

> Because of their special technique of investigation, Masters and Johnson may not be able to detect why women find deep penetration essential for the development of adult orgastic fulfilment. This depends not only on the contractions of the orgastic platform but also on a more feminine mode of vaginal functioning: the spreading intense sensations which arise from rhythms of tension and release in the unstriated vaginal muscles and those in the circumvaginal plexus – an inner activity which need not express itself in visible changes.
>
> (Benedek 1968: 420)

Therese Benedek also believes, as had Deutsch before her, that a woman's sexual identity is invested more in her aspiration to bear children and be a mother than in orgasm.

Sherfey's paper was taken up more sympathetically by Gillespie in Britain than it had been in the United States:

> in view of what we have learned from Masters and Johnson, we should reconsider very carefully the question whether clitoral excitation is necessarily associated with the urge to penetrate and act the male; may not clitoral excitation on the contrary lead to the wish *to be penetrated* in order to satisfy its proper erotic aim in the physiological manner that has been described? In the former case, penis envy indeed seems an inevitable and therefore normal consequence of anatomy; but in the latter case *penis desire*, i.e. the desire to be penetrated and so stimulated both vaginally and clitorally, is the outcome to be expected in a normal female psychosexual development.
>
> (Gillespie 1969: 497)

Moustafa Safouan (1976), a follower of Lacan, states that the transfer from clitoridal to vaginal orgasm is a mythical idea of femininity and that what is important from the psychoanalytic point of view is not the transformation of clitoridal to vaginal but of auto-erotic libido into object libido (a point also made by Grunberger).

In this whole debate there is often a shift of ground to adult sexuality. It was not Freud's contention that the clitoris is not involved in adult femininity; indeed it is the 'pine shavings [which] can be kindled in order to set a log of harder wood on fire' (1905). What he is positing is the central role of the clitoris in *pre-Oedipal* sexuality and its accompanying active impulses. The wish to be penetrated and the recognition of the vagina will occur only subsequently.

Masters and Johnson's work took to extremes the myth that quantified physiological investigation will throw light on the mystery of the 'dark continent'. The answer can only lie in the unconscious meaning attributed by each individual to the clitoris as organ of masculinity or of femininity. It has to be accepted that advances in biological and physiological knowledge have not and cannot resolve the mystery — because this mystery represents the unknowable of human existence, of man's origins, of the non-rational, and because psychology goes beyond the purely physiological. Nevertheless the work has had, in spite of its limitations, an — often silent — influence on psychoanalytic thinking about female sexuality and helped to counteract a stereotyped image of 'the feminine woman' proposed by some of Freud's followers (though not by Freud himself).

Following a spurt of papers in the United States on the female orgasm, interest in the types and nature of this orgasm receded in the light of a move away from a concern with drives in psychoanalytic theory generally, replaced by a greater focus on object relations in the understanding of human development and unconscious structures.

In 1976, six years after the translation of Chasseguet-Smirgel's book in English, and ten years after Sherfey's paper, a special issue of the *Journal of the American Psychoanalytic Association* edited by *Blum*, was devoted to female sexuality. The key concepts of the original debate of the 1920s are here too reconsidered, in particular the age-old, thorny question of 'penis envy'. While Freud saw penis envy as initiating feminine development and hence central, most of these authors view penis envy as secondary in importance in the development of femininity. While the authors of Chasseguet-Smirgel's book considered the defensive aspects of penis envy, the authors of the Blum collection, although they do propose some defensive aspects (for instance, Lerner) for the most part consider penis envy to occur 'naturally'; they believe it, however, to be an *impediment* to femininity rather than initiating femininity as in the classical theory

(Blum; Parens *et al.*). Its importance and specificity is also reduced by seeing it as a way of representing more general narcissistic injuries (Grossman and Stewart).

Galenson and Roiphe stand out from the other authors of the American collection in that they believe that penis envy and the feminine castration complex exert crucial influences upon feminine development. However, in contradistinction to Freud, for whom the castration complex initiates femininity, they see the castration complex as shaping an already developing sense of femininity stemming from early bodily and affective experiences with both parents. From their direct observational studies they come to the view that patterns of sensuous interaction of mother and child involve the genital zone from the very beginning of life, not only in the course of the mother's fondling and bodily ministrations and during feeding, but also in connection with transmitted pressure and excitation from the adjacent anal and urinary areas. They talk about 'a true early genital phase' which precedes the phallic–Oedipal phase (Galenson and Roiphe 1976: 34).

There is a renewed interest in the role of early vaginal sensations by all the authors of the Blum collection. While the role of penis envy is minimized (except by Roiphe and Galenson), it is replaced by the importance of 'inner-genital' sensations which are believed by these authors to play a special and important role in the development of the girl.

Specific to these American psychoanalysts is the postulation of a conflict-free source of femininity prior to the perception of sexual difference. This departs from the European perspective of Klein and of Chasseguet-Smirgel, for whom feminine identity comes out of the gradual integration of relational and conflictual phenomena. This is part of a general theoretical difference between the American 'ego psychologists', who believe that there is a conflict-free ego zone where cognition is straight-forward, and the European psychoanalysts, who are radically against the idea that there is an area of cognition free of ambiguity, conflict and sexuality. The psychoanalytic model in these papers has shifted towards ego psychology and a concern with adaptation to reality and cognitive functions. The attempt to integrate child observation and psychological research means at times a change in focus away from the unconscious and towards both biological and social factors. The approach is at times 'prospective' observations rather than 'retrospective' elucidation of unconscious meanings. Distinct and central to this view is the concept of *gender identity*, which is the awareness of belonging to one sex and not the other. Femininity becomes the role assignment. There is a sliding from sexuality to self-concept, from desire to perception. This view differs from all others (Klein, Lacan, Freud) in that identity is here seen as given

15

and unified rather than the result of integration. Cognitive functions, seen by these psychoanalysts as independent of unconscious conflicts, play a central role, and femininity refers to the knowledge that 'I am a girl'. Kleeman expresses it like this:

> Though a number of authors have contradicted Freud by ascribing vaginal sensations to the very young female . . . , the answer to the question of when femininity begins would seem to lie in a study of the origins of the little girl's gender identity. Studying how a girl acquires her sense of being female (the early phase of which we call *core gender identity*) by a variety of methods, including direct observation of children, reveals that the assignment of gender at birth is a crucial moment. One cannot understand gender identity or gender role without giving proper credit to the moment of assignment, which in turn sets in motion a whole process of acculturation which teaches the little girl that she is female and what and how a female is supposed to think, to feel, and to act in the family and in the segment of society that family represents. *Innate* differences exist between male and female infants and children, but even more crucial for gender–identity formation are the *learning* experiences of the young child. Parents relate differently to girls and boys from birth. The expectations and selective reinforcements conveyed to a girl are different from those conveyed to a boy, though the process is usually subtle. The known socialization inputs to the two genders are sufficiently dissimilar to produce known gender differences in dependency and aggression, as well as other traits (Mischel 1966). The learning experiences are powerful enough to make them the predominant factor in determining core gender identity (Money *et al.* 1955; Stoller 1968a, 1968b). Taken together, these facts confirm the existence of a primary femininity in infancy.
>
> (Kleeman 1976: 11–14)

Core gender identity, according to Stoller, who coined the term, has no implication of role or object relations; it is part of narcissism and is made up of a biological force, the sex assignment at birth, parents' attitudes about the infant's sex, early postnatal effects caused by habitual patterns of handling the infant, and sensations, especially from the genitals. These are the factors which make up 'primary femininity'. This is the first of two stages he postulates in the development of femininity in females. This first stage is *non-conflictual* in origin and contributes to a sense of femaleness. The second phase, which is the one described by Freud, is the result of conflict, especially Oedipal conflict. Although Stoller talks about primary femininity as a true self, he contradicts this when he writes that the second phase is one which 'produces a richer and more compli-cated femininity *not merely one of appearances*, but one enriched by desires to perform with the substance, *rather than just the façade, of femininity*' (Stoller 1976: 77; italics mine).

While Freud (1925), Greenacre (1948, 1958) and Erikson (1964) emphasized the impact of anatomical difference on the maturation of certain ego-functions and sexual identity, the approach of the contributors to the Blum volume emphasizes the cognitive developmental aspect of gender learning. In particular the child's labelling herself a girl is seen as coming first, even before identification. The cognition in the parent — My baby is a girl — also organizes a whole set of cues, selective rewards and sanctions, and directives to the child. Parental attitudes, originating partly in the culture and expressed in the family setting, reflect normative and pathological gender-identity issues in those significant adults.

We can see how the new explosion of papers in the 1960s and 1970s lead in various directions. Nothing was resolved; if anything, they engendered greater diversity even if at first glance one aim was united around doing justice to women. Certain concepts might appear similar, but in fact they refer to different things. For instance, the primary femininity of the American authors is conceptually different from the early femininity which Horney or Klein wrote about and which referred to an instinctual and object-relational disposition rather than to a unified cognitive apperception.

Nevertheless, certain writings had an undeniable and world-wide impact. The work of Masters and Johnson, though hailed as ethically dubious by all, had an unquestionable influence on psychoanalysis, practice as well as theory.

Lacan's work has also had a profound influence in France and the Latin countries, though little direct influence in the Anglo-Saxon world of psychoanalysis until very recently, when his ideas do seem to be slowly permeating.

Diachronic versus synchronic: a cultural divide

The difference in perspectives, largely diachronic (that is, developmental) in Anglo-Saxon writings, largely synchronic (that is, ahistorical and structural) in French writings, originates in wider cultural traditions, with the more empirical Anglo-Saxon approach and the more philosophical French tradition. In the French tradition there is also a greater reverence for and scholarly interest in 'the text'; in this case, the Freudian text. The continual return to Freud's text is considered as important as clinical practice.

Dialogue across national barriers can be difficult when theoretical premises are not made explicit and understood. These theoretical differences are at the centre of the debate on femininity, since this debate concerns the relationship of the biological and the psychological, and the role of observational data, and since this is the foundation of the discord between the models. The synchronic approach is concerned with structures of the mind and their interconnections (at any one point in time without reference to the historical past or notions of causality) while the diachronic approach, which is more tied to the biological, is concerned with the development of the child into the adult. Freud's perspective is bifocal with diachronic and synchronic components. Although he proposed a theory of development (diachronic approach), he also, for instance, did not revise his theory following the reports of vaginal sensations in little girls because his considerations rested on the unconscious representation of femininity in his adult patients (synchronic approach).

French psychoanalysis has for a large part an antipathy for the genetic perspective and has opted for the synchronic approach. André Green, for instance (1986), not a disciple of Lacan, deplores a reduction of the structural dimensions of psychoanalysis to the merely genetic. He points out that the idea that studying the child as a way of finding greater simplicity to the complexity of the adult, as an explanation, is a fallacy (1979). Direct observation cannot account for the essential dimension of psychoanalysis, which is to do with how the environment is interpreted and internalized. The study of the child or the psychoanalysis of the child does not offer greater simplicity, merely difference (Green, Diatkine) just as the mentality of the savage is not simpler, only different. Secondary processes do not develop from primary processes but always coexist and conflict (Pontalis). Green (1979) writes that the observation of the child is only of the order of day residues in relation to the dream. Psychoanalysis comes into its own only in that construction of childhood as in the construction of the dream. Direct observation of the child cannot prove or disprove theory, he says, it only confirms the theory which impregnates the perception of the situation. Direct observation without theoretical hypotheses is unintelligible and cannot supply new knowledge to psychoanalysis (Diatkine 1979). Green (1979) suggests that there is a place for the child in psychoanalytic thinking, and that is to stimulate ideas if we can allow the child in us to speak, much as we use countertransference in the clinical setting.

Whereas in the United States there is a bias, on the contrary, towards direct observation and a developmental model and an important theoretical place is taken by ego-functions and the appraisal of reality, in Britain synchronic and diachronic mingle. In particular, there is a special emphasis on the distinction between the historical child and the internal child, always the result of projections and introjections, and

and reality is always an experienced reality. Observation is seen as secondary to prior psychoanalytic insights, whereas observation in the work of Margaret Mahler (for instance) takes on a primary function. As for infant observation, which is part of the training of psycho-analysts and psychotherapists in Britain, an important function of it is to be a powerful emotional experience from which the observer will learn by his response to it, much as Green advocates (see Rustin 1989). More importantly, there is a significant strand of Kleinian think-ing, starting with Bion, which gives a special place to knowledge and the quest for meaning within the psychical apparatus and is less concerned with the genetic. Klein herself moved towards a more synchronic approach; in the latter part of her work she is particularly concerned with structures of thinking with the fluctuation of mental organizations between paranoid–schizoid and depressive positions, and it is this aspect of her work which has been the most influential on con-temporary British psychoanalysis.

Nevertheless, there remain important theoretical differences between the British and the French approach, and I think that the concept of '*Nachträglichkeit*' encapsulates this. *Nachträglichkeit* meaningfully translated as '*après coup*' in French but inadequately as 'deferred action' in English – a more apt translation has recently been given as 'after revision' by Benvenuto and Kennedy (1986). It was Lacan who first pointed out the importance of this concept in the work of Freud. The concept of '*après coup*', little found in Anglo-Saxon writings, is central to French think-ing, not just amongst the followers of Lacan. It refers to the fact that experiences and memory-traces take on new meaning to fit in with new experiences. The expression in French, '*après coup*', gives it the sense of a sudden revelation bestowed on something which has already happened.

Of special importance are the times of psychic reorganization with the attainment of a new stage of development when meaning is given *retrospectively* to those memory-traces. This is relevant to our topic, because the castration complex refers to *the* privileged moment of psychic reorganization where previous perceptions and events take on a new meaning. This perspective of *Nachträchlichkeit* underlines a view of psychical temporality and causality which departs from historical progression. It rules out a view of the subject's history reduced to linear determinism which envisages only the action of the past on the present (Laplanche and Pontalis 1973). For Klein, on the other hand, everything has a meaning from the beginning (de Mijolla 1973) and influences later development, and this is a crucial theoretical difference. This linear determinism, of course, does not mean simple cause and effect, but the castration complex (for instance) is not seen by Klein as a moment of retrospective psychic re-structuring or a privileged moment but only as lived out in function of earlier developments.

This opposition between a conception of a linear development and one which moves around moments of privileged re-structuring makes for a fundamentally different conception of the unconscious and psychic development, and creates a cultural divide between French and Anglo-Saxon psychoanalysis which can make dialogue meaningless if this is not understood. It is not just that the French are more interested in the castration complex and the British in the early pre-genital stages or in a very early Oedipus complex; it is a whole conception of psychoanalysis which is at variance.

For Freud, and this is highlighted by Lacan, the castration complex refers to that privileged moment in which earlier experiences are reorganized and given special meaning, initiating the meaning of masculinity and femininity. It is not reducible to earlier experiences; 'castration' is a 'primal phantasy' which organizes phantasy life, irrespective of personal experiences. It is, as it were, imposed on the individual. For Klein the Oedipus complex and the castration complex are part of a progressive and 'natural' evolution, evolving out of lived and instinctual experiences.

'The body never stops haunting the presumed autonomy of the unconscious'

Lacan's understanding of Freud is explicitly grounded in a structuralist model, but equally important to our topic is the French existentialist tradition of Sartre and de Beauvoir. It is this rejection of essentialism – the notion of a female essence – which has led to Lacan's work being espoused by many feminist thinkers (analysts and non-analysts).

But is it so simple to do away with essence? Direct criticisms of Lacan's theory of femininity have come in particular from women analysts who were at one point disciples of Lacan, such as Michèle Montrelay and Luce Irigaray. They take note of Lacan's schema, but they assign to femininity an origin prior to the mark of symbolic difference and 'the law', an origin before language. Couched in different terms, it is a return to the earlier debate and the question of whether there is a femininity prior to the castration complex. Lacan responds to this in his latest writings by still maintaining that there is no prediscursive reality, no feminine outside language. However, he introduces the idea that woman has a 'supplementary *jouissance*' which the man knows nothing of. He uses the term 'supplementary' to avoid 'complementary' which is the conception of male and female as having two separate libidos that he is criticizing. It seems that in introducing this notion of 'supplementary *jouisssance*' he is implicitly recognizing that feminine sexuality is more than – has a 'supplement' to – the lack of phallus.

Lacan's model, cannot, by definition, incorporate the area of experience which is prediscursive, and I think it is relevant that such experiences as reverie or intuition which belong to this realm and to the earliest mother-and-baby relationship have tended to be talked about as 'feminine'. This prediscursive mode of relating does not exclude the triangular situation, since the father is always present for the mother.[4] It is also relevant that words related to such experiences have to do with the 'inside' of the body: 'inner thoughts', 'inner space', 'container', 'containment', 'holding' – a representation of the maternal figure which is not just lack of phallus. It could be possible to think of such representations as being in the same relationship to the actual womb or breast as the relationship of phallus to penis, but this time it is a representation of prediscursive phenomena which in my mind any useful model must be able to incorporate. This 'feminine' (in the linguistic sense used by Lacan) side seems to be strikingly absent in Lacan's work in which a person's sense of self is in continual flux and dependent on the Other rather than secured around an internalized developmental experience born out of a sense of containment.

Luce Irigarary suggests that there is in women a direct and unsymbolized relationship to the mother – not mediated by language. The girl, says Irigaray, 'has the mother, in some sense, in her skin, in the humidity of the mucous membranes, in the intimacy of her most intimate parts, in the mystery of her relation to gestation, birth, and to her sexual identity' (Irigaray 1988: 133). It is in this light that one can understand the poignancy of the threat of psychic annihilation for the girl and the consequent defensive attempts at differentiation from the mother by recourse to 'masculinity' in anorexia nervosa and homosexuality, for instance (Breen 1988, 1989b).

Lacan's work is important in stressing that psychoanalysis is about unconscious desire which is not in a direct relationship to 'nature', which is also not a desire which can be fulfilled in reality. In that sense, as Moustafa Safouan points out, 'anatomy is not destiny', even though it does shape the form the castration complex takes (1976: 13). But if it shapes the form the castration complex takes, if it introduces a differential account of the Oedipus complex and its dissolution, can one so easily remove the body from the semiotic? As Andrew Parker puts it:

> the body never stops haunting the presumed autonomy of the unconscious, never stops littering the field of psychoanalysis. . . . Anatomy, then, is neither fully destiny nor lack of destiny in its psychoanalytic conceptuality: it is instead what might be termed its a-destiny, that which prevents psychoanalysis from completely coming into its own as Theory, from thinking that it escapes the body when it defines itself against it.
>
> (Parker 1986: 102)[5]

If the body cannot be ignored, and I do not believe it can be, what is the role of the female body in the structuring of the feminine unconscious? Can we think of the role of the body without falling into a biologizing trap of equating biology and psychology? The richness of Freud's thinking is that he did not in fact omit one or the other sides of the problematic. There is not a one-to-one relationship between body and mind but nor can the body be ignored. The body for Freud is always representation of the body. And if that is so, then it is possible to think that femininity includes both a representation of lack (which has nothing to do with the biological body since in reality there is nothing missing in the female apparatus), and also the representation of an inner space and heterosexual attraction more tied to biological and anatomical reality. The work concerned with specific feminine biological experiences tied to the life cycle of women comes into place here (Benedek 1956; Bibring 1959; Pines 1982, 1989, 1990; Breen 1974, 1989a).

Both conceptions coexist in Freud's work – in a rather unhappy marriage – hence the out-of-focusness which is hard to grasp, but I am suggesting that it is the nature of the beast which makes it an unhappy marriage.

A contradiction structures the feminine unconscious

A way forward is to speak of a duality in feminine sexuality. Dolto in France and Kestenberg in the United States look at this duality from a developmental perspective. Dolto (1965) describes two stages to penis envy. The first she calls '*envie de penis centrifuge*' (centrifugal penis envy), which accompanies castration anxiety and which is experienced as lack or infirmity unfairly inflicted; the second, '*envie de penis centripète*' (directed inwards), accompanied by pride in her genital which permits an identification with her mother and brings with it the desire to receive the penis (penis envy in the sense of penis desire). Kestenberg (1980) distinguishes between an 'inner-genital phase' in the third year of life in which inner-genital impulses are externalized and expressed in the handling of baby dolls, and a phallic phase, divided into a 'phallic negative-Oedipal phase' with intense penis envy and a 'phallic positive-Oedipal phase', where phallic sadistic wishes turn against herself. There seems to be a certain contradiction in these two accounts with envy of the penis and a sense of lack coming before the wish to receive the penis for Dolto, while it is the other way around for Kestenberg. This suggests that it may be more apt to speak of coexistence than stages. (Klein, we saw, does not speak of stages or coexistence, but for her, penis envy is mainly a defence.)

Michèle Montrelay goes further; she stresses that there is a contradiction between a phallic and a 'concentric' character to feminine sexuality, and suggests that it is this contradiction itself which structures the feminine unconscious. Braunschweig and Fain also believe that both 'Freudian' and 'Kleinian' conceptions of female sexuality coexist and that this coexistence is usually conflictual; the woman lives two Oedipal conflicts, one quasi-biological linked to the maternal role and which minimizes the role of the man with the penis experienced as being inside the mother (Kleinian), the other which enhances the role of the clitoris and the subordination of maternity to paternity (with the role of the external father). The wish to have a child (basic feminine desire) and the wish to have a child from the father (substitute for a wish for the penis) are in basic opposition.

Although most contemporary work still opts for one or the other, thinking in terms of a contradiction and opposition between a more biologically based experience of femininity (a positive femininity) and a femininity constructed from the experienced of lack (a negative femininity) goes a long way, I believe, towards understanding the historical oscillations and disputes in the literature and also encompasses a greater range of clinical phenomena. In the case of psychoanalysis it cannot be said that 'the proof is in the pudding' because there is always an important gap between the theory and the clinical data, and clinical data are always interpreted data and subject to further interpretation. However, both the experiences of lack, and the experience of a basic 'positive' femininity seem to come back with sufficient consistency as central and determining to warrant thinking of them as coexistent and conflictual.

Mainly about men

A silent revolution in the psychoanalytic understanding of men

The same basic question of the relationship of mind and body is of course present too in the study of masculinity, and Lacan's solution applies to masculinity as it does to femininity, since he removes the body altogether from the psychoanalytic understanding of masculinity and femininity which he sees as a division in language. This question, however, has not on the whole been a focus since in Freud's model there is not, with masculinity, the same disjunction and hence such a clear bifocality as with femininity. In his scheme masculinity has a more natural and central place for the boy than femininity has for the girl, femininity being achieved by the girl only as the result of a lengthy process.

23

In fact, there *has* been a revolution in the psychoanalytic understanding of masculinity, but it has been more silent and has gone almost unnoticed.

Although it could be said that more has *implicitly* been written on male sexuality since it is with and in himself that Freud's theories first originated with little Oedipus becoming the norm, the study of masculine sexuality is remarkable by the relative paucity of papers specifically devoted to it.

Most of the early papers on female sexuality did make reference to male sexuality. The role of pre-Oedipal phenomena was explored in relation to men but often with a time lag. Understanding of men's masculinity came in the wake of the debates on femininity.

Following Freud's discovery of the importance of pre-Oedipal phenomena in girls he suggested that the pre-Oedipal phase should be investigated in boys too, but he did not go on to do it himself. Others did, and this lead to three major discoveries; first, that the boy's early relationship to the mother could be strongly aggressive, while Freud believed that the mother—son relationship was the least ambivalent of all relationships; secondly, that the boy faces the difficult task of negotiating passive strivings in relation to the mother; and thirdly, for some authors, that there is an early feminine phase with sexual strivings towards the father.

Those analysts who had been part of the Freud—Jones debate and asserted that the girl has an early knowledge of the vagina, also postulated an unconscious knowledge of the vagina in boys and a fear of it. They also questioned the validity of a typical phallic stage in boys as well as in girls (Jones, Horney and Klein).

> If we seriously accept Freud's dictum that the sexual theories formed by children are modeled on their own sexual constitution, it must surely mean [. . .] that the boy, urged on by his impulses to penetrate, pictures in fantasy a complementary female organ.
>
> (Horney 1967: 140).

Jones believed that the boy denies the existence of the vagina because he can thus avoid jealous conflicts (in avoiding knowledge of the parental intercourse) and castration. 'The idea of the vulva must precede that of castration. If there were no dangerous cavity to penetrate into there would be no fear of castration' (Jones 1938: 577). Horney suggests that fear of the father's penis is put forward to hide the intense dread of the vulva (Horney 1932: 353). Klein explained this fear of the mother's body as resulting from the projection of sadistic impulses into her. In addition, Horney saw as critical the boy's fear of ridicule owing to his knowledge that his penis is not large enough to satisfy the mother.

The authors who retained Freud's notion of phallic monism also recognized the importance of an early phase in boys, but their view of that has differed markedly, particularly from Klein's description of early Oedipal phenomena coloured by pre-genital components. Ruth Mack Brunswick, in her paper based on her discussions with Freud, stresses that the phenomena of the pre-Oedipal phase should be described in their own terms and not in the terms of the Oedipus complex. During this pre-Oedipal phase the father is not yet a rival, there is no sexual differentiation between individuals since the boy takes for granted the universal possession of the penis, and the pre-genital zones outweigh the genital one in importance.

With their theory based more on instinct, these authors became particularly preoccupied with the notion that the boy has to make a change from passivity to activity. Ruth Mack Brunswick thought that this was not too problematic because there is always a natural passage from passivity to activity on the part of the child. It learns to sit instead of being held; it reaches out for its own bottle instead of merely receiving it; each bit of activity is based to some extent on an identification with the active mother. The problem, she says, is greater for the girl, who will need to effect the difficult passage to the 'passive Oedipus complex'.[6] On the contrary, 'the boy seems to pass with relative ease out of this predominantly passive, pre-Oedipal attachment to the mother into the characteristically active, normal Oedipus complex'. In the case of an unduly strong, persistent Oedipus complex in the small boy, which is given up with extreme difficulty, much of the fixation is passive instead of active and pre-Oedipal instead of Oedipal (Mack Brunswick 1940: 248). Activity is impaired in the boy due to regression or fixation at the pre-Oedipal level or a 'constitutional inability to overcome the primary inertia'.

Jeanne Lampl-de Groot, on the contrary, thought that the early passive component *was* problematic for the boy. The passive libidinal strivings which are first satisfied by the mother in the pre-Oedipal phase will form the pre-history of the positive attachment to the father, which is a 'passive feminine' or 'homosexual' one (the negative Oedipus complex). While the girl's passive attachment falls within normal development, in the boy it contributes to pathological trends which may later disturb his normal sexuality (Lampl-de Groot 1946: 76–7). Sylvia Payne goes still further, and states that the boy's development might well be *more* difficult than that of the girl – the reverse of what was originally believed. Although the boy does not have to change the sex of is love object, he does have to change the character of his relation to the primary object from an oral-receptive sucking to an active aggressive penetrating and discharging relationship, whereas the girl can displace oral-receptive sucking tendencies from mouth to vagina (Payne 1936: 22).

A number of early papers counterbalance Freud's emphasis on the girl's penis envy by discussing the boy's envy of the mother and her procreative capacity (Boehm 1930; Groddeck 1923; Horney 1926; Jacobson 1950; Bettelheim 1955; Van der Leeuw 1958), Klein believing it to be a more fundamental envy (in both sexes) than penis envy. Felix Boehm writes about an early, feminine phase of development in which the boy's feelings are very much like those of a girl and leads to envy of the woman's functions. This 'vagina envy', he says, looks very much like the woman's penis envy. But he concludes:

> I do not think the material I have quoted in this paper enables us to decide with any certainty whether the man's envy is as closely related to narcissism as the woman's or . . . whether it is substantially influenced by a passsive-homosexual attitude towards the father.
>
> (Boehm 1930: 466–7)

Melanie Klein in her early work also describes a 'femininity phase' in boys as well as in girls. It results from a turning away from the mother towards the father and an identification with the mother. The 'femininity complex', parallel to the castration complex in girls, consists in the frustrated desire for the organs of conception, pregnancy and parturition. In this phase the boy has an oral-sucking fixation on his father's penis. He wants to rob the mother of her internal possessions, including babies, and the father's penis felt to be inside the mother, and also to destroy her babies out of jealousy. He fears punishment by having his body mutilated and dismembered and castrated by the mother. This combines with the dread of castration from the father for attacking his penis inside the mother. Hence the superego is formed from the persecuting images of both the mother and the father. The anxiety associated with the femininity phase drives the boy back to identification with the father.

At first Klein explained the turn away from the mother to the father as the result of deprivation due to weaning in particular; later she came to believe that there is an inherent ambivalence towards objects. In her later writings Klein dropped her concept of a feminine phase altogether.[7] Development is then described as proceeding in both boys and girls through the integration of active and passive trends in relation to each parent, within the context of a very early Oedipal configuration. Klein's description of male and female development runs parallel, and the different outcome rests on instinctual differences and how the instinctual trends are dealt with. Anatomical sexual differences have repercussions too in Klein's view: the girl has a greater tendency for introjection due to the receptive nature of her sexuality; the boy, on the other hand, possesses with the penis what is felt to be both an instrument of cruelty due to the urethral sadistic phantasies connected with it, and an instrument of reparation through its life-giving and pleasure-giving function. The penis also offers the boy possibilities of alleviating anxieties. For the boy as for the girl, the sadistic attacks on the mother's body makes her body a place full of dangers. However, the boy has a specific way of being able to deal with these anxieties. He uses the fact of having a penis to overcome his fear of internal and external dangers and prove his superiority over the dangerous external and internal objects. Because of this, the boy develops his sense of the omnipotence of excreta less strongly than the girl, replacing it in part by the omnipotence of his penis.

> He endows his own penis with destructive powers and likens it to devouring and murderous beasts, firearms, and so on. His belief that his urine is a dangerous substance and his equation of his poisonous and explosive faeces with his penis go to make the latter the executive organ of his sadistic tendencies ... his penis and his sense of omnipotence become linked together in a way which is of fundamental importance for the man's activity and his mastery of anxiety.
>
> (1932b: 243)

The mother's body is a permanent anxiety object for him, but this also increases the attraction of women because it is an incentive to overcome his anxiety.

> the boy's phantasies of taking possession of his mother's body by copulating with her form the basis of his attempts to conquer the external world and to master anxiety along masculine lines. Both as regards the sexual act and sublimations he displaces his danger-situations into the outer world and overcomes them there through the omnipotence of his penis.
>
> (1932b: 243–4)

For Klein both the boy and the girl have to struggle with the primitive psychotic anxieties which threaten the boy's penis and the girl's internal organs, through to a progressive integration and acceptance of the self's impulses. For the boy there are helpful factors in that reassurance is more easily afforded due to the external nature of his genital, in so far as he can make direct reparation to the mother in phantasy with his penis and in so far as his envy of the mother is compensated by his being able to turn to a possession of his own.

Klein minimized her departure from Freud, but her model is significantly different in this area of thinking. It is not just that Klein describes early forms of castration anxiety or forerunners of the castration complex. In her model, castration anxiety is primarily a consequence of sadistic attack on the object and only one form of retaliation feared from both mother and father. This conception departs radically from that of Freud, for whom the castration complex is specifically linked to the prohibition on incest, hence is always part of an Oedipal situation, and marks a definite and structuring moment in mental development.

This still marks a fundamental theoretical difference between psychoanalysts, though it often remains implicit. Generally speaking, however, in spite of this difference there has been a significant move in Britain, in the United States and in France (with the notable exception of Lacan) towards recognizing the importance of the pre-Oedipal phase (or in Kleinian terminology pre-genital and early Oedipal), whether or not the castration complex is considered to be a privileged moment of structuring significance. While the questioning of social roles and structures in the 1960s had a very vocal and colourful expression in the feminist movement and in the discussions around female sexuality, this move towards recognizing the importance of the pre-Oedipal phase in men formed part of a quieter revolution which was brooding, its seeds already sown before the 1960s, leading to a complete about-face in the understanding of masculinity. This understanding developed from the 1960s in the following ways.

First, while authors in the 1930s had begun to note the more difficult task facing the boy because of the need for him to change his aim from passive to active (Payne), after the 1960s psychoanalysts started to note the boy's *greater vulnerability in terms of the development of his masculine identity* due to his early involvement with the mother. This view is in some ways pre-dated by Freud's discussion of Leonardo da Vinci's homosexuality which he links to the absence of a father. But whereas Freud considered the absence of the father in terms of the Oedipal situation, psychoanalysts now concentrated on processes of identity formation.

Greenacre (1953) had already stressed the importance of the first eighteen months to the boy's masculine development and secure gender identity.

Stoller, in his now classical study (1972), shows that transsexual boys had mothers who treated them as an extension of themselves, hence the boys' sense of femininity. Greenson thought that the threat of fusion with the mother or of re-engulfment was fundamental. He writes:

> The girl too must dis-identify from mother if she is to develop her own unique identity, but her identification with mother *helps* her establish her femininity. It is my contention that men are far more uncertain about their maleness than women are about their femaleness. I believe women's certainty about their gender identity and men's insecurity about theirs are rooted in early identification with the mother. I am using the term 'dis-identify' in order to sharpen my discussion about the complex and interrelated processes which occur in the child's

struggle to free himself from the early symbiotic fusion with mother.
. . . The male child's ability to dis-identify will determine the success
or failure of his later identification with his father. These two
phenomena, dis-identifying from mother and counter-identifying with
father are interdependent and form a complementary series.

(Greenson 1968: 370)

The refusal of femininity and the lack of knowledge of the feminine
organ (a point in common for both sexes, according to Freud) is
understood less as bedrock and more as a defence against fusion with the
mother, with its consequent loss of identity (Stein 1961).

Greenson suggests that although women envy men, men at a more
deeply unconscious level harbour an intense envy of women, in particular
the mother, behind a façade of contempt, and he thinks that this envy
is destructive of men's gender identity. He suggests that the dread of
homosexuality, which is the fear of losing one's gender identity, is stronger
and more persistent in men than in women.

Secondly, the role of the father has shifted in the conceptualization
of masculine development. The positive relationship to the father
(described as 'negative Oedipus complex' or 'homosexual attachment')
had been mainly seen by earlier authors as threatening to the development of masculine sexuality (for example, Lampl-de Groot 1947: 76).
Recent thinking stresses the reverse. Klein (1945) had already described
how a positive picture of the father's penis as a good and creative organ
is a precondition of the boy's capacity to develop his positive Oedipus
desires.

For only if the boy has a strong belief in the 'goodness' of his male
genital – his father's and his own – can he allow himself to experience
his genital desires towards his mother. When his fear of the castrating
father is mitigated by trust in the good father, he can face his Oedipus
hatred and rivalry. Thus the inverted and positive Oedipus tendencies develop simultaneously and there is a close interaction between
them.

(Klein 1945: 411)

Increasingly psychoanalysts stress the crucial *importance of the boy's positive
relationship to the pre-Oedipal father* as facilitating the important task of dis-
identification from the mother. Greenson writes:

How much of the boy's identification with the father is a counter-
identification, actually a 'contra'-identification, a means of counteracting
the earlier identification? Is it not in this area where we can find an
answer to why so many men are uncertain about their maleness? Perhaps
it is the shaky basis of their identification with the father, their contra-

identification, which makes them so reactively contemptuous of women and so envious, unconsciously.

(Greenson 1968: 373)

Loewald (1951) sees the father as a positive force against the threat of re-engulfment which precedes the identification heir to the Oedipus complex described by Freud. Glasser also describes the father as an alternative object which can protect against the mother (Glasser 1985). Within Mahler's framework the father is seen as a facilitator to the separation—individuation process. Abelin describes an 'early triangulation' around eighteen months where a toddler identifies with the rival father's wish for mother. Using Piaget and Lacan's work, within the framework of Mahler's research, he suggests that this early triangulation assures the passage from a mirroring, one-to-one interaction to symbolic representation of more than one object in space, including the self.

The role of the father has been increasingly understood as fundamental to psychic functioning in that it is the father who introduces reality between mother and child. The actual absence of the father does not mean absence of representation, since a child without a father constructs the father. For the same reason the introjected father is very different from the reality. Limentani (1991), in re-considering the clinical material from his work with sexual deviants, notes the absence of the father from the material, which he speaks of as a lack of internalization of the father. Chasseguet-Smirgel suggests that the sexual deviant minimizes the role of the father while creating the illusion that he himself is the main object of the mother's sexual interest. For Lacan, the absence of the representation of the father marks psychosis. The reason for the absence of representation remains open to question. If the absent father is constructed, maybe one needs to be thinking more of a refusal of representation of the father, similar to the refusal of acceptance of the parental relationship described by Britton (1989).

American psychoanalysts, from the perspective of ego psychology, speak of a non-defensive pre-Oedipal identification of boys with the father (Tyson 1986), and consider the role of the early relationship to the father with his special characteristics (deep voice, different way of handling babies, and so on).

Thirdly, most theoretical perspectives now consider the role of *early genital phenomena*, though not all agree as to their significance. Galenson and Roiphe describe an early genital phase before the Oedipus complex, beginning between fifteen and twenty-four months of age. Genital arousal at this time provides a channel for tension discharge and for pleasure but *without* any Oedipal resonance. From their observational studies they conclude that the early awareness of sexual difference is less disturbing for boys than for girls because boys deny sexual difference, by avoiding confrontation with female genitals and by a turn to the father and identification with him. They suggest that this extensive use of denial interferes with the boy's capacity for symbolic elaboration in fantasy and interferes with body schematization (Galenson and Roiphe 1980: 817). The emergence of Oedipal strivings threatens the strategy of denial and identification with the father.

In Kleinian theory, on the other hand, early genital impulses are thought to be accompanied by Oedipal phantasies. There is a certain collapsing of distinctions, since the Oedipus complex is thought to arise before the classical genital phase (Freud's phallic phase), so that the term 'pre-Oedipal' is dropped in favour of pre-genital, which means before the stage of genital *primacy*. In the Kleinian conception there is an interaction of impulses from primary zones rather than a linear sequence as in the Freudian model, and the attainment of the genital stage merely means a strengthening of the genital impulses. For instance, O'Shaughnessy (1976) writes that the anal zone enters into the infant's awareness from the beginning in an important way and that anal primacy is a defence; when it persists and predominates it belongs to pathology (see also Heimann 1962). Similarly and significantly, the phallic phase is also seen by Kleinian psychoanalysts not as a normal passage to loving the object but as a narcissistic defence which impedes the negotiation of the Oedipal situation and mature male sexuality (Brenman Pick 1985).

Fourthly, the place and understanding of *castration anxiety* has changed. In classical theory the castration complex describes a set of relations and fears linked to the prohibition on incest. It initiates a differential account for the boy and the girl, bringing about the dissolution of the Oedipus complex for the boy, initiating it for the girl. The word 'complex' denotes its all-encompassing character and role as psychic organizer marking an important moment in development. Masculinity and femininity come into being at that point with the awareness of difference. For both sexes, its mode of resolution will have a determining effect, not just in the area of sexuality but also of character.

Lacan points out that what is important in Freud's account is not the actual body and the perception of the absent penis, nor is it actual prohibitions from the father, but it is the presence of a symbolic threat which marks the condition of being human. The castration complex hence refers to a prohibition against incest which goes beyond the individual experience and belongs to the human order; this distinguishes the human race within the animal kingdom. This understanding of castration with its central place in instigating sexual difference sets Freud apart from all other contributors to this field of study, all of whom relied on a biological explanation for the difference between the sexes – and this on either side of the Freud–Jones debate (Mitchell 1982).

As early as the 1920s the link between castration with the prohibition on incest and the resolution of the Oedipus complex, as well as the primary place of castration in the formation of masculinity, were questioned. It was suggested that castration anxiety represented other losses, the nipple (Starcke 1921), or the womb (Alexander 1922; Rank 1924). Later, Klein also suggested that other factors contributed to the dissolution of the Oedipus complex.

> While I . . . fully agree with Freud that castration fear is the leading anxiety situation in the male, I cannot agree with his description of it as the single factor which determines the repression of the Oedipus complex. Early anxieties from various sources contribute all along to the central part which castration fear comes to play in the climax of the Oedipus situation. Furthermore, the boy experiences grief and sorrow in relation to his father as a loved object, because of his impulses to castrate and murder him. . . . His feelings of guilt about his aggressive impulses towards his father increase his urge to repress his genital desires.
>
> (Klein 1945: 417)

Hence it is not just fear, but in a large measure love which for Klein contributes to the development of the Oedipus complex and its passing. In fact, if anxieties and frustrations are too great, the Oedipus situation cannot develop.

A number of contemporary authors also stress the narcissistic factors involved in the passing of the Oedipus complex (Person 1986), something which Freud and also Horney had already referred to.

Although castration fears are still considered important, the castration complex as such does not in contemporary writings hold the place it did for Freud, except for psychoanalysts who adhere to a largely classical position.

'Castration' is generally understood to represent for both sexes the acknowledgement of incompleteness, of human limitations, the abandonment of the belief in one's omnipotence and the possession of all attributes including the sole possession of the mother's love. It represents acknowledging the mother's relationship to a third party. More specifically, castration anxiety is often understood as integrating and organizing more primitive anxieties (Duparc 1986), often of a psychotic nature – persecution, loss of identity and annihilation. Stoller, David and others suggest (David 1975) that in paranoia, the fear of castration is more than the fear of losing the penis; it is the fear of losing the sense of self, the fear of 'depersonation' rather than just the fear of 'depersonalization' (David 1975).[8]

Tyson considers that castration anxiety can be understood as a developmental metaphor:

> Fears of castration that appear to have primarily pre-Oedipal elements in later life, that is, fears of the 'phallic castrating woman', suggest an early disturbance in the mother–child relationship, unmediated by father, so that the resulting feeling of lack of safety, fears of helplessness, vulnerability, or lack of trust become organized around a fear of castration.
>
> (Tyson 1986: 6)

Phyllis Tyson suggests that castration anxiety is not only an anxiety about the loss of the penis, but also relates 'to the overall sense of masculine identity and fear of one's masculinity being undermined' (Tyson 1989: 1060). She writes that castration anxiety, 'rather than coming into florescence and completion in the phallic phase, as Freud thought, is something the boy must overcome from the beginning of the separation process' (1989: 1056).

Freud's notion of the castration complex has been so diluted that Limentani (1991) even doubts whether castration anxiety 'will ever regain again its position at the very centre of a discussion of male sexuality. Nowadays, almost all analyses tend to deal more and more with early components within the framework of the mother–child relationship.' I think that this can be understood in the sense both that castration anxiety is now more generally seen as being only one form of persecutory anxiety (in relation to mother and to father) and also in the sense that male sexuality is seen to integrate many elements beside the 'phallic' penetrating function. Monique Schneider (1988) says:

> Man is not only phallic. I even think that he could not be tolerated as penetrating if he were not enveloping at the same time. Generally, psychoanalysis doesn't want to know anything about this enveloping power because it reactivates a sort of deep feminine and maternal identification.

The debate is, however, by no means over, and Rangell in a 1991 paper rejects the idea of castration as metaphor and returns to the more classical view of it as 'a pathological belief operative in the unconscious which originated during the period of childhood sexuality' (Rangell 1991: 3); he suggests that if castration anxiety has become a subject of the past it is because psychoanalysis focuses now more on interactional aspects at the expense of reconstruction.

Fifthly, *bisexuality* is given a more important place and more generally recognized as an essential psychological balance of identifications, and an internal balance necessary for sexual and psychic integration.

Freud had oscillated in using the term 'bisexuality' to denote biological facts and psychological facts, and between 'bisexuality' as a given from which the child progressively moves away in order to gain a sexual identity, and 'bisexuality' as an internal state necessary for psychic and sexual integration (David 1975; Laplanche 1970). It is the latter meaning which is given increasing importance. David writes that bisexuality should not just be understood as a negative concept (1975: 823), but needs to be considered as having an important positive and creative aspect. He suggests using the concept of a pre-genital or pre-Oedipal psychobisexuality which refers to an early introjection of a sexual differentiation, prior to the phallic stage.

Meltzer proposes to use the term 'ambisexual' to refer to the appearance of both heterosexual and homosexual acts, as distinct from 'bisexual', which does not refer to pathology but is a metapsychological and biological concept. He relates the bisexual nature of mental states to the introjective identification with internal parental objects and not as a direct expression of the id. This avoids relating masculine and feminine to pre-specified dichotomies such as active—passive, intellectual—intuitive and so on.

Winnicott describes the female and the male elements in both sexes in the following way: the 'pure female element' in both men and women relates to the experience of 'being'. This sense of being antedates being-at-one-with, since baby and object are one. The male element, in contrast, presupposes separateness and is object-relating:

> on the male element side, identification needs to be based on complex mental mechanisms, mental mechanisms that must be given time to appear, to develop, and to become established as part of the new baby's equipment. On the female element side, however, identity requires so little mental structure that this primary identity can be a feature from very early, and the foundation for simple being can be laid (let us say) from the birth date, or before, or soon after. . . .
>
> Psychoanalysts have perhaps given special attention to this male element or drive aspect of object-relating, and yet have neglected the subject—object identity to which I am drawing attention here, which is the basis of the capacity to be. The male element *does* while the female element (in males and females) *is.* . . .
>
> It seems that frustration belongs to satisfaction-seeking. To the experience of being belongs something else, not frustration, but maiming.
>
> (Winnicott 1971: 80–1)

Hence the feminine for Winnicott is that state of primary non-differentiation (in both sexes) which means that men have a more fragile sexual identity and *greater* bisexuality because of the early relationship to the mother.

The recognition of the role and importance of feminine identification in male sexuality and masculine development both as a threat to masculinity but, more importantly, as positive for intrapsychic and interrelational balance has been a major line of development in the recent decades. This psychobisexuality is increasingly understood to be fundamental not just for sexuality but for psychic integration and structuring more generally (McDougall 1989). For Kleinian authors psychic bisexuality, which derives from early identificatory processes and the introjection of each parent, rests on the capacity to have a differentiated image of the two parents in interaction with each other. While Freud believed women to be more bisexual than men because of the early relationship to the mother, the understanding of identity formation has shifted perspective to considering the large part played by feminine identification in men.

A number of authors have pointed out a confusion in the literature between homosexuality and femininity (Meltzer 1973; David 1975). Freud himself in his analysis of Schreber does not distinguish between a homosexual wish and a feminine wish (David 1975: 812). Bergler (1969) writes that it is important to make a distinction between a passive feminine position in men often referred to erroneously as homosexual, and true homosexuality. It is now also generally recognized that true homosexuality itself covers a number of different psychological structures (McDougall 1989; Limentani 1989; and so on).

Sometimes, the term 'homosexual' is used simply to refer to the positive, loving relationship of son to father necessary to psychic health.

Some French psychoanalysts (E. Kestemberg 1984; Sullivan and Weil-Halpern 1984) use the term 'primary homosexuality' to refer to a primary identification of the son to the father, pre-supposing a distinction of maternal and paternal object and proceeding from a narcissistic object choice. This primary homosexuality rests on a shared phantasy between parent and child of the same sex in the context of the primal scene, and serves as an important foundation to the formation of sexual identity. It facilitates later identifications and thus helps to guard against the second 'narcissistic homosexuality' (Frejaville 1984).

Denis (1982) suggests that for the boy there is a primary homosexuality in relation to the mother at a stage before sexual differentiation, when the mother is conceived as like the self, and from which relation will develop tenderness. The recognition of sexual difference will put an end to this primary homosexuality and organize psychic bisexuality. Heterosexuality and secondary homosexuality now appear and give retrospective meaning to the past. From this perspective it is no longer the case

35

that the boy keeps the same object while the girl has to change hers, but the difference is that there is a change which gives retrospectively a different meaning to the object, homosexual for the girl and heterosexual for the boy after the perception of sexual difference.

There certainly has been no simplification or unification of views on masculine development. Nevertheless, what most psychoanalysts have now recognized is the particular fragility of masculine identity, and this makes for a complete about-face from classical theory. While for Freud there was an important disjunction between mind and body in the case of little girls, with femininity only the end result of lengthy process, boys' masculinity, was described as taking a more 'natural' course, leading without explanation required to the Oedipus complex (at which point the resolution of the castration complex would determine its destiny). Recent researches suggest that the early (or subsequent) course is far from straightforward and that the 'fear of femininity' Freud describes stands on even deeper and more basic foundations than he believed. Now, even more than then, the out-of-focusness is evident, the important disjunction yet connectedness of mind and body in the male psyche.

At the end of this rapid overview, which can do no more than indicate the major issues, it will be seen that there are two important, related but not identical, questions in the debate on female sexuality, a debate which maximally highlights the question of the place of the body in psychoanalysis since it is in regard to women that, according to classical theory, psychology is at odds with the actual body. On the one hand, the question of whether there is a specific positive feminine experience 'outside' or 'before' or 'alongside' the experience of lack, on the other hand, the question of whether the early relationship to the mother is to be considered masculine or an intrinsic part of femininity, and conjointly whether the clitoris is a masculine or feminine organ, psychologically speaking.

What stands out beyond the important theoretical differences is the duality at the heart of the feminine in contrast with the greater unity of masculine sexuality, as well as the continuing greater 'mystery' of femininity which some ascribe to its prediscursive component and others relate to the specific nature of the bodily schemata. At the same time, the greater understanding of bisexuality and of the importance for the boy as well as for the girl of the earliest relationship to the mother, has brought a much more complex and differentiated understanding of male sexuality beyond the apparent simplicity. A retreat to the concept of bisexuality, however – an important concept in itself – cannot be an explanatory solution but, more, a working tool. It can only be useful in conjunction and in tension with the concept of the Oedipus complex.

While Freud's genius was to point towards the relative independence of psychological from biological, he none the less believed that 'the ego is first and foremost a bodily ego' (Freud 1923: 26).

For some, the real Freud is the one who separates psychoanalysis from biology, while for others the biological substratum is basic to an understanding of sexuality. I have tried to show that this can be understood as an inherent contradiction and duality which rests at the heart of psychoanalysis and of sexuality – the study of unconscious meanings and fantasies which have the body as their seat. There is a disjunction yet complex articulation of biological and psychological, and of anatomical and psychological. It is in relation to female sexuality that in the classical model the disjunction is greatest, that the construction of sexuality is least straightforward. The issue, as we have seen, is complex and has been debated from various positions, with Montrelay, for instance, arguing for a duality of 'quasi-biological' and 'phallic' development, with Braunschweig and Fain or Gillespie arguing for the 'femininity' of the clitoris.

Psychoanalysis is always confronted with the question of the links of body and psyche, and its foundation comes at the point of rupture between the two (Gantheret 1971). If it is the prerogative of the psychoanalytic approach to stress the *relative* independence of the psychological from the biological, and if in order not to forget this independence it has sometimes had to be taken to extremes, it still holds true that identificatory and interactional processes are woven around and in a loose association with impulses and body schemata. It is a 'criss cross and overlap' (Wittgenstein) in which nothing can be assumed but in which the body cannot be ignored either. However, the body we are talking about from a psychoanalytic point of view is always a representation of the body and hence come the open possibilities, so that understanding the representation of a 'concentric' feminine sexuality need not mean a reductionist biologistic approach. I have argued for an understanding of femininity which encompasses both an unconscious representation of lack and an unconscious representation of its 'concentric' aspects.

The papers chosen for this book – all from the last two or three decades – come from Britain, France and the United States; the selection does not, of course, aim to be fully representative of the work on this vast topic.

In the papers selected to illustrate the themes of this book I have not been concerned so much with covering specific topics relating to the many aspects of femininity and masculinity which have been written about, as with structures of the mind. The Oedipus complex and bisexuality, the first and last sections (Parts One and Four), define such structures.

In Parts Two and Three I address more specifically the central issue I discussed in this introduction relating to the debate around the question of whether femininity is or is not based on a lack, and more generally to the relationship of body and mind.

Masculinity and femininity is a field of study probably more typified by its disparity than by unity. A certain coherence in this collection of papers comes from my own thesis, that the tension beween 'anatomy is destiny' and keeping 'psychoanalysis separate from biology', which has coloured the debate about female sexuality, has not gone away, that attempts to resolve it by putting psychoanalysis firmly in the 'symbolic' register have proved unsatisfactory, and that a way forward is to make theoretical use of the contradiction. Part Two addresses this issue directly, while Part Three considers issues of body representation which go beyond the 'phallic question'.

Ultimately it is, from a psychoanalytic perspective, the underlying phantasy which determines whether an act is masculine or feminine. But the phantasy takes the body as its foundation and incorporates bodily characteristics and sensations. Understanding masculinity and femininity means understanding that interplay, means tolerating the out-of-focusness.

Notes

1 Lampl-de Groot in her 1927 paper, 'The evolution of the Oedipus complex in women', pre-dated Freud's understanding of the early attachment to the mother, referring to it as the girl's 'negative Oedipus complex', which she believed was identical to the boy's positive Oedipus complex.

2 Within academic and feminist circles the work of Lacan took on importance in Britain following the publication of Mitchell's book, *Psychoanalysis and Feminism* (1974), written before she became a psychoanalyst.

3 Lacan also disregards the role of affects. His theory does not incorporate the 'memories in feeling' or indeed any pre-discursive phenomena which form such a central part of British psychoanalytic theory.

Green (1986) suggests that in the early years (the years to which Lacan goes back) Freud placed an emphasis on representations rather than affect because of his concern with demonstrability and scientific status and his wish to keep psychoanalysis separate from hypnosis and catharsis, but in his later work there is an increasing place given to affect, which is now granted unconscious status.

4 In this sense there is always a three-person situation, something both Klein and Lacan would agree on.

Laplanche and Pontalis (1973) even ask if we can really speak of a 'pre-Oedipal phase' which implies a period characterized by a two-person relationship between mother and child, since for Freud the father is present at the beginning as a 'troublesome rival', and his use of the term 'negative complex' may be more appropriate to his meaning.

5 Mack Brunswick suggests the use of the terms 'active' and 'passive' Oedipus complex rather than positive and negative Oedipus complex. According to this new terminology the pre-Oedipal sexuality of the girl becomes her active Oedipus complex with the mother as its object; her passive Oedipus complex has the father as its object. For the boy, the active Oedipus complex denotes the positive Oedipus complex with the mother as object; his passive Oedipus complex has as its object the father.

6 Klein's interest in a femininity phase declined when she became interested in the depressive position, that is, with the conflicts of love and hate towards the same object.

7 The debate amongst feminist theoreticians continues around the role of the body, with Braidotti, for instance, arguing that 'feminist theoreticians should re-connect the feminine to the bodily sexed reality of the female'. See Sayers' book, *Biological Politics* (1982), for a discussion of the place of biology within feminism.

8 David (1975) uses the term 'depersonation' to contrast with 'depersonalization'.

PART ONE

The Oedipus complex

Introduction

The Oedipus complex formed the kernel of Freud's understanding of human sexuality, and he comments: 'None of the findings of psycho-analytic research has provoked such embittered denials, such fierce opposition – or such amusing contortions – on the part of critics as this indication of the childhood impulses towards incest which persist in the unconscious'. (Freud, SE4, 1900; footnote, 1914: 263).

The tragic story of Oedipus, who killed his father and married his mother, which is on the level of phantasy for the human individual, is subject to repression. It is the unconsciousness of the desire (Oedipus did not know they were his parents since he had been separated from them at birth), as well as its prohibition, which describes human sexuality from a psychoanalytic point of view. When Oedipus discovered his incestuous actions he stabbed his eyes out (symbolic castration) and fled from the land he had polluted. The prohibition of the incestuous act is what leads the boy towards adulthood through repression of the desire and identification with the father. The authority of the father or the parents is introjected into the ego, forming the nucleus of the superego and perpetuating the prohibition against incest. The libidinal trends are desexualized and changed into impulses of affection.[1]

The recognition of sexual difference in classical theory has a momentous but not identical consequence for the boy and the girl. The sight of the female genital engenders in the boy the fear that he could lose his penis, giving new, retrospective meaning to earlier threats of castration or experiences of loss (of the feeding breast, of his own faeces). In order to eschew this possibility, the boy abandons and represses his wish to take his father's place in relation to his mother.

The moment of recognition, on the other hand, arouses anger and envy in the little girl, who up until then was 'a little man' in that she too took her mother as her love object, her phallic strivings towards her coming from her clitoris. Acceptance of 'castration', and the anger with the mother who deprived her of a penis, will instigate her turning to her father as her love object and to the babies he can give her as a substitute for the penis. This desire will be gradually given up because it is never fulfilled. Whereas the recognition of sexual difference and the fear of castration ultimately leads to the dissolution of the Oedipus complex for the boy, for her the recognition of sexual difference initiates the Oedipus complex when she gives up her wish for a penis and puts in place of it a wish for a child,

> and with that purpose in view she takes her father as a love-object. Her mother becomes the object of her jealousy. The girl has turned into a little woman ... this new situation can give rise to physical sensations which would have to be regarded as a premature awakening of the female genital apparatus.
>
> (Freud 1925: 256)

The girl's turn to the father is more than just a change of object, Freud says. Active trends which have been frustrated are abandoned, and some of the passive trends too. The transition to the father-object is accomplished with the help of the passive trends in so far as they have escaped the catastrophe. The path to the development of femininity now lies open to the girl, to the extent to which it is not restricted by the remains of the pre-Oedipal attachment to her mother which she has surmounted. Because the turning to the father is accomplished with the help of the passive trends, a masochistic attitude will be important to female sexuality, while the narcissistic wound of her discovery of sexual difference will lead her to identify her whole body with the phallus in a narcissistic way. Because there is no threat of castration for the girl, the Oedipus complex does not come to an abrupt end as it does for boys, and hence the formation of the superego will suffer.

The Oedipus complex is still, as it was for Freud, considered to be central to the development of masculinity and femininity, shaping identifications, and central to the understanding of deviant sexual development. All psychoanalysts agree upon this. What differs is the timing of the Oedipus complex, what phenomena it encompasses and the understanding of its origin, in particular the role of 'castration' in instigating the girl's Oedipus complex which only 'classical' theorists uphold. Its 'pre-history' is now generally granted greater importance than it had for Freud, but there is controversy as to what forms the Oedipus complex, with Kleinian writers including manifestations from the pre-genital phase, while for others the Oedipus complex denotes only those manifestations of three-person attraction and rivalry which have a genital basis. There is also a controversy as to when genital sensations take on Oedipal meaning, again with Kleinian authors dating this much earlier than most.

The relationship between pre-Oedipal and Oedipal elements is conceptualized in two different ways. In the one conceptualization, to the classical Oedipus phase is added an earlier, discrete phase. This is Lampl-de Groot's perspective; she suggests that the separation of sexuality from tenderness which Freud first described as common in men could be understood in terms of the mother of the pre-Oedipal phase and the mother of the Oedipal phase:

> the admired and honored woman is chosen according to the mother image of the period of the Oedipus complex. She is the heiress to the great love of little Oedipus for Jocasta. The degraded sexual partner, on the other hand, is the heiress to the image of the mother of the pre-Oedipal phase: she has inherited the intense hostility that the little boy may have felt for her. That hostility, in turn, stems from his early ambivalence toward the mother and is reinforced by the fact that the mother has later become his rival in his love for the father. The adult man can vent his anger against the degraded sexual object; he can mistreat her, can force her to satisfy all his needs and desires, even perverse ones, and can compel her to attend to his wants as he wished his mother to do when he was a little boy.
>
> (Lampl-de Groot 1946: 76)

In the other conceptualization. Oedipal and pre-Oedipal are more closely interconnected. Blanck writes:

> Although Freud applied the Oedipus myth to the normal family, it does not describe a normal family constellation. The normal Oedipal situation requires that there shall have been a pre-Oedipal family life in which preponderantly positive self representations and positive representations of both parents develop out of positive affective experiences. These attenuate the murderous wishes of the Oedipal phase. One questions whether the normally developing child can wish unambivalently to kill the parent of the same sex with whom she or he has built up positive cathexes over the pre-Oedipal years. Murderous wishes have to be transient, not even necesssarily restricted to Oedipal wishes, but more broadly attributable to normal quantities of negative affect. I am not persuaded that the Oedipal wish can overthrow all that went before, although I acknowledge its power.
>
> (Blanck 1984: 336)

Blanck does at the same time recognize the Oedipus complex as 'a critical period in Spitz's sense of convergence of drive maturation with ego development' (1984: 337).

In the case of the girl, while Freud described a definite developmental move from one object to the other following disappointment, the relationships to mother and father are now conceived as more fluid. Ogden (1987) points out that disruption of the pre-Oedipal relationship to the mother as described by Freud at the time of the change of object would be expected to lead to the erection of narcissistic and omnipotent defences rather than to Oedipal love as the foundation of healthy love relationships. The early relationship to the father is now recognized, and there is seen to be a constant move between negative and positive complex (Laufer 1984). The role of the father before the Oedipus complex is recognized, both in his direct interaction with the child and indirectly in consequence of his interaction with the mother (Formanek 1982). The role of the mother or the parent's unconscious phantasies and desires in structuring the sexuality of the child has been emphasized (Le Guen 1984). Lichtenstein (1961) believes that the infant is given an identity by the mother, he is 'the organ, the instrument for the fulfillment of the mother's unconscious needs'.

For Klein's followers there is an early Oedipus complex, early femininity and no normal phallic phase since they do not accept the theory of phallic monism (see also Blanck de Cereijido 1983). The Oedipus complex is described as biologically determined since it does not result from the perception of 'castration'. Most other authors retain the classic phallic phase, even when they describe an earlier 'primary femininity', which modifies considerably the classical picture (Phyllis Tyson). Edgcumbe and Burgner (1975) make a further distinction between a 'phallic-narcissistic phase' during which the narcissistic investment of sexually differentiated aspects of the body assumes particular importance, and an 'Oedipal phase' in the later part of the phallic phase when triangular Oedipal relationships are established.

Roiphe and Galenson (1980), using Mahler's framework, suggest that the *rapprochement* crisis is more troubled for girls than it is for boys, because their recognition of sexual difference is not denied as it is by boys and leads to a heightened aggressive aspect of the ambivalence to the mother and a turning to the father, in preparation for the future positive Oedipal constellation.

Using Klein's later formulations, Kleinians make a distinction between less mature (or early stages of) and more mature forms of the Oedipus complex. While the paranoid-schizoid mode of functioning predominates, the Oedipal conflict will be experienced in a very split fashion (with one parent or part-object idealized and the other experienced as persecuting). The Oedipus complex in its more mature form (which is the true Oedipus complex) is thought to be intrinsically related to the depressive position in that it describes a relationship to whole objects. In fact one could say that the traditional Oedipus story as it is told, although referring to whole objects, operates at the level of murder and talion, which is the paranoid-schizoid mode of functioning. Segal suggests reserving the term 'Oedipus complex' for the relationship to the parents as whole people of the depressive position, and that what sometimes appears as an Oedipus complex is not a true triangular relationship but the projection of the hated aspects of the breast onto the penis. This will have the appearance only of an Oedipus complex in the boy.

Whatever the theoretical orientation, and whatever the debates about what is true Oedipus complex and what is not, and about when to locate it in time, the Oedipus complex is still generally thought to have a fundamental role in the structuring of sexuality, in spite of the increasing place given to pre-Oedipal or pre-genital phenomena. An important difference remains around whether it is conceived of as developing in progressive continuity or seen as imposing a distinctive new structure which reorganizes and gives new meaning to earlier perceptions. For instance, Denis (1982), taking up Freud's own formulation, suggests that although sexual differences are perceived early and play a role as precursors, it takes an extra element (the Oedipus complex and castration) to initiate later a Copernican revolution leading to all differences being re-organized around the sexual difference, which then takes on special and fundamental significance. Hence early bodily experiences and parental attitudes become determining retrospectively. Some contemporary Kleinians have shifted the perspective from the classical Oedipus complex as described by Freud. They suggest that the true Oedipus complex is recognizing the couple as a creative relationship which produces the baby and recognizing the hate, jealousy and envy it provokes.

> The fantasies of going off with daddy or going off with mummy are really defensive structures against those feelings, an Oedipal myth as distinct from the reality underneath. Any deviation from sexuality of that kind is an internal attack on the parents as a couple, and in that sense is not really a complete healthy development.
>
> (Segal 1990)

Britton (1989) calls them 'Oedipal illusions', intended to deny the Oedipus situation.

Maxwell Gitelson, reviewing the role of pre-genital conflicts in pathology, concluded in 1952 that 'the Oedipus complex thus has a typical importance not so much as the nucleus of the neuroses but as the nucleus of normal character structure and as the basis of mature life' (1952: 354). This view is still generally held, in spite of the differences in perspective.

The formative role of negative as well as positive Oedipal constellations is also generally recognized. The papers of both Blos (1984) and

Laufer (1984) included in Part One, written on either side of the Atlantic, one describing masculine development, the other feminine development, illustrate current thinking which emphasizes a constant fluctuation between positive and negative Oedipus complex rather than a strictly linear development, and progressive change rather than discrete times of trauma and resolution.

In his paper, Blos stresses the importance of the negative Oedipus complex in the formation of masculine identity with its important roots in the pre-Oedipal relationship to the father.

Eglé Laufer describes the vicissitudes of the girl's giving up of the phantasy of being able to keep the mother's love for herself, which goes along with her acceptance of 'castration'; that is, the acceptance of her body and of being of the same sex as the mother. She views this as 'an organizer' which lays the foundation to her relationship to herself as a woman.

Part and parcel of the Oedipal situation is the recognition by both sexes that the parents have a relationship to each other. Britton (1989) describes in his paper, from a Kleinian perspective, the function of this 'triangular space' and the defensive manoeuvres and organizations which take place when that recognition of the parental link cannot be tolerated.

Note

1 The Oedipus complex came to mean for Freud more than this 'positive version' and to denote more broadly the child's situation in the triangle, both 'homosexual' and 'heterosexual', thus emphasizing the centrality of bisexuality.

1

Son and father

PETER BLOS

As the title of this presentation indicates, I shall limit myself to a narrowly confined aspect of object relations. It is a topic that defies precise circumscription partially due to its vast ramifications and to its still contentious and unsettled place in psychoanalytic theory. The fact that my chosen subject is one of momentous importance in human life requires no persuasion nor testimony. In choosing it I emphasize a current trend in clinical and theoretical psychoanalysis. I shall begin with a brief overview of recent developments as well as the historical ones in the orbit of son and father.

The discovery of the Oedipus complex, its fateful role in life and, particularly, in neurosogenesis has led to an ever-deepening investigation of its complexity. Originally, gender polarity represented a core configuration in Oedipal conflict formation; this fact is still discernible today in Oedipal terminology when we speak of the positive and the negative Oedipus complex. For brevity's sake I shall refer in this text simply to the 'positive complex' or the 'negative complex'. As far as I propose modifications of their classical definitions, I trust that my presentation as a whole will convey the qualifications in psychoanalytic theory I intend to suggest.

The case of Dora permits us to contrast early and contemporary views of Oedipal dynamics. Dora illustrates the pathogenic valence that Freud (1905) attributed to the positive complex and its influence on her life, even though he gave ample evidence of his suspicion or, indeed, his conviction that the negative complex was at the root of her illness. This he stated clearly in the case study itself (pp. 60–1) and in a letter to Fliess (14 October 1900), even though it played a minor role in the analytic work with the girl — at least, as far as we can glean from the clinical report. The degree as well as the kind of pathogenic valence the clinician

49

assigns to pre-Oedipality and to one or the other of the two complexes in their dynamic inter-play, often remain a matter of emphasis or preconception. In contrast to the treatment of Dora, the pathogenicity of pre-Oedipal object relations is taken for granted in almost any case today, and afforded a prominent place not only in the evolutionary history of a given neurosis, but explicitly and increasingly in the analytic work itself.

The polarity of gender – son–mother, daughter–father – has dominated the concept of the Oedipal constellation since its inception and has weighed heavily in the etiologic formulation of the neurotic conflict. However, clinical observations have attributed an increasingly persuasive significance to isogender early object relations. Indeed, both constellations, namely those of isogender and allogender partnership, have received slowly, at times reluctantly, the recognition of equal significance in the theoretical formulations of normal and pathological development. This historical reference might sound groundless or overstated at its first hearing, yet we cannot deny that the positive complex and its resolution have received far more attention in the analytic literature than the natural history as well as the resolution of the negative complex ever has.

It was this extreme sparseness of investigations in male isogender object relations from the earliest stages of development onward that prompted me to inquire into these neglected issues. My analytic work had convinced me that early isogender experiences not only dominate and shape the son–father relationship at infancy, but influence critically the boy's creation of his self and object world for a lifetime. This complexity of the son–father relationship has always been known, even if never sufficiently illuminated. Freud has described the contrasting roles played by the father in the son's life.

The Oedipal father is by definition the restraining and punishing father under whose threat of retaliation the little boy abandons his competitive strivings, as well as his patricidal and incestuous animus. There has never been any doubt that this father picture is incomplete and misleading because we know that the typical father also acknowledges and elicits his little son's self-assertion; being emulated by the son fills the father with pride and joy as does the junior toddler's phallic, narcissistic and exhibitionistic exuberance.

A well-known comment by Freud will remind us that we revisit old and familiar territory: 'As regards the prehistory of the Oedipus complex ... [W]e know that the period includes an identification of an affectionate sort with the boy's father' (Freud 1925: 250). This early experience of being protected by the father and caringly loved by him becomes internalized as a lifelong sense of safety in a Boschian world of horrors and dangers. It seems to me that too exclusive a contribution to the sense of bodily integrity has been attributed to the early mother. We have ample occasion to observe in the analysis of adult men the enduring influence of this father imago, especially when it remains unaltered by reality. The 'over-idealization of the analyst and analysis' reflects the father's role in the child's life during the first two years (Greenacre 1966). The resistance aroused whenever the analytic work threatens to deprive the patient of his father-illusion confirms the life-sustaining influence of the early child–father relationship. The patient will not let go of it easily ... the terrifying impression of helplessness in childhood aroused the need for protection – for protection through love – which was provided by the father' (Freud 1927: 30). The little boy seeks by active and persistent solicitation the father's approval, recognition and confirmation, thus establishing a libidinal bond of a profound and lasting kind. Some questions force themselves upon us: Where do the origins of those affections lie? At which stage of object relations do they flourish? Under what conditions do these hallmark emotions of the negative complex seemingly vanish or what transformations do they undergo? One receives the impression from the literature that the negative complex declines by the ascendancy and subsequent resolution of the positive complex or, in other words, that the fully developed triadic configuration effects by its sheer ascension the resolution or transformation of the negative complex. Of course, every analyst knows that this is not the case. Yet, until recently, very little attention has been paid to the process or the timing of this particular kind of isogender attachment resolution. We are presently justified to say that the qualitative and pathogenic specificity of this closeness derives from an unaltered perpetuity in the son–father relationship, the beginnings of which are to be found in a quasi-maternal bonding by substitution.

It is a well-known historical fact that with the establishment and growth of child analysis the frontiers of psychoanalytic practice and, consequently, of theory-building were pushed out farther and deeper into the realms of infancy as well as adolescence, namely, into those two epochs of life during which psychic structure formation, initiated by physical matura-tion, proceeds on a grand scale. Detailed and direct child observation provided a wealth of new and subtle details with regard to psychic differentiation and developmental moves, thus amending and altering in precision and complexity our previous knowledge of psychic structure formation as derived from reconstruction. These exploratory penetrations into the developmental terrains of both infancy and adolescence delivered findings that enriched the general body of psychoanalysis and, conse-quently, widened the scope of our science. Instead of relying largely on the reconstruction of infantile trauma and object relations, of internalization processes, of psychosexual and ego development from the analysis of adults, it became possible to observe them in their germinal states and follow their growth. Observing first-hand what had previously been largely inferred, enhanced our knowledge of a more exact schedule – comprising sequences and timing – of infantile and adolescent development.

As a first consequence of psychoanalytic infant research, the pre-Oedipal mother moved prominently to center-stage, eclipsing Oedipality to a considerable degree in the etiological determination of mental disturbances as they became manifest later in life. By virtue of distinguishing more clearly the pre-Oedipal determinants in pathogenicity generally, the limits and the criteria of analyzability became more sharply delineated. What I want to call attention to at this point is the importance of the pre-Oedipal father in the life of the male child. Here we find ourselves on territory not yet fully charted, but with sufficiently explored contours of the terrain to know in which directions to advance our search. The findings just alluded to not only have changed our knowledge of timing as to paternal recognition by the infant, but have also drawn a sharper outline of the earliest stages of parental imitation, internalization and identification. The dating of core gender identity to an earlier period relegates many classical psychoanalytic tenets of psychosexual development to the archives of our science.

I have devoted the major portion of my professional life to the investigation of the adolescent process. Adolescence thus became the focus of my clinical observations from which my theoretical constructs radiated backwards and forwards into the proto-adolescent and the meta-adolescent stages of the life cycle. I refer here to my adolescent research because the theme of this paper is launched from these observations and their theoretical inferences. Edging my way into the substance of this presentation, I state now a proposition which I advanced some years ago. I share the well-established opinion that the male child arrives at a resolution of the positive complex prior to his entry into latency, but beyond that, I have postulated that his negative complex, having its origin in the dyadic stage of object relations, survives in a repressed, more or less unaltered, state until adolescence (Blos 1974). Developmentally speaking, the necessity arises to differentiate between a dyadic and a triadic positive and negative complex.

Whatever course the individual resolution of the positive complex will take, its achievement is always reflected in the formation of a new structure, the superego. Dual parental pre-Oedipal determinants are always recognizable in the final superego structure. What appears, however, to acquire prominence in the male superego is the dominant voice of the father principle which is, at its dyadic origin, not yet instinctually conflicted but belongs to a pre-competitive, idealizing stage of the 'good father'. Both father and mother complex operate at this level more or less reactively and compensatorily rather than in an antagonistic libidinal entanglement. The prototypical dyadic split into pleasure and unpleasure parental figures precludes by its very nature the formation of an internal conflict. This pre-conflictual state is further upheld by the attribution of pain to the external world, the 'not-me' realm of perception and the attribution of pleasure to the 'me' experience, inclusive of the pleasure object; within this dawning affective awareness lies the emergence of the self. Precursors of this process are apparent from early infancy on; they become organized and stabilized in psychic structure with the decline of the Oedipal phase. All this is well-established psychoanalytic knowledge. It is also well known that positive and negative components of the complex are inseparably intertwined but nevertheless distinguishable by the preponderance or dominance of one or the other in their constant ebb and flow. Alongside these differentiating processes in the male child – so I submit – the negative complex is not subjected to as radical a transformation during pre-latency as the positive one is. In other words, its definitive transformation into psychic structure is delayed until adolescence.

With the advent of sexual maturation arrives the biological imperative for definitive and irreversible sexual identity; as a coefficient of this imperative we can isolate, observe and define adjunct identities of a social, cognitive and self-representational nature. They form in their synergic evolution the post-latency personality. This process of psychic restructuring affects every facet of the adolescent's life and promotes forcefully the terminal resolution of the negative complex. What had appeared to me earlier in my work as the resuscitation of the positive complex which, by deflection, transformation and displacement turns in an apparently pre-determined fashion to extra-familial heterosexual object-finding, gradually acquired in my clinical judgment the character of a largely defensive operation. Here I have in mind the fact that the boy's dyadic father relationship which fluctuated between submission, self-assertion and sharing the father's grandeur is drawn into the sexual realm with the advent of puberty. The regressive pull is counteracted by sexual gender assertion. I came to see ever so clearly that this defense springs into action in the wake of a resurgence of the boy's negative complex which reaches, at puberty, the apex of its conflictuality.

The defensive state I speak of is transitory in nature and declines with the definitive resolution of the negative complex at the closure of adolescence. I am fully aware that this exposition does not tell the whole story, but I highlight here intentionally what appears to me a neglected stage in the ontogeny of mature male object relations and of the mature self. This particular comprehension of male sexuality at adolescence gained further clarity and plausibility from the analytic observation that inordinate, compulsive, heterosexual activity or, conversely, anxiety arousal due to heterosexual inaction or passivity, subsided markedly with the resolution of the negative complex. I noticed that the decline of this conflict introduces a kind of heterosexual attachment behaviour which possesses a different quality: to this we refer as a mature (or more mature) love relationship in which the defensive nature of the attachment has dropped away and recognition as well as appreciation can be extended to the uniqueness of the partner as a whole person. When the defensive quality of the immature bonding between sexually mature partners has gradually dissipated, then the formation of the adult personality is reasonably assured.

The termination of adolescence constitutes a critical and contributory stage in the formation of the adult neurosis. Indeed, it is the persistent incapacity of the young man to surmount his negative complex which leads to the consolidation of the manifest and definitive neurosis of his adult life. By inferring that the Oedipus complex as a dynamic totality does not yield normally to a post–Oedipal level of object relations until the closure of adolescence, I simultaneously postulate that the structuralization of the adult neurosis cannot be thought of as completed until adolescence has passed. I shall not elaborate here on the far-reaching consequences of the adolescent process, delivered or aborted, on the ultimate attainment of emotional maturity or psychopathology, but continue on the path that brings us closer to the core of my presentation.

In accordance with the Oedipal schema just outlined, I am now ready to say that the resolution of the Oedipus complex in its totality advances in a biphasic fashion: the resolution of the positive component precedes latency − in fact, facilitates its formation − while the resolution of the negative component has its normal timing and takes its normal course in adolescence or, to be more precise, in late adolescence when it facilitates the entry into adulthood. This schema became further complicated by my analytic observation that the flight of the adolescent boy to the father, defensively manifested by rising oppositionalism and aggression, is usually commensurate to the intensity and urgency of the son's need for a protective closeness to him *vis-à-vis* the magnetic and mysterious female to whom he is irresistibly drawn. This drive constellation is too frequently and too readily identified with homosexuality; such a simplistic equation demands a vigorous disclaimer. What we observe is the male's defensive struggle against passivity in general, not against homosexuality in particular. I must insert at this point that I am aware of having left aside some well-known and relevant facts about the boy's competitive and antagonistic struggle with the Oedipal father. After all, adolescence is the stage in life when the universal polarities of active and passive are in conflict and in final combat on a Promethean scale. In the analysis of the adolescent boy it is imperative that this double-faceted defensive struggle − against submissiveness and passivity as well as against self-assertion and patricide — becomes disentangled. How this dilemma appeared in a treatment and was acted out in the transference, I shall illustrate with a clinical episode.

A late-adolescent boy had reacted for some time to my interpretations of his violent behaviour toward his parents, especially the father, as proof of my taking sides with them and considering his accusatory and demeaning comments about them as amoral and demented. This reaction had reached paranoid proportions. I abstained from interpreting his acting out in the transference because I knew that repeated interpretations too often lose their credibility. During a session which I shall now describe, the patient accused me in a highly agitated state of thinking of him as a helpless and weak child, scared to stand up against his father. He was obviously trying to pick a fight with me and stand his ground. When his shouting attack mounted and threatened to get out of hand, I told him firmly and stentorially that he had to stop telling me what is on my mind or leave. His outburst suddenly subsided; he became calm and pensive. After a long silence, he said quietly: 'I just remembered a dream I had last night. I am wrestling with my father, not fighting, just wrestling. Suddenly I feel that I'm coming — I cannot control it — I get panicky and I yell: "No, no — I don't want to make up with you!" I repeat these words again and again, getting more and more desperate. I can't stop the orgasm. I have it.' After the recall of this dream neither patient nor analyst had much difficulty in recognizing son and father's sporty playfulness which was a rare event in the boy's early and middle childhood. 'I hardly ever played with my father. He was not there — especially when I was afraid of my mother. I saw just enough of him — or perhaps more than enough of my mother — to know how much I missed him.' The dream reflects the son's present struggle between a murderous defense against submission and a passionate yearning for paternal acknowledgment of his manhood. The paranoid reverberations of his past, examined in the struggle of his adolescent life, freed the young man from the fixation on the pre-Oedipal father and facilitated his advance toward the Oedipal level. Alongside this developmental progression, the compulsive and defensive need for 'having sex' gave way to a wish and a budding capacity to form a relationship of a sexual as well as a personal, emotional and romantic nature.

Returning to the discussion of analytic developmental theory, I must admit that much of what I had attributed to the triadic relationship in my first realization of the adolescent boy's libidinal attachment to the father had to be relegated to the dyadic phase. In other words, the father of the negative complex is intrinsically fused with the father of the pre-Oedipal period. The regressive pull to the father of the dyadic phase becomes apparent when the adolescent boy is viewed in a developmental continuum, as outlined above. Pursuing this course of thinking and developmental allocation in the analytic work with adolescent boys and adult men, it became apparent to me that the loved and loving father of the pre-Oedipal and Oedipal period (that is, the father of the negative complex) ascends to a paramount conflictual position at the terminal stage of adolescence. Once alerted to this phenomenon, I became used to its omnipresence as a normal constituent of the male adolescent process and I gradually desisted from relegating the manifestations of these inordinate passions to the realm of abnormal development or Oedipal psychopathology. It is no uncommon observation, especially if derived from the microscopic scrutiny of the tidal currents of emotions as is possible in analytic work, that isogender libidinal drives break through after their relative calm of the latency years has passed. These urges do not represent prima facie a homosexual inclination or disposition, but rather confirm that the normal adolescent formation of male sexual identity is on its way. What we observe, then, are the emotional and expressive manifestations of the normal negative complex in transition.

As early as 1951, Loewald made the following comment of a general developmental nature: 'Against the threat of the maternal engulfment the paternal position is not another threat of danger, but a support of powerful force.' Mahler (1955) confirmed this finding by saying that 'the stable image of a father or of another substitute of the mother, beyond the eighteen-months mark and even earlier, is beneficial and *perhaps a necessary prerequisite* [italics added] to neutralize and to counteract the ego-characteristic oversensibility of the toddler to the threat of re-engulfment by the mother'. Of course, both statements refer in equal measure to boy and girl infant. A psychoanalytic researcher and clinician who paid particular attention to the development of the early relationship between infant and father during the dyadic period is Abelin (1971, 1975; Panel 1978); Ross (1977, 1979) has written a comprehensive overview of the literature that deals with the role of the father in the development of the young child from its beginnings through the early formative years; and Herzog (1980) has contributed original research in this field.

Returning to the mainstream of my deliberations, I have so far submitted two theoretical statements which are the outcome of my analytic work with adolescent boys. As the next step, I endeavour to integrate them into the body of psychoanalytic theory, its schema of development, and the dynamics of neurosogenicity. One of the two propositions, as stated above, attributes to adolescence the final resolution of the negative complex, implying that the resolution of the Oedipus complex proceeds in a biphasic progression. The other proposition states that much of what had been generally attributed to the revival of the Oedipal father in adolescence is more profitably understood – as to origin and nature – if related to the pre-Oedipal father imago of the dyadic period. Such an adjudication requires some evidence to be persuasive.

At this point a differentiation – even a tentative and incomplete one – between the son–father relationship of the dyadic and of the triadic period should be welcome. The pre-Oedipal father takes over from the early mother some significant portions of the infantile attachment emotions, inclusive of the split in good and bad object. Should the father at this stage serve only as a simple replacement of the mother, then the relationship can be expected to become pathogenic; should the father, however, be perceived and used differently by his son, then a healthy expansion and enrichment of the child's incipient personality becomes discernible. The father assumes for the little boy, early in life, a charismatic quality in his physical presence which is different in its constitutional disposition and bodily responsiveness from that of the mother. The respective quality of the way the father or the mother holds the infant or plays with him demonstrates well the variance or disparity of which I speak. The father of the dyadic period is indeed a facilitator who, in conjunction with the mother, activates the individuation process and finally becomes for his son a saviour from the beckoning regression and the threatening re-engulfment during the *rapprochement* subphase (Mahler 1955). This father, i.e. the dyadic father, has been called 'uncontaminated' due to the fact that he has never been a full-fledged symbiotic partner. He belongs to the post-differentiation, pre-ambivalent, idealizing stage of early object relations. Jealousy is indeed noticeable and so is the quest for total object possession. However, the son's turn to the father is not yet affected or burdened by sexual jealousy, patricidal conflict and retaliatory anxiety. These emotional discordances belong to the father of the Oedipal era. The idea of a belated resolution of the negative complex at adolescence forced itself on my mind by the eloquent role this emotional conflict plays in the analysis of every male adolescent.

When I once made a comment to an older male adolescent about his complacent, unconflicted and timeless dwelling in analysis, he responded with the recall of a blissful feeling, similar to the one that suddenly had welled up in him when I spoke. He remembered the precious occasions when he was permitted as a little boy to sit quietly in his father's study while his father worked at his desk. He re-experienced in the analytic situation the dyadic bliss of his childhood. In pursuit of this recollection, he came to realize that his life-long thirst for great accomplishments and fame was not only due to the meekly attempted and prematurely abandoned competition with his father, but – more basically – it embodied his passionate quest for his father's love, indeed, for union and oneness with him. When the patient gleaned this insight through the vehicle of transference interpretations he was deeply moved and said: 'It feels like being accepted for the first time in my father's arms or to have a life of my own, not just playing at it.' I came to realize that what originally had led to the neurotic stalemate was his need for dyadic bonding which, in turn, left only make-believe or inauthentic action open to him in his never-ending effort to transcend his fixation.

The dyadic father attachment and the sharing of father-greatness became arrested in this case on the level of reflection and imitation. It never progressed to the level of identification. He admired the father who could work, while he, the son, could only keep frantically busy, propelled by exalted anticipations. In his despair of ever fulfilling his father's expectations and giving him the pleasure of gratification, the young man finally blamed his father for not using his extraordinary mind to the fullest and doing great things which, in turn, would provide the son with hope and trust in himself by reflection. The awareness of his emotional father involvement was summarized by the patient saying: 'If I'll ever be able to let anything or anybody go for good — and what else is growing up all about — I have first to say goodbye to my father.' We might paraphrase his words to read: 'goodbye to my pre-Oedipal father.' The character pathology of this case was one of a pernicious, debilitating pseudo purposefulness and incompleteness of action. The patient's insight into the problems just outlined led to a forward move toward identifications along the father series of which the analyst was one if not, indeed the first. The fact that the patient could not tolerate the de-idealization of the father at adolescence fixated his emotional development at the terminal stage of childhood, thus consolidating his neurosis on the threshold to adulthood. I speak here of the adolescent de-idealization of the father as a symbolic patricide which sets the son free by setting into motion the de-idealization of the self.

At this point I have to introduce a correction in the portrayal of the dyadic son—father relationship of which — I fear — I have inadvertently given too idyllic a picture. What has to be introduced are the father's ambivalent emotions towards his infant son which throw dark shadows over his infantile exuberance and lust for life. Even when love, pride and devotion are the father's manifest emotions, negative feelings drift into the relationship. They usually are not acknowledged by the father; they remain unconscious. However, if not neutralized to some degree, they tend to affect adversely the early son—father attachment. The father who harbors feelings of envy, resentment and death wishes toward his son is dramatically represented in the Greek myth by King Laius who set out to kill his infant son Oedipus by abandoning him in the wilderness to certain death. The inference that the unnatural deed Laius committed was initiated by the voice of the oracle only speaks of the ubiquitous danger of hostile emotions which the birth of an infant son unleashes in the father. Normally they are reduced to insignificance under the onrush of joy and elation evoked by paternity. Ross (1982) has written a persuasive paper on this issue, designating this particular component of the son–father configuration as the Laius complex which every son has to face when he becomes the father of a son.

Two comments are in order here. One refers to a component of the common oppositional and self-assertive stance of the son *vis-à-vis* the father as a defense against passivity. This dynamic explication is convincingly supported by the fact that the analysis of repressed passivity transmutes disorganized and disorganizing oppositionalism into adaptive and organized behavior, solidifying in its course a stable as well as harmonious sense of self. The second comment refers to the theme, which I shall call the search for the loving and loved father. This facet of the father complex assumes in adolescence a libidinal ascendancy that impinges on every fact of the son's emotional life. The quality of this longing as observed in male infants has been called 'father hunger' by Herzog (1980) or 'father thirst' by Abelin (Panel 1978). The terminology itself expresses both authors' assumption that the affect of father-yearning is experienced in early childhood within the oral modality.

The resolution of the Oedipus complex finds its ultimate completion in the resolution of the pre-Oedipal father relationship at adolescence. This statement does not alter nor invalidate the overriding importance of the boy's conflict with the Oedipal father, but addresses itself to an intrinsic component of the male father complex as a whole. Clinically, the theorem is not restricted to adolescence because it assumes, more often than not, a major role in the analysis of the male adult. The fact of not having surmounted or resolved the father complex, as in the case of an aborted adolescence, lays bare its pathogenic role in the neurotic nexus of any adult male patient. I shall illustrate the theorem just outlined as it emerged in the analysis of a middle-aged man. His emotional bondage to his father was as extreme as his father's unrelatedness to his son and his uncompromising need that his son submit to his will. Way into manhood, the patient was shaken by the fear that the slightest show of self-assertion *vis-à-vis* his father would leave him disinherited, namely abandoned, starving, lost. The love for his father — which indeed was 'father hunger' — emerged in the analysis and was acknowledged. In an outburst of tears and sobbing, he stammered the words: 'I love that man.' Consciously, the son had resented and hated the father all his life. Entering analysis, he announced: 'I cannot hate my father for the rest of my life. It kills me.' A recent succession of anxiety attacks and a turn to heavy drinking brought this tortured man to psychoanalytic treatment. In contrast to hating his father, he had always adored his mother about whom nothing disparaging could ever be said. It was only after the analysis of the negative complex that he could see her in a new light. He began to express doubts about her loving nature. Scrutinizing his illusory positive complex he found an old, managerial caretaker who had 'never hugged or kissed me.' The patient realized that he had cast her in a madonna image when his desire for emotional closeness to his father had become a lost cause. Now the adult son could say: 'I loved my father too much.' He ceased to endear himself to father figures and concomitantly he ceased to canonize women. With these changes, his addictiveness faded away and so did his compulsive and superficial and promiscuous relatedness to women.

As a cogent complement to my analytic experience just cited, I am reminded of Freud's remark about the girl's resolution of her Oedipus complex. In his work with women patients he was struck by the fact that the positive complex pales into insignificance with the deepening of the analytic work, while the negative complex moves to the forefront. The analysis of the Oedipus complex – and Freud refers here to its positive component as the one subjected to analysis – comes to a standstill. Freud (1924) writes: 'At this point our material – for some incomprehensible reason – becomes far more obscure and full of gaps' (p. 177). In the perplexing pursuit of this problem he came to realize that the pre-Oedipal period exerts an influence on the emotional development of women that equals or even exceeds the influence of the positive Oedipal position. Freud (1931) states 'it would seem as though we must retract the universality of the thesis that the Oedipus complex is the nucleus of the neuroses.' He concludes, that 'this correction' is not necessary if we include in the Oedipus complex the negative component of the girl's exclusive attachment to the mother and realize that the girl reaches the positive position only after 'she has surmounted a period before it that is governed by the negative complex' (p. 226).

What arouses my attention in this context is the fate of the dyadic father in the boy's formation of the positive complex or, more specifically, the fate of the negative complex, its resolution and its neurosogenic valence. It should be obvious that this comment of mine refers to a far broader context than that of homosexuality. In fact, it would be appropriate and clinically supportable if we made a differentiation between the boy's negative complex of the triadic constellation and the boy's dyadic father complex, which belongs to an earlier stage of object relations, as well as their respective influence on a man's love life and on his sense of self.

I hasten to add that the residues or fixations pertaining to the positive complex are as clearly apparent throughout male adolescence as we have always considered them to be. However, our attention is aroused by the boy's conflictual, i.e. active and passive, father engagement and disengagement, both reflecting a specific quality of emotional exigency and motivational forcefulness.

Contemplating the period of the pre-competitive son–father attachment as well as the confidence and security the little boy derives from his father's control and domination, the conjecture presents itself that an indestructible residue of this early father-trust carries over into the tumultuous arena of the triadic struggle. This is to say that the restraining and punishing father is also the rescuer of the son from being taken over by infantile delusions; this so-called rescuer is the early personification of the reality principle who makes growing into manhood an attainable expectancy.

I have traced a roadblock in the path toward this achievement to a father's need for an intense closeness to his isogender infant offspring; in this closeness, the father gratifies vicariously and belatedly his lifelong father hunger. An emotional involvement of this kind always comprises a three-generational network. Under these auspices a potentially liberating infantile attachment turns into an oppressive bondage. One might say that the abandoned seduction theory has re-entered here along an unexpected course and in an unexpected guise.

I have observed this kind of interaction between father and son in the analyses of several men who derived excessive pleasure from the caretaking ministrations of their infant son. In one case the child responded to the father's need by becoming a nightly visitor to his bed, always bypassing the mother. No disciplinary interference could keep the now four-year-old child in his room because he kept responding to the father's unrelenting, unconscious wishes for physical and emotional closeness to him. When the patient's deprivation of physical and emotional contact with his early father emerged in the analysis, the little boy began to listen to the request to stay in his room. The nightly commuting to the father's bed faded away with the patient's mounting realization that he gratified vicariously his own pre-Oedipal 'father hunger' via his little son's bodily closeness.

In a considerable number of my adult male patients, ranging in age from their twenties way into their late fifties, the negative complex appears often as the rock bottom of their neurotic illness. I remind you here of Freud's 1931 paper on female sexuality which I quoted earlier. There, he calls attention to some of his women patients' all-encompassing fixation on the pre-Oedipal mother lying at the root of their neuroses. One cannot help but wonder why the boy's negative complex, being of equal neurosogenic valence, has never received an equal measure of attention. This neglectfulness persisted despite the fact – as quoted by Mack Brunswick (1940) in her classic paper (written in collaboration with Freud) on the pre-Oedipal phase – that Freud had commented at the time: 'on the basis of this new concept of early female sexuality, the pre-Oedipal phase of the boy should be thoroughly investigated' (p. 266). This admonition was never fully heeded.

The residues of the pre-Oedipal attachment experience of son to father lie, to a large extent, buried under a forceful repression once adolescence is passed. This infantile emotional experience, when roused into reanimation during analysis, remains usually inaccessible by sheer verbalization. It finds expression via affectomotor channels, such as uncontrollable weeping and sobbing, while the patient is tormented by overwhelming feelings of love and loss in relation to the dyadic father. One man in his fifties exclaimed at such a moment, choked by tears: 'Why did I love my father so much — after all, I had a mother.' In contrast to these passionate affects, the manifest and remembered son—father relationship had usually been distant, often hateful, admiring or submissive, governed by fear of rejection and grudgeful with a sense of disappointment.

The foremost structural achievements of both Oedipal conflict resolutions at the imminence of latency and, later, of adulthood, are respectively the superego and the adult ego ideal. The male superego preserves for good the circumstances of its origin, namely, the interdiction of incest under the threat of chastisement; it remains an agency of prohibition. The infantile ego ideal, in proximity to object idealization, promotes a forward move in libidinal disengagement, identified in psychoanalytic theory with 'the decline of the Oedipus complex'. In contrast, the adult ego ideal is an agency of autonomous aspiration; as such it is guarded as a cherished and beloved personality attribute whose archaic origin lies in father attachment, father idealization or, briefly, in the negative complex, i.e., the adult ego ideal is the heir to the negative Oedipus complex. 'Genetically' as Bibring (1964) commented, 'it [the ego ideal] derives its strength mainly from positive libidinal strivings in contrast to the superego, in which aggressive forces prevail' (p. 517). This view is supported by the clinical fact that the adult ego ideal holds unambivalently to its position, once acquired, with steadfast loyalty. Here Nunberg's (1932) comment comes to mind: 'Whereas the ego submits to the superego out of fear of punishment, it submits to the ego ideal out of love' (p. 146). It seems that without the dual challenge of Oedipal anxiety and guilt as well as pre-Oedipal father attachment and father hunger, the personality development of the boy is seriously endangered; a disposition in the direction of social and libidinal malfunction might be in store for him. To particularize the inferences I just made, I submit a contribution from the phenomenology of the ego ideal in transition during adolescence.

We are familiar with the adolescent boy's proverbial hero worship and his search for models of emulation, characteristically expressed in his construction of a personal hall of fame. We observe that the personalities on posters and albums, inhabiting the inner sanctum of the adolescent's world, represent his transient but intense idealizations and trial identifications. These imaginary relationships, while highly emotional, are devoid of sexual, i.e. genital constituents and are – due to sublimatory transformations – devoid of infantile attachment emotions. The ego-syntonic affects are exclusively those of admiration, idealization and devotion to the respective hero's qualities of excellence and perfection, most frequently attached to personalities in the field of sports, music or stage. The bearers of these qualities are predominantly acclaimed performers and almost exclusively male. We witness here in *statu nascendi* the socialization of the infantile ego ideal alongside the structuring of the adult ego ideal during adolescence.

Adolescence cannot be comprehended by the classical psychoanalytic recapitulation theory because certain emotional experiences and tasks do not find their normal timing until adolescence, when the developmental progression confronts the child with novel, maturationally evoked, conflictual constellations. A major one is singled out for my deliberation in this paper. The event of sexual maturation, i.e. puberty, is the biological signal that the passing of childhood has arrived; any undue prolongation of it becomes an indication of a developmental derailment. The shift in object choice or the adolescent displacement of the primary love object is well understood in the son–mother relationship. What is less understood is the fate of the son's libidinal father attachment. Simple displacement along isogender lines is observed only when a durable fixation prevents libidinal modulation to advance in puberty toward a heterosexual identity. Simple displacement onto object relations of the father series will endanger the son's heterosexual identity or weaken, indeed prevent, its formation and irreversible constancy.

Having discarded the protective envelope of childhood, the safekeeping of purpose and meaning of life passes over into the guardianship of the self. I conceive the dynamics of this personality change as intrinsically related to the resolution of the dyadic father relationship which becomes increasingly divested of infantile dependency needs. In other words, its resolution in the male is not and cannot be effected by object displacement, but only by the formation of a new psychic institution, which is to say, by a structural innovation. I postulated that the object libido which gave life to the negative complex is compelled and propelled by sexual maturation to undergo a transformation into a psychic structure which is sustained by narcissistic libido. In this new structure I recognized the adult ego ideal (Blos 1974).

The proposition of a biphasic resolution of the Oedipus complex would logically be followed by the conclusion that the definitive organization of the adult neurosis has its timing during the terminal stage of adolescence. It is stating the obvious to say that contributary and essential contributions to the construction of a neurotic illness are identifiable all through the stages of proto-adolescent development. Evoking the image of the arch, it is also obvious that its construction remains incomplete and its ultimate self-support and solid rigidity are not achieved until the keystone is dropped into place. In an analogous fashion, the definitive neurosis, i.e. the adult neurosis, remains incomplete until the closure of adolescence declares that the psychobiological period, called childhood, is passed. Whenever a derailment of the phase-specific differentiation in object relations or an abnormal consolidation of psychic structure occurs during childhood, the developmental injury meets a last chance of spontaneous healing during adolescence. Beyond that, temperamental ingenuity and ego resourcefulness present a myriad of adaptational potentials, one of which is the neurotic compromise, the neurosis. The assertion that the decline of the Oedipus complex proceeds in two stages of pre-adulthood implies the view that psychological childhood comes to its close at the end of adolescence. To this assertion has to be added that the dyadic isogender attachment experience of the male child contributes a basic determinant in the neurotic formations as they appear later in his life. I would not be surprised if the outcome of my research and its claim for amendments to the classical theory are met both with agreement and incredulity. I do acknowledge that my propositions are not supported by extensive research. All I can ask from the audience is a response of critical attention and a testing by clinical observation.

I mentioned earlier in this presentation that the dyadic state operates in polarities which are reflected in the split into the 'good' and 'bad' object. The cognitive level of thought, when restricted to the exclusive use of polarities, is of a primitive nature and of limited efficiency because complexities are dealt with in terms of simple dichotomies. The advance to the triadic level lifts the thought process onto a higher level or, rather, it establishes the precondition for this advance. We might say the triadic complexity of object relations and its implicit experience of a higher-level conflict produce an infinite multitude of possible diversity within its realm; of these, a selected few are retained and stabilized in transcending the triadic stage. The Oedipal complexity of interpersonal experiences is reflected on the cognitive level in the emergence of the dialectic process. We recognize in this process the triadic nature of thesis, antithesis and synthesis. The complexity of this thought process permits by the choice of determinations an endless sequence of possible cognitive combinations or permutations, each pressing forward toward a resolution on an ever higher level of thought.

From postulating a biphasic resolution of the Oedipus complex it would follow by implication that the so-called higher levels of thought make their appearance at the time of its terminal resolution, which occurs at the adolescent period. This theoretical assumption finds a validation in the adolescent research by Inhelder and Piaget (1958). To quote: 'The adolescent is an individual who begins to build "systems" or "theories" in the largest sense of the term ... the adolescent is able to analyze his own thinking and construct theories' (p. 339). The capacity to execute such mental operations declares the readiness of the adolescent mind to deal with the abstractions inherent in ideologies, philosophy, epistemology and science. The child does not possess a thought faculty of this kind. The researchers claim that these higher thought constructs serve the purpose of furnishing 'the cognitive and evaluative bases for the assumption of adult roles. They are vital in the assimilation of the values which delineate societies or social classes as entities in contrast to simple inter-individual relations' (p. 340).

I have commented that the primitivity of thought, anchored in dyadic affectivity, stands in stark contrast to the intricacy of the dialectic thought process. The triadic state is concerned with self, object and identity, as well as with object-directed emotional and sexual issues; it transcends, so to say, its infantile origin and instinctual involvement by perpetuating its existential nature in the cognitive sphere, namely, in the interminable effort to comprehend the world and the self in ever more complex terms and configurations.

Summary

I have traced in my deliberations the mutual influence of drive and ego development throughout the male child's dyadic and triadic father-relatedness as it proceeds within a changing soma and social surround during the first two decades of life. I have made the effort to conceptualize the normal developmental progression in male personality formation with explicit reference to the fate of the boy's dyadic father-relationship as well as his negative Oedipus complex in general. These considerations, restricted as they are in scope and gender, assign to the dyadic father complex a nuclear role in neurosogenesis as well as recognize in it an etiological factor in relation to specific forms of psychopathology throughout the male life cycle.

Note

Plenary lecture presented at the Fall Meeting of the American Psychoanalytic Association, New York, 17 December 1982.

References

Abelin, E. (1971). The role of the father in the separation-individuation process. In *Separation-Individuation: Essays in Honor of Margaret S. Mahler*, ed. J.B. McDevitt & C.F. Settlage. New York: Int. Univ. Press, pp. 229–52.

—— (1975). Some further observations and comments on the earliest role of the father. *Int. J. Psychoanal.*, 56: 293–302.

Bibring, G.L. (1964). Some considerations regarding the ego ideal in the psychoanalytic process. *J. Amer. Psychoanal. Assn.*, 12: 517–21.

Blos, P. (1974). The genealogy of the ego ideal. *Psychoanal. Study Child*, 29: 43–88.

Freud, S. (1887–1902). *The Origins of Psychoanalysis: Letters to Wilhelm Fliess, Drafts and Notes.* New York: Basic Books, 1954.

—— (1905). Fragment of an analysis of a case of hysteria. S.E., 7: 7–122.

—— (1924). The dissolution of the Oedipus complex. S.E., 19.

—— (1925). Some psychical consequences of the anatomical distinction between the sexes. S.E., 19.

—— (1927). The future of an illusion. S.E., 21.

—— (1931). Female sexuality. S.E., 21.

Greenacre, P. (1966). Problems of overidealization of the analyst and of analysis. *Psychoanal. Study Child*, 21: 193–211.

Herzog, J.M. (1980). Sleep disturbance and father hunger in 18- to 28-month-old boys. *Psychoanal. Study Child*, 35: 219–33.

Inhelder, B. & Piaget, J. (1958). *The Growth of Logical Thinking from Childhood to Adolescence.* New York: Basic Books.

Loewald, H.W. (1951). Ego and reality. *Int. J. Psychoanal.*, 32: 10–18.

Mack Brunswick, R. (1940). The preoedipal phase of libido development. In *The Psychoanalytic Reader*, ed. R. Fliess. New York: Int. Univ. Press, 1948, pp. 261–84.

Mahler, M.S. (1955). On symbiotic child psychosis. *Psychoanal. Study Child*, 10: 195–212.

Nunberg, H. (1932). *Principles of Psychoanalysis.* New York: Int. Univ. Press, 1955.

Panel (1978). The role of the father in the preoedipal years. R.C. Prall, reporter. *J. Amer. Psychoanal. Assn.*, 26: 143–61.

Ross, J.M. (1977). Toward fatherhood: the epigenesis of paternal identity during a boy's first decade. *Int. Rev. Psychoanal.*, 4: 327–47.

—— (1979). Fathering: a review of some psychoanalytic contributions on paternity. *Int. J. Psychoanal.*, 60: 317–27.

—— (1982). Oedipus revisited: Laius and "the Laius complex." *Psychoanal. Study Child*, 37: 169–200.

2

The female Oedipus complex and the relationship to the body

M. EGLÉ LAUFER

Women's lives and their own view of themselves have changed dramatically over the past 50 years since Freud wrote his last paper on the subject. Moreover, the opposition to Freud's view, voiced by some analysts at that time, has gained support both from analysts and women themselves. Janine Chasseguet-Smirgel (1984) said, 'the works of Kestemberg, Galenson, Roiphe . . . have in my view invalidated and discredited the claims of the theory of phallic monism to be regarded any longer as the gospel truth. In fact, it is not simply a question of rejecting this infantile sexual theory as purely defensive, but of drawing the consequences of this rejection for psychoanalytic theory overall. If the girl stands in the first place not for *deficiency*, but primordially for *receptacle*, then our conceptions of psychosexual evolution must change direction or even be reversed, the site of what is most instinctual and animal to the human being must be rediscovered' (p. 169). I think what she is saying here expresses something that we have all been aware of for a long time in our clinical work.

Like Chasseguet, I have, of course, also been impressed by the findings of child and adult analysts who have shown convincingly that the little girl's awareness of her own body is not primarily that of lacking a penis. She has a much earlier awareness of her body as containing an inside space and of the openings in her body, the mouth, anus, and possibly the vagina. I believe, however, that we must now understand how these circumstances relate to the early history of the development of the girl's *relationship* to her own body and how it will shape and determine her future development.

From my own clinical observations of disturbed adolescent girls and women who had experienced a psychotic or depressive breakdown following the birth of their first child, it seemed to me that the conflicts underlying the path toward pathological development were in fact not so different from those described by Freud and others and that it was therefore more a matter of finding a different way of understanding the concepts that Freud had made central to the understanding of pathology. It was for this reason that I have chosen to examine the theme of the castration complex in feminine development which Freud made central to his theory of female development (1931). What I have tried to clarify is that the *significance* of the early, infantile, masturbatory activity and sensory experiences together with their accompanying fantasies, which include the awareness of inner space and of body openings, lies in the relationship that this establishes between the girl and her own body and the extent to which this relationship then facilitates or hinders the child's ability to detach herself from her dependence on the mother. The ongoing *early* Oedipal conflict can then be understood as inevitably leading to a later point in development where the awareness of reality — the separation from the mother and the impingement on the child's omnipotent fantasies of the unrivaled role of the father in relation to the mother — *has* to be acknowledged by both the male and female child. With this acknowledgment the child, boy or girl, also has to make an accompanying change in the relation to his or her own body and its contents. The outcome of this change, the resolution of the Oedipal conflict, whether it takes on a defensive character, and to what extent this defensive character will affect the child's capacity for the perception of reality will point the way to future pathology or normality (M. Laufer 1982).

Freud (1905) saw the role of sexuality in mental life as inextricably linked with pathological development and symptom formation. He postulated that there can be no disturbance in mental functioning without an accompanying disturbance in the sexual life of the person. I think we have taken a long time to understand that this is not simply a statement about genital functioning as such — i.e., of orgastic or reproductive capacity. It is a way of saying that in order to remain free of pathology, as adults, we have to be able to experience our bodies as a source of pleasure and instinctual gratification. But although we cannot 'give up' the pleasure principle as the source of infantile omnipotence, we must find a way to accommodate external reality so that we can maintain an area of our lives in which the pleasure principle can still reign supreme.

Freud, it seems to me, was the first to recognize the girl's biologically determined, *relative* difficulty in achieving this — relative, that is, to the boy. I believe that girls behave as if they 'lacked something', however much they may have been told or been aware that they didn't and that they had other powers or capacities. Penis envy may appear outdated, in our present social climate, but behaviorally the concept still has a validity and the power to shape women's lives. It is for this reason that I have started out on the assumption that although the findings of Klein (1928), Horney (1923) and Jones (1927) must be included in our thinking as well as the change in women's awareness of themselves, the problem is how to include them rather than perpetuating a controversy as to who has the 'complete truth'.

Similarly, I too have, of course, been aware that the little girl's attachment to her father does not *begin* when she turns away from her relationship to her mother. Clearly, the child has an intense and libidinized relationship to the father before the actual pressure to resolve the Oedipal situation becomes imperative. I would see the developmental task or problem more simply: how far can the girl relinquish the libidinal tie to the mother without having to find some symptomatic compromise solution through identification with the father or a masochistic submission to the father. Clinically, in the transference, it has seemed to me more a question of whether the relationship to the father and later to men is allowed into the space the girl has been able to create between herself and her internalized mother, or whether his presence continues to act like an ineffectual shadow in her life that is felt as a threat which comes between her and the internalized mother.

My own conclusions are still changing in the light of my clinical experiences and those of others. These have come from work with adolescent girls who are developmentally faced with the task of changing their relationship to their body from that of the prepubertal child to that of a sexual adult woman, or of pregnant young women where the task is one of changing the relationship to themselves to that of identifying with their own mother's maternal role. In both these situations the pathological, defensive symptomatology which may result demonstrates the genetic history of the earlier development of the relationship to their bodies. What has impressed me most has been the capacity of some women to deny the reality of the changes taking place in their bodies or their compelling need physically to attack their own bodies or later that of their babies during these critical developmental periods.

In order to explain these pathological phenomena I think we have to take seriously the events in our patients' lives as biological realities and not only as a metaphor that can have interchangeable meanings in fantasy. This makes the issue of the timing and function of the resolution of the Oedipal conflict a critical issue. If we regard the resolution of the depressive position as the central issue and hence only see the resolution of the infant's relationship to the breast as central to the therapeutic task, I think we risk entering into the patient's own delusional system when applying it to clinical work with the disturbed adolescent or the psychotic areas of functioning in the adult patient. We then leave them without having made conscious their relationship to their adult sexual body and

and their internal experience of it. For this reason the timing of the resolution of the Oedipal conflict is still central to our controversy.

Yet it seems to me that it would be most helpful if we were to change the emphasis of the argument of whether a so-called 'pre-Oedipal period' exists or whether the Oedipal situation is there from much earlier – that is, about when the relationship to the parents begins to take on a competitive and triangular meaning to the child – to when does this ongoing conflict *have* to find some resolution. My own answer would be that while the infant or the 'pre-Oedipal' child can avoid the task of *resolving* the Oedipal conflict for a prolonged period by the creation of its own fantasy and later by masturbatory activity which maintains the infantile omnipotence, this effort has to succumb at some point to the realization of the differences between the sexes. It is the defenses against this awareness which we see as the 'psychical rigidity' Freud (1933: 134) spoke of in the pathological development of women.

The way I have understood the significance of the earlier phase is that it is the period in which the relationship to the girl's own body becomes established. The decisive factor is the extent to which she is left with a narcissistic libidinal cathexis of her body rather than vulnerable to her self-destructive impulses, because the predominance of a narcissistic cathexis will help her to negotiate possessing a female body and becoming a mother who can enjoy her child's body. Or, as Freud (1933) said,

> But the phase of the affectionate pre-Oedipus attachment is the decisive one for a woman's future: during it preparations are made for the acquisition of characteristics with which she will later fulfil her role in the sexual function and perform her invaluable social tasks.
>
> (p. 134)

The significance of the Oedipus complex in development, and specifically the manner in which it is dissolved in the girl's development by the end of the Oedipal period, have been, and still are, the focus for much theoretical disagreement. Central to the past and present controversies has been the idea that Freud created a false view of female development because he was influenced by the idea of the supremacy of the phallus and that he subordinated women to this idea. In fact, it is as if Freud has come to represent what we have learned to recognize – that in society there is, and always has been, a deep unconscious need to idealize the penis into a symbolic phallus and that this need is common to both men and women. But I believe that the framework of the questions that Freud laid down as requiring an answer about the differences he observed in the development of males and females still does help us to understand how such a fantasy can come into being and how it comes to exercise such a dominating influence on the unconscious and on the capacity to live with the reality of one's body.

I will limit myself to three main themes in Freud's formulations which are central to these questions. First, Freud defined the girl's perception of her body as being 'castrated' and assumed that the manner in which she dealt with this formed the basis of her castration complex and determined her future sexual development. Second, I shall describe the nature of the early attachment to the mother and ask whether it is different from that of the boy from the beginning, or whether it only takes on a different course at some later point in development, as suggested to Freud by the observation that girls have a longer period of attachment to the mother than boys; or, putting it another way, is there something different in this early relationship that then makes it more difficult for the girl to detach herself from the mother? Third, I repeat Freud's very fundamental question: what is it that enables the girl to give up the homosexual object at all and to make a heterosexual object choice, i.e. to turn from the mother to the father as a libidinal object? And must this result, as Helene Deutsch (1930) suggests, in a masochistic libidinal surrender to the father, through turning the acceptance of castration into the fantasy of the castration wish?

Although I can no longer accept the description Freud (1925) gives of the little girl's reaction to the sight of the penis as constituting an actual event that then signals a landmark in her development,[1] I do believe that something has to occur, optimally as part of a gradual process rather than contained in a traumatic event, which functions as an organizer of all the earlier experiences and perceptions and which will lay the foundation for the way the girl will relate to herself as a *woman* in her adult life. That is, however much I have come to understand the essential part played by the early experiences in the capacity for normal development, as in the capacity for object relationships and in the relationship to oneself and one's body, I think that the manner in which the existing psychic organization of the little girl reacts to the inevitable demand to see herself as belonging to the same sex as her mother (and one that differentiates her from the father) crucially impinges on her previously established narcissistic organization and leads her into a different developmental path from that of the boy, whether it is toward normality or a more pathological development. To view herself as 'not having a body that enables her to become a man' which is how I understand the term 'castrated' irrespective of her awareness of her receptive capacities or of having a vagina, means that at some point in her development she must give up the fantasy of being able to keep her mother's love to herself, because it simultaneously implies an understanding that there exists a longed-for satisfaction which her mother can obtain from the father, *and* that it is one which the girl can never hope to replace (Lampl-de Groot 1927).

71

Up to this time, the girl (like the boy) has been able through her masturbatory fantasies and the accompanying sensory experiences to invest her body and its products with the omnipotent power of being both the potential giver of gratification to the mother, or of being able to take over the role of 'frustrator' of the mother through the discovered capacity to achieve her own gratification by using her own body. The meaning of these early fantasies of using the body and its products, in the infant's attempts to maintain infantile omnipotence, and as a defense against the primitive anxieties of being destroyed, was investigated by Melanie Klein (1928) who has made an important contribution to our understanding the intensity of the persecutory anxieties that help to attach the girl to her mother. I also think that if the masturbatory experiences help the girl to internalize a positive relationship to her actual body, they will enable her to risk being less dependent on the mother for her survival and gratification, and can then act as a basis on which she is better able to accept her castration with less persecutory anxiety.

The libidinal relationship to the father is initially contained in the fantasy of the overlapping, interchangeable relationship in the images of both mother and father, where the parents (insofar as they can become gradually separated in the child's mind) are experienced as gratifying each other – but initially only through the same means that are available to the child, i.e. through mouth, anus, breast, feces, clitoris, or penis, where the father can be both giver and receiver, as can the child and the mother. In this respect, I cannot see that the girl's awareness of an extra opening, the vagina, adds to the awareness of a difference in her potential role of giving or receiving. Paula Heimann (1952) summarizes this early stage of development of the Oedipus complex as 'the infant . . . divines that there are physical intimacies between his parents – and in so far recognizes a reality; but he conceives of these intimacies in terms of his own impulses, in other words, his notions are determined by projection and by so much are a gross distortion of reality. The parents do to one another what he himself would like to do' (p. 163). Even if we conceptualize the infant as perceiving the mother as *containing* the father's penis in the early oral relationship (as described by Melanie Klein, 1928), this does not add anything of special significance to the girl's early development of the awareness of herself as female and different from the male, since its significance is the same for both the boy and the girl – that of seeing the mother as the primary object who frustrates the desire for gratification and thus is responsible for the narcissistic injury this inflicts on the infant.

Freud (1931) made it clear that he too was aware of how these early frustrations at the breast constitute a narcissistic injury to the infant's sense of omnipotence, but he still laid stress on the difference between

72

these early and gradual developments of the infant's sense of reality of his own helplessness and the specific nature of the later injury that the lack of a penis evokes in the girl. Melanie Klein's work provides us with details of the destructive fantasies against the mother who not only contains the penis but the babies inside her body which both the boy and the girl feel deprived of in their wish to identify themselves with the mother. But it is the anxiety aroused by the destructive fantasies related to this blow to her omnipotence which the girl, as different from the boy, feels unable to allay through finding a means in the use of her body. Possessing at least the potential of a potent penis, the boy can use it as a defense against the anxiety of his projected fantasies of a devouring, unsatisfied and envious mother. It is here that Melanie Klein has contributed, for me, to answering Freud's question not only why there is so much aggression exhibited by the girl to the mother, or why she appears to blame the mother for all the deprivation (including the lack of a penis), but to the understanding of how her relative inability to detach herself from the mother, relative (that is) to that of the boy, derives from the anxiety coming from the projection onto her mother of the fantasy of her own dissatisfaction and disappointment. Detaching herself can then only be felt as depriving her mother of her satisfaction.

But I think this view of the girl as needing a penis in order both to feel she can satisfy the mother and to maintain her belief that the mother can still satisfy her own wish for a baby confirms Freud's view that penis *envy*, the wish for the penis, in the girl is an expression of the wish to live out her primary libidinal aim — of giving or being given a baby by the mother, while the fantasy of actually possessing a penis is a secondary pathological structure whose aim is defensive and related to persecutory anxiety (Jones 1927).

Freud (1931) talked of the girl's 'acceptance of castration' as being simultaneous with the time at which the libidinal tie to the mother is given up. Reviewing his description of the options that are then open to the girl, I have found it helpful to make use of my clinical experience of the transference relationship in the analysis of adolescent girls and young adult women. This seems to indicate quite clearly that the libidinal tie to the mother has very often not been given up at all. Sublimatory as well as sexual activities in women are still extremely vulnerable to inhibition and other defenses because of the intense anxiety aroused either by the mother's envy or by the identification with the forbidden possession of the father's penis. Freud also points to this problem in his comment on the high incidence of frigidity in women, which he sees as an inhibition of sexuality. He said (1931), 'Indeed, we had to reckon with the possibility that a number of women remain arrested in their original attachment to their mother and never achieve a true change-over towards men' (p. 226).

73

Further clinical evidence for this view comes from the high incidence of postnatal depression in women after the birth of their first child. This can be understood as the final process of mourning for the loss of the tie to their mother that becoming a mother involves. In addition, it can also be understood as representing an identification with the fantasy of a dissatisfied and depressed mother who has to be kept appeased by the daughter's giving up or inhibiting her own potential satisfaction and enjoyment of having produced her own child. For some women this conflict can become so intense that the reality of the baby has to be disavowed altogether, the relationship to the baby cannot become established, and instead the woman will experience an acute psychotic state with all the subsequent danger of violence either against herself or the baby.

In severely disturbed adolescent girls, what can be observed clinically is how the effort to defend against the still existing libidinal attachment to the mother — which has now the added danger of becoming an incestuous homosexual tie to the mother — can lead to the compelling need to direct aggression against their own body in an attempt to detach themselves from their sexual body and its meaning, as in suicide attempts, self-cutting, anorexia, bulimia, and so on.

Freud describes the outcome of the castration complex as resulting in either an eventual 'acceptance of castration' or a setting up of the masculinity complex as an attempt to maintain the 'disavowal' of castration. He makes the point that both the boy's and the girl's first reaction to the task of allowing the perception of the 'absence of a penis' into their awareness — that is, their first recognition of the difference between male and female — is one of disavowal. But once the girl has accepted herself as being without a penis, i.e., castrated, the most significant difference between the boy and the girl is that in the girl it leads to a repression of her sexuality. He makes it clear that he is here referring specifically to a phallic sexuality — that is, the relation of the girl to her own genitals both as a source of pleasurable experience and as containing her active aims to give her mother satisfaction or a baby — and these have to be repressed because 'they have proved totally unrealizable'. He continues, however, to say that

> the passive [i.e., the receptive] trends have not escaped disappointment either. With the turning-away from the mother clitoral masturbation frequently ceases as well; and often enough when the small girl represses her previous masculinity a considerable portion of her sexual trends in general is permanently injured too. The transition to the father-object is accomplished with the help of the passive trends in so far as they have escaped the catastrophe. The path to the development

of femininity now lies open to the girl, to the extent to which it is not restricted by the remains of the pre-Oedipus attachment to her mother which she has surmounted.

(p. 239)

Later he makes it clear that if the girl is to develop normally, she must take the father as a sexual object in the final stage of her Oedipus complex and before its final resolution. I think this view has aroused some of the most intense criticism of the psychoanalytic theory of female sexuality since it lends itself to the equating of the 'passive aims' with the idea of 'masochism' as if masochism were an essential part of normal female sexuality.

From my clinical observations of adult women who showed a marked masochistic trend in their sexual relations, I would be more inclined to say that if the girl has been able to give up the libidinal attachment to the mother, resulting from the acceptance of herself as castrated, and with it her hatred of the mother, then the passive aims which she uses to maintain a relationship to the father have more of a narcissistic wish attached than the directly sexual wish of castration or penetration. The satisfaction that the girl seeks, I think, is that of still feeling her body valued and desired, even though it now appears to contain only her pregenital passive wishes. But once a libidinal aim is included in the passive, wishful fantasy directed at the father, it must take on a masochistic meaning since the 'acceptance of castration' has now taken on a wishful quality and has become a 'castration wish'. And the 'castration wish' then forms the basis for a masochistic fantasy of being castrated by the father through penetration. This occurs only where there is a displacement of the aggression related to the still unbroken tie to the mother and not as a result of detachment from the mother. It represents a compromise in order to keep repressed the existence of the libidinal tie to the mother through the possession of the fantasy penis which the father must take from her, while the hatred of the mother becomes internalized into the superego structure.

Normal latency fantasies for the girl are of being chosen instead of having to choose, of being desired instead of experiencing sexual desire herself. These wishful fantasies, and the wish for a baby, can allow the passive pregenital longings to continue to find expression, without the anxiety of regressive longings for the mother. But I do not see this suppression of sexuality during latency as necessarily leading, as Freud (1931) suggests, to the extinction of the girl's sexuality in her adult life. Rather it seems to me to be an expression of the fantasy depicted in 'The Sleeping Beauty' that everybody has to remain asleep, the girl princess as well as her parents the king and queen, until she is discovered and her resistance surmounted by the prince. This fable is not so much a

75

story of passive masochistic surrender to the man, but of the need to control both the parents and her sexuality and her own 'prickly' hatred, during latency, in order later to allow the prince to gain entry to the palace and to discover the girl's hidden vagina.

The other alternative is the formation of a masculinity complex. Although Freud comments that if it persists into adulthood, it can lead to a homosexual object choice, it is often confused with penis envy. From a diagnostic point of view a careful distinction must be made between the two. Penis envy and competitive behaviour with men express the wish for a penis, while the masculinity complex contains the fantasy of possessing a penis. The distinction marks the difference between normality or neurotic development, even distorted by envy and the need to compete with men, and more severe pathology, which may contain a psychotic area at its core. The continued disavowal of castration into adulthood through the construction of a fantasy of a body that includes a penis must distort the relationship with reality to a degree that leaves the woman with the potential for a psychotic breakdown when faced by reality with a challenge to that fantasy, as Freud (1931) points out when he talks of the normal first disavowal by the girl.

A young woman who had retained a fantasy of possessing a penis into young adulthood, for instance, felt consciously free of all anxiety in a satisfactory homosexual relationship, but then felt compelled to break off the relationship when it began to force her to acknowledge that she could neither give nor receive a baby. The initial lack of anxiety about her homosexuality resulted from her ability to gratify the wish to continue to deny castration. The wish for a baby, however, brought with it the anxiety of experiencing a break with the reality of her body in order to maintain the disavowal of castration, and with it the danger of severely damaging attacks on her own body as an expression of her hatred and disappointment in its failure.

I have observed similar transitory paranoid states in adult women who feel dependent on the need to masturbate, where the paranoid reaction becomes comprehensible only when it becomes clear how it relates unconsciously to masturbatory activity and fantasies. I think such evidence in the transference of psychotic anxiety in connection with masturbatory activity must always relate to the fantasy that the body includes a penis and differs from more neurotic anxiety seen in the transference as the fear of the analyst's disgust or contempt. However, it could also be argued that the fantasy of possessing a penis can be used as a defense, without necessarily posing a danger of an underlying psychosis, until the first experience of penetration of the vagina. It is only then that the masculinity complex must finally be given up, if the construction of a psychotic body image is to be avoided and the subsequent pull toward a homosexual object choice. The importance of the first act of penetration is referred to by Freud (1918) when he examines the custom in some primitive societies of allowing the first act of penetration to be carried out by a person other than the prospective husband. He attributes this to a fear of the hostility that is aroused in a woman and becomes directed at the man who carries out the act. He makes it clear that the aggression is related to a fantasy that the act of penetration is a renewed confirmation of lacking a penis.

In discussing female development in terms of the significance of the castration complex, and the special nature of the girl's relationship to her mother, I have said little about the girl's relationship to the father beyond my discomfort at, or perhaps disbelief in, the concept of the girl turning to her father when she has succeeded in detaching herself from the mother, before the final resolution of the Oedipus complex. I think, as do many analysts, that there is a much earlier libidinal attachment to the father. The idea of the 'Oedipus complex' being made up of a constant move between the negative and the positive complex, beginning from the time when the child – boy or girl – first begins to differentiate between himself or herself and the nurturing object, seems more correct nowadays than to assume that there is a sudden shift to the father. However, the basic dependence on the mother as the nurturing object exerts a constant force on the girl, as well as on the boy, to relinquish the libidinal attachment to the father and to put an identification with him in its place – an identification which then allows the child to continue to feel in exclusive possession of the mother. The girl therefore certainly forms much earlier libidinal attachments to her father, but she also has to relinquish them because of her greater anxiety. The final dissolution of the Oedipus complex marks the resolution of the conflict between the positive and negative Oedipal situation by the giving up of both attachments and maintaining only an 'affectionate tie' as Freud (1924) described it for the boy. This then allows the girl to move into latency and to use her identifications with both parents as the basis of her sublimatory activity.

The third possible outcome of the castration complex proposed by Freud consists in a general revulsion from sexuality by the girl. It is to be distinguished from that of the girl who, although also giving up masturbation, still remains sufficiently in touch with her passive wishes with which to turn to the father. The crucial issue for future development would therefore be whether in thus rejecting her own sexuality, the relationship to the father also has to be renounced. A father who is overtly sexual toward his daughter may have to become an 'object of revulsion' for the girl because of her need to keep her own sexual feelings repressed. In the normal adolescent girl such an attitude may be revived as her initial reaction to the awareness of the penis in its sexual role,

77

but she can gradually come to relate to the male's penis as she is able to relate more positively toward her own genitals. If the revulsion toward her own sexual body remains too intense, however, the problem of relating to a man's penis can remain unresolved. This may again lay the adolescent girl open either to regressing to the pregenital relationship to the mother or to seeking a homosexual relationship. Although I agree that in the course of normal development a relationship to the father has to become established after the dissolution of the negative Oedipal complex, I do not believe that the wish for a baby with which the girl turns to the father has to imply an instinctual wish for gratification. If it does, as I said earlier, I believe it must contain a masochistic fantasy, the aim of which is to deflect and keep repressed the intense violent and sadistic impulses that still tie the girl to the mother.

I now turn to some clinical material of an 18-year-old adolescent girl who began analysis after a severe suicide attempt. Because the relationship to the father had never been established in the early pre-Oedipal period in a way that could then lead to a normal Oedipal conflict, the girl remained attached to the mother and had no means of feeling that she could relate to her female sexual body other than as an identification with that of her mother's. This in turn compelled her to attempt to destroy it because of the conflict aroused by her effort to feel that she could be in control of her own body. The castration complex had been resolved by the disavowal of castration and men were seen by her as violent intruders into the fantasy of union of herself with the mother – that is, as a projection which contained her own hatred of the mother.

In a preliminary interview Mary described herself as having 'been dead' since the age of 16. It had therefore not been any particular event which finally led to her attempt to kill herself. She said she hated her body and related it to her disgust with her mother's body because her mother suffered from a colonic disorder and she did not want to have to think about her mother's body. She had in fact ceased to have any interest in her own body and its appearance at the age of 16 at the time of her mother's illness. This followed shortly after she had been away from home for the first time, staying with another family. An elderly male relative of that family had kissed her in a sexual way and had frightened and disgusted her. At that time she also gave up seeing a boyfriend with whom she had gone out once, on the grounds that her mother didn't approve of him. From that time onward she retreated into her studies and only went out when accompanied by her mother or her female friends. Her suicide attempt was preceded by a period during which she secretly and compulsively stuffed herself with food; as a result, she then felt disgusted with her own body. It was as if what she had experienced at 16 was the failure of her capacity to allow a man to relate to her body sexually because she had been unable to integrate her own sexual development in any way other than as something disgusting and repelling.

When she was seen at 18 for assessment, she was dressed in a little girl's dress covered over by a coat which she kept on in order to keep her body completely hidden. She knew that her problems were related to her mother; she felt that she either had to allow herself to be completely dominated and 'eaten up' by her mother or that by removing herself and becoming independent she would cause her mother to collapse and 'to starve'. She saw her attempt to kill herself as the only independent action that she had been able to do and that she had felt forced into by her terror and despair at her own helplessness. She used her relationship to her father to feed herself with the fantasy that he preferred her to her mother and that her mother wanted to be rid of her in order to have the father to herself. At these times she felt afraid that her mother was trying to poison her.

In the transference she experienced the analyst both as an intruder into her fantasy in which she was together and united with her mother and her body, while at the same time trying to keep repressed her wish to give in to the analyst and be dominated by her with the fantasy that this would destroy the mother. Her body was used to live out this fantasy in alternately repelling the analyst by silence and secretiveness and later in falling asleep throughout the sessions.

Her first 'attempt' at sexual intercourse was initiated by her inviting a man to stay the night in her apartment and then furiously fighting with him when he tried to approach her sexually. The following day she reported triumphantly that she had proved that she could be strong enough to prevent a man from raping her. In this way she succeeded in living out her fantasy that I, the analyst, would love her and that we could remain united as long as she could prevent the act of penetration which would compel us both to acknowledge a man's penis and our own helplessness as castrated women and therefore our hatred of each other.

As long as she could feel strong enough to keep the man's penis outside and from intruding into her own and my reality, we could remain in her fantasy as totally dependent on each other for our needs. Men, she felt, were there only for us to be seen together with so that we appeared normal like other women. Her fear of even that wish was of being seen with a man who might then be the admired one and she would be left out feeling jealous. In this way she expressed her wish to deny the existence of the penis completely, even as something that she could own and use in relation to other women. Only in this way could she feel in control of her own hatred and jealous feelings.

Her sexual life was dominated by the fantasy of being given an enema, as she had once experienced when 4 years old from her mother. This fantasy provided the motivation for making her feel that if she could not control her bodily needs (as in eating), she would have to reject her body altogether, as in killing herself, because of her disgust with it. The predominance of the anus in her mental life could deny both her own vagina and the penis and therefore the sexual difference between male and female. In this way she could continue to see herself as able to satisfy her mother's needs and feel in control of her own needs.

For this girl, the absence of a libidinal relationship to the father meant that even a shift away from the mother by displacement onto the father of the masochistic wish to be castrated was not open to her. When she began analysis, she lived with a constant belief that her parents were about to separate. Mary had already experienced herself as an object of disgust during latency, as was shown in the repeated nightmares she reported having had of being covered by crawling insects or skin diseases making her feel 'like a leper, untouchable'.

The actual experiences of her infancy could not be established, and thus we did not know how far this relationship to her body was defensive against the terror of an excessive intrusion in infancy or how far it was based on her belief that she had had insufficient bodily care. Probably both were true since her mother presented herself to me as someone who needed to be told how to look after her daughter while at the same time showing me that she would adhere to any instructions I might give in a frightened and rigid way, as if I was a baby book recommending four-hourly feedings. She described her daughter as having been terrified of strangers at 8 months and clinging to her mother and rejecting everyone else. This seemed to be repeated within the transference where I was initially treated as a dangerous stranger who could not be identified as a caring object but only as one who came between her and her mother.

This case seems to me to illustrate how the relationship which the girl forms to her own body in the early pre-Oedipal years determines how the Oedipus complex is *finally* resolved: in turn, this then shapes the girl's subsequent ability to form a relationship to her own sexual body after puberty.

Note

1 In 'Female Sexuality' (1931) Freud himself modifies this view.

Bibliography

Chasseguet-Smirgel, J. (1984). The femininity of the analyst in professional practice. *Int. J. Psychoanal.*, 65: 169–78.

Deutsch, H. (1930). The significance of masochism in the mental life of women. *Int. J. Psychoanal.*, 11: 48–60.

Freud, S. (1905). Three essays on the theory of sexuality: S.E., 7: 125–243.

—— (1918). The taboo of virginity. S.E., 11: 191–208.

—— (1924). The dissolution of the oedipus complex. S.E., 19: 173–179.

—— (1925). Some psychical consequences of the anatomical distinction between the sexes. S.E., 19: 248–58.

—— (1931). Female sexuality. S.E., 21: 223–43.

—— (1933). Femininity. S.E., 22: 112–35.

Heimann, P. (1952). Certain functions of introjection and projection in early infancy. In *Developments in Psycho-Analysis*, pp. 122–68. London: Hogarth Press.

Horney, K. (1923). On the genesis of the castration complex in women. *Int. J. Psychoanal.*, 5: 50–65.

Jones, E. (1927). The early development of female sexuality. In *Papers on Psycho-Analysis*, pp. 438–51. London: Baillière, Tindall & Cox.

Klein, M. (1928). Early stages of the oedipus conflict. *Int. J. Psychoanal.*, 9: 169–180.

Lampl-de Groot, J. (1927). The evolution of the oedipus complex in women. *Int. J. Psychoanal.*, 9: 332–45.

Laufer, M. (1982). The formation and shaping of the oedipus complex. *Int. J. Psychoanal.*, 63: 217–27.

Laufer, M. & Laufer, M.E. (1984). *Adolesence and Developmental Breakdown*. New Haven: Yale Univ. Press.

Laufer, M.E. (1982). Female masturbation in adolescence and the development of the relationshp to the body. *Int. J. Psychoanal.*, 63: 295–302.

3

The missing link: parental sexuality in the Oedipus complex

RONALD BRITTON

For Freud the Oedipus complex was the nuclear complex from its discovery in 1897 to the end of his life (Freud 1897, 1924d). It remained central in the development of the individual for Melanie Klein. She adopted the term 'Oedipal situation' and included in it what Freud had referred to as the primal scene, i.e. the sexual relations of the parents both as perceived and as imagined (Klein 1928).

From the outset of her work with children Melanie Klein was impressed at the ubiquity of the Oedipal situation and its unique importance; she also thought that it began much earlier than did Freud and that it began in relation to part objects before evolving into the familiar Oedipus complex, which related to the two parents perceived as whole objects – that is, as persons. So for her it began in infancy with phantasies of a relation to breast and penis and phantasies of the relationship between these two part objects, which would be succeeded by ideas about the parents under the influence of these earlier phantasies. She felt that the child's attitude and relationship to this unfolding situation was of profound significance for the urge to learn, which she called the epistemophilic impulse, and for the individual's relationship to reality.

In 1926 she wrote,

> at a very early age children become acquainted with reality through the deprivations it imposes on them. They defend themselves against reality by repudiating it. The fundamental thing, however, and the criterion of all later capacity for adaptation to reality is the degree in which they are able to tolerate the deprivations that result from the Oedipal situation.
>
> (Klein 1926)

This was written more than a decade before Mrs Klein was to describe what she called the 'depressive position' – that period of integration and recognition which entailed a realization of the nature of the world outside the self and of the nature of the internal ambivalent feelings towards it, in other words, the beginnings of a sense of external and internal reality and the relationship between them. Since the delineation of this central concept of Kleinian thinking, it has become increasingly evident that the capacity to comprehend and relate to reality is contingent on working through the depressive position. Klein repeatedly emphasized that the Oedipus complex develops hand-in-hand with the developments that make up the depressive position, and I have suggested elsewhere that the working-through of one entails the working through of the other (Britton 1985).

This initial recognition of the parental sexual relationship involves relinquishing the idea of sole and permanent possession of mother and leads to a profound sense of loss which, if not tolerated, may become a sense of persecution. Later, the Oedipal encounter also involves recognition of the difference between the relationship between parents as distinct from the relationship between parent and child: the parents' relationship is genital and procreative; the parent–child relationship is not. This recognition produces a sense of loss and envy, which, if not tolerated, may become a sense of grievance or self-denigration.

The Oedipus situation dawns with the child's recognition of the parents' relationship in whatever primitive or partial form. It is continued by the child's rivalry with one parent for the other, and it is resolved by the child relinquishing his sexual claim on his parents by his acceptance of the reality of their sexual relationship.

In this chapter I want to suggest that if the encounter with the parental relationship starts to take place at a time when the individual has not established a securely based maternal object, the Oedipus situation appears in analysis only in primitive form and is not immediately recognizable as the classical Oedipus complex. In the first part of the chapter I describe a patient who illustrates this situation.

In less severe disorders it is the final relinquishment of the Oedipal objects that is evaded. An illusional Oedipal configuration is formed as a defensive organization in order to deny the psychic reality of the parental relationship. I emphasize that it is a defence against psychic reality because these defensive phantasies are organized to prevent the emergence of facts already known and phantasies already existent. The parental relationship has been registered but is now denied and defended against by what I call an Oedipal illusion. These illusional systems provide what Freud called a domain . . . separated from the real external world at the time of the introduction of the reality principle . . . free from the demand of the exigencies of life, like a kind of reservation.

(Freud 1924e)

In the same passage, he describes the person who creates such a domain in his mind as

lending a special importance and secret meaning to a piece of reality which is different from the reality which is defended against.

(ibid)

In the second part of this chapter I discuss patients who exemplify such Oedipal illusions.

In contrast to the fixity of these Oedipal illusions, the Oedipal rivalry both in the positive (heterosexual) form and in the negative (homosexual) form provides a means of working through the depressive position. In each version one parent is the object of desire, and the other is the hated rival. This configuration is retained, but the feeling changes in relation to each parent. Thus good becomes bad and vice versa as positive changes to negative. My contention is that the evasive use of this switch is halted by the full recognition of the parents' sexual relationship, their different anatomy, and the child's own nature. This involves the realization that the same parent who is the object of Oedipal desire in one version is the hated rival in the other.

The acknowledgement by the child of the parents' relationship with each other unites his psychic world, limiting it to one world shared with his two parents in which different object relationships can exist. The closure of the Oedipal triangle by the recognition of the link joining the parents provides a limiting boundary for the internal world. It creates what I call a 'triangular space' – i.e., a space bounded by the three persons of the Oedipal situation and all their potential relationships. It includes, therefore, the possibility of being a participant in a relationship and observed by a third person as well as being an observer of a relationship between two people.

To clarify this point it is helpful to remember that observed and imagined events take place in a world conceived of as continuous in space and time (Rey 1979) and given structure by the Oedipal configuration. The capacity to envisage a benign parental relationship influences the development of a space outside the self capable of being observed and thought about, which provides the basis for a belief in a secure and stable world.

The primal family triangle provides the child with two links connecting him separately with each parent and confronts him with the link between them which excludes him. Initially this parental link is conceived in primitive part-object terms and in the modes of his own oral, anal and genital desires, and in terms of his hatred expressed in oral, anal and genital terms. If the link between the parents perceived in love and hate can be tolerated in the child's mind, it provides him with a prototype for an object relationship of a third kind in which he is a witness and not a participant. A third position then comes into existence from which object relationships can be observed. Given this, we can also envisage *being* observed. This provides us with a capacity for seeing ourselves in interaction with others and for entertaining another point of view whilst retaining our own, for reflecting on ourselves whilst being ourselves. This is a capacity we hope to find in ourselves and in our patients in analysis. Anyone, however, who has treated a psychotic patient or been involved in a psychotic transference will know what I mean when I refer to times when this seems impossible, and it is at those times that one realizes what it means to lack that third position.

A patient who exemplifies difficulties in the first encounters with the Oedipal situation

In my early work with this patient, Miss A, I was hardly aware that my difficulties in understanding her had anything to do with the Oedipus complex. What gradually became evident was that she lacked the 'third position' described above. She could not conceive of relationships between others, and it was intolerable for her to feel that I was communing with myself about her.

Miss A came into treatment after a psychotic breakdown in midlife. She was relatively soon afterwards able to carry on an ostensibly normal life in the outside world, but she remained for many years in a psychotic state of mind in her sessions and in relation to me.

I came to learn that she could not allow the notion of parental intercourse to exist because she could only anticipate it as a disaster. The possibility of my communicating with a third object was unthinkable for her, and so the third position I refer to was untenable.

As a consequence it seemed impossible to disentangle myself sufficiently from the to-and-fro of the interaction to know what was going on. In the early years of her analysis I found that any move of mine towards that which by another person would have been called objectivity could not be tolerated. We were to move along a single line and meet at a single point. There was to be no lateral movement. A sense of space could be achieved only by increasing the distance between us, a process she found hard to bear unless she initiated it. What I felt I needed desperately was a place in my mind that I could step into sideways from which I could look at things. If I tried to force myself into such a position by asserting a description of her in analytic terms, she would become violent, sometimes physically, sometimes by screaming. When it became a little more contained, she could express it in words: she shouted: 'Stop that fucking thinking!' I came to realize that these efforts of mine to consult my analytic self were detected by her and experienced as a form of internal intercourse of mine, which corresponded to parental intercourse. This she felt threatened her existence. If I turned to something in my mind later on, when things were not so primitive, she felt I was eliminating my experience of her in my mind. The only way I found of finding a place to think that was helpful and not disruptive was to allow the evolution within myself of my own experience and *to articulate this to myself,* whilst communicating to her *my understanding of her point of view.* This, I found, did enlarge the possibilities and my patient could begin to think. It seemed to me that it was a model in which parental intercourse could take place if the knowledge of it did not force itself in some intrusive way into the child's mind. Should it do so, it appeared to be felt to be annihilating the child's link with her mother both externally and internally.

In an attempt to understand this clinical situation, I have called on Bion's concept of the 'container and contained', in addition to Melanie Klein's theories of the early Oedipus situation. Bion (1959) has described the consequences for some individuals of a failure of maternal containment as the development within them of a destructive envious superego that prevents them from learning or pursuing profitable relations with any object. He makes it clear that the inability of the mother to take in her child's projections is experienced *by the child* as a destructive attack *by her* on his link and communication *with her* as his good object.

The idea of a good maternal object can only be regained by splitting off her impermeability so that now a hostile force is felt to exist, which attacks his good link with his mother. Mother's goodness is now precarious and depends on him restricting his knowledge of her. Enlargement of knowledge of her as a consequence of development and his curiosity are felt to menace this crucial relationship. Curiosity also discloses the existence of the Oedipal situation. This in the development of every child is a challenge to his belief in the goodness of his mother, and a reluctance to admit it into his picture of his mother is normal. In the child already menaced by any enlargement of his knowledge of his mother because of her existing precarious status in his mind, the further threat of acknowledging her relationship with father is felt to spell disaster. The rage and hostility that would be aroused by this discovery is felt to threaten his belief in a world where good objects can exist. The hostile force that was thought to attack his original link with his mother is now equated with the Oedipal father, and the link between the parents is felt to reconstitute her as the non-receptive deadly mother. The child's original link with the good maternal object is felt to be the source of life, and so, when it is threatened, life is felt to be threatened.

In some personalities, therefore, the full recognition of parental sexuality is felt as a danger to life. The emergence in the transference of the full emotional significance for them of an idea of the primal scene is followed by panic attacks and fear of imminent death. Greater knowledge of the Oedipal situation is also felt to initiate a mental catastrophe.

Faced with this — as Klein (1946) and Bion (1956) have pointed out — the psychotic mutilates his mind in order not to perceive it. In schizophrenic patients the mental apparatus is splintered, and thinking becomes impossible. The patient I am describing, Miss A, appeared to have preserved a great deal by a violent severance of her mind so that some parts were protected from knowledge and only emerged in a psychotic breakdown or in analysis.

There was in her an 'infantile' self that appeared ignorant of anything other than an ideal breast and a state of persecution. The persecutor was a hovering male presence, which she feared might oust the good mother, and she was terrified she might be left alone with this figure. Interruptions in analysis and any interruptions in the flow of good experience were felt to be the result of violent attacks from this hostile object. At times I was taken to be this hostile object; at other times I was felt to be the victim of it. I was also familiar with it in the form of my patient attacking me. As progress was made and communications between us became more possible, her internal situation became clearer. She contained a hostile object, or part of herself in fusion with a hostile object, that interfered in her attempts to communicate with me. At times this had the power to control her speech, and she could not articulate. At others she whispered words, and broken phrases were managed. If I could demonstrate that I really wished to know her, which I could only do by demonstrating some minimal understanding, her capacity to communicate would be recovered. The way I came to understand that often-repeated sequence was that she needed some experience of my taking her in *before* I could return in her mind as the good maternal object she could talk to. Otherwise I might be what she called the 'wrong person'.

The 'wrong person' looked like the right person but had connections with father. For many years she was threatened by the fear of these crucially distinguished figures becoming confused. The thought of her idealized mother becoming united with father was her greatest fear. In the transference it took the form of a fear that the different aspects of my relationship with her would not be distinct from each other. Some of my functions were regarded as good; others as bad, such as my going away. She kept them distinct in her mind as if they were different transference figures. 'Don't become one thing,' she would say at times, in terror. From this patient I learnt how essential it was to distinguish between the integration that is sought for as a means of working through the depressive position, and a fusion of elements that are not stabilized and distinguished in their qualities and attributes, and whose union produces a sense of chaos.

If any pressure towards precocious integration was felt to come from me, it provoked great anxiety and either violent refusal or abject masochistic submission. This latter reaction turned out to be based on a phantasy of submission to a sadistic father and was regarded by my patient as profoundly wicked but always tempting. It appeared to serve the purpose of substituting herself for mother; such substitution provided both perverse gratification and an avoidance of the phantasy of the parents uniting.

She felt I must not become 'one thing' — i.e., a monstrous amalgamation of the separate maternal and paternal identities she had attributed to me. The amalgam that would result from this union was an ostensibly loving maternal figure who had inside her a contradiction of her own nature; a presence that made all her apparent good qualities treacherous. I was always reminded of descriptions of demonic possession, in which the devil was felt to have infused all the characteristics of the person with hidden evil. The horror she felt about this figure was to do with its contradictory nature. She called it 'unnatural' and regarded the emergence of this idea of me in the transference as disastrous because it destroyed not only all good but also all meaning previously established.

This fearful outcome corresponds to Melanie Klein's description of the child's terror of the combined object as a persecutory phantasy of the parents fused in permanent intercourse. I would describe my patient as having an infantile phantasy that her father was of such a nature and power that he could penetrate her mother's identity in such a way as to corrupt her goodness, and maternal goodness, although precariously idealized, was my patient's only concept of goodness. It always impressed me that for such a patient the very concept of goodness was at stake and not simply its availability or presence.

It is not my intention here to go into the factors in the patient's disposition and life circumstances that contributed to this inability to surmount the earliest stages of the Oedipus situation in any detail. I would simply like to say that in my view it was the initial failure of maternal containment that made the negotiation of the Oedipus complex impossible. The personality and intrusiveness of her father into her mother's mind were very significant, but these were combined with the patient's own considerable difficulty in tolerating frustration. The phantasy of parental intercourse was constructed from a combination of projections of herself and perceptions of her parents.

My wish is to draw attention to the reality of her belief that catastrophe was associated with the emergence of the Oedipal situation and that consequently she resorted to violent splitting to prevent it occurring. The result was an internal division within her mind organized around separate parental objects whose conjunction she believed must be prevented.

External reality may provide an opportunity for benign modification of such phantasies, or may lend substance to fears. It may also provide material for the formation of psychic structures that are meant to prevent the recognition of the Oedipus situation. The situation in the family of my patient enabled her to construct an internal organization of herself and her objects which had three main parts with no integration of them.

Her everyday relationship with the outside world, which was superficial, undemanding and reasonable, was based on her relationship with her sibling. Internally she had one self in loving union with an idealized mother and another self in alliance with a father seen as epitomizing anti-mother love. The link between these two selves was missing, as was the link between the internal parents.

What these two 'selves' did have in common, when it eventually emerged, was hatred of the parents as a loving couple. Initially the two parents could only be perceived as being linked in hate and mutual incompatibility, which meant that their coming together was a disaster. The gradual reclaiming by the patient of projected parts of herself in the course of a long and very difficult treatment led to the emergence of the idea of a couple who could unite willingly and pleasurably. New difficulties then arose with the eruption of envy and jealousy; these emotions were felt to be unbearable and seemed to become almost pure psychic pain.

I would like to distinguish the problems of this patient from the others referred to in this chapter whose difficulties with the Oedipus situation were not so early, total or primitive. The difference clinically could be summarized by saying that in this patient they were in the manner and mode of the paranoid–schizoid position. I think aetiologicaly the difference lay in the failure to establish a securely based, good maternal object before encountering the vicissitudes of the Oedipus complex.

Oedipal illusions

As described briefly above, Oedipal illusions are a developmentally later phenomenon than the primitive wiping out of the parental relationship with delusional developments that I have described in the previous section. When these illusions are paramount, the parental relationship is known but its full significance is evaded and its nature, which demonstrates the differences between the parental relationship and the parent–child relationship, is not acknowledged.

The illusion is felt to protect the individual from the psychic reality of their phantasies of the Oedipal situation. These I have found, in such cases, to be expectations of an endlessly humiliating exposure to parental triumphalism or a disastrous version of parental intercourse. This latter is perceived either as horrific, sado-masochistic or murderous intercourse, or as depressive images of a ruined couple in a ruined world. However, whilst such illusions are perpetuated as evasions of the underlying situation, the Oedipus complex cannot be resolved through the normal processes of rivalry and relinquishment.

I think that in normal development such illusions are frequent and transitory, producing cycles of illusionment and disillusionment that are the familar features of an analysis. In some people, however, the persistence of an organized Oedipal illusion prevents the resolution of the complex and in analysis the full development of its transference counterpart.

These illusions are often conscious – or almost conscious – versions of actual life situations. For example, I heard about a young woman in supervision: she was a musician who gave to her professional relationship with her music teacher the secret significance of preparation for a love affair. Once she was in analysis, her ideas about her analyst were suffused with the same erotic significance and the belief that it would end in marriage.

These wish-fulfilling ideas are often undisclosed in analysis, where they take the form of the patient's belief in a secret understanding between patient and analyst that transcends that formally acknowledged, as Freud points out in his paper 'Observations on Transference-love' (Freud 1915a). The illusory special relationship may take much less conspicuously sexual forms than the example I have quoted, whilst still having an erotized basis.

The transference illusion is felt to protect the patient from what is imagined to be a calamitous transference situation. As such, it poses considerable technical problems. Whilst it persists, all the analyst's communications are interpreted by the patient in the light of the illusional context.

I would like to illustrate the fears defended against by such an illusional construction from the analysis of a male patient. He had originally been a refugee from a foreign country but now worked as a government scientist. He regarded his parents as having lived separate lives, although they shared the same house. It became clear that the reality of their relationship had given some substance to this idea but also that his fixed mental picture was a caricature. It served as the structure for phantasies involving each parent separately, phantasies that were never integrated, and, though mutually contradictory, they remained adjacent to each other, as it were in parallel.

He transferred his picture to the analytic context in a rigidly literal way. He had a slight acquaintance with my wife in his professional context but never brought any thoughts from that context to his ideas of me as his analyst. He developed pictures in his mind of his analyst and of his analyst's wife in entirely separated contexts. Two wishful outcomes of his analysis lay side by side. One was of a permanent partnership with me in which he and I were alone together; the other was my death coinciding with the end of analysis, when he would marry my widow.

This formed the basis of a complex psychic organization in which the patient was able to oscillate between such contradictory beliefs without ever giving them much reality, or ever giving them up. Whilst this mode was operating in the analysis, things were always about to happen but never did; emotional experiences were about to occur but never materialized. The consequence for the patient's own mental operations was profound. Despite his considerable intellectual gifts, he was not able to bring things together in his mind, which resulted in learning difficulties as a child and a lack of clarity in his thinking as an adult, which had limited his originality. The consequences for his emotional life were a pervasive sense of unreality and a constant feeling of unfulfilment. There was a quality of nonconsummation in all his relationships and projects in life.

When change did begin to occur in his analysis, it provoked phantasies of great violence. Initially they were confined to the night-time. They took the form of murderous intercourse between the primal couple, which filled his dreams in many forms, and when they could not be contained within his dreams, they erupted as transitory night-time hallucinations of a couple who were killing each other.

In contrast to this, the analysis was for a long time an ocean of calm. Calmness was his aim, not fulfilment, and calm detachment was idealized. For a long time this was thought by him to be the aim of analysis and the aspiration of his analyst. Thus he thought his task was to facilitate this in both of us by forever finding agreement. His dreams were enormously informative but were a vehicle for getting rid of his thoughts into me, so that he could relate to my interpretations instead of to them, and therefore to himself second-hand. What his dreams made clear to me was his belief that bringing his parental objects together in his mind would result in explosion and disintegration. When the relationship between us did begin to feel rather different in the sessions, so that we both made more contact and yet were at greater variance, it led to fears of imminent catastrophe.

One form this took was a fear of sudden death. In particular, he had attacks of panic when he thought his heart was about to stop beating. His fearful expectation of violent collision took a concrete form in the emergence of a new fear of driving. Prior to this I had been hearing a lot about 'contra-flow systems' in his sessions — both in dreams and in reports of daily life. (At that time, some years ago, contra-flow traffic systems were a novelty on our motorways and in the news.) I took them to be a representation of the way my patient had segregated so carefully two different and contradictory streams of thought. I had wondered if their appearance in the analysis indicated that things were coming closer together in his mind. My patient then developed a panicky conviction when driving that unless there was a central barrier on the road, the streams of traffic would crash into each other. It reached such proportions that for a time it stopped him driving. This heralded changes in the transference relationship, which now did develop within it some conflict and opposition. The fear of finding within himself the violence that previously had only appeared in projected forms as violent parental intercourse became prominent for the first time. It is best conveyed by a dream he brought after a weekend break, at a time when weekends were very difficult and full of anxiety:

He is about to be left alone in a room with a dangerous, wild man by a couple who are going to the theatre. This man has always been locked up and restrained – he should be in a straitjacket. The patient is terrified that the man will destroy everything in the room. On his own he will not be able to reason with him. The man begins to speak. Previously, it seemed, he had been a mute. Help comes in the form of a Senior Negotiator from the Ministry (where the patient worked in reality). The Negotiator can speak to the Man, but if the Man realizes that the Negotiator has connections with the law, this will provoke him to even greater fury. (In reality, the Negotiator was concerned with terrorists in prison.)

The patient had many associations to this dream, and they made it clear that there was a situation in the patient's life involving a sense of betrayal by a woman and sexual jealousy that was connected to the dream. They also made clear that the couple went to the 'Theatre of the Absurd'. This, in turn, was associated with a debate he had participated in once as to whether a theatrical performance in a church could include the word 'fuck'. It was clear, I thought, that the man who represented that aspect of himself that had been mute and locked up was wild with jealousy. That was the new element, in my patient, in his analysis. The debate as to whether the idea of a 'fucking couple' could be allowed in the 'church' of the transference was still taking place in his analysis. My patient's dream suggested that he thought it an 'absurdly' dangerous venture to admit into his mind phantasies of his analyst, as one of a sexual couple, provoking a violent emotional reaction inside him. I interpreted myself as represented by the Negotiator as well as by the parental couple. The law that would further inflame the wild man was, I think, the law of the Oedipus complex – the law that distinguishes the sexes and the generations, provoking not only jealousy but also envy of the parental couple for their sexual and procreative capacities. My intention in describing briefly some aspects of the analysis of this patient is to illustrate some of the fears and conflicts from which the Oedipal illusion was felt to protect the patient.

Summary

The Oedipal situation begins with the child's recognition of the parents' relationship. In severe disorders development founders at this point, and the Oedipus complex does not appear in recognizable classical form in analysis. The failure to internalize a recognizable Oedipal triangle results in a failure to integrate observation and experience. This was the case in the first patient I described. I suggest that it is a consequence of a prior failure of maternal containment.

In the second part of the chapter I described what I call Oedipal illusions as defensive phantasies against the psychic reality of the Oedipus situation, and suggested that if they persist, they prevent the normal 'working through' of the Oedipus complex, which is done through sequences of rivalry and relinquishment.

Finally, I would like to clarify my view of the normal development of the Oedipus complex. It begins with the child's recognition of the nature of the parental relationship and the child's phantasies about it. In the Oedipus myth this would be represented by the story of the infant Oedipus abandoned on the hillside by his mother – a tragic version in the child's phantasy of being left to die whilst the parents sleep together. The complex unfolds further in the development of the child's rivalry with one parent for absolute possession of the other. This we see exemplified in the myth by the meeting at the crossroads where Laius bars the way, as if representing the father's obstruction of the child's wish to re-enter mother through her genital. This is what I regard as the psychic reality of the Oedipus complex, as are the fears of personal or parental death as imagined consequences.

What I have called Oedipal illusions are defensive phantasies meant to occlude these psychic realities. In the myth I see the Oedipal illusion as the state in which Oedipus is on the throne with his wife/mother, surrounded by his court, turning a 'blind eye', as John Steiner has put it, as to what they already half know but choose to ignore (Steiner 1985).

In this situation, where illusion reigns supreme, curiosity is felt to spell disaster. In the phantasied tragic version of the Oedipus complex the discovery of the Oedipal triangle is felt to be the death of the couple: the nursing couple or the parental couple. In this phantasy the arrival of the notion of a third always murders the dyadic relationship.

I think this idea is entertained by all of us at some time; for some it appears to remain a conviction, and when it does it leads to serious psychopathology. I have suggested that it is through mourning for this lost exclusive relationship that it can be realized that the Oedipal triangle does not spell the death of a relationship, but only the death of an idea of a relationship.

References

Bion, W.R. (1956). Development of schizophrenic thought. *Int. J. Psycho-Anal.*, 37, 344—6. [Reprinted in *Second Thoughts*. London: Heinemann, 1967.]

—— (1959). Attacks on linking. *Int. J. Psycho-Anal.*, 40, 308—15. [Reprinted in *Second Thoughts* (pp. 93—109). London: Heinemann, 1967.]

Britton, R.S. (1985) The Oedipus complex and the depressive position. *Sigmund Freud House Bulletin, Vienna, 9,* 7—12.

Freud, S. (1897). Letter 71. Extracts from the Fliess Papers. S.E.1 (pp. 263—266).

—— (1915a). Observations on transference-love. S.E. 12 (pp. 157—71).

—— (1924d). The dissolution of the Oedipus complex. S.E. 19 (pp. 171—9).

—— (1924e). The loss of reality in neurosis and psychosis. S.E. 19 (pp. 183—7).

Klein, M. (1926). The psychological principles of early analysis. *Int. J. Psycho-Anal.*, 7. [Reprinted in *The Writings of Melanie Klein, 1* (pp. 128—38). London: Hogarth Press, 1975.]

—— (1928). Early stages of the Oedipus conflict. *Int. J. Psycho-Anal.*, 9, 167—80. [Reprinted in *The Writings of Melanie Klein, 1* (pp. 186—98). London: Hogarth Press, 1975.]

—— (1946). Notes on some schizoid mechanisms. *Int. J. Psycho-Anal.*, 27, 99—110. [Reprinted in *The Writings of Melanie Klein, 3* (pp. 1—24). London: Hogarth Press, 1975.]

Rey, J.H. (1979). Schizoid phenomena in the borderline. In J. LeBoit & A. Capponi (Eds.), *Advances in the Psychotherapy of the Borderline Patient* (p. 449—84). New York: Jason Aronson.

Steiner, J. (1985). Turning a blind eye: The cover up for Oedipus. *Int. Rev. Psychoanal., 12,* 161—72.

PART TWO

The phallic question

Introduction

Within the psychoanalytic community it was not the Oedipus complex but the views Freud subsequently developed on female sexuality which elicited fierce opposition, in particular his paper on the anatomical distinction between the sexes (1925) in which he describes the wound to a woman's narcissism for her lack of a penis: 'she develops, like a scar, a sense of inferiority'. She blames her mother for her lack and abandons masturbation which reminds her of her inadequacy: 'the little girl's recognition of the anatomical distinction between the sexes forces her away from masculinity and masculine masturbation on to new lines which lead to the development of femininity' (Freud 1925: 256). It is only at this point, and as a consequence of her recognition of lack, according to Freud, that the girl turns to her father and hence enters her Oedipus complex. Hence, femininity, for Freud, is a purely psychological development based on this original disappointment. It is not, as it is for other theorists, a consequence of a biological drive.

Freud's notion of phallic monism whereby there is an early non-existence of the vagina even in the unconscious became the centre of the heated debate in the 1920s and 1930s known as the Freud–Jones debate.

For Freud, and this is taken up by Deutsch and Lampl-de Groot, femininity is acquired only after an earlier masculine phase in which the 'masculine' clitoris is the only sexual organ. Penis envy is seen as primary and derives from the fact that the clitoris is felt to be inferior to the penis, which the girl blames her mother for not giving her. Jones (1927), on the other hand, believed that 'men analysts have been led to adopt an unduly phallo-centric view of the problems in question, the importance of the female organs being correspondingly underestimated' (Jones 1938: 556).

Karen Horney and Melanie Klein were the main proponents of the so-called 'English school' of which Jones became the champion ('English', presumably, because of Jones since Horney moved to the United States from Berlin in 1932 after her earliest papers had been written and Klein moved to England only in 1926). Josine Muller, basing her view on the direct observation of children and on the analysis of women suffering from frigidity, also joined their view (1932). The basic difference from Freud's view in the English school rested on the belief that there is an early feminine phase in which the vagina is known and plays a role; early vaginal sensations are believed to be of fundamental importance and lead to specific anxieties and defences. These sensations also mean that there is an early, primary heterosexual impulse to receive. A certain amount of penis envy is understood as primary, but in its largest part it is thought to be defensive by these psychoanalysts.

Horney (1926) writes that the little girl experiences from the very beginning vaginal sensations and corresponding impulses, and hence she has from the outset a lively sense of the specific character of her own sexual role, and that therefore a primary penis envy of the strength postulated by Freud is hard to account for. She makes a distinction between a primary penis envy based on the anatomical difference between the sexes due to the narcissistic mortification of possessing less than the boy, and the desire to be a man in adult women which has little to do with this and is a secondary formation to the Oedipus complex. In renouncing the father as a sexual object, the girl recoils from the feminine role.

The attraction to the opposite sex operates from early on and penis envy is an expression of it: 'in the associations of female patients the narcissistic desire to possess the penis and the object-libidinal longing for it are often so interwoven that one hesitates as to the sense in which the words "desire for it" are meant' (Horney 1926: 68–9). For Horney there is a specific and biologically determined form of feminine anxiety which stems from the tremendous difference in size between the genitals of the father and the little girl, and leads to a fear of destruction. In contradistinction to this, the boy's specific genital anxiety is a wounding of his self-esteem ('my penis is too small for my mother'). 'Hence carried back to its ultimate biological foundations, the man's dread of the woman is genital-narcissistic, while the woman's dread of the man is physical.' She suggests that direct genital masturbation is often given up by girls because of the anxieties which cannot be assuaged as the boy can by direct perception. Sometimes it becomes

confined to the clitoris with its lesser cathexis of anxiety and everything connected with the vagina – the knowledge of its existence,
vaginal sensations and instinctual impulses – succumbs to a relentless
repression. Castration phantasies are a secondary formation: 'When the
woman takes refuge in the fictitious male role, her feminine genital
anxiety is to some extent translated into male terms – the fear of vaginal
injury becomes a fantasy of castration' (1926: 69). The fiction of maleness
enables the girl to escape from the female role which is linked with guilt
and dread of internal injury.

Melanie Klein's views were fairly similar on these points. She
rejects the notion of a 'phallic phase' in boys and girls in which only
one genital, the male one, would be known (1945). Klein believes
that both the girl's and boy's development include, from early infancy,
genital sensations and trends which constitute the first stages of the
Oedipus complex in its positive and inverted forms when they mingle
with oral, urethral and anal desires and phantasies. Hence the part-
object nature of the early Oedipus complex. The positive Oedipal
situation reaches its climax during the stage of genital primacy (Freud's
phallic stage) when there is a whole-object relationship.[1] In her early
writings Klein considers, as Freud did, that the girl's turning to the
father is based on hate for the mother, but for her it is due to frustration from the breast rather than to disappointment for her lack
of the penis. She later in fact comes to believe that it is love, not
hate, which propels the search for new objects (1945). Underlying this
for Klein, it is the girl's 'dominant feminine instinctual components'
which bring about the Oedipus impulses: 'what she [the girl] primarily
wants is not to possess a penis of her own as an attribute of masculinity,
but to incorporate her father's penis as an object of oral satisfaction'
(Klein 1932a: 196). The leading anxiety for the girl is the dread of
internal injury; while for Horney the threat came from the father
and his physically large penis, for Klein the attacks come from the image
of a mother containing a hostile penis inside her. This fear results
from the projection of the girl's own hostility. The wish for a child,
which for Klein is primary, leads to an Oedipal rivalry with the mother
expressing itself in the impulse to rob her mother of the father's penis
(phantasized inside the mother) and babies and consequently to the dread
of retaliation from the mother. This is a specific feminine castration
anxiety[2] and is the leading anxiety situation for the girl – the dread
of attack from the mother on her feminine organs and her capacity
to bear children. This dread is later transferred to the father with
a consequent fear in relation to the penis. The dread of the mother
may impel the girl to give up identification with her and to identify with the father instead. It is the girl's fears concerning the inside

of her body which contribute 'in addition to the operation of biological factors' to prevent the emergence of a clear vaginal phase in early childhood. Nevertheless, 'the mental representation of the vagina exerts its full share of influence no less than the mental representation of all the other libidinal phases, upon the infantile genital organization of the female child' (Klein 1932a: 211). In the Kleinian view sexual identity will develop from the ability to see the parents as differentiated and in a relationship to each other with the self as separate.

Jones proposed to make a distinction between the 'proto-phallic' phase and the 'deutero-phallic' phase. In the first there is no conflict, and it is assumed that everyone has a satisfactory male organ, penis or clitoris. In the second there is a conscious discovery of the sex differences and this results in envy and imitation. It is really about the deutero-phallic phase that there is an argument. Whereas for Freud the passing of this deutero-phallic phase ushers the Oedipus complex (that is, turning to the father), 'in London, on the other hand, we regard the deutero-phallic phase as essentially a defence against the *already existing* Oedipus complex' (Jones 1938: 614). The desire to possess a penis of her own is a defence against the dangers of the Oedipus complex. The girl deflects her libido into the safer auto-erotic direction (of the wish for the penis) which marks the denial of her femininity. This 'phallic position' is an emotional attitude rather than a stage in libidinal development. Jones concludes that a woman's femininity develops from the promptings of an instinctual constitution. 'In short, I do not see a woman [...] as *un homme manqué*, as a permanently disappointed creature struggling to console herself with secondary substitutes alien to her nature. The ultimate question is whether a woman is born or made' (Jones 1938: 616).

Joan Rivière, a Kleinian analyst, also believed that 'womanliness' is always present (even in the most completely homosexual woman), but it can also be used to hide the possession of masculinity 'much as a thief will turn out his pockets and ask to be searched to prove that he has not the stolen goods' (Rivière 1929: 306). She suggests that there is not a radical difference between genuine womanliness and 'masquerade'. Womanliness always exists but in some cases is used to avoid anxiety rather than as a primary mode of sexual enjoyment.

Those who argued in favour of a primary femininity used as argument the evidence of vaginal sensations in little girls. Freud acknowledged the reports of female analysts of early vaginal sensations but did not feel the need to revise his theory. He writes:

It is true that there are a few isolated reports of early vaginal sensations
... but it could not be easy to distinguish these from sensations in
the anus or vestibulum; in any case they cannot play a great part. We
are entitled to keep to our views that in the phallic phase of girls the
clitoris is the leading erotogenic zone.

(Freud 1933: 118)

It may be a certain shift, though, that Freud says 'leading' and not
'only' erotogenic zone. There is no doubt that a certain amount of
revision did take place. Mack Brunswick, in a 1940 paper arising
from her earlier 'collaboration with Freud, begun in 1930', writes
that, 'contrary to our earlier ideas, the penis wish is not exchanged
for *the baby wish which . . . has long preceded it*. In the course of normal
development the impossible is given up and the possible retained'
(Mack Brunswick 1940: 245) (italics mine). Mack Brunswick traces
this wish for a baby back to an identification with the active mother
and the wish to have everything the omnipotent and all-possessing
mother has. Later in the anal phase, there is an active wish to present
the mother with a baby. The girl gives up this active baby wish when
she accepts her own castration and consequent inability to impregnate
the mother. Although this is different from Klein's early Oedipal
wish for a baby, it is nevertheless a step away from the view expressed
in Freud's writings of the wish for a baby replacing the wish for
a penis.

The 'Freud–Jones debate' as such ended in the 1930s in an impasse
because, as Mitchell suggests, 'the concepts did not tally', because the
battle could never take place

because it was being fought on two completely different fields. . . .
Horney and Jones believed that the biological division of the sexes
was directly reflected in the mental life of each sex. . . . Freud,
roughly speaking, was arguing for a theory in which there is an
important gap between, on the one hand, biological femaleness
and maleness, and on the other psychological femininity and masculinity. He is also arguing against a theory of symmetry between the
sexes.

(Mitchell 1982: 129–30).

The debate, however, remains to this day, implicit or explicit, with Lacan
the main upholder of Freud's theory of sexual monism and the structuring
role of penis envy. Others recognize penis envy to be important if not
exclusive in femininity. Kestenberg writes:

The phase of intense penis envy is not to be construed as detrimental to feminine development. It is not identical with the parallel phase in the boy, but is a typically feminine avenue for identification with the opposite sex. It paves the way to heterosexuality and the acceptance of male children.

(1980: 327)

On the whole, penis envy in contemporary writings is widely believed to be, at least in large part, defensive in nature — displaced from the envy of the breast (Klein), aimed at repressing feminine desires (Gibeault, Torok, Braunschweig and Fain), wished for in order to repair a flaw in self-esteem and the relationship to the mother (Tyson 1989), aimed at avoiding fusion with the mother and the consequent loss of identity (Stein 1961) and so on. Phyllis Tyson concludes that penis envy can no longer be regarded as the major organizer of femininity:

It is an important part of the early phallic phase and as such might be considered as the developmental organizer of those masculine aspects found in the broader sense of gender identity, but we must look to the early identifications with the idealized mother-ego ideal in order to understand the greater portion of the feminine personality organization.

(1982: 77)

Some consider the use of the terms 'castration anxiety' or 'castration complex' to be highly unsatisfactory when applied to the girl's reaction to the discovery of genital difference (Tyson 1982: 73), while others retain the term 'castration anxiety' to include persecutory anxieties directed to the inside of the body (Duparc 1986).

While many writers on the subject believe that there is an early vaginal awareness and a subsequent repression of the vagina (Barnett 1966; Gutton 1983) and its representation in the unconscious (Chasseguet-Smirgel 1964), the question of whether the 'phallic' phase or components should be considered 'masculine' or part of 'femininity' remains open.

The papers in this chapter include contemporary views on Freud's notion of phallic monism and the role of 'castration' in the development of femininity. Chasseguet-Smirgel (1976) looks to Freud's own clinical writings to put into question this assumption, and suggests that lack of knowledge of the vagina results from splitting of the ego or from repression. She suggests that the theory of phallic monism aims at eradicating the narcissistic wound springing from the child's helplessness and smallness. Gillespie (1969) considers clitoridal excitation to lead to the feminine wish to be penetrated rather than to penetrate.

The last three papers, Braunschweig and Fain (1971), Montrelay (1978) and Gibeault (1988), I believe, show a way forward because, each in its own way, goes beyond the opposition of the Freud–Jones debate to show a duality which coexists in femininity, or in the case of Gibeault, two modes of thinking which coexist.

Braunschweig and Fain suggest that women live two Oedipal conflicts, one quasi-biological where the man's role is limited and where there is a primary desire to have a child as described by Melanie Klein, the other one which comes under the aegis of the law of the father and the castration complex as described by Freud. They suggest that there is a general misrecognition of female sexuality which separates clitoris and vagina out of castration anxiety and gives increased importance to the clitoris in a fetishistic way – coming from the projection onto the girl of a phallic phase – at the expense of the vagina. In this latter view feminine sexuality is subordinated not to male sexuality as such or to the penis as instrument of Eros but to phallic-narcissism (which is opposed to Eros). At the same time this phallic-narcissistic organization enables the woman to disengage from conflicts in relation to the mother (when the conflict is directly in relation to the mother who possesses the penis inside her in the 'Kleinian' Oedipal conflict). Montrelay goes further in suggesting that the very incompatibility of a phallic and a 'concentric' character of feminine sexuality is specific to the feminine unconscious. If femininity is a dark continent, it is, she suggests, because it ignores repression. The early knowledge of femininity and the vagina, however, far from facilitating maturation, prevents it in so far as it maintains erotism outside of the representation of castration. In so far as it impedes symbolization, this 'concentric' femininity remains, according to Montrelay, the 'dark continent', while the 'mature' woman is the one who reconstructs her sexuality in a sphere which no longer relates to her sex but to a castrated male sex. Braunschweig and Fain also consider the repression of the vagina to be part of normal development, and its non-repression to be problematic.

Looking from a different vantage point, Gibeault (discussing Cosnier's book) considers in both men and women two modes of thinking: a phallic logic which is an infantile theory based on sexual monism which protects the individual from primitive anxieties, and a genital logic which acknowledges the opposition and difference of masculine and feminine, and that both coexist. Gibeault suggests that the binary system of the phallic/non-phallic mode simplifies differences and hence has a role in organizing and reassuring both sexes. In its reference to the penis as an anatomical organ, this sexual theory plays a role in repressing Oedipal conflicts. The bedrock, according to Cosier, is really a psychological one in that the refusal of femininity in both sexes (penis envy in the woman, passivity in the man) relates to the unconscious attack on the contents of the mother's body. This is similar to Klein's view of the centrality of primary envy of the mother's creativity, body and contents, and the far-reaching defensive consequences of it.

Notes

1 Klein uses the term 'pre-genital' rather than 'pre-Oedipal' to denote the earliest phases which have other organs than the genital one as their focus of importance, since for her the Oedipus complex is present at a much earlier stage than the classic phallic stage.

2 François Duparc (1986) points out that the first to mention this feminine castration anxiety is Lou Andreas-Salomé in a letter to Freud of 19 October 1917: 'Castration anxiety in girls (e.g. after masturbation threats) frequently takes the form of a fear of being incapable of bearing children . . .; the emphasis is on this aspect instead of on threatened loss as in the case of the boy.' She also writes that 'What emerges as something quite new, not arising from anal-erotic memories, is in the case of the girl the fear of the male penis, though this is closely allied to the wish to possess one for oneself, or to appropriate it for oneself while possessing the man – the idea of being violated etc.'

4

Freud and female sexuality: the consideration of some blind spots in the exploration of the 'dark continent'

JANINE CHASSEGUET-SMIRGEL

Because time is limited it will not be possible for me to deal with Freud's ideas on female sexuality in their entirety, even less to compare them with opposing views expressed by other psychoanalysts. I shall therefore speak about only those issues which have caused the greatest controversy.

Let me open this discussion with a remark of a general nature: if a subject as fundamental as female sexuality causes such disagreement among analysts after almost 80 years of clinical experience, it must be because it stirs up certain internal factors in a particularly intense way which somehow interfere with our progress towards knowledge. Our differences of opinion about female sexuality are such that in the mêlée we lose sight of the truth.

A correlative comment comes to mind: divergencies in our understanding of female sexuality inevitably breed corresponding differences of opinion concerning male sexuality. Bisexuality, the notion of a 'complete' Oedipus – both negative and positive – the necessity for dual identification, all conspire to cast the shadow of the 'dark continent' on to male sexuality. It seems to me artificial and fallacious to abstract the study of female sexuality completely from that of the femininity common to both sexes and of human sexuality in general.

I shall therefore restrict my study of Freud's work on female sexuality to the discussion of some essential points; but at the same time I find myself forced to broaden the scope of these very same issues.

I shall examine the theory of *sexual phallic monism* and its most important consequences; I shall try to formulate certain hypotheses which I have developed on other occasions, with the idea in mind of showing how Freudian theories of female sexuality have endured in spite of the opposing clinical material which has come to light, in spite of the undeniable contradictions these theories reveal, and finally in spite of those theories which have lent a completely different dimension to female sexuality. I shall express a personal view on these matters, particularly on the topic of penis envy; yet my study will remain very much within a Freudian perspective; my basic assumptions being rooted in the question of 'human prematurity', which is linked to the child's early *helplessness (Hilflosigkeit)*.

The *Midrash*, a Talmudic commentary, recounts that when a child is born he is endowed with universal knowledge; but an angel appears, touches the new-born's upper lip with his finger and the child's knowledge vanishes into oblivion. It would seem that this legend, which one can imagine as representative of primary repression, is illustrative of theories of infantile sexuality and, in particular, the central one of sexual phallic monism and the correlative ignorance of the vagina, which is shared by both sexes. These theories replace what is probably an innate knowledge. We know, however, that for Freud sexual phallic monism and ignorance of the vagina are not defensive elaborations tied to repression: the vagina is non-existent for both sexes, *even in the unconscious*, and this lasts until puberty. This postulate is repeated throughout his work, beginning with the 'Three Essays' (Freud 1905); it appears again in 'Femininity' (Freud 1933) and finally in the 'Outline' (Freud 1940). (An important 'watershed' expression of this idea can be found in Freud 1923.) It is noteworthy that in the latter texts Freud is aware of the controversy inspired by the existence of early vaginal desires but he dismisses it abruptly. In 'Femininity' he writes (Freud 1933: 118): 'It is true that there are a few isolated reports of early vaginal sensations as well, but it could not be easy to distinguish these from sensations in the anus or vestibulum; in any case they cannot play a great part.'

In the 'Outline' we find in a note Freud's refutation of the 'supporters' of the vagina: 'The occurrence of early vaginal excitations is often asserted. But it is most probably that what is in question are excitations in the clitoris — that is, in an organ analogous to the penis. This, does not invalidate our right to describe the phase as phallic' (Freud 1940: 154).

In his article on 'Female Sexuality' Freud (1931) answers his opponents on this idea for the first time; his answer is astonishing:

> A man, after all, has only one leading sexual zone, one sexual organ, where-as a woman has two: the vagina — the female organ proper — and the clitoris, which is analogous to the male organ. We believe we are justified in assuming that for many years the vagina is virtually non-existent and possibly does not produce sensations until puberty. It is true that an increasing number of observers report that vaginal impulses are present even in these early years. In women, *therefore* [my italics], the main genital occurrences of childhood must take place in relation to the clitoris.
>
> (p. 228)

It is obvious that when Freud refutes these theories he takes into account the existence or non-existence of early vaginal sensations; but he does not recognize that the existence (at least unconscious) of the vagina would completely upset the theory of female sexuality, particularly in our understanding of the female Oedipus, of the girl's wish for the paternal penis and the wish to have a child, all of which would become in this respect, *primary* and fundamentally feminine. The boy child is completely unaware of the vagina's existence and imagines that all human beings possess a penis, including his mother. This is stated plainly in the 'Three Essays' (Freud 1905), while at the same time, erections of the penis before puberty and concomitant wishes for penetration are denied. ('The processes at puberty thus establish the primacy of the genital zones; and in a man, the penis, which has now become capable of erection, presses forward insistently towards the new sexual aim – penetration into a cavity . . .') In his paper 'On the Sexual Theories of Children' Freud (1908) takes into account a number of observations stemming from the case of Little Hans (Freud 1909). What he describes is quite apropos of what I am trying to say here:

> If children could follow the hints given by the excitation of the penis they would get a little nearer to the solution of their problem. That the baby grows inside the mother's body is obviously not a sufficient explanation. How does it get inside? What starts its development? That the father has something to do with it seems likely; he says that the baby is *his* baby as well. Again, the penis certainly has a share, too, in these mysterious happenings; the excitation in it which accompanies all these activities of the child's thoughts bears witness to this. Attached to this excitation are impulsions which the child cannot account for – obscure urges to do something violent, to press in, to knock to pieces, to tear open a hole somewhere. But when the child thus seems to be well on the way to postulating the existence of the vagina and to concluding that an incursion of this kind by his father's penis into his mother is the act by means of which the baby is created in his mother's body – at this juncture his enquiry is broken off in helpless perplexity. For standing in its way is his theory that his mother possesses a penis just as a man does, and the existence of the cavity which receives the penis remains undiscovered by him.
>
> (Freud 1908: 218)

It is noteworthy that later Freud (1924, and especially 1940) pictures the male child wishing only to be near his mother, indulging in vague and imprecise contacts which imply his penis only in an obscure way.

I would like to take up here some aspects of the observations in the Little Hans case (Freud 1909) which seem to me to contradict the

107

'fuzzy' quality of the excitation of the little boy's penis and to bring into question the entire theory of sexual phallic monism, or rather, to put into very evident relief its essentially defensive nature; thus, simultaneously, we can raise the issue of the equally defensive character of the sexual theories of children in general. We perceive that a complete and intuitive knowledge of sexuality (which is quite unacceptable for many reasons), underlies these theories; this knowledge is complete and intuitive because it is instinctual. How can we possibly imagine the girl to be unaware of the fact that she possesses a vagina when Freud (1917) attributes to the dream the power to discover early on all of the organic changes to come (this is the dream's 'diagnostic aptitude'). Why should the unconscious, which possesses the means for awareness of our bodily intimacy, be blocked when it comes to the vagina? Why should the boy not be aware of an organ complementary to his own since Freud postulates elsewhere the existence of innate primary fantasies?

When Hans was three and a half years old, his little sister Hanna was born. His father jotted down in his notebook that day:

> At five in the morning, labour began, and Hans's bed was moved into the next room. He woke up there at seven and, hearing his mother groaning asked: 'Why's Mummy coughing?' Then, after a pause, 'The stork's coming to-day for certain . . . ' . Later on he was taken into the kitchen. He saw the doctor's bag in the front hall and asked: 'What's that?' 'A bag', was the reply. Upon which he declared with conviction: 'The stork's coming to-day.' After the baby's delivery the midwife came into the kitchen and Hans heard her ordering some tea to be made. At this he said: 'I know! Mummy's to have some tea because she's coughing.' He was then called into the bedroom. He did not look at his mother, however, but at the basins and other vessels, filled with blood and water, that were still standing about the room. Pointing to the blood-stained bed-pan, he observed in a surprised voice: 'But blood doesn't come out of *my* widdler.'
>
> (Freud 1909: 10)

It seems to me that this excerpt reveals that Hans *knew* that delivery was painful because he was able to link his mother's groaning to the coming of the stork. For certain reasons (he probably felt invaded by those sensations connected to his sadistic feelings and the subsequent feelings of guilt) he still preferred to transform the groans into coughs, which are less worrisome. He also connected, at the same time, the doctor's bag and the arrival of the stork. He therefore knew very well that everything was going to happen inside his mother's body. Moreover, without having been present at the birth, he was aware that the child had come out through the mother's genital organs since he associates his and her 'widdler' with the blood.

108

It should be noted that nothing justifies Freud in assigning to the widdler ('wiwi-macher') an exclusively male meaning throughout the text; and when Hans asks his mother if she has a widdler too and she answers, 'Of course, why?' (p. 7), it is not necessary to think that she was lying to him because she too possesses genito-urinary organs; Hans's question could be understood as expressing his curiosity concerning the differences between the sexes, of which he was very well aware on a certain level. To demonstrate this idea, let us turn to some of the facts. Just before the outbreak of his phobia he went into his mother's bed in an attempt to seduce her, saying: 'Do you know what Aunt M. said? She said: "He *has* got a dear little thingummy"' (p. 23). Yes, a dear thingummy, but a *little* one. Not a big one like the horses. This was the beginning of a constant theme, the comparison between his *little* penis and the big penises of animals he envied; this provoked in him a fear of horses biting his fingers and a more vague fear with regard to animals possessing obvious phallic traits: the giraffe (because of its long neck), the elephant (because of its trunk), the pelican (because of its bill). Freud writes that Hans's statement, 'my widdler will get bigger as I get bigger', allows us to conclude that in the course of his observations Hans never stopped comparing and remained forever unsatisfied with the dimensions of his widdler (and in fact one can imagine that a part of his phobia derived from his wish to steal the big widdlers of the horses and the other phallic animals, which would then come back to threaten him. The fallen horses, the objects of Hans's terror, can be considered, on a certain level, castrated: fallen being the opposite of erect);[1] his wish for a big widdler remained an issue for a long time. Hans's father, like Freud, concluded that Hans feared 'that his mother did not like him, because his widdler was not comparable to his father's'. The fulfilment of this wish is played out in the fantasy of the plumber coming to give him a big widdler. Where does this wish for a penis as big as the father's originate, if Hans has no idea that his mother possesses an organ that his 'dear little thingummy' is incapable of (ful)filling? His knowledge of the mother's vagina appears in two fantasies he tells his father: (1) 'I was with you in Schönbrunn where the sheep are; and then we crawled under the ropes, and then we told the policeman at the end of the garden and he grabbed hold of both of us' (p. 40); (2) 'I went with you in the train, and we smashed a window and the policeman took us off with him' (p. 41). The idea that his penis is too small for his mother's vagina appears again, I think, in his fear that his mother would drop him during his bath into the big bathtub. That this fear issued from his wish that his mother would drop Hanna during her bath does not invalidate this hypothesis. Like the child who said apropos of the new arrival in his nursery, 'the stork should take it away again' (Freud 1908: 212), Hans was just as capable of sending

Hanna back where she came from (the mother's vagina). Later Hans talked about the big box (the mother's womb): 'Really Daddy. Do believe me. We got a big box and it was full of babies; they sat in the bath' (Freud 1909: 69). To my mind, this is the vagina.

We cannot fail to recognize in little Hans's fantasies and phobia an *Oedipal wish implying the genital possession of the mother with the help of a penis robbed from his father.*

But what is striking is that Freud sees this too — the material leaves little room for any other interpretation — and yet, in spite of this, he continues to uphold the theory of sexual phallic monism and the accompanying ignorance of the vagina. He says, in fact (Freud 1909):

> Some kind of vague notion was struggling in the child's mind of something he might do with his mother by means of which his taking possession of her would be consummated; for this elusive thought he found certain pictorial representations, which had in common the qualities of being violent and forbidden, and the content of which strikes us as fitting in most remarkably well with the hidden truth. We can only say that they were symbolic phantasies of intercourse.
>
> (pp. 122–3)

And further:

> But this father . . . had been his model . . . his father not only knew where children came from, he actually performed it — the thing that Hans could only obscurely divine. The widdler must have something to do with it, for his own grew excited whenever he thought of these things — and it must be a big widdler too, bigger than Hans's own. If he listened to these premonitory sensations he could only suppose that it was a question of some act of violence performed upon his mother, of smashing something, of making an opening into something, of forcing a way into an enclosed space — such were the impulses that he felt stirring within him.
>
> (pp. 134–5)

At this point, when we think Freud is on the verge of identifying the existence of the vagina at least on the preconscious level in little Hans's psyche, he surprises us with this strange conclusion:

> But although the sensations of his penis had put him on the road to postulating a vagina, yet he could not solve the problem, for within his experiences no such thing existed as his widdler required. On the contrary, his conviction that his mother possessed a penis just as he did stood in the way of any solution.
>
> (p. 135)

Freud's conjectures here appear contradictory: firstly, contrary to what he claimed (Freud, 1905) and to what he continued to claim in later works, the boy's wishes for penetration exist well before puberty and so does the 'obscure' and 'premonitory' existence of the vagina. It would be impossible to prove in any decisive way if at any moment Hans thought that his mother's widdler was a penis, and even so, this representation would have to be superimposed on that of the vagina. One might ask: if his conviction does indeed stand in the way of any solution, as Freud has written, is this representation then perhaps a defensive one – and if this is true, how? One can imagine Freud's answer: the fear of castration would drive the little boy to see a penis where there isn't one. But the fear of castration springing from the sight of the female genital organs without a penis is all the more powerful, according to Freud, precisely because the child is ignorant of the vagina's existence. He therefore imagines a sex not just different from his own, but – horrors! – an absence of sex.

I believe, in fact, that none of these difficulties would arise if, like with the child in the *Midrash*, we considered that little boys and girls were completely knowledgeable about sexuality; but that this knowledge is then tampered with by a series of repressions, of a defensive nature, which result first from the pressure of unbearable excitations, and then afterwards from conflictual situations. (The idea of an 'instinctive knowledge' and even an 'instinctive patrimony' stemming from the processes of sexual life and constituting the nuclear centre of the unconscious was not foreign to Freud, 1918, but he refuses, in my opinion, to draw the logical consequences which necessarily follow. Freud was perhaps afraid that this conception would be exploited for the purposes of Jungian theory.) This would explain why the child shapes his own sexual theories according to his stage of development. The child lives on two planes: that of his profound knowledge, possessed instinctively, of sexuality, and that of his development, his wishes, his defences which gauge the information the child receives during the course of his growth. Sexual education is therefore caught between two dimensions: the child's unconscious on the one hand, to which nothing can be taught which it does not already know and, on the other, his own sexual theories which he elaborates for his own purposes and which give answer, in principle, to what he feels he can stand at any one stage of his development. When children are informed of sexual matters there is always the possibility that the adult will find himself in Hans's father's situation when he said to him (Freud 1909: 95) 'but you know quite well boys can't have babies', to which came the reply, 'Well yes. But I believe they can, all the same.'

My hypothesis is that the theory of sexual phallic monism corresponds not to the lack of knowledge of the vagina but to a splitting of the ego ('Well, yes.

But I believe they can, all the same') *or to the repression of an earlier piece of knowledge*. This hypothesis has already been formulated by Josine Muller, Karen Horney, Melanie Klein and Ernest Jones. However, I hope to put my subject into a different perspective.

Before presenting my hypothesis in full, I would like to discuss another famous clinical text of Freud's, the analysis of the Wolf Man (Freud 1918). If little Hans's phobia is focused on the positive Oedipus, the 'infantile neurosis' of the Wolf Man is focused on the negative Oedipus, the wish to *assist the paternal coitus*, to take the mother's place in the primal scene. We know that the child witnessed at the age of one and a half the famous scene of coitus *a tergo* between his parents and that he dreamed his wolf-dream when he was four years old. In Freud's estimate, the reactivation of the primal scene in the dream directed the child towards genital organization, a discovery of the vagina (cf. Freud 1918: 64). This is in contradiction with his theory of the discovery of the vagina in puberty. In a strange way Freud assumes that observing the coitus *a tergo* convinced the child 'that castration was the necessary condition of femininity' (p. 78). Our first objection is that in this position the vagina is not visible. Furthermore, we are again faced with the equivocal role the vagina plays in the masculine castration complex, because, in this instance, the vagina is held responsible, above all, for the Wolf Man's castration fears: the vagina is precisely the wound the father leaves after castration. Freud claims, nevertheless, that the child represses his knowledge of the vagina, and adopts instead his first theory of anal sexual intercourse:

> But now came the new event that occurred when he was four years old. What he had learnt in the meantime, the allusions which he had had to castration, awoke, and cast a doubt on the 'cloacal theory'; they brought to his notice the difference between the sexes and the sexual part played by women. In this contingency he behaved as children in general behave when they are given an unwished-for piece of information — whether sexual or of any other kind. He rejected what was new (in our case from motives connected with his fear of castration) and clung fast to what was old. He decided in favour of the intestine and against the vagina ... He rejected the new information and clung to the old theory.
>
> (Freud 1918: 79)

Here again we come across theoretical suggestions which contradict other statements we find elsewhere in his work. Freud (1937) describes passivity, in any form, as sufficient to stir up fears of castration in men; actual penetration is not necessary to awaken these fears of losing the penis. Anal penetration, *a fortiori*, does not prevent man from fearing castration. The fear of passivity, we know, is the 'bedrock' of the psychoanalysis of males:

At no other point in one's analytic work does one suffer more from an oppressive feeling that all one's repeated efforts have been in vain, and from a suspicion that one has been 'preaching to the winds', than . . . when one is seeking to convince a man that passive attitude to men does not always signify castration and that it is indispensable in many relationships in life.

(Freud 1937: 252)

Furthermore, it is striking that the wishes for penetration by the father's penis were active in the Wolf Man's case when he observed the parental coitus (at the age of one and a half) and were revived in his dream (at four years of age), and yet the same wish for penetration arises in the girl's case only in puberty. The Wolf Man, like Schreber (Freud 1911) wished to have a child by his father, an instinctual wish tied to his feminine identification, while the girl's wish is only a substitute for, an ersatz version of, her penis envy (Freud 1925). The man's feminine wishes to be penetrated and to have babies by the father would therefore be more direct than the woman's. We should bear in mind that these wishes constitute for the male individual the nucleus of delusion.

Moreover, we know that Freud (1931: 229) asserts in his article on 'Female Sexuality': 'It is only in the male child that we find the fateful combination of love for the one parent and simultaneous hatred for the other as a rival.'

Freud considers the pre-Oedipal phase more significant in the woman's case than in the man's. He claims (Freud 1931) that sometimes the girl never attains her positive Oedipal phase, and during the phase of her negative Oedipus complex 'a little girl's father is not much else for her than a troublesome rival' (p. 226). If the girl does reach the positive Oedipal phase, her relationship to her father is merely a continuation of the relationship she enjoyed with her mother: 'Except for the change of her love-object, the second phase had scarcely added any new feature to her erotic life' (p. 225).

If we carry these statements to their logical conclusion, can we not say that in Freudian theory the father is more of an object for the boy than for the girl?

Penis envy, in the girl's case, is a derivative of sexual phallic monism. The Freudian conception implies that from the moment when the girl discovers the penis's existence, a discovery that antecedes the Oedipal phase, to the moment in puberty when she discovers the existence of her vagina, she is, in her own eyes, a castrated individual with a truncated penis; the clitoris. This fact makes her turn away from her mother who did not offer her a penis and drives her into the Oedipus complex so as to obtain from her father the desired organ, a desire which in happy circumstances turns into the wish for a child, and preferably a male one. The woman's sexual desire for the penis is absolutely subordinate to or has been flattened out by her narcissistic envy. *Penis envy is primary, the feminine erotic wishes are secondary.*

But, as we all know, the woman's psychosexual trials and tribulations do not end here. Since the little girl's sexuality is in the final account male, and exclusively focused on the clitoris – the external 'feminine' genital parts, as Freud significantly calls them, do not come into play at all, even in seduction. Once the girl arrives at puberty she has to give up her cathexis of her 'male' organ (the clitoris) and turn towards her internal feminine organs. 'What is thus overtaken by repression is a piece of masculine sexuality' (Freud 1905: 221). The clitoris that remains the focus (it should only serve as a transmitter of excitability, 'pine shavings' for the kindling of a fire) is at the root of female frigidity and predisposes the subject to the neuroses, most particularly hysteria. Gillespie (1975) poses the following question in relationship to this issue: 'Does not Freud's theory of the pseudo-masculine clitoris which has to be given up imply an insistence that the female *must* be castrated . . .?

We know that the clitoris plays a role for the entire duration of the sexual act and for the duration of a normal woman's lifetime. Jones (1933) implied this when he wrote that 'after all, the clitoris is a part of the female genital organs'.

I think that we can now list the principal points which have been raised in my discussion of the Freudian theory of female sexuality as it stands in relationship to the theory of sexual phallic monism:

the boy's ignorance of the mother's vagina;
the girl's ignorance of her own vagina;
the girl's exclusive cathexis of the clitoris, the equivalent to a truncated penis;
the necessary renunciation of this cathexis at puberty;
the girl's psychosexuality is dominated by the unsatisfiable envy for the male organ;
the boy's wish to be penetrated by the father's penis and to have his babies is more direct than the girl's;
the positive Oedipal phase is never attained by some women;
the female positive Oedipus complex is only the displacement of the woman's relationship to her mother on to her father;
maternity is an 'ersatz' masculinity which in fact can never be attained.

Female sexuality is therefore a series of lacks: the lack of a vagina, lack of a penis, lack of a specific sexuality, lack of an adequate erotic object, and finally the lacks which are implied by her being devoid of any intrinsic feminine qualities which he could cathect directly and by her being forced to give up the clitoris. We can add the relative lack of a superego and the capacity for sublimation, issues which I shall not be able to discuss here. The boy's sexuality is so much more full: he possesses an adequate sexual organ, a sexuality which is specific from the outset, and two love objects to satisfy the requirements of both tendencies of the Oedipus complex.

Now the woman as she is depicted in Freudian theory is exactly the opposite of the primal maternal imago as it is revealed in the clinical material of both sexes. This could be a mere coincidence, but the contradictions we have been able to discern throughout Freud's work on the problem of sexual phallic monism and its consequences, force us to take closer notice of *this opposition between the woman, as she is described by Freud, and the mother as she is known to the Unconscious.*

What astonishes us in all of this is not that Freud's pathways to knowledge were blocked in certain areas of his work, but that in spite of this he was able to pursue his researches so successfully and so far. The issue is this: this theory still enjoys a solid reputation because, ultimately, it has withstood the contra-indications of certain clinical and theoretical arguments, and has withstood the pressure of its own internal contradictions.

The theory of sexual phallic monism (and its derivatives) seems to me to eradicate the narcissistic wound which is common to all humanity, and springs from the child's helplessness, a helplessness which makes him completely dependent on his mother.

As early as 1895, in the 'Project' (Freud, 1950) Freud already began to place emphasis on the human being's condition of helplessness in infancy, and the situation of dependency it entails. Subsequently (Freud 1915) he attributes the separation between the ego and non-ego to the infant's helplessness (*Hilflosigkeit*): 'the primal narcissistic state would not be able to [develop] if it were not for the fact that every individual passes through a period during which *he is helpless* [my italics] and has to be looked after and during which his pressing needs are satisfied by an external agency' (p. 135*n*).

Later, (Freud 1926) he again mentions the helplessness of the human being, whose

intra-uterine existence seems to be short in comparison with that of most animals, and it is sent into the world in a less finished state. As a result, the influence of the real external world upon it is intensified and an early differentiation between the ego and the id is promoted. Moreover, the dangers of the external world have a greater importance for it, so that the value of the object which can alone protect it against them and take the place of its former intra-uterine life is enormously enhanced. The biological factor, then, establishes the earliest situations of danger and creates the need to be loved which will accompany the child through the rest of its life.

(pp. 154–5)

The human being's dependency on his mother, who is absolutely necessary for his survival, causes for the most part, as we all know, the formation of an omnipotent maternal imago. As the child grows, he gains, through his psychophysiological maturation and identifications greater and greater freedom. Nevertheless, his psyche remains forever marked by his primary helplessness, especially since it follows hard upon an earlier state of completeness in which every need was automatically satisfied (I am alluding to the foetal state and to the very short period when we can assume that the ego and non-ego are not yet differentiated). Because the child is faced with a discrepancy between his incestuous wishes and his ability to satisfy them, a discrepancy which springs from man's biological chronology – this is a point that Grunberger (1956, 1966) has stressed – the child's experiences of these wishes become a real drama. Here again, helplessness is at the heart of the problem.

Let us remember the bleak picture Freud (1920) paints of the Oedipal child:

The early efflorescence of infantile sexual life is doomed to extinction because its wishes are incompatible with reality and with the inadequate stage of development the child has reached. The efflorescence comes to an end in the most distressing circumstances and to the accompaniment of the most painful feelings. Loss of love and failure leave behind them a permanent injury to self-regard in the form of a narcissistic scar, which in my opinion, as well as in Marcinowski's . . ., contributes more than anything else to the 'sense of inferiority' which is so common in neurotics. The child's sexual researches, on which limits are imposed by his physical development, lead to no satisfactory conclusion; hence such later complaints as 'I can't accomplish anything; I can't succeed in anything.' The tie of affection, which binds the child as a rule to the parent of the opposite sex, succumbs to disappointment, to a vain expectation of satisfaction or to jealousy over the birth of a new baby – unmistakable truth of the infidelity of the object of the child's affections. His own attempt to make a baby himself, carried out with tragic seriousness, fails shamefully. The lessening amount of affection he receives, the increasing demands of education, hard words and an occasional punishment – these show him at last the full extent to which he has been scorned.

(pp. 20–1)

Renunciation of the Oedipal object, in this context, seems to be tied to the child's pained recognition of his smallness, of his insufficiencies. This is the tragedy of lost illusions. The theory of sexual phallic monism maintains these illusions. McDougall (1972) has pointed out that the sight of the female genitalia without a penis not only inspires the child with fright because it confirms the possibility of castration, but it also requires the child to recognize the role of the father's penis and to accept the primal scene.

In my opinion, reality is not only founded in the difference between the sexes, but also in the absolute correlative, the difference between the generations. The reality is not that the mother has been castrated but that she possesses a vagina that the child is utterly unable to (ful)fill. The reality is that the father possesses a penis that the little boy does not have (the big widdler that Little Hans envied), and genital faculties the child does not possess. When the child is forced to heed the difference between the sexes and their complementarity, he simultaneously comes to realize the difference between the generations. *This causes a narcissistic wound that the theory of sexual phallic monism tries to erase*: if in the Oedipal phase the child was devoid of any wishes to penetrate his mother, of any knowledge of his mother's vagina, he would have no reason to envy his father whose capabilities would then be not much different from his own; if his mother were willing, and his father did not object, he too could engage in those vague and imprecise 'contacts'. The Oedipal boy preserves in this way a measure of his narcissism. In fact, this corresponds to the perverted temptation to render pregenital wishes and satisfactions (within the little boy's reach) equivalent to, or even to value them more highly than genital wishes and satisfactions (which are only within the father's reach). A very clear expression of this temptation is to be found in the analysis of Little Hans, when he states his wish to beat horses and finally, as he confesses, to beat his mother: for a little boy, it is, in fact, easier to do this than to attempt to have genital coitus with an adult woman.

Other narcissistic advantages are contained in the theory of sexual phallic monism: if the mother is without a vagina, the little boy, in terms of the inverted Oedipus complex, can satisfy the father just as much as the mother can. Many homosexuals entertain this fantasy; they believe that the anus, which they have genitalized, and the vagina are equivalent. The supposed lack of knowledge of the vagina offers the male child narcissistic benefits on both the negative and positive planes of the Oedipus complex.

The need for sexual phallic monism finds its origin in two different dimensions of the child's relationship to the mother: on the one hand, the archaic omnipotent mother and on the other, the Oedipal mother; in both instances the child experiences with pain the inadequacy linked

117

to his helplessness. The wish to break away from the primal mother drives children of both sexes to project her power on to the father and his penis, and to more or less decathect specifically maternal qualities and organs. If the relationship to the mother has been a sufficiently good one (for external as well as internal reasons) the male child will choose his father as his model (as in the case of Little Hans) so he can be like him and one day possess his mother. He will then cathect his own penis with an actual sexual and narcissistic value, but one which is to be truly realized only in the future. He will not, however, entirely abandon his narcissistic cathexis of the maternal faculties and organs: breasts, vagina, the possibility of bringing children into the world. This process leads him to develop according to the norms of his own sex, yet without, in a state of reaction, devaluating the feminine elements; he will thus be able to integrate his femininity and increase his capacity to understand the wishes of his partner in love relationships. If his relationship to the archaic mother has been very sour, he can completely remove his narcissistic cathexis from the maternal prerogatives and place it entirely on the paternal penis and his own. Because he will so thoroughly disdain the maternal traits, he will find great difficulty in integrating his femininity, if he does not find it simply impossible. He rejects any re-sexualization of his passive homo-sexual impulses; he finds it horrifying. Re-sexualization is rejected by the ego precisely because the reaction-cathexis of the penis has absorbed the bulk of the narcissistic libido; femininity is thereafter divested of this libidinal content. This would help to explain, in my opinion, the conflicting character of the male's passive homosexual wishes, because the erotism driving the subject towards his father is connected precisely to a devaluation of femininity, and therefore to that of his own. In these cases a violent opposition breaks out between homosexuality and narcis-sism. I think this is one of the reasons amongst the many others cited by other analysts, why with patients revealing paranoid features it is necessary to analyse the maternal relationship early on in treatment.[2]

Freud attributed to man a 'natural scorn' for women. This scorn originated in the fact of their lack of a penis. My experience has shown me that underlying this scorn one always finds a powerful maternal imago, envied and terrifying (see also Chasseguet-Smirgel 1964).

A passing devaluation of the mother and women is 'normal' and allows the boy to cathect narcissistically his own sexual identity, but it should not be prolonged into adulthood except in the guise of protective feelings towards the woman. Scorn in the adult is never 'normal' and reveals personal uncertainty about one's own self-worth. It can be, among other things, the manifestation of a phallic-narcissistic regression. Of course what I said earlier about the defensive nature of the theory of sexual phallic monism does not expel Jones's theses, for instance his thesis on the

118

phallic phase, but contributes to our understanding (at least I hope it does this) of the defensive character of that phase that protects the subject not only from his fears of castration on the Oedipal level but also from the narcissistic wound tied to his intrinsic insufficiencies.

In contrast to the subject presenting paranoid symptoms stands the transsexualist who through plastic surgery removes his male characteristics to fabricate a vagina in their place. For precise 'historical' reasons linked to his relationship to his parents he was probably unable to project his ego ideal on to his father and his penis. His narcissistic cathexis never detached itself from the maternal feminine attributes of the archaic mother. The male's femininity, his homosexual position are, because of the complex factors we have just described, borne by multiple defensive and instinctual forces:

classical regression before the Oedipal phase and fear of castration by the father;

impossibility of identification with a sadistic father;

'normal' identification with the mother in the primal scene, on the level of the inverted Oedipus complex and the integration of femininity;

the envious wish to acquire the father's big penis through incorporation, with the goal in mind of paternal identification in the hope of possessing the mother in the positive Oedipus complex;

the wish *to be* the omnipotent mother and to possess her attributes which continue to be narcissistically cathected (this wish can, consequently, be perfectly ego-syntonic);

the wish to be the mother so that fusion can occur and separation-anxiety be avoided;

the wish to be penetrated passively by the mother's anal phallus (I can only allude to this position here);

the wish to escape the omnipotent mother by decathecting those attributes which belong to her, and by 'gluing' oneself to the father and his penis.

The need to detach oneself from the primal omnipotent mother by denying her faculties, her organs and her specifically feminine features, and by investing in the father, seems to be a need which both sexes share. Bachofen (1861) has studied the transformation of matriarchies into patriarchies. The existence of matriarchal civilizations raises many problems, but Bachofen's work nevertheless touches upon a profound psychological truth, because we can thus observe projected on to the history of civilizations the individual adventure of development in men and women.

A psychoanalyst to the end, Bachofen answered Momsen, who had challenged his theses, that personal reasons must underlie Momsen's refusal to accept the existence of matriarchies. Bachofen thought that Aeschylus'

Eumenides described the transition from matriarchal to patriarchal law. We know that this play is the narrative of Orestes' trial after he murdered his mother. He had acted to avenge his father, Agamemnon, who had been assassinated by Clytemnestra. The Erinyes, who at the end of the play become the Eumenides, are daughters of the night, chthonian, subterranean divinities who reigned before the time of Zeus (like the mother who reigns before the father). They are the prosecutors at the trial. They are described as 'the gloomy children of the night'. Apollo, at whose specific command Orestes had set out to avenge his father, heads the defence. Orestes appeals to Athene who was born without maternal involvement; she was born straight from the head of Zeus, fully armed and helmeted and thus escaped primal infantile helplessness. She creates a court, the Areopagus, in the very place where the Amazons had been, before they had been defeated by Theseus; in this way the Erinyes lose their legal prerogative as judges. The Erinyes protest:

> Here is overthrow of all
> the young laws, if the claim
> of this matricide shall stand
> good, his crime be sustained.

The Erinyes believe that Clytemnestra's crime is less of an offence than Orestes' because 'The man she killed was not of blood congenital.' Orestes makes the astonishing retort: 'But am I then involved with my mother by blood-bond?' Apollo supports Orestes:

> The mother is no parent of that which is called
> her child, but only nurse of the new-planted seed
> that grows. The parent is he who mounts. A
>   stranger she
> preserves a stranger's seed, if no god interfere.
> I will show you proof of what I have explained.
>   There can
> be a father without any mother. There she stands,
> the living witness, daughter of Olympian Zeus . . .

Athene approves of this speech and claims to be 'strongly on [her] father's side'. (This conception of birth should be compared to the one Sade postulates on several occasions.) Orestes is acquitted. The Erinyes lament:

> Darkness of Night, our mother, are you here to
>   watch? . . .
> Gods of the younger generation, you have ridden
>   down
> the laws of the elder time, torn them out of my
>   hands

120

and threaten the country with the worst disaster. The Erinyes are finally promised that they will be made into a cult. They calm down, are made the Eumenides; the play has a happy, festive ending.

It is noteworthy that Athene, a woman, and Apollo, a man, band together to deny the maternal prerogatives.

The girl's penis envy seems to me not to rest upon her ignorance of the vagina and her subsequent feelings of castration (although certain conflicts which arise in this relation almost oblige her to repress her knowledge of this organ; this repression is perhaps normal as has been indicated by Braunschweig and Fain (1971) but on her need to beat back the maternal power.

I would like to report a session which I mentioned at the last London Congress. I think it very clearly illustrates what I am driving at. I hope that those who are already familiar with this material will forgive me for repeating it here:

The woman patient was the third in a family of five children. She has two older brothers. A brother and then a sister were born after her. She began the session by complaining about her being with a woman analyst; since women are inferior to men, she was not going to get anything out of being with me (this was a recurring theme). Then she told her dream. She is in a theatre. A woman is standing on the stage exposing one breast which is very big, round and swollen. The patient said that the previous day she had read in an article about an actress who was in a very special kind of show in Paris in which she would undress in a very obscene way while insulting the public whom she mocked and humiliated. In her dream the patient is in the hall, amongst the spectators, with her brother and a friend of his. At the actress's feet there is a little 18-month-old boy. At a particular moment the actress throws herself back, lifts up her skirts and reveals her sex. The patient's brother and his friend become very agitated, mock the woman and make a cutting motion with their fingers, a gesture which is aimed at letting her know that she is castrated. The patient continues and relates a fantasy: she could pull on her husband's penis, and his body would empty like a balloon being emptied of its air. It should be noted that she had always felt that her husband was the-son-of-her-mother-in-law, but not a person in his own right. It seems to me that this example very clearly illustrates that underlying her devaluation of the woman (myself in the transference) a very powerful maternal imago is to be found which upsets her status by producing other children after her and by offering them her breast (she was 18 months old when her younger brother was born, the same age as the little boy in the dream). This mother had humiliated her as the

121

actress had done to her public in the day residue. Her resources for overcoming her narcissistic wound were limited, and she chose therefore to indicate the pitfall and failure in the maternal power, i.e. the absence of a penis. It is the only way to triumph over the mother. But to achieve this it is better to be equipped with a penis, like the two young men in her dream who flout their power in the way she could have if she had been the little 18-month-old boy in her dream. In the fantasy that follows the dream, the patient attacks the mother's breast directly by emptying it, the husband's body representing the breast, and his penis the nipple. The husband is then like a deflated balloon, in other words, like a limp breast. On another plane, the husband also represents the little brother whom she castrates and destroys.

My experience with women patients has shown me that penis envy is not an end in itself, but rather the expression of a desire to triumph over the omnipotent primal mother through the possession of the organ the mother lacks, i.e. the penis. Penis envy seems to be as proportionately intense as the maternal imago is powerful.

It goes without saying that the narcissistic decathexis of the maternal organs and qualities which then follow makes identification with the mother and the acceptance of femininity rather difficult. Passive feminine homosexuality is very conflictive and, because of this, integrating it is very problematical. Idealization of the father and his penis perturbs the psychosexual life of women. Athene, the daughter of Zeus, says:

> There is no mother anywhere who gave me birth, and, but for the marriage, I am always for the male side with all my heart ...

We could pursue in the area of sociocultural activities the undeniable effects of our universal need to escape our primal dependence on the mother, but unfortunately there is no time for that here.

In spite of his views on female sexuality which reflect, in my opinion, our fundamental conflict with the maternal object as it arises in our state of helplessness in infancy, Freud, because he did not recognize the determining force of the child within man, implicitly assigned to the mother the important role that is hers. Bachofen felt that moving from a matriarchy to a patriarchy was equivalent to the subordination of material principles to spiritual principles, the subordination of the chthonic law of subterranean maternal powers to celestial Olympian law. Psychoanalytic theory does not escape this struggle between maternal and paternal law. If we underestimate the importance of our earliest relations and our cathexis of the maternal imago, this means we allow paternal law to predominate and are in flight from our infantile dependence: if we neglect the organizing effects of the Oedipus complex, which includes the experience of whole objects, of the paternal superego, of the penis, we restore the maternal primal power which, even if it does intimidate us, is an undeniable source of fascination. Our personal conflicts may cause us to forget that we are all children of Men and Women.

Notes

Presented as part of a Dialogue on 'Freud and Female Sexuality' at the 29th International Psycho-Analytical Congress, London, July 1975.

1 Freud's interpretation of the fallen horse phobia leads him to the scene where Fritzl hurts his foot and bleeds. Freud identifies the fallen horses with Fritzl and Hans's father. He thus arrives at the death-wish rather than the castration-wish.

2 We know that Schreber's (Freud 1911) mother was absorbed, so to speak, by her husband who had usurped her maternal functions. In this case, as in all cases of male paranoia, what is significant is the absence of a narcissistic cathexis of femininity.

References

Aeschylus *Eumenides* (transl. R. Lattimore). Chicago Modern Library, 1942.

Bachofen, J.J. (1861). *Das Mutterecht*, 2 vols. Basle: Benno Schwabe, 1948.

Braunschweig, D. and Fain, M. (1971). *Eros et Anteros*. Paris: Petite Bibl. Payot.

Chasseguet-Smirgel, J. (1964). The feminine guilt and the Oedipus complex. In J. Chasseguet-Smirgel (ed.), *Female Sexuality: New Psychoanalytic Views*. Ann Arbor: Michigan Univ. Press, 1970.

Freud, S. (1905). Three essays on the theory of sexuality. S.E. 7.

—— (1908). On the sexual theories of children. S.E. 9.

—— (1909). Analysis of a phobia in a five-year-old boy. S.E. 10.

—— (1911). Psycho-analytic notes on an autobiographical account of a case of paranoia (dementia paranoides). S.E. 12.

—— (1915). Instincts and their vicissitudes. S.E. 14.

—— (1917). A metapsychological supplement to the theory of dreams. S.E. 14.

—— (1918). From the history of an infantile neurosis. S.E. 17.

—— (1920). Beyond the pleasure principle. S.E. 18.

—— (1923). The infantile genital organization: an interpolation into the theory of sexuality. S.E. 19.

—— (1924). The dissolution of the Oedipus complex. S.E. 19.

—— (1925). Some psychical consequences of the anatomical distinction between the sexes. S.E. 19.

—— (1926). Inhibitions, symptoms and anxiety. S.E. 20.

—— (1931). Female sexuality. S.E. 21.

—— (1933). New introductory lectures on psychoanalysis: XXXIII. Femininity. S.E. 22.

—— (1937). Analysis terminable and interminable. S.E. 23.

—— (1940). An outline of psycho-analysis. S.E. 23.

—— (1950). Project for a scientific psychology. S.E. 1.

Gillespie, W. (1975). Woman and her discontents. A reassessment of Freud's views on female sexuality. *Int. Rev. Psycho-anal.* 2, 1–9.

Grunberger, B. (1956). La situation analytique et le processus de guérison. In *Le Narcissisme*. Paris: Payot, 1971.

—— (1966). Oedipe et narcissisme. In *Le Narcissisme*. Paris: Payot, 1971.

Jones, E. (1933). The phallic phase. *Int. J. Psycho-anal.* 14, 1–33.

McDougall, J. (1972). Primal scene and sexual perversion. *Int. J. Psycho-Anal.* 53, 371–84.

5

Concepts of vaginal orgasm

W.H. GILLESPIE

On this special occasion in the history of *The International Journal of Psycho-Analysis* there are few psychoanalysts still active among us who have been subscribers ever since Volume 1 appeared. My own regular subscription began with Volume 13, which contained the translation of Freud's paper, 'Female Sexuality' (1931).

If one takes a remote bird's-eye view of the most obvious changes in the climate of psychoanalytic interest and opinion that have made themselves felt in the pages of the *Journal*, and elsewhere, over these 38 years, one may think perhaps of the controversy between Freud and Jones over female psychosexual development; the full unfolding of the Kleinian theory and its applications, with its stress on the earliest stages and the most primitive fantasies and relationships to breast and to mother, together with the prolonged controversy resulting therefrom; and the development of the structural theory from the basis laid down by Freud, a development which owes much to Anna Freud. The further extension of ego psychology initiated by Hartmann before he left Vienna and greatly elaborated in America by himself and others is less adequately represented in the *Journal*, since much of this work was published elsewhere.

However, these main streams by no means constitute the whole of psychoanalytic progress over the years, even if they are the most purely psychoanalytic. Technical progress in extra-analytic fields has revealed various facts highly relevant to psychoanalysis, though unknown at the time of Freud's work. I am thinking in particular of recent work on sleep and dreaming which should take us back to reconsider *The Interpretation of Dreams* and the 'Project' that preceded it; and I think also of the remarkable findings resulting from Masters and Johnson's researches into the anatomy and physiology of the human sexual response, as well as the detailed and complex knowledge that has been accumulating recently of the process of sexual differentiation in the human embryo; this latter should lead to a fuller understanding of the meaning of bisexuality than was possible in Freud's time.

The last two subjects were recently presented to psychoanalysts (not without a certain bias, to be sure) by Mary Jane Sherfey and following this they were discussed at length at a meeting of the American Psychoanalytic Association, reported in its journal (1966): they were brought especially to the attention of the British Psycho-Analytical Society in February 1969, by Drs Rey and Pines. This is the area in which the discoveries of Masters and Johnson most obviously call for a reconsideration if not a revision of traditional psychoanalytic theory and attitudes; here we have a good example of how we may profitably take up again an issue which was debated many years ago at the highest level in the pages of this *Journal*.

I wish to comment only on one limited part of Freud's (1931) paper, 'Female Sexuality', the part to which Masters and Johnson's work is particularly relevant; the latter provides certain hitherto unknown facts which may possibly call for some modifications in Freud's formulations concerning female libidinal development. I refer to Freud's view that the female must not only change the sex of her love object, but must also overcome an initial phallic stage of development in which the leading erotogenic zone is the clitoris and the aim an active one directed towards the mother in the first instance; she must, said Freud, substitute the vagina for the clitoris as the leading zone, and must accept a passive aim in place of her original active one. This can be accomplished successfully in such a way as to produce a truly mature woman only if she can succceed in overcoming the very strong earlier attachment to the clitoral[1] zone with its active aim, a task which many women fail to accomplish satisfactorily.

This view of the relation between clitoris and vagina and of the difficult task of making the transfer had been reached by Freud at least as early as 1897, when he wrote about it to Fliess (Freud 1950), bringing it into relation with the abandonment of other, earlier, sexual zones, i.e. pregenital ones. Even more relevant is a passage in 'Three Essays on the Theory of Sexuality' (Freud 1905). After speaking of 'pubertal repression' in women Freud writes:

> When at last the sex act is permitted and the clitoris itself becomes excited, it still retains a function: the task, namely of transmitting the excitation to the adjacent female sexual parts, just as — to use a simile — pine shavings can be kindled in order to set a log of harder wood on fire.

The following passage (especially when one recalls subsequent formulations) seems to indicate that this piece of insight, with its remarkable foreshadowing of the findings of Masters and Johnson, quickly became converted for Freud into the idea that the 'transfer of excitation' from clitoris to vagina implied a developmental process in which the clitoris should normally *give up its excitability* in favour of the vagina, and that its failure to do so in less normal cases is associated with anaesthesia of 'the vaginal orifice'.

One of the outstanding features of Masters and Johnson's researches is that they have literally thrown light in dark places, namely on the processes that occur in the female genitalia during sexual activity, using colour cinematography with the help of special apparatus. For my present purpose I will pick out only one or two of their findings; my references will be to Sherfey's (1966) paper and its quotations, since this may be more accessible than the Masters and Johnson monograph (1965).

First, then, Masters and Johnson state (Sherfey 1966: 66):

> From an anatomic point of view, there is absolutely no difference in the response of the pelvic viscera to effective sexual stimulation, regardless of whether stimulation occurs as a result of clitoral area manipulation, natural or artificial coition, or, for that matter from breast stimulation alone . . . The female's physiologic responses to effective sexual stimulation . . . develop with consistency regardless of the source of the psychic or physical sexual stimulation.

It should be carefully noted, of course, that it does not follow from this that the *psychological* response is necessarily uniform.

Secondly, as regards orgasm, Masters states (Sherfey, p. 69):

> the female responds to sexual stimulation . . . in a manner essentially akin to the localized congestive reaction which accompanies erection in the male penis . . . [And] actual orgasmic experiences are initiated in both sexes by similar muscle components.

Finally, let us look at the role of the clitoris as elucidated by Masters and Johnson. As Sherfey remarks (p. 74):

> One of the most significant findings of Masters and Johnson is the fact that the clitoral glans is kept in a state of continuous stimulation throughout intra-vaginal coition even though it is not being touched and appears to have vanished

owing to erection and retraction into the swollen prepuce. Masters and Johnson state (Sherfey, p. 74):

> A mechanical traction develops on both sides of the clitoral hood subsequent to penile distension of the vaginal outlet. With penile thrusts, the entire clitoral body is pulled towards the pudendum by traction exerted on the wings of the minor labial hood.

When the penile shaft is withdrawn during active coition, traction on the clitoral hood is somewhat relieved and the body and glans return to the normal pudendal overhang positioning.... This rhythmic movement of the clitoral body in conjunction with intravaginal thrusting and withdrawl of the penis develops significant secondary tension levels. It should be emphasized that this same type of secondary clitoral stimulation occurs in every coital position, when there is full penetration of the vaginal barrel by the erect penis.

Sherfey goes on (p. 78):

Furthermore, it is also obvious why the thrusting movements of the penis will necessarily create simultaneous stimulation of the lower third of the vagina, labia minora, and clitoral shaft and glans as an integrated, inseparable functioning unit with the glans being the most important and, in by far the majority of instances, the indispensable initiator of the orgasmic reaction. With these observations, the evidence seems overwhelming: *it is a physical impossibility to separate the clitoral from the vaginal orgasm as demanded by psychoanalytic theory.*

Now if we accept these findings and statements, what becomes of the supposed distinction between clitoral and vaginal orgasm, and the value judgement which sets so many sophisticated Western women in pursuit of the elusive 'vaginal orgasm'? It seems probable that we must agree that an orgasm is an orgasm, and that one differs from another not in kind but in degree or completeness, or in the emotional satisfaction that accompanies it.

I wish to propose that in future if and when the term 'vaginal orgasm' is used we should no longer think of that as something excluding an outgrown clitoral erotogenicity; the term should instead be used exclusively to denote an orgasm that is *brought about* by thrusting movements in the vaginal barrel, whether or not such movements are indirectly producing excitation of the clitoris. The term 'clitoral orgasm' would then denote *orgasm produced by local stimulation* in the vicinity of the clitoris, not by thrusting movements in the vagina.

Having in this way eliminated the probably misleading idea that female maturity necessitates an outgrowing or 'repression' (to use Freud's early description) of clitoral erotogenicity, we can proceed to consider what obstacles actually stand in the way of vaginal orgasms as defined above; and here we shall find ourselves on familiar psychoanalytic ground and shall be concerned with many psychological problems, such as fear of penetration or invasion, problems of penis envy, masculine identification, and countless others. But one bogey will be out of the way, and I believe this will be a real advance in the psychoanalytic understanding of female sexuality.

I should like to suggest further that, in view of what we have learned from Masters and Johnson, we should reconsider very carefully the question whether clitoral excitation is necessarily associated with the urge to penetrate and act the male; may not clitoral excitation on the contrary lead to the wish *to be penetrated* in order to satisfy its proper erotic aim in the physiological manner that has been described? In the former case, penis envy indeed seems an inevitable and therefore normal consequence of anatomy; but in the latter case *penis desire*, i.e. the desire to be penetrated and so stimulated both vaginally and clitorally, is the outcome to be expected in a normal female psychosexual development.

Finally, it should be said that an incomparably fuller discussion of the problems of female sexuality is to be found in the *Journal of the American Psychoanalytic Association* of July 1968. In particular, the semantic ambiguities in current uses of the term 'vaginal orgasm' are considered in great detail in an admirable paper by Glenn and Kaplan. My excuse for the present publication is that there may be an advantage in picking out one particular theme for discussion from among the very complex issues that face us in the study of female sexuality, if in this way one particular tree may be clearly visualized and distinguished from the wood. I make no apology for the symbolism.

Note

1 I am aware that the correct form is 'clitoridal', but this is so clumsy and unpronounceable that I prefer to be incorrect.

References

Freud, S. (1905). Three essays on the theory of sexuality. *S.E.* 7.
—— (1931). Female sexuality. *S.E.* 21.
—— (1950). Extracts from the Fliess papers: Letter 75. *S.E.* 1.
Glenn, J. and Kaplan, E.H. (1968). Types of orgasm in women: a critical review and redefinition. *J. Am. Psychoanal. Ass.* 16, 549–564.
Masters, W.H. and Johnson, V.E. (1965). *Human Sexual Response*. Boston, Mass.: Little, Brown; London: Churchill, 1966.
Sherfey, M.J. (1966). The evolution and nature of female sexuality in relation to psychoanalytic theory. *J. Am. Psychoanal. Ass.* 14, 28–128.

6

The phallic shadow

DENISE BRAUNSCHWEIG and MICHEL FAIN

Going through the writings which compare the sexual maturation of the little girl and the little boy, you find that in spite of the divergences which separate them, there is often a shared error which brings them together. A confusion appears between the penis as object of phallic narcissism and the penis as instrument of Eros. This confusion leads to the idea that the boy, possessor of the penis, is more capable of integrating his drives than the girl. Now narcissism and eroticism don't get on well together, as we will often have occasion to recall. There is an ordinary expression which signifies this:'sexual impotence'. Potency is a narcissistic quality. The fact is that the impotent man thinks of his sexual activity as a form of potency, and this, moreover, is why he is not impotent, but inhibited in his erotic capacity. And it is the narcissistic investment, fixated onto this instrument which he fears losing if he uses it, which leads to this state. Phallic narcissism, a direct consequence of the castration complex, constitutes for the man a way of emerging from the Oedipal conflict. If the superego is the inheritor of the Oedipus complex, then phallic narcissism is an inheritance which comes from the father, and to a certain extent, like any inheritance, it consecrates the father. This inheritance contains in particular the reality principle. So the boy who has developed in normality-inducing conditions treats the core of anxiety hysteria that he experiences at the moment of his Oedipal conflict in a way that ensures its repression and thus issues in a phallic narcissism pregnant with an ego ideal based on the reality principle. Our reason for having just given this explanation is above all to make it clear that this course of development determines a libidinal economy which is different according to sex, and we insist on the term 'different', for the affirmation that the penis, by its very existence, ensures a better integration of the drives is a judgement which shows that the reality defined by phallic narcissism is not always the truth. Rather, the presence of the penis as a perception experienced via the parents sets going a series of reactions which are of primordial importance in the determinism of sexual identity. So we can expect that the difference of the sexes will be pregnant with a different libidinal economy, and that the absence of a visible penis in the girl entails for her a set of responses which will make her adopt an economic system that cannot be superimposed on the boy's. Our point of view already allows us to sense in advance that the famous masculine protest has to do with this mode of distribution of the libidinal economy.

In the outcome of her Oedipal conflict, the little girl cannot therefore treat her core of anxiety hysteria in the same way as the little boy. Moreover, it is usual to agree that the outcome of the Oedipal conflict is less clear-cut with the girl. That amounts to saying that the core of anxiety hysteria is going to persist and lead to a series of manifestations which, further, will be able to undergo a regression to the level of the anal stage, whether in part or completely. On the other hand, the constitution of her superego, less assured than that of the boy, includes a paternal origin which the girl has every interest in maintaining, for it constitutes, right inside her personality, the transgression which is just what this presence should avoid. This transgression occurs in a displaced mode, through an attitude of masochistic provocation on the part of the ego in relation to the superego, a provocation which is usually at the root of the tendency to failure. The direct consequence of these differences is translated by the fact that the reality principle does not succeed in ensuring a complete primacy for itself, that a significant quantity of object-libido is not transformed into narcissistic libido and remains free, and comes to reinforce the pleasure principle as a result.

The pleasure principle, when it is dominant, in no way constitutes a capacity for eroticism. It simply marks a tendency to discharge excess libido so as to return as quickly as possible to the optimum level. Whatever the conceptions that have been developed by psychoanalysts, the fact is that girls only belatedly become conscious of their vaginas, and that, as a result of this fact, sexual desire for them is elaborated in such a complex way that it becomes extremely fragile. The fact of the non-recognition of the vagina as an erogenous zone during childhood is so well established, and thus so much follows an implicitly defined organization, that we are obliged to characterize as 'abnormal' the cases observed from time to time in clinical practice of 'premature' recognition of the vagina as an erogenous zone. It is a matter of a real syndrome appearing in a family constellation containing certain specific elements, while it is possible to observe some differences on the basis of these common elements. The reason why we consider it necessary to discuss this here now is above all to see what differences this premature recognition of the vagina entails in these women's development, in comparison with the most usual form of development. So what we have is a family marked by the following characteristics: the girl is the elder sister of a brother, who is the chosen object of the mother, with whom he lives in a state of continuing symbiosis. The sister is only considered interesting by the mother to the extent that she helps in maintaining this symbiosis, a fate which she shares with her father. It is in the girl's reactive attitude in relation to the mother—son couple and the possibilities this situation offers her for getting close to her father, the acceptance or rejection of these possibilities, that the differences in each case are constituted. But however this may be, the dominant elements of such a constellation come down to these facts: first, the mother—son couple constitutes a unity in which narcissistic and erotic tendencies are satisfied, tendencies which do not go by way of the mother's vagina and do not, for this reason, confer a primacy on the mother's genital organs.

Secondly, faced with this couple, another is set up, the father and the daughter, a fact which in no way bothers the mother. The father—daughter couple is a miserable get-together, sanctioning the paternal downfall and his inability to imprint his law on the family. To sum up, we could say that the mother's indifference to her daughter's sexual development, an indifference that has been manifest ever since her birth, and the father's inability to ensure his power, seem to play an important part in this premature recognition of the vagina as an erogenous zone. In fact, it is not possible for us to respond with certainty to the question which then emerges: would it not be the maintenance of vaginal sexual pleasure as a conscious memory which would be unusual? – a pleasure which begins around the age of three, perhaps even before, goes through the whole latency period without modification and is maintained after puberty. Wouldn't there always be a recognition of the vagina which would subsequently be repressed? We will discuss this important question later on, our aim for the moment being to grasp what usually happens, on the basis of these 'irregular' cases. The little girl here is leading a triple life. In the first place, she is the servant of the mother—son couple and so her attitude seeks to show honour to the son. In the second place, she is the love object of the excluded father and in a dim way she perceives his desire. Finally, she has her secret life, in the course of which, through fantasies, generally sado—masochistic ones, she experiences authentic vaginal orgasms. These fantasies are not accompanied by masturbation, which is to say by the use of the hands. (In general, but not always, the legs are crossed and squeeze the sex tightly.) Always, in these fantasies, neither the man's penis, nor penetration, is evoked. However, these fantasies contain the representation of a strong character who has been able to bring the mother into line. So these little girls really do have a double life, each split off from the other. On the one hand, they are the priestesses of the cult of the little brother, and in addition the consoler, and even more the fellow sufferer of the father — here it is a matter of their official life — and on the other, they have an intense fantasy life accompanied by numerous orgasms. When they become adult, they experience considerable sexual difficulties, since they do not manage to reunite their two ways of life. But then we find that a whole section of their development has remained in an embryonic state. They are not aware of the possibilities for seduction that they could exercise in utilizing their wiles, whether these methods are physical or intellectual. In place of the development of their desires for seduction, identifications with the mother are substituted, which are meant to please the brother. Their elegance is subject to the principle of not making the brother ashamed. So this fantasy life with intense vaginal orgasms seems to have taken the place of what for other women ends up with an interest in the possibilities for seduction offered by their own bodies. In some way, the preparation for masculine desire seems in these cases not to have been elaborated. It is true that these little girls have only got close to the father in so far as he is neglected, and that nothing was turning them in the direction of seduction. Through these examples of premature recognition of the vagina as an erogenous zone, we are led to think that, without a penis, girls are led to cathect their own bodies — not, as in the cases cited, the vagina. But we think it is not possible to compare, or to establish an equivalence between the narcissistic investment that the little boy performs on his penis, and the girl's cathexis of her body. She invests in it, at least in part, in the manner of an object of love, with an object-libido which for this reason does not undergo the same narcissistic transformation. So what we have is a movement which includes a large element of auto-eroticism. The little girl likes to make herself pretty. So this auto-eroticism comes to compensate for what she experiences as a narcissistic wound. It is no less certain that this auto-eroticism undoubtedly takes on a meaning with an anal origin. The notions of 'dirty' and 'ugly' are there in the background. It is interesting to note that the epithets 'dirty' and 'ugly' are used to designate the little girl who has stolen her mother's make-up and then devoted her adorable little face to some expert cosmetic operations. So feminine coquettishness includes the relatively late integration of an anal element. This element is allowed from a certain age onwards, and in particular after the loss of virginity.

In any case, this integration shows a different utilization of anality from the boy's, which is one of the arguments tending to place in doubt the idea of a shared and identical stem in the development of boys and girls. Here too, the latency period is instructive for us. The resurgence of anality promoted by the Oedipal failure will in both sexes take routes whose apparent divergences only serves to underline their complementarity. It is not a divergence but already a tendency to intersection.

As we discussed earlier on [referring to an earlier chapter not included here — Editor's note], the group of little latent males is marked by the dominance of the active ego ideal, contemporary with the anal period, over the passive ego ideal, more primal, marked by the omnipotence of passivity, which has raised itself up in the wake of the failure of the immediate satisfaction of desires and of their hallucinatory realization. Oedipal failure, followed by the introjection of the superego, would tend to bring about a massive displacement of the penis libido in the direction of the anus, and cause pleasure to be sought in anal passivity in relation to the father. Narcissistic investment of the penis is generally opposed to such a step, and reacts by mobilizing the anal ego ideal, advocating active domination and mastery. For the little girl, the same step results in an apparent submission, not to the paternal penis, but to the delegated power which it confers on the mother in the imposition of the reactive forms. If these are going to serve in part to build up the coquettishness we spoke of above, and all the more during the latency period because maternal authority is experienced as subordinated to the father and 'dirty' anality is now abandoned to obtain his love, it is none the less the case that the little girl's 'cleanliness' instantly demands to be dirtied by the little boy, and this cleanliness represents a first draft of a sexual and receptive organ in relation to the future partner of adulthood. This cleanliness thus already appears as something very different in nature from the kind of reaction formation that could appear in another little girl showing a significant regression promoted by an anal fixation.

The process of integration which concludes with the transformation of anal drives into coquettishness comes to be added, without conflict, to this appearance of reaction formations. Faecal matter on view conserves a vivid attractive power leading to the definite feeling of disgust. This feeling translated the immediate introjection into the psychic apparatus of the fantasies represented by faecal matter and the immediate attempt at rejection which it brings with it. The whole art of make-up consists in recovering this attractive power of faecal matter — a power which even has a penetrative aspect — while suppressing the reactions of repulsiveness which usually follow this initial moment of attraction. And an overdone use of cosmetics goes back to this repellent anal quality. This integration of anality is not only translated by make-up, which is only its most visible aspect, but also by a whole mode of behaviour, including in particular a certain way of carrying the body — to give it an image, let us call it a certain 'rough' look which must not, any more than the make-up, exceed a certain limit. If the little girl represses this type of anal integration and principally cathects the 'little boy' mode which, although it is there in normal cases, is dominated by the first one, then she becomes frankly repulsive. Her anality takes on the value of a symbol of destructive power stuck to her, which does not make her only a phallic woman, but also the representation of a primal scene during which anality becomes representative of the father's threat of castration. A man's reaction when faced with a woman presenting anal traits that are not concealed follows the reactivation of the memory-traces linked to the primal scene and to the anal type of aggressions which it arouses.

In her study of female homosexuality, Joyce McDougall has ably demonstrated how the mothers of homosexual women, because of a significant anal fixation, hinder the development which goes from reaction formations to coquettishness. A division is produced between the hated 'clean' mother and the coquettish, feminine woman who becomes the erotic object, the father remaining the repulsive object onto whom all anality is projected. We would like to add a complementary detail to this remarkable description: the father in such a case receives the anal charge which is usually invested in the little boy. This fact allows us to understand that the idealization of the paternal penis benefits from the anal charge which is normally invested in the boy, for if you say idealization you say defaecalization.

Having said this, we think, along with Joyce McDougall, that a little girl has more need to be loved by her mother in the course of her excremental activity than the little boy. Passive pleasure linked to a valorized anality tends to maintain the dominance over active anal omnipotence of the ego ideal centred on the passive omnipotence lost in the past. So the desire to receive remains in the foreground.

B. Lewin has published an article in which he discusses a fantasy found in a number of patients, during which the woman thinks she is smearing herself with faecal matter. The associative chain which brings on this fantasy starts with the idea of menstruation experienced as a form of anal incontinence. Lewin thinks that this fantasy of anal incontinence is a reassurance that is both narcissistic and auto-erotic, against the resurgence of the impression of castration linked to periods. It represents a desire to extend the erogeneity of the mucous membrane of the anus to the entire skin surface, a fantasy activated by the acceptance of castration.

Lewin's point of view confirms ours on two points. First, the pleasure derived from beautifying her own image because of the impossibility of transforming object libido into narcissistic libido centred on the penis, like the little boy, can be regressively doubled by the erotic pleasure, through extending anal sensibility to the entire skin of the body, of dirtying herself with faecal matter — which, so the little girl thinks, could make her into the 'dirty' little boy.

Secondly, after the displacement of all the anal charge on to periods, make-up, creams and the slightly 'rough' bearing, all accentuate the sexual attraction. It is not only a question of identification with an attractive woman, but also of the result of a whole relationship to the body, charged with erotic pleasure. It is probable that impure periods, following the Bible, concentrate the whole faecal aspect onto themselves, whereas make-up preserves the initial attractive power of faecal matter.

At any rate, the fantasy described by Lewin emphasizes a distinctive aspect of the renewal of anal omnipotence, without there being a decathexis of passivity and of the pleasure of the anal mucous membrane extended to the skin. We think that this aspect, typically feminine, only exercises a dominant action over a completely different aspect, nearer to the little boy, an aspect in which the active anal ego ideal also reappears so as to bandage up the wounds linked to the Oedipal failure.

The entire preceding description looks as though it is taking no account of the classical displacement of penis envy onto the desire to have a child. This is not entirely true. The auto-erotic cathexis of the body seems to us a more logical sequel not just to the acceptance of the visible lack of a penis, but above all to the set of environmental responses entailed by the fact of being one of the female sex. This way of looking at things remains in the general line of thinking which would say that to any narcissistic wound there corresponds a tendency to auto-erotic activity. The desire to have a child, which, as Melanie Klein stressed, certainly has a very deep origin, is at the same time the desire which the little girl can officially declare. So this desire, on the one hand an innate one, is on the other hand put forward as a reparation, although this does not happen without the maternal state which it implies at the same time reflecting a pressure to reduce specifically feminine sexual desires. This seems to us sufficiently complex to require postponing its discussion until later.

We are aware that while for any psychoanalyst, and even for a high proportion of educated people, it can be acknowledged that what is considered feminine narcissism is the counterpart of a basic narcissistic deficiency, on the other hand to assert that this same deficiency, linked to the absence of a penis, would make it possible to develop a greater capacity for erotic pleasure can appear as a real scandal, renewing the shock produced by Tiresias. These are not things that should be said — but are they true? The narcissism—eroticism opposition does not seem to us any less reliable than the observations that have been presented. It is certainly valid to make the objection that in less unusual cases, the identifications with the protagonists of the primal scene in the inverted Oedipal positions cast a different light on things. And it is also true that in the little girl's and even the woman's conscious — or easily made conscious – experience, she, just like Freud and all who have followed him in this line, believes that her sexual organs are not worth as much as the boy's in terms of their resources for pleasure. Wouldn't there rather be a reciprocal overestimation of the erotic possibilities of the other sex, with this counter-invested for the boy by the narcissistic cathexis of the penis, and generally remaining completely unconscious? Such an over-valuation might be at the root of the myth of the androgyne in Plato's *Symposium*, taken up by Freud in a different context (*Beyond the Pleasure Principle*): the desire to possess the sex that one does not have, and to which are consequently attributed exceptional qualities, without losing the one that is naturally one's own, especially if one is a boy. Freud also described the overestimation of the love object as being characteristic of the state of being in love in men; so might not the unconscious projection of superior erotic capacities onto the woman be part of the nature of erotic attraction? The women we have discussed, and who had a premature awareness of their vaginas, do not develop a real bodily narcissism and did not go through penis envy which opens up for seduc-tiveness the desire to be desired. Maria Torok has told us about penis envy, its unfortunate consequences for feminine sexuality, and its unconscious defensive significance in the relationship to the anal and Oedipal mother; a desire can be satisfied, she says, but never an envy; penis envy signs the girl's renunciation of the autonomous possession of her body and *jouissance* by means of the penis; but this envy encounters a complicity in the other sex, where envy for the vagina has to remain unconscious not just because of the fears of castration it would engender, but also because this envy, in the Kleinian sense, is addressed to the mother, who in the unconscious, as much for boys as for girls, still commands all the capacities for pleasure and creativity in her primary omnipotence. When we get to this point we can see that we have made almost no progress by making the objections that could be offered against us to ourselves.

Another angle then appears: the wish often expressed in child psychotherapies through the associative material to see the difference of the sexes suppressed. This wish in fact appears to be highly complex. It emanates from an ego already provided with an organization reflecting the opposition brought out by Freud in an initial formulation, between ego instincts and sexual instincts. Generally speaking, the perception-consciousness system is maintained in a state of underdevelopment in sexual matters. The understanding to which it is entitled concerning the relationships which govern family life does in fact follow the line of the wish expressed. The child is not deemed to know about his parents' sexual life, any more than they are deemed to be authorized to know about the child's sexual life. This is why the repression of infantile masturbation (we are not talking here about adolescent masturbation) takes on such a tragic quality. What we have is a repression which does not know what it is repressing. It is not a simple ban, but a prohibition issued by the parents' superego against perceiving what is going on with the child. This is also why the masturbation which is officially accepted because of the erroneous principles of sex education, but denied at the level of its Oedipal significance, in the last analysis undergoes the same repression. At several points, Freud mentions that the infantile masturbation that takes place at the time of the Oedipal conflict frequently leads to real castration threats on the part of the adults. In fact, these threats are rare, and even when they are made it is probable that they are not taken seriously. We think that in this area Freud believed, as he did with hysteria, in the reality of the threat which is thereby situated at the level of the perception-consciousness system, whereas in fact it is a question of an unconscious construction. It is the parents' anxious reaction, an anxiety in the face of their superego, which does not accept their access to the meaning of the young child's masturbation, which gives a very great force to the castration threat which gets associated with infantile masturbation. The quasi-universal belief in this threat can only take on its strength, which is not altered by surface reassurances, through an instinctual manifestation which is blind to all reasoning. Now as Freud stressed over and over again, the superego derives its huge force from the id. The threat in question is as incapable of being altered by reasoning as a fully constituted phobia. This is why the reality principle as a group phenomenon contains a shared negation of the castration threat – a negation which derives its strength in the dynamics of a crowd, and one which gives way if the bonds constituting the group are dissolved.

We are thus led to think that the wish that there be no sexual relationship between the parents – in other words, that it should not be possible to call up a representation of the primal scene – has something to do with the repression by the parental superego of infantile masturbation.

We should recall that infantile masturbation is developed in an initial period as a defence against the primal scene. Actually, the primal scene provokes two contradictory experiences, on the one hand an onrush of stimulations, and on the other a feeling of exclusion. Masturbation through a concentration on the pleasure accompanied by fantasies enables the afflux of excitation to be isolated, at the same time as it creates a very rich internal narrative. But the parental reaction breaks in on the distance which had been created in this way, all the more forcefully in that it is a mirror image: the very small child's masturbation tends to make them conscious of just what the child was running away from in its masturbatory activity.

This leads us to a second point: is the transgression, in so far as it can be conceived of by the young spectator of the narcissistic unity formed by the mother and her newborn baby, beyond sex, as one could think it might be? To the older child, the baby appears to be libidinally endowed with economic possiblities which she or he no longer has: it sucks its mother's breasts, defaecates and urinates in its nappies; its whole body and all its functions seem to have become the object of the mother's special attention. So there is a lack of harmony between the older one's instrumental capacities, which are well developed, assuring him of an obvious superiority which makes him an older one, whereas in libidinal terms he feels very inferior to the newborn child. From this point there is only one step to believing throughout his life that the young will always be better provided for than him, and it is rapidly made. We can say that in the elder one's eyes, even if he considers that he has a bigger penis than the new baby, it is also a repressed penis, whereas the baby has methods at its disposal that he can no longer command. It is a matter of a transgression which is perhaps beyond sex, but not a transgression of the sexual in the wide sense of the term.

The little girl who is the spectator of the same scene certainly relives an identical conflict. All her desire to possess her mother, her lack of a penis to do this, can be strongly reactivated. She can find compensations because of the mother's being partially on leave as the father's wife, and the counter-Oedipal position of the father which is often reinforced in such circumstances. But the little girl also has another compensation: she becomes conscious of the importance conferred on the woman's body by motherhood. This attenuates her narcissistic wound linked to the lack of a penis, even though it also reactivates her double Oedipal conflict. While in one way this valorization of the woman's body helps the girl to effect her change of object by making her desire a child from her father, just at this point when he is more available, in another it also reactivates the more primitive form centred on the desire to seize the paternal penis, a partial object, which at this point is confused with the mother's baby. The small boy cathects his penis with all his narcissism and so makes out of an old instrument of pleasure, now greatly devalued in itself, the representative of a shared cult. The small girl gets into playing with dolls, and often devotes to her doll a genuine love, whereas the little boy displaces the cult devoted to the penis onto substitute representations which will form the basis of the ego ideal modified by the Oedipal conflict. Here we reach a paradoxical conclusion, opposed to the general view: the 'transgression beyond sex' of the new baby, a transgression which puts in question the apparent superiority of the elder male child and confirms him in his phallic narcissism, seems in contrast to bring the little girl a reparation for a more ancient narcissistic wound and open the way to love for her. This is why women are mature more quickly than men, even though they do not seek to achieve as much as them.

The universal need, which is narcissistic in essence, to project the phallic shadow onto the female genital organs, correspondingly diminishes their original capacity for being able to give pleasure. It is because of this need that in some African tribes, little girls are made to undergo various manipulations very early on which are meant to enlarge the shaft of the clitoris. Completely opposite in appearance, this practice is related to the excision practised in other tribes.

Masters and Johnson made a study of 'sexual response' which is curious in a number of ways. We can follow their conclusions only with a certain degree of reluctance, given the experimental methods used. However, they have the merit of showing in their way the extent to which this projection of the phallic shadow entailed a misrecognition of female sexual pleasure. We know that some surgeons have gone so far as to lower the position of the clitoris, thinking that frigidity is due to the impossibility of contact with the penis during intercourse. Doctors have injected cortico-suprarenal extracts 'to increase the size and sensitiveness of the clitoris'. In fact, these practices mask with the jargon of rationality the same fantasy as the one operating in the African tribes cited above. To put it in more ordinary terms, the majority of men (and many women too) imagine that in sexual relations, the clitoris follows a course which can be superimposed onto that of the penis. In fact, what happens is the opposite: the clitoris, which is swollen at the start of sexual excitation, is completely retracted at the moment of orgasm; and on the other hand it tends to become tumescent again, and even painful, if orgasm has not been reached. In fact, the clitoris is a unique organ of its kind, it has a purely erotic function and plays a prominent role because of its very rich supply of nerves in the perception of sexual excitement. In the adult woman, it opens the way to the desire for vaginal penetration. A sensitive organ, it does not particularly call forth a desire for direct contact, provoking too sharp an excitation, but plays an important role in the pleasure linked to the excitation of the surrounding erogenous zones, the mons Veneris, the labia minora, in this way contributing to the general erotogeneity of the female genital organs.

Attention has been drawn to the importance acquired by urethral excitation in the little girl. A fixation of this kind is to a large extent derived from the shadow of the penis, an organ which condenses both sexual and urinary functions. But the clitoris has no connection with the female urethra and no need of it.

In fact, female genital activity develops naturally towards a whole starting from organs which are apparently separate whose function in no way corresponds to that of the penis. This apparent separation entails psychological reactions centred on the notion of castration, for the man as well as the woman, reactions which contribute to a disturbance in the woman's sexuality. The penis, a visible unity, grouping together genital and urethral eroticism, leads to the notion of synthesis, whereas female functional unity is perceived as fragmented.

A commonplace fantasy concerning anal eroticism reinforces this error: for the male, the anus is fantasmatically in direct communication with the penis and the aim of the fantasies of incorporating the paternal penis is to make the child grow a big penis. It is not impossible, as René Diatkine has observed, that the origin of this kind of fantasy is to be found in erections accompanying the pleasure of defaecation.

The clitoris, in contrast, is not included in a similar fantasy – and if it is, this occurs in a mode of reinforced masculine protest, with nothing to grip onto, which tends to separate it from its function of integrating into an ensemble. A fantasy identical to the boy's tries, without succeeding in this, to re-create a feeling of unity which, because it is modelled on that of the boy, risks destroying the female functional unity.

It does not escape us that these considerations describe the active phallic phase, common to both girls and boys, in another light, or at least that they incline us towards thinking that it is more a tradition that has created it in the girl, and not a natural movement. To put this another way, the projection of the phallic phase onto the little girl would come from a general way of thinking and in short would be identical in its origin to the manipulations which little girls are made to undergo in some African tribes. If this explanation seems to distance us from the classical opinion developed by Freud and brings us close to that of Melanie Klein, at the same time it is not so far from the Freudian hypothesis about fetishism. Human beings of both sexes give the female genital organs a simultaneous double meaning and in this way integrate a false conception of the clitoris, a true generalized fetishism and one that because of this forms part of a general way of thinking.

The notion of fetishism leads to the discussion of the concept of reality, limiting this of course to our subject. Reality is a provisional notion defined by a given group. The way in which this notion is constructed for each individual to the point of becoming an integral part of an ego-function is a long story which is not our concern here. We will limit ourselves to the question concerning the castration threat. This is experienced by the group as an absolute reality, secondarily denied. This secondary denial is in no way a rectification, but a collective rejection. The neurotic who acts and thinks without being able to maintain this negation is very badly thought of for this reason. Our project is to show that the influence of this denied reality, a reality which is not a truth, has contributed to warping the understanding of what female sexuality is. The little boy's 'No, such a thing does not exist' when he perceives the absence of a penis in the little girl, is an echo of the general negation of the group. The little girl can only register this vast echo which 'does not want to know', and for this reason transforms her sex not into lack, but into a general misrecognition. Her clitoris, on the other hand, receives an accentuated recognition to the detriment of the vagina. From this point, a woman must wait for a partner of one or other sex to come and reveal to her a truth that is not a reality. The reality of the group derived from the law of the father first of all denies the existence of the female sex, a representation of castration, and valorizes the clitoris in a fetishistic mode, thus erroneously detaching it from the vagina, and then simultaneously recognizes the existence of the female sex in a way which ultimately remains impregnated with the initial mistake.

We can then wonder whether a basic error of this kind has not shaped an aspect of the female character: women, when it comes down to it, are not particularly interested in reality, and are completely contemptuous of masculine logic. They know that their truth makes them escape from the reality of the group dominated by the law of the father. It is therefore not surprising that Melanie Klein pronounced some first truths about female sexuality, and on that basis some theories that were incisive because they were unconcerned with a masculine reality that she did not recognize. It seems to us that what Maria Torok describes in relation to penis envy is close to our opinion: in order to come to terms with the group error erected into reality, the woman is obliged to find a substitute to ensure the counter-investment of her true desire: she says she desires the fetish when in fact she is seeking the functional unity which is her sex and which is presented to her as a truncated, fragmented and non-existent grouping.

If we now go back to those little girls we discussed above and who, following a certain type of conflict linked to unusual circumstances, brought about a premature recognition of the vagina as an organism playing a part in female eroticism, we could say that in discovering this truth they were turning away from reality and behaving as psychotics. Indeed, it was stressed at the same time that this premature recognition occurred within a constellation where the law of the son, the maternal penis, was more powerful than the law of the father.

We also rediscover another point of view developed at the beginning and concerning the difference of the sexes: whereas the little boy's narcissistic valorization of the penis, a valorization occurring to the detriment of the pleasure that the genital organization can procure, is included in the reality principle, the existence of an integrated female sexuality whose basic elements all exist early on is part of a specifically feminine pleasure principle. This is why the Freudian and Kleinian conceptions about female sexuality are not opposed but coexist. The attempt, which has often been made to integrate them with each other proceeds from the same movement as the construction of a symptom, for their coexistence is normally conflictual. Melanie Klein, moreover, brings out the tight connection that exists early on between female sexuality and the desire to have children. In this we once more come across an element which has been amply developed in relation to men's sexuality: the antagonism between the narcissistic valorization of the penis (which because of this becomes a phallus unfit for pleasure) and the maternal instinct.

The woman thus lives two Oedipal conflicts, one proceeding from a quasi-biological law inscribed in the destiny of being a mother, and which would tend to minimize the role of the man – the angle defended by Melanie Klein – and another conflict marked by the law of the father which contains in itself the simultaneous negation and affirmation of female sexuality, the separate valorization of the clitoris and the subordination of maternity to paternity.

This conception makes possible a better understanding of the deep roots of the virulent aggressiveness of what are called masculine women in relation to men. The virile woman valorizes the existence of an illusory phallus that she knows is illusory. This constrains her into demanding from others that they recognize the existence of what does not exist. Men only recognize in them a fetish, and definitely not a phallus. From this arises the protest demanding that the invisible be perceived in her. Women like this who have suffered from the ritual negation of their own sex, placed in a repetition compulsion, demand that the man accords them recognition of a sex which, in their personal lives, has already caused their own to disappear. The demand for inclusion of their own sex in the reality of the group is displaced onto the demand that they are given the recognition for a phallus: you might as well try to fill the barrel of the Danaïdes, the female murderers of the father. So women like this have structured themselves solely according to the Oedipal conflict placed under the law of the father, and despite their masculine look they are completely subjected to it. The feminine woman, without displaying it, has managed to circumvent this law at the same time as recognizing it, ultimately knowing how to use it to her advantage. Her superego holds in balance maternal and paternal images, the maternal instinct and love for the bearer of the penis.

We think that our way of understanding this part of the development of women's sexuality takes account of the complexity of its structure, even though it has barely broached it. At the level of eroticism, the aspect emphasized by Melanie Klein insists on the active desire to take the penis into the inside of the body and keep it there, with the man then being no more than a practically functional object, whereas the part described by Freud, essentially more psychological, gives eroticism a different quality, in particular through the idealization of the object which it enables – different in comparison with this preceding aspect, which is unequivocally marked by instinct.

Basically, this double aspect only describes a banal truth: the male is only momentarily useful for the perpetuation and safeguard of the race, a fact which in many species, and particularly in the human species, has not stopped him from installing a primacy which has transformed the systems of relationship and done so in a practically irreversible way. The movement from the desire to have a child, a primal need which fully confers her sex on the woman, to the desire to have a child from the father – substitute for envy for the omnipotent phallus, reparation for the negation of the female sex by the law of the father – does not constitute a linear path, but a structure laid down very early on containing two antagonistic aspects. The woman is naturally the site of a permanent conflict.

What emerges from this first approach to the problem is that female sexuality has been imprinted with a direction which subordinates it not to male sexuality, but to phallic narcissism. This being essentially anti-erotic, it is just as necessary for the man to disengage himself from it as for the woman not to knock and nag against it, in order for them to be able some day to find themselves once more in each other's arms. But this subordination of female sexuality to phallic narcissism is often more apparent than real, for in the end, this organization enables the woman to disengage herself from deeply embedded conflicts with her mother, thanks to the defensive possibilities she is offered by the paternal law.

None the less, this orientation of cathexes which follows the Oedipal conflict – an orientation which, so it would seem, constitutes the human framework for the difference of the sexes – plays so dominant a role that it seems to us necessary to establish more precisely the elements involved.

Notes

Translated by Rachel Bowlby

1 This fact has on a number of occasions led to diagnostic errors, being labelled 'epileptic' (L. Kreisler).

7

Inquiry into femininity

MICHELE MONTRELAY

> ... like all women you think with your sex, not with your mind.
> (A. Artaud)

Why was the theory of femininity in psychoanalysis articulated from the start in the form of an alternative? What does it mean for analysts that they must choose between two contradictory conceptions of women: that of Jones and that of Freud?

The posing of these questions makes it necessary to recall briefly the contents of the two doctrines and the basis of their incompatibility. For Freud, libido is identical in the two sexes. Moreover, it is always male in essence. For it is the clitoris, an external and erectile part of the body, and hence homologous to the penis, which is the girl's erotic organ. And when, at the moment of the Oedipus complex, she desires a child from the father, this new object is again invested with a phallic value: the baby is nothing but a substitute for the penile organ of which the girl now knows she is deprived. Thus feminine sexuality is constantly elaborated as a function of phallic reference.[1]

For Jones, and for the English school (Klein, Horney, Müller), feminine libido is specific. From the start, the girl privileges the interior of the body and the vagina: hence the archaic experiences of femininity which leave an indelible trace. It is therefore not enough to give an account of feminine sexuality from a 'phallocentric' point of view. It is also necessary to measure the impact that anatomy and the sexual organ itself, has on the girl's unconscious.[2]

Thus Jones and his school were answering the Viennese school when they proposed the precocious, even innate character of femininity. Freud spoke of one libido, whereas Jones distinguished two types of libidinal organization, male and female.

145

Forty years have passed: the problem of femininity continues to be posed on the basis of the Jones–Freud contradiction. Can this contradiction in fact be surpassed?

Phallocentrism and concentricity

The investigations conducted by Smirgel and a team of analysts, published as the *Recherches psychoanalytiques nouvelles sur la sexualité féminine*, have recently shown that it is possible to get past the contradiction. It is an advance which is possible from the moment one abandons all polemical preoccupation and sticks to clinical practice.

Predictably, the book starts with a detailed analysis of the confrontation of the two schools. But having completed the history of this long and burning dispute and disengaged its parameters, the authors do not take sides. Leaving the scene of the debate, they take us to the analyst's: there where the one who speaks is no longer the mouthpiece of a school, but the patient on the couch.

It is rare to be given an account of large fragments of the cure; still more rare for it to be given *à propos* of feminine cases. Here we have the freedom to follow the discourse of female patients in analysis in its rhythm, its style, and its meanderings. We are taken into the interior of the space that this discourse circumscribes, a space that is that of the unconscious where, as Freud has seen, negation does not exist, where consequently the terms of a contradiction, far from excluding one another, coexist and overlap. In fact, anyone who tries to take bearings from these researches is referred to Freud *and* to Jones. For this book not only talks of femininity according to Freud, but it also makes it speak in an immediate way that one does not forget. An *odor di femina* arises from it, which cannot be explained without reference to the work of the English and Viennese.

Thus the *Recherches* calls for a double locating, which is worth explicating at greater length here. Let us return to Freud: the essential modalities of the organization of feminine desire cannot be grasped without taking up in its own right the idea of phallocentrism so decried by Freud's contemporaries. The book makes constant and explicit reference to it – but specifying that the phallus cannot be identified with the penis. In fact, far from signifying an anatomical reality, the phallus designates, according to this book, the ideas and values that the penile organ represents. By freeing the concept of the phallus from the organic context with which it is still often confounded, the authors enable us truly to grasp the nature of phallocentrism: 'There is every reason for separating the study of penis-envy from any consideration of the penis itself as a thing.'[3] It is necessary, on the contrary, to specify the ideal dimension to which the male organ refers: 'penis–envy is always envy of the idealized penis'.[4]

Simultaneously, the models that are put forward in order to account for feminine desire make clear on the clinical level the real implications of 'phallocentrism': the authors are not fooled by a patient who declares herself impotent and humiliated on the pretext that she is 'only a woman'. The penis envy latent in these remarks is not reducible to an instinct. It is impossible to legitimate it 'through an alleged state of castration for which phylogenesis would bear the responsibility'.[5]

On the contary, the desire for the penis can be analyzed only in as much as it arises from a complex elaboration, constructed in order to maintain the phallic power of the father. Only those patients whose fathers' prestige and symbolic status had been threatened posit the possession of the penile organ as indispensable. Their sufferings and their symptoms appear in order to make plain that the essential is withdrawn from them, namely, the penis confounded in the imagination with the phallus. Thus the phallic power of the father is fantasmatically assured.

In the other accounts of homosexual or 'normal' women, in every case, a particular form of relation to the paternal phallus can be traced, in which it is always a question of maintaining an inaccessible term, so that desire can subsist. It is a subtly constructed relation, but one that does not differ in its nature from that set up by the man: as the detailed account of a masculine case of perversion makes clear enough.[6]

In showing that desire is only ever pure artifice, the book thereby discards the hypothesis of the innateness of desire that the English school had advanced in relation to femininity. It confirms the correctness of Freud's reservations in regard to this 'natural' femininity on which Jones insisted so much.[7]

And yet the *Recherches* takes up the main point of the clinical work of the English school. The article by Grunberger, especially, insists on the specifically *concentric* organization of feminine sexuality.[8] He shows that it is as if the woman, more so than the man, remains dependent on the drives, in which the authors see, like Jones, the intrication of archaic, oral, anal, and vaginal schemas.

'Often, for the little girl, it is the mouth which takes up symbolically, and for reasons on which Jones has insisted, the value of a vaginal organ,' Luquet-Parat remarks.[9] And further on Maria Torok develops the theory of the English school:

M. Klein, E. Jones and K. Horney have indicated long before we did, the precocity of the child's discovery and repression of vaginal sensations. We, for our part, have observed that the encounter with the other sex was always a reminder of the awakening of our own.

Clinically, penis-envy and the discovery of the sex of the boy are often seen associated with a repressed memory of orgasmic experiences.[10]

Thus two theoretical positions, hitherto considered incompatible, are both verified within the framework of a clinical study. The Jones–Freud contradiction therefore appears to be surpassed.

The contradiction displaced

But this transcendence remains implicit. The authors never formulate it as the outcome or culmination of their work. Let us look at these few lines where Grunberger analyses feminine narcissism, 'That which', characterizes '. . . the libidinal cathexis of the woman, is its concentric character *and* at the same time the phallus.'[11]

To simultaneously affirm the 'concentric' and phallic character of feminine sexuality is to declare that both Freud and Jones are right. But surely it then becomes necessary to formulate a new point of view through which the truth of the two schools would be maintained?

This point of view is not formulated within the framework of the book; rather, the Freud–Jones contradiction seems to gradually lose its relevance in the face of clinical practice. And yet the verification of two incompatible propositions does not do away with the contradiction that links them. The fact that phallocentrism and concentricity may be equally constitutive of feminine sexuality does not prove that they make up a harmonious unit. It is my contention, that, on the contrary, they coexist as incompatible and that it is this incompatibility that is specific to the feminine unconscious.

Thus the most important thing about this work, that is, the displacement to which the authors submit the basic contradiction, is not sufficiently brought out. They should have stressed that the Freud–Jones incompatibility, although it was first articulated as a polemic, is far more than a disagreement of two schools. For, once this disagreement and the passions it arouses have subsided, the contradiction emerges again as a play of forces which structures the feminine unconscious itself. Phallocentrism and concentricity, both simultaneously constitutive of the unconscious, confront each other according to two modes: the first, the more spectacular, appears as *anxiety*; but the same relation of forces, plays, inversely, in *sublimation*. Each of these determining processes of the unconscious economy will be seen at play in the incompatibility of the two aspects of femininity analyzed by Jones and Freud.

The dark continent

The representation of castration

Let us start with anxiety in general, from what we know of this in so far as it is common to both sexes. This global approach will allow us to situate better in what follows the specifically feminine processes of anxiety.

Anxiety in psychoanalysis is most often described as 'castration anxiety', that is to say, as the horror that seizes the child on discovering the penis-less body of the mother. It is this discovery that engenders the fear of one day undergoing the same fate.

It is true that in each cure, the analyst must reckon with the 'imprescriptable' force of this fear of mutilation.[12] But this is not anxiety: to represent to oneself the motive of one's fear, is already to give a reason for it. But anxiety is *without reason*. What we mean is that it supposes the impossibility of any rational thought. In other words, anxiety appears as the limit–moment when conscious and unconscious representation are blocked off.

How are we to analyze this blockage? By specifying at first the nature of the representation that is its object. Three positions based on Lacanian theory will serve us as points of reference:

1 The unconscious is a structure or combinatory of desires articulated as representations.
2 These representations can be called representations of castration, inasmuch as their literal articulation effectively deprives the subject of a part of *jouissance*[i]
3 The stake is this *jouissance*, whose loss is the price of representation.

Let us take these three propositions:

1. Unconscious representation, which is what this article is concerned with, refers to different processes from those currently designated by the term 'representation'. The latter, ordinarily, concerns the conscious; it explains the reflexive activity that applies itself to the reality of the (philosophic) subject and to objects. Unconscious representation, on the contrary, neither reflects nor signifies the subject and its objects. It is a pure cathexis of the word as such. How is this possible? An example will make it clear to us: consider the distinction between conscious and unconscious representations of castration.

2. The conscious representation of castration in the child does not designate any real mutilation. It is an imaginary evocation: either it is the other who threatens by uttering a prohibition (the case of the boy);

or the little girl in order to explain the absence of the penis to herself images: 'someone must have taken it from me'.

Such a representation takes on an unconscious status at the moment at which it no longer refers to anything but the words that constitute it. Taken out of reality, it no longer refers to anything other than its form: what is now cathected, both in the prohibiting utterance and the phantasmatic imagination, is their specific articulation and the multiple puns, the play of sonorities and images that this articulation makes possible. But how can words become the objects of such a cathexis? Why do they mobilize all the strength of the unconscious? Leaving these questions open and referring the reader back to Freud,[13] let us remark only that the words, in the first moments of life, extended the body of the mother and simultaneously circumscribed the place of *suspension* (suspense) of her desire. In words, therefore, the most real of *jouissance* and the furthest of the phallus were conjoined. Perhaps, in the unconscious, the power of words remains the same?

3. Consequently, the unconscious representation is only a text. But the text produces effects: since sexuality is organized as we have seen, not according to some instinct, some 'tendency', but according to what has been said. Consequently, discourse makes impossible any direct and peaceable relation to the body, to the world, and to pleasure. It turns away from *jouissance*: it is in this sense that it is castrating. In other words, the unconscious representation of castration is, in the first place, a castrating representation.

But, at the same time, the term 'representation' must be taken in a second sense. For the sequence of discourse having once marked us, endlessly reproduces itself. And we can define the unconscious as the place where these re-presentations are indefinitely staged. This fact of repetition, of the eternal return of words, has been sufficiently demonstrated for us to take it as given here: if the representation then does not cease to represent itself, how can it disappear? Yet, the analyst must reckon with this effacement. For the patient, who expresses anxiety after the event, is speaking of a time when nothing was thinkable: then, the body and the world were confounded in one chaotic intimacy that was too present, too immediate – one continuous expanse of proximity or unbearable plenitude. What was lacking was a lack, an empty 'space' somewhere. Indeed, it seems in these clinical cases that the castrating dimension of representation is missing. Consequently, it is as if representation, at least in its effects, had wiped itself out.

Oedipus and the stake

To explain the persistence of the representation as well as its vacillation in anxiety, let us pause at the hypothesis we set out a moment ago. Let us imagine that at certain moments, the representation is indeed produced, but without castrating effects: emptily circulating, it would lose the power of turning the subject away from *jouissance*. This, not as a function of facts inherent in representation itself, but from an intrusion, a violence, emanating from the real. Perhaps a reading of Sophocles' drama *Oedipus Rex*, will serve as clarification.

At the begining of the drama, Oedipus appears as he whose relation to representation is sufficiently assured to unravel the enigmas of the Sphinx. And yet, the tragic action will progressively disclose the ruin of this representation.

The ancients used to say that this ruin was willed by the gods. The analyst declares that Oedipus was led to it by his incestuous desires. We must hold simultaneously to the idea of gods who persecute and to that of the subject who desires. For the theme of the fateful mistake, of the plan controlled by external forces, emphasizes this essential fact: that the realization of unconscious desire is always so catastrophic that the subject can never bring it about on its own.

It is one thing to desire, another to realize this desire. We have seen that to desire is to represent the lacking object (the other), that is to say, to 'enjoy' (*'jouir'*) exclusively in the form of words. To satisfy this desire is, on the contrary, to decathect words to the profit of reality: in other words, enjoyment of the mother leads back to a recuperation of the stake that, endlessly replayed, is normally the guarantee of representation.

This is why it is necessary that desire should not be realized. Hence the repression that ensures that one does not think, nor see, nor take the desired object, even and above all if it is within reach: this object must remain lost.

But in Oedipus, the gods, or chance, restores the object of desire: Oedipus enjoys Jocasta. But, simultaneously, repression continues to take place, and in an ever more pressing manner: the successive recourses to Tiresias, to sacrifices, and to the law show a desperate effort to avoid seeing the cause of the pestilence. An effort that is ineffectual: repression is no longer anything but a gigantic pantomime, powerless to assure the throwing back into play of the stake of desire. We know that, for want of a stake, representation is not worth anything.

Thus Oedipus' tragedy enables us to emphasize both the economy and the failure of representation at the same time. But it also suggests the cause of this failure. Why does the encounter with the Sphinx take place immediately before the drama? To what does the Sphinx refer, this reasoning and devouring hybrid being, which beats its wings as it talks? Why does this monster, a woman with the body of a beast, take up her place at the gates of Thebes?

Does not the encounter with this enigmatic figure of femininity threaten every subject? Is it not she who is at the root of the ruin of representation?

Freud, asking himself about feminine sexuality and assessing the small purchase that it offers analytic investigation, compared it to a 'dark continent'.

The *Recherches nouvelles* begins by recalling this formula. How appropriate! And yet it is as if the authors do not see the threatening shadows that they call forth by these words. For feminine sexuality is not a dark, unexplored continent through any provisional insufficiency of research: it is unexplored to the extent that it is unexplorable.

Of course one can describe it, give an account of it in clinical or theoretical work. But it is elsewhere, in the framework of the cure, that femininity stubbornly resists analysis. On the couch, a discourse analogous to that whose style the book renders so well, is enunciated: 'live' discourse, whose very immediacy seems to be a sign of life. But it is this immediacy, this life, which is an obstacle to analysis: the word is understood only as the extension of the body that is there in the process of speaking. It seems no longer to be hiding anything. To the extent that it does not know repression, femininity is the downfall of interpretation.

It is femininity, not women, that can take on such a status. Let us specify what meaning will be given here to the three terms: woman, femininity, repression:

- the word 'woman' will designate the subject who, like the man, is an effect of unconscious representation;
- by 'femininity' will be understood the set of the 'feminine' drives (oral, anal, vaginal) in so far as these resist the processes of repression;
- finally, repression will be distinguished from *censorship*:[14] the latter is always submitted to; the former, on the contrary, has the value of an act. In fact, the obstacles the censor opposes to libidinal development appear as the result of the experiences of the Other's desire. Regressions or fixations have made it impossible for the mother or the father to symbolize this or that key-event in the child's sexuality. And from then on, this 'blank', this unspoken, functions like a check; the censor that is set up appears as the effect of an absence of representation. It is therefore unrepresentable, and consequently 'uninterpretable'. Repression on the contrary, presupposes a symbolization: as we have seen, it allows the representation to be cathected as such, while the real satisfaction, renounced, becomes its stake. Repression is always a process that structures on the level of the psychic economy.

As we will see, feminine eroticism is more censored, less repressed than that of the man. It lends itself less easily to a 'losing itself' as the stake of unconscious representation. The drives whose force was demonstrated by the English school circumscribe a place or 'continent' that can be called 'dark' to the extent that it is outside the circumference of the symbolic economy (foreclosed).

What are the processes which maintain femininity 'outside repression', in a state of nature, as it were?

The first, of a social order, concerns the absence of prohibitions: the girl is less subject than the boy to the threats and to the defenses that penalize masturbation. We keep silent about her masturbation, all the more as it is less observable. Françoise Dolto[15] has shown that, sheltered by their privacy, the girl, the woman, can live a 'protected' sexuality. One tends to refer to the anxiety of rape and penetration without emphasizing that, in reality, on the contrary, the girl risks little. The anatomy of the boy, on the other hand, exposes him very early to the realization that he is not master either of the manifestations of his desire or of the extent of his pleasures. He experiments, not only with chance but also with the law and with his sexual organ: his body itself takes on the value of stake.

In relation to castration, therefore, the position of the man differs from that of the woman whose sexuality is capable of remaining on the edge of all repression. Under certain circumstances, then, the stake of castration for the woman finds itself displaced: it consists in the sexuality and the desire of the other sex, most often that of the father and then, of the masculine partner. Which is why Perrier and Granoff have been able to show 'the extreme feminine sensibility to all experiences relating to the castration of the man'.[16]

Yet other processes, of an instinctual and not a social order, maintain feminine sexuality outside the economy of representation — the intrication of the oral–anal drives with vaginal pleasure. Jones, Klein, and Dolto have insisted on the fact that the girl's archaic experiences of the vagina are organized as a function of pre-established oral–anal schemas. At the further extreme, precocious sexuality 'turns' around a single orifice, an organ that is both digestive and vaginal, which ceaselessly tends to absorb, to appropriate, to devour. We find again here the theme of concentricity disengaged by the authors of the book.

If this insatiable organ–hole is at the center of precocious sexuality, if it inflects all psychic movement according to circular and closed schemas, it compromises woman's relation to castration and the law: to absorb, to take, to understand, is to reduce the world to the most archaic instinctual 'laws'. It is a movement opposed to that presupposed by castration: where the *jouissance* of the body loses itself 'for' a discourse that is Other.

Here, we will not therefore question the truth of the clinical observations produced by the English school: all experience of child analysis confirms the precocity of the 'knowledge' of the vagina. More generally, it is quite true that the very small girl experiences her femininity very early. But, simultaneously, it must be stressed that such a precocity, *far from favoring a possible 'maturation', acts as an obstacle to it*, since it maintains eroticism outside the representation of castration.

Anxiety and the relation to the body

A third series of processes stand in the way of repression: those concerning the woman's relation to her own body, a relation simultaneously narcissistic and erotic. For the woman enjoys her body as she would the body of another. Every occurrence of a sexual kind (puberty, erotic experiences, maternity, etc.) happens *to* her as if it came from another (woman): every occurrence is the fascinating actualization of *the*[ii] femininity of all women, but also and above all, of that of the mother. It is as if 'to become woman', 'to be woman' gave access to a *jouissance* of the body as feminine *and/or* maternal. In the self-love she bears herself, the woman cannot differentiate her own body from that which was 'the first object'.

We would have to specify further what is only intimated here: that the real of the body, in taking form at puberty, in charging itself with intensity and importance and presence, as object of the lover's desire, reactualizes, reincarnates, the real of that other body, which, at the beginning of life was the substance of words, the organizer of desire; which, later on, was also the material of archaic repression. Recovering herself as maternal body (and also as phallus), the woman can no longer repress, 'lose', the first stake of representation. As in the tragedy, representation is threatened by ruin. But at the root of this threat there are different processes: for Oedipus, the restoration of the stake proceeded by chance, from the gods; it was effected *in spite of* a prohibition. Nothing, on the contrary, is forbidden for the woman; there is no statement or law that prohibits the recovery of the stake since the real which imposes itself and takes the place of repression and desire is, for her, the real of her own body.

From now on, anxiety, tied to the presence of this body, can only be insistent, continuous. This body, so close, which she has to occupy, is an object in excess that must be 'lost', that is to say, repressed, in order to be symbolized. Hence the symptoms that so often simulate this loss: 'there is no longer anything, only the hole, emptiness'. Such is the *leitmotif* of all feminine cure, which it would be a mistake to see as the expression of an alleged 'castration'. On the contrary, it is a defense produced in order to parry the avatars, the deficiencies, of symbolic castration.

The analyst often finds a 'fear of femininity' in connection with feminine anxiety, especially in the adolescent. We have tried to show that this fear is not a result of fantasies of violation and breaking in (effraction) alone. At bottom, it is fear of the feminine body as a non-repressed and unrepresentable object. In other words, femininity, 'according to Jones', that is, femininity experienced as real and immediate, is the blind spot of the symbolic processes analyzed by Freud. Two incompatible, heterogeneous territories coexist inside the feminine unconscious: that of representation and that which remains 'the dark continent'.

Defenses and masquerade

It is rare for anxiety to manifest itself as such in analysis. It is usually camouflaged by the defenses that it provokes. It is a question of organizing a representation of castration that is no longer symbolic, but imaginary: a lack is simulated and thereby the loss of some stake — an undertaking all the more easily accomplished precisely because feminine anatomy exhibits a lack, that of the penis. At the same time as being her own phallus, therefore, the woman will disguise herself with this lack, throwing into relief the dimension of castration as *trompe-l'oeil*.

The ways in which this can occur are multiple. One can play on the absence of the penis through silence just as well as through a resounding vanity. One can make it the model of erotic, mystical, and neurotic experiences. The anorexic refusal of food is a good example of the desire to reduce and to dissolve her own flesh, to take her own body as a cipher. Masochism also mimes the lack, through passivity, impotence, and doing nothing ('*ne rien faire*'). The observations of Helene Deutsch and those of the *Recherches nouvelles* could be understood in this way. Castration is similarly disguised in the register of erotic fiction: where the feminine orifice, O, is 'falsely' represented in its successive metamorphoses.

Here, I would rather turn to the poets, those who have written in the novelistic or made films out of the feminine drama ('*cinema*'), since the limitations of this article rule out any detailed consideration of clinical cases.

Take Fellini, the director of *Juliette of the Spirits*, a film so baffling, no doubt, because it brings out the presence of the 'dark continent' so well. The dimension of femininity that Lacan designates as masquerade, taking the term from Joan Rivière,[iii] takes shape in this piling up of crazy things, feathers, hats, and strange baroque constructions, which rise up like so many silent insignias. But what we must see is that the objective of such a masquerade is to say nothing. Absolutely *nothing*. And in order to produce this nothing the woman uses her own body as disguise.

The novels of Marguerite Duras use the same world of stupor and silence. It could be shown that this silence, this non-speech, again exhibits the fascinating dimension of feminine lack: Duras wants to make this lack 'speak' as cry (*Moderato Cantabile*), or as 'music'. Here, let us simply recall what is said in the *Ravishment of Lol V Stein*: 'what was needed was a word-absence, a word hole ... it could not have been spoken, it could only be made to resound'.[17]

Thus the sex, the vagino-oral organ of the woman, acts as obstacle to castration; at the same time, 'falsely' representing the latter in its effects of allurement, which provoke anxiety. This is why man has always called the feminine defenses and masquerade *evil*.

Woman is not accused of thinking or of committing this evil, but of incarnating it.[iv] It is this evil that scandalizes whenever woman 'plays out' her sex in order to evade the word and the law. Each time she subverts a law or a word that relies on the predominantly masculine structure of the look. Freud says that Evil is experienced as such when anxiety grips the child in front of the unveiled body of his mother. 'Did his desire then refer only to this hole of flesh?' The woman affords a glimpse of the Real, by virtue of her relation to nothing – that is to say, to the Thing. At this moment, the Symbolic collapses into the Real. Freud also says that the pervert cannot see the castrated body of his mother. In this sense, every man is a pervert. On the one hand, he enjoys without saying so, without coming too close – for then he would have to take upon himself a terrible anxiety, or even hate; he enjoys by proxy the thing he glimpses through the mother. On the other hand, he does not appear to understand that her relation to the thing is sublimated. It is this evil which has to be repressed.

A film like *Day of Wrath*[v] lays bare all the masculine 'defenses' against femininity and woman's direct relation to *jouissance*. The man is terrorized by the threat that femininity raises for 'his' repression. In order to reassure him and convince him, the woman always advances further along her own path by explaining herself, wishing to speak the truth. But she does not understand that her discourse will not and cannot be received. For the fact of bypassing the law of repression precisely by *saying all* contaminates the most precious truth and makes it suspect, odious, and condemnable. Hence masculine censure.

The frustrations, interdictions, and contempt that have weighed on women for centuries may indeed be absurd and arbitrary, but they do not matter. The main thing is the fact of imposing the definitive abandonment of *jouissance*. The scandal can then come to an end – the feminine sex bears witness to castration.

The analyst, for his part, cannot define feminine castration simply as the effect of his strictures. If the exemplar of the hysterical, neurotic woman is *one who never lets up wishing to be her sex*, inversely, isn't the 'adult' woman *one who reconstructs her sexuality in a field that goes beyond sex?* The principle of a masculine libido upheld by Freud could be clarified as a function of this 'extraterritoriality'.

Jouissance and sublimation

Feminine castration: hypotheses

Once again, let us take an example from literature. Klossowski's portraits of women easily lend themselves to a clinical commentary. We might be surprised at the astonishingly virile attributes (both anatomical and psychical) with which the author endows his heroines and deduce from them some perversion. It is also possible to see in these attributes the material of a moral fable outlining a type of perfected femininity: the 'true' woman, the 'femme' woman would be drawn as she who has *'forgotten' her femininity*, and who would entrust the *jouissance* and the representation of it to another. For this reason, Klossowski's heroine, Roberte, could in no way talk about herself, her body or 'the word that it conceals'.[18] It is someone else's task to hold the discourse of femininity, in love and/or in a novel.

Under the sign of this forgetting a second economy of desire, where the stake is no longer the same, can effectively be described. The stake is now precocious femininity and not the penis or masculine sexuality: precocious femininity becomes the material of repression. 'According to Jones' one or several periods of latency correspond to this decathexis of sexuality, periods during which the little girl and the woman disentangle themselves from their own bodies and their pleasures. This is why periods of frigidity in analysis can often be considered as an index of progress: they mark the moment when the patient decathects the vaginal–oral schemas, which till then were alone capable of providing access to erotic pleasure.

The decisive step by which the feminine unconscious is modified lies, not so much in the change of love object[19] as in the change in the unconscious representative. Masculine, phallic representatives are substituted for the first 'concentric' representatives. The law and the paternal ideals of the father that are articulated in her discourse constitute

157

the new representatives capable of supplanting the models of archaic representations (feminine Oedipus).

Let us note that this substitution does not mutilate the woman and deprive her of a penis that she never had, but *deprives her of the sense* of precocious sexuality. Femininity is forgotten, indeed repressed, and this loss constitutes the symbolic castration of the woman.

For clarity's sake, let us draw a diagram of these hypotheses on the economy of the feminine unconscious.

	Stake	*Representative*	*Relation to* jouissance
Economy I (according to Jones)	masculine sexuality (phallocentrism)	vagino-oral orifice (concentricity)	anxiety
Economy II (according to Freud)	precocious femininity (concentricity)	signifying order (phallocentrism)	sublimation

This diagram calls for three comments.

1 The parameters of the feminine economy still refer to Jones and to Freud, but in opposite directions.
2 In clinical practice, such a clear-cut distinction is not observed. The two forms of economy usually coexist, with one predominating (provisionally or definitively) over the other.
3 The notion of sublimation has been introduced.

If we can show that in an economy of type II all relation to *jouissance*, including sexual pleasure, is of a sublimatory kind, then not only will a specific dimension of feminine sexuality be clarified, but a misinterpretation of sublimation will also be avoided: that which consists in seeing in sublimation a passage from the sexual to the non-sexual.

Sublimation and metaphor

In the cure and more specifically, in the transference (i.e., the set of unconscious modifications produced by the enunciation of discourse on the couch), the dimension of pleasure can emerge.

In the *Recherches* M. Torok speaks of its manifestation: 'when one of my patients has understood an interpretation, when, consequently, an inhibition is lifted, a frequent indication of this advance is that the patient dreams and in this dream she has an orgasm' (a description of one of these dreams follows).[20]

M. Torok, by insisting on the fact that a pleasure arises when a new representation is elaborated, tells us what is essential about this pleasure. Contrary to what one might think, this pleasure does not lie in the lifting of an inhibition, that is, in the releasing of a tension, contained for too long. On the contrary, the pleasure, far from being explicable by the cliché of release ('*défoulement*'),[vi] arises from the putting in place of *new* representations. Let us note that these were first enunciated by the other, the analyst, who, in interpreting, verbally articulates something of a sexuality maintained till then in the state of nature, in the 'dark'.

Here, therefore, pleasure is the effect of the word of the other. More specifically, it occurs at the advent of a structuring discourse. For what is essential in the cure of a woman is not making sexuality more 'conscious' or interpreting it, at least not in the sense normally given to this term. The analyst's word takes on a completely different function. It no longer explains, but from the sole fact of articulating, it structures. By verbally putting in place a representation of castration, the analyst's word makes sexuality pass into discourse. This type of interpretation therefore *represses*, at least in the sense given to the word here.

Understood in this way, interpretation can perhaps help us to locate a certain cultural and social function of psychoanalysis. The Freudian theory of sexuality was developed (*mise en place*) in relation to women and femininity. We can ask whether psychoanalysis was not articulated precisely in order to repress femininity (in the sense of producing its symbolic representation). At the same time, Freud's reservations about Jones would make sense: the attempts to 'make' femininity 'speak' would surely jeopardize the very repression that Freud had known how to achieve.

Let us return to our example. What pleasure can there be in the repression that is produced at the moment of interpretation? First, let us say that interpretation, as it is analyzed here, does not consist so much in explaining and commenting, as in articulating. Here again, it is the form of words which must be emphasized. In response to the analysand's fantasy, the analyst enunciates a certain number of signifiers necessarily relating to his own desire and his listening-place. These words are *other*: the analyst's discourse is not reflexive, but different. As such it is a *metaphor*, not a mirror, of the patient's discourse. And, precisely, metaphor is capable of engendering pleasure.

First Freud and then Lacan analyzed the motives of this pleasure with regard to the joke. We laugh when we perceive that the words speak a text other than that which we thought. And if the other laughs, if the misapprehension plays on one more register, the pleasure becomes keener still. What function does this other text, this other ear, have? It has the function of engendering a metaphor, that is to say, of substituting itself for the preceding text and listening-place. Pleasure arises the moment this metaphor is produced. Lacan says that it is identified with the very meaning of the metaphor.[21]

In what then, does this meaning, bereft of signification, consist? We can define it as the measure of the empty 'space' induced by repression. The metaphor, by posing itself as that which is not spoken, hollows out and designates this space. Freud said that the pleasure of the joke lies in the return of the repressed. Does it not rather, lie *in putting the dimension for repression into play on the level of the text itself?*

It is this pleasure of the joke that can be evoked in relation to all sublimation. For it is an operation that consists in opening up new divisions and spaces in the material that it transforms. In the transference, the patient's orgasm took note of an interpretation. Surely this is best represented as a breath of air between two signifiers, suddenly opened up by the metaphor?

The orgasm, like a burst of laughter, testifies to the meaning — insignificant — of the analyst's word. We must now try to rediscover this dimension of 'wit' in pleasure and *jouissance*.

Pleasure and jouissance

Feminine erotic pleasure varies considerably in its nature and effects. There is variety in the places of the body cathected, in the level of intensity, in the outcome (orgasm or not), and in the effects: a 'successful' sexual relation can cause calm or anxiety. Let us also remember that a neurosis cannot necessarily be inferred from frigidity: and that, reciprocally, psychotics and very immature women have intense vaginal orgasms.[22]

How are we to make sense of the exuberance, the bizarreness, and the paradoxes of these pleasures? By referring less to the varieties of form and intensity than to their function in the psychic economy. Here again, we will distinguish two types of sexual pleasure: the precocious and the sublimated.

The first was earlier seen to be the effect of the experience of archaic sexuality. Even if it involves two people, even if it presents the appearance of an adult sexuality, it merely re-actualizes or raises to the highest pitch in orgasm, the *jouissance* that the woman has of herself.[23] In this type of pleasure, the other's look and his desire further reinforces the circularity of the erotic relation. Hence the anxiety that arises before and after the sexual act.

Inversely, pleasure can be structuring in its effects. The sort of 'genius', of inspiration that the woman discovers after love, shows that an event of an unconscious nature has occurred, which has enabled her to take up a certain distance from the dark continent.

We will call sublimated pleasure that which takes the same form as incestuous pleasure while none the less presupposing and confirming woman's access to the symbolic. This pleasure is no longer derived from femininity as such, but *from the signifier*, more precisely, *from the repression that it brings about*: this is why sublimated pleasure is identified with the pleasure derived from the joke.

Such a transformation is on a par with the mutation which has been outlined above as the passage from Type I to Type II sexual economy. The latter assumes, on the one hand, the forgetting of precocious femininity, and on the other, the setting in place of a new representative or signifier of castration. Does not the sublimated sexual act constitute for the woman, one of the ways of putting a Type II economy into place, where:

1 the signifier would be actualized in the rhythm, the periodic return of the penis;
2 the stake would consist of the repressed feminine drives,[24] inseparable from the penis itself;
3 pleasure would be the meaning of the metaphor through which the penis 'would repress' the body, feminine sexuality.

Let us be more precise: the penis, its throbbing, its cadence, and the movements of love-making could be said to produce the purest and most elementary form of signifying articulation, that of a series of blows that mark out the space of the body.

It is this which opens up rhythms all the more ample and intense, a *jouissance* all the more keen and serious in that the penis, the object which is its instrument, is scarcely anything.

But to state this is to state a paradox: the penis produces *jouissance* because it incarnates a finitude. Sublimation always implies a de-idealization. The phallic signifier, detached from the terrifying representations of the superego that revolve around the imaginary phallus, must appear as an object of not-much-meaning.[25]

This step, usually suspended during childhood, takes place after the first sexual experiences of adulthood. Is it a question of unconscious processes? Provided the ground has been prepared, life and a certain ethic undertake this work. To the extent that romantic idealization is successfully mourned (relinquished), to the extent that the dimension of the gift predominates, the penis can objectify, by its very insignificance, the 'difficulty to be' of the couple, in which *jouissance* is lost. Thus it can no longer be separated in its consistency from the material of this archaic, feminine *jouissance* that has been renounced. It embodies it as lost, and all of a sudden restores it a hundredfold. For it deploys this *jouissance* in direct proportion to the forgetting, which is in itself infinite.

Thus, ethics is indissociable from a 'certain' relation to *jouissance*. The de-idealization that it implies alone makes possible the occasional coming together and binding of two perfectly distinct, heterogeneous spaces. The voluptuous sensation of an aspiration of the whole body in a space absolutely Other and consequently, infinite, cannot simply be explained as the effect of the perception of the vaginal cavity. It implies that this cavity is hollowed out by repression, that is to say, by a symbolic operation.

Consequently, pleasure, far from being reduced to the excitation of an organ, on the contrary, *transports* the woman into the field of the signifer. Sublimated pleasure, like the dream and hypnosis, like the poetic act, marks a moment when the unconscious representation takes on an absolute value: in other words, when the act of articulating produces on its own the meaning of discourse (meaning nothing). Sweeping away all signification, it lays hold of the woman and catches her in its progression and its rhythms.[26]

For the man, exceptions aside,[27] this transportation into the signifier cannot be produced in so violent and radical a way. In fact, how could he abandon himself to that which he himself controls, and from whose play he gives pleasure (*jouissance*)? Moreover, this game (play) involves the risk of detumescence,[28] and also the vertigo and anxiety aroused by the absolute of feminine demand: the woman expects and receives all there is of the penis at the moment of love.

If we no longer consider what is properly called pleasure, but the orgasm usually designed as '*jouissance*' by the analyst, a similar distinction must be made between *jouissance* of Type I and the orgasm that is produced in a sublimated economy. In the former, the residue of pleasure comes to a dead end, since the woman again found herself powerless to maintain the unconscious economy. This form of orgasm, registering pleasure outside significance (*signifiance*), bars access to the symbolic. Sublimation, on the contrary, transports not only pleasure but the orgasm into metaphor. Orgasm, endlessly renewed, brought to a white heat, explodes at the moment of pleasure. It *bursts* in the double sense of the French term *éclater*: the sense of deflagration and that of a revelation. There is therefore a continuity of the ascent of pleasure and of its apogee in orgasm: the one carries the signifier to its maximum incandescence; the other marks the moment when the discourse, in exploding under the effect *of its own force*, comes to the point of breaking, of coming apart. It is no longer anything.

To break *itself*, to disjoint *itself*, in other words, to articulate itself through a meaning that endlessly escapes. Orgasm in discourse leads us to the point where feminine *jouissance* can be understood as *writing* (*écriture*) – to the

162

point where it must appear that this *jouissance* and the literary text (which is also written like an orgasm produced from within discourse) are the effect of the same murder of the signifier.

Isn't this way Bataille, Jarry, and Jabès speak of writing as the jouissance of a woman? And why that which she is writing is the Name?[vii]

Notes

Translated by Parveen Adams, with acknowledgement to Jacqueline Rose for her invaluable advice.

1 S. Freud, compare, on this subject in particular: 'Three Essays', (1905), *The Standard Edition of the Complete Psychological Works of Sigmund Freud*, vol. VII; 'Femininity' (1932), vol. XXII; 'The dissolution of the Oedipus Complex' (1924), vol. XIX.

2 E. Jones, 'The Early Development of Female Sexuality', *International Journal of Psycho-analysis* (1927), vol. VIII; 'The Phallic Phase' (1933), vol. XIV; 'Early Female Sexuality' (1935), vol. XVI.

3 J. Chasseguet-Smirgel, C.J. Luquet-Parat, B. Grunberger, J. McDougall, M. Torok, C. David, *Recherches psychoanalytiques nouvelles sur la sexualité féminine*, Payot, 1964. M. Torok, 'La signification de l'envie de phallus chez le femme', p. 184.

4 *Ibid.*, p. 186.

5 *Ibid.*, p. 132.

6 *Ibid.*, p. 65–90.

7 On phallocentrism and the innateness of desire, see 'La phase phallique', *Scilicet* 1, Seuil: a rigorous restatement of the theoretical positions of Freud and Jones on femininity from the position of Lacanian theory; trans. in J. Mitchell and J. Rose (eds) *Feminine Sexuality: Jacques Lacan and the école freudienne*, Macmillan, 1982.

8 *Recherches*, p. 103.

9 *Ibid.*, pp. 124–5.

10 *Ibid.*, p. 191.

11 *Ibid.*, p. 103 (author's emphasis).

12 *Ibid.*, p. 67.

13 S. Freud, 'Repression' and 'The Unconscious', *SE*, vol. XIV.

14 This distinction is not always made. These two types of process are usually designated by the term 'repression' (primary and secondary).

15 F. Dolto, 'La libido et son destin féminin', *La psychanalyse*, VII.

16 W. Granoff and F. Perrier, 'Le problème de la perversion chez la femme et les idéaux feminins'. *La psychanalyse*, VII. This article is essential for theoretical work on feminine sexuality.

17 Marguerite Duras, *La Ravissement de Lol V. Stein*, Gallimard, p. 54.

18 P. Klossowski, *Les Lois de l'hospitalité*, p. 145.

19 The 'change of object' designates the renunciation of the first love object, the mother, in favor of the father. On this problem see J. Luquet-Parat, 'Le changement d'objet', *Recherches*, p. 124ff.

20 *Recherches*, p. 192.

21 Apropos of metaphor, see J. Lacan, 'The agency of the letter in the unconscious', *Ecrits: A Selection*, trans. A. Sheridan, Tavistock, 1977, and 'Les formations de l'inconscient', *Séminaire 1956–1957*. On pleasure by the same author: 'Propos directifs pour un congrès sur la sexualité féminine', *Ecrits*, Seuil, 1966, trans. in J. Mitchell and J. Rose (eds), *Feminine Sexuality: Jacques Lacan and the école freudienne*.

22 See F. Dolto.

23 See P. Aulagnier, *Le Desir et la perversion*, Seuil.

24 Drives repressed both in the course of earlier Oedipal experiences as well as in the *present*, by the very fact of the *presence* of the penis.

25 This paragraph and the following one were added to the earlier *Critique* article in 1976 in order to clear up a misunderstanding. Only someone who idealizes the signifier could interpret the fact of relating to *jouissance* to an operation of sublimation and to the putting into play of the signifier's 'frenzied idealization' (C. David). I take as a tribute – no doubt unintended – what someone exclaimed apropos of this article: 'So, the *jouissance* of the woman is produced by the operations of the Holy Ghost!' It can happen!

26 If the woman, at the moment of orgasm, identifies herself radically with an unconscious representation, articulated by the other, then does she not find herself again precisely in the archaic situation where the maternal representation was the sole organizer of fantasy? The reply could be in the affirmative for orgasms of the psychotic or neurotic (acute hysteria) type. In these cases, pleasure and orgasm are nothing more than the manifestation of, among other things, a sort of *direct seizure* of the woman by the Other's discourse. For the woman, who, on the contrary, assumes her castration, this relation is *indirect*: it passes through the (paternal) metaphor of the maternal discourse, a metaphor that, as we have seen, presupposes an economy of desire in which the woman puts herself at stake.

27 Except in the case of actual homosexuality. We must be careful, however, not to set up too clear-cut a distinction between the sexuality of the man and that of the woman. Without pretending to settle the whole problem of bisexuality here, let us only say that every masculine subject is cathected as the object and product of his mother: he was 'part' of the maternal body. In relation to the masculine body and unconscious cathexis, then, one could also speak of 'femininity' as implied in maternal femininity. Would not the sexual act be structuring for the male subject to the extent that, putting into play the repression of femininity, he would produce each time the

coupure that separates the man from his mother, while 'returning' to her the femininity of his partner.

28 On the question of detumescence, cf. Lacan *Séminaire 1967–1968*. See also 'The Signification of the Phallus', *Ecrits: A Selection* and 'Propos directifs pour un congrès sur la sexualité féminine', *Ecrits*, Seuil.

Translator's notes

i The word *jouissance* is impossible to translate. Its meanings include: enjoyment, enjoyment of property or privilege; pleasure; and the pleasure of orgasm. It is necessary, however, to distinguish between *jouissance* and *plaisir* (pleasure), which are two theoretically distinct concepts in Montrelay's text.

ii The article *la* of *la* femininité is italicized in French: see J. Lacan, 'Dieu et la jouissance de la femme', *Séminaire livre XX: Encore*, Seuil, 1975.

iii In Womanliness as Masquerade', *International Journal of Psychoanalysis* X (1929), pp. 303–13.

iv In the earlier version of this article, which appeared in *Critique* 278 (1976), this sentence ends with 'since it consists in confronting desire with a bodily lack (which is carnal)'.

v Directed by Carl Dreyer, 1943.

vi The French is *défoulement*, a pun on the French word of repression: *refoulement*.

vii *Nom* puns on the French negative *non* and also refers to *Le Nom du Père* (Name of the Father).

8

On the feminine and the masculine: afterthoughts on Jacqueline Cosnier's book, *Destins de la féminité*

ALAIN GIBEAULT

You Isolde
I Tristan
No more Tristan!
No more Isolde!
No names,
No parting,
Newly perceived,
Newly kindled
Ever, unendingly
One consciousness . . .

Can the feminine be defined? And can we imagine a precise, univocal definition which would make it possible to grasp the mystery of the 'dark continent' to which Freud alluded? Freud's approach is well known: situate the feminine in the opposition of masculine and feminine and separate out its antecedents in infantile sexual development on the basis of other oppositions: between subject and object at the object stage, between active and passive at the sadistic-anal stage, between masculine or castrated genital organ at the time of infantile genital organization (the stage of phallic sexual monism, when '*maleness* exists, but not femaleness'). And Freud goes on to clarify:

> It is not until development has reached its completion at puberty that the sexual polarity coincides with *male* and *female*. Maleness combines [the factors of] subject, activity and possession of the penis; femaleness takes over [those of] object and passivity. The vagina is now valued as a place of shelter for the penis; it enters into the heritage of the womb.[1]

All the same, we know that this sequence of stages, which could be understood as an *Aufhebung* which both suppresses and maintains the preceding oppositions, in fact corresponds to an ideal sequence in Freud's thinking, and that it is contradicted by the Freudian theory of phallic sexual monism, which defines the masculine as the positive and the feminine as the negative. A refusal of maternal femininity, the place of the uncanny and of death, as Jacqueline Cosnier emphasizes in her book on the 'destinies of femininity'.[2] A need for protection against the primitive maternal imago, according to Janine Chasseguet-Smirgel, in its situating of the whole of female sexuality 'under the sign of lack', 'lack of vagina, lack of penis, lack of a specific sexuality, lack of an adequate erotic object, lack of her own capacities invested in the self and necessity, ultimately, of "lacking" a clitoris'. To these may be added the relative lack of a superego and of capacities for sublimation. On the other hand, the boy's sexuality is 'complete': he possesses an adequate sexual organ, a specific sexuality from the outset and two erotic objects for the two sides of the Oedipus complex.[3]

This is the conception of masculinity and femininity which leads Freud to understand the refusal of femininity at the origin of interminable cures as a 'biological bedrock'. Jacqueline Cosnier's aim is to conceive of this refusal, this repudiation, as a 'psychological bedrock', which comes down to understanding femininity not as a negative notion, which would confirm an acceptance of powerlessness, but as a positive and intelligible notion.

It is this positive approach to femininity which I want to clarify here, starting from a number of themes taken from Jacqueline Cosnier's recent work: primary identification with maternal femininity; female masochism and phallic and/or genital logic. This will be a way of considering the integration of the feminine body in more depth, not so much by emphasizing female sexuality on its own, as by studying the feminine in its articulation with the masculine, in both men and women, and beginning with questions of identification and the drives.

1. The primary identification with maternal femininity

We must first of all consider the opposition between masculine and feminine not just as the end-point of a course of development, in this case as the result of sexual maturation at puberty which would give its full meaning to the difference of the sexes, but as the very principle of this development, at the moment of the Freudian object stage and the subject/object opposition. This assumes, first, that we think of this development less according to a genetic sequence, in the sense of a succession of phases, as we might think from a first look at Freud, obeying a linear causality of the past over the present, than as a metapsychological sequence: in this case, the reality of this passage from one stage to another is indeed attributed to biological *maturation*, which at a predetermined moment arouses activity of more or less significance on the part of an erogenous zone; but it is secondary in relation to the history of the *conflict* installed at this point, and in relation to the deferred effects which introduce a retrospective causality of the present over the past. Second, we have to distinguish the masculine—feminine opposition from the male—female opposition (or rather, as Cosnier, following Christian David, reminds us, from the opposition of *maleness* and *femaleness*):[4] in other words, distinguish between the *psychical representation of the body* — which is more a fantasmatic body than a real body, a body of drives which privileges the *felt* and the not immediately figurable — and the *body that is objective and spatialized* according to anatomy, based more on vision and the external apprehension of sexual difference.

This opens up a perspective whereby masculine and feminine are relative to what is lived in terms of identifications and drives, which leaves a space for a psychical topography, rather than deriving only from the perception–consciousness system. This does not rule out taking account of the consequences of the objective apprehension of sexual difference (as we know, Freud accords major significance to vision in the organization of the castrastion complex), but a psycho-sexual approach to masculinity and femininity requires that this dimension not be the primary one.

From this point of view, the opposition of masculine and feminine is contemporary with primary identification, of which Freud says first, in *The Ego and the Id*, that it involves an 'identification with the father in his own personal prehistory', only to correct this in a footnote and say 'with the parents'.[5] This is a movement of interiorization which follows the two periods of the organization of auto-erotism: first, the period of a primordial 'sense of oneself', of a primitive reflexivity of the body that correlates with the hallucination of satisfaction and the double reversal of the drive; the reversal into the opposite, in the passage from passivity to activity inherent in hallucinatory satisfaction, and the reversal onto the subject's own self, in the passage from object to subject, are evidence of this primary identification with the mother, with her femininity. In this way, a rhythm between inertia and constancy is installed, relative to the mother's function as protective shield, which progressively enables the child to *experience* itself and not to figure itself as a unity distinct from the mother, to feel the limits of its body and the lack which could be fulfilled: thus the child is in a position to cathect its vital functions and erogenous zones as the mother does, in spite of the juxtaposition of extreme and discontinuous sensations. At the moment of the 'object stage', contemporaneous with the perception of the mother as a total object and her differentiation from what is non-mother, this 'sense of itself' becomes a 'representing itself' correlative with primal repression, in other words with the anticathexis of hallucinatory satisfaction and the displacement onto the object of experiences of pleasure-unpleasure linked to the satisfaction of needs.

In this context, Cosnier says that 'the feminine identification is the synthesis of primary identification and the secondary identification with the differentiation of ego/non-ego resulting from the homosexual investments that precede the recognition of sexual difference ... and sexed identification'.[6] Is it a question of a feminine identification or already of a bisexual identification in which the interiorization of the difference between masculinity and femininity is correlative to the psychical bisexuality of the mother? The censure of the [woman] lover[7] or the alpha function of the mother[8] linked to her 'capacity for daydreaming' are some of the ways of designating the presence of an internal third person which the mother transmits to her child, by giving a functional meaning to everything in bodily contact with her child which involves a pleasure whose cause must be unknown; in other words, what the child's body represents for her unconscious.

The differences between presence and absence, between good and bad, and between the inside and the outside are thus correlative both with the primitive differentiation between what is mother and what is non-mother, and with the difference between masculine and feminine within the mother herself. Representations of the ambisexed mother or of the parents combined would be evidence of this primary identification with the parents, by condensing the two sexes into a single image: at the origin of psychical bisexuality, this imago of the archaic mother would refer to the image of a total integrity of the subject guaranteeing its narcissism and its omnipotence; 'proto-representation of femininity', as Jacqueline Cosnier puts it — which could also, it seems to me, be considered as a 'proto-representation of masculinity', from the very fact that this archaic image can figure receptiveness and joining in relation to bodily experiences, at the same time as their breaking in and penetrating action. This is perhaps what leads Cosnier to speak of secondary identification in connection with the ego/not-ego differentiation, to designate this primitive and condensed differentiation of masculine and feminine, whereas secondary identification in the strict sense refers to the successive and structuring post-Oedipal identifications, to the differentiated imagos of the mother and the father.

How, then, should we understand the articulation between this primary identification with the mother and the early constitution of a core of gender identity, as Robert Stoller has succeeded in defining it? From this point of view, the boy and the girl would follow an identical path, whereas we know that gender distinctions are acquired very early. Around the second half of the second year, the child can identify itself and others as male or female, through a process where psychological and social factors operate more than anatomical factors.[9] Belief in being a boy or a girl precedes the organization of sexual difference and does not contradict the attribution of a penis to every human being.

For Freud, while the fundamental riddle spurring on the child's 'instinct for knowledge' was often the question of the origin of babies, he did not put aside the idea that gender [genre] distinction, the division of the human race [genre] into two sexes, represented a major problem to solve, necessitating the construction of 'sexual theories'.[10] As we know, the phallic phase and the theory of castration constitute what is at issue in these researches during childhood: we can suppose that the primary identification with the other, as a movement aimed at the narcissistic identity of the sexes, and the accession to gender distinction, are the two elements which, through their dialecticization, open the way to the organization of sexual difference, to the moment of the *identification* of the sexes, to their *delimitation* according to their respective psychical characteristics.

This involves giving up the early undifferentiated representations and identifications, which are then considered to be inappropriate in relation to gender, and the recognition of the limits imposed by the other sex. The development of sexual identity implies coming out of this original matrix where all sexes are possible, and elaborating for each sex its wish for the prerogatives of the other sex: penis envy for the girl, envy of reproductive capacities for the boy. This is one of the main destinies of primary femininity, and for both sexes.

2. Female masochism

At this level, the integration of maternal femininity which is analogous in the two sexes is relative to primary masochism, as a cathexis of pain related to hallucinatory satisfaction; in other words, as investment of the rupture of pleasure/unpleasure, *jouissance*/suffering, hallucinated pleasure/pleasure received. [*Jouissance* refers to a more intense and erotized excitation than pleasure — Editor's note.] The primary masochism of which Freud says that it 'still has the self as its object'[11] is identical here to primary sadism, for if one opens the way to auto-erotism, the other opens the way to the object. Freud has a tendency, as we know, to sexualize these 'pairs of opposites'. In 1905, in the *Three Essays*, he was writing:

It is . . . a suggestive fact that the existence of the pair of opposites formed by sadism and masochism cannot be attributed merely to the element of aggressiveness. We should rather be inclined to connect the simultaneous presence of these opposites with the opposing masculinity and femininity which are combined in bisexuality – a contrast which often has to be replaced in psychoanalysis by that between activity and passivity.[12]

We can now understand how these masculine/sadism/active connotations opposed to feminine/masochism/passive are at the origin of the Freudian description of feminine masochism – not in the woman, but . . . in the man! Feminine masochism because, as Jacquline Cosnier reminds us, masochism is for Freud 'characteristically female': its features, 'being castrated, or copulated with, or giving birth'[13] would go back to an identification with the mother in the sexual act. Cosnier insists in her work on separating feminine masochism from femininity as such, and she sees in it a deferred effect of primary masochism 'inseparable from the early relationship' to the mother, and valid for both sexes. This involves a fantasmatic compromise between 'the desire for fusion effacing the difference from the mother, and the desire for separation which would make it more extreme'[14] which, in the deferred effect of the infantile neurotic organization and puberty, would pick up again the issues involved in primary identification and primary homosexuality.[15]

This is a point of view not so far away from the one presented by Florence Bégoin-Guignard in a lecture on 'The Cat's Smile'. On the other side of the regressive aspects whereby 'being castrated, or copulated with, or giving birth' are lived as pain and would be a result of the exercise of paternal violence, we should acknowledge a more archaic and forward-orientated dimension of masochism, where boy and girl would have to take on the loss of the first object, enjoy the penetration of the maternal penis (early genital instincts) and introject the mother as a protective shield. The first period of femininity would be inseparable from the fantasmatic integration of masochism, as a libidinal co-excitation of receptivity.[16] For her part, Jacqueline Cosnier also emphasizes the positive dimension of feminine masochism as an acceptance of passive desires which enables a disengagement from the fantasmatic dangers linked to childhood powerlessness and the narcissistic wounds of the needs of dependency. The struggle against passivity, on the other hand, would be evidence of the impossibility of integrating feminine masochism as a component in auto-erotism, and would entail the risk of a fatal masochistic ascendancy.

The question then arises as to what would then be the interest of maintaining the concept of 'feminine masochism', since in this perspective it goes back to primary masochism. In addition, to sexualize masochism in this way would be to bail out the Freudian affirmation which makes masochism 'truly feminine'.[17] But as we know, Freud himself admits that 'the concepts of "masculine" and "feminine" . . . are among the most confused that occur in science',[18] and that neither anatomy nor psychology can succeed in specifiying their connotations. Anatomy and biology may perhaps be able to characterize what is masculine or feminine through the difference of genital organs and reproductive cells, but biological bisexuality forbids the determination of pure masculinity or pure femininity.

Psychology is in no better a position, for Freud, for ultimately the reference to activity and passivity is not finally conclusive. He himself often had recourse to the opposition of active and passive to determine the masculine and the feminine: he even calls it an 'essential' meaning, 'the most serviceable in psychoanalysis'.[19] But in his lecture on 'Femininity', he ends up criticizing this assimilation, which is not confirmed in either the animal or the human world. As he himself says in relation to human sexual life, there is a lack of conformity between the two oppositions, for both in what is sexual in the narrow sense (in suckling, for instance) and in what is sexual in the wider sense (social life), activity is not foreign to the female world. Freud does for a moment speculate that femininity could be characterized not by passivity, but by 'giving preference to passive aims', since 'to achieve a passive aim may call for a large amount of activity'. But here as well the essence of femininity slips away, because it is necessary to consider sociological factors which 'force women into passive situations'.[20]

The investigator is confronted with the same problem as the child, boy or girl, seeking to understand sexual difference. In both cases, says Freud, they are in the position of 'purely thinking beings, from another planet', who would be amazed to find on earth 'the existence of two sexes among human beings, who, though so much alike in other respects, yet mark the difference between them with such obvious external signs'.[21] The invention of phallic logic and phallic sexual monism makes it possible to install a momentary 'order' and to respond to this fundamental question.

3. Phallic logic and/or genital logic

If boys and girls have similar destinies from the point of view of feminine masochism and the primary identification with maternal femininity, none the less the phallic logic contemporaneous with the Oedipus complex introduces a difference between boys and girls in terms of phallic and castrated, of more and less, of positive and negative. The distinction between the sexes as a perceptual experience dating from the beginning of life and entering consciousness around the age of two finds here an 'understanding' and a 'conceptualization', as an instinctual experience more articulated with the 'anatomical destiny'. A great deal is at stake, because this involves confirming the disidentification with the archaic mother and making possible the secondary re-identifications, while also promoting the decondensation of the erogenous zones. Cosnier correctly notes that the activity–passivity polarity which Freud wanted to distinguish from the masculine–feminine polarity is sexualized, and comes to be condensed in a more or less solid way into the phallic–castrated polarity.

It is the theory of phallic sexual monism which, through its link with the anal organization of the libido, for both sexes only grants the penis the value of a detachable 'little one',[22] and refuses any possible meaning to the difference between the penis and the female genital organs. Primacy of the *penis* as occasion for feminine excitation – which thus enters into a series of symbolic substitutions (faeces – penis – baby)[23] – and displacements onto every bodily and intellectual activity, which confirms the privileged role of this sexual organ in a semantic dimension of the symbol. Primacy of the *phallus*, if we want to use the reference to the Graeco-Latin term to emphasize the structuring function of the penis in the differentiation of the sexes:[24] the symbolic function of the phallus serves to make explicit the bodily and sexual anchoring of gender distinction and the central place of the castration complex, in conformity with the syntactical dimension of the symbol (on this difference between the semantic function and the syntactical function of the symbol, see my article).[25] The binary system of phallic/non-phallic simplifies the difference of the sexes, but by the same token it has a function of organization and reassurance for both sexes.

Does this theory refer to a reality or to a fantasy? As we know, Freud attributes a primacy of the masculine to both sexes and does not think that there can be any function for a representation of the vagina before puberty: he thinks that in childhood the 'vagina is still undiscovered by both sexes'. In relation to the little girl, he clarifies: 'It is true that there are a few isolated reports of early vaginal sensations as well, but it could not be easy to distinguish these from sensations in the anus or vestibulum; in any case they cannot play a great part'.[26] As for the little boy, we should remember that in the case of Little Hans, Freud would have let the boy move on, 'if matters had lain entirely in my hands': then he would have been able to offer him a confirmation of 'his instinctive premonitions by telling him of the existence of the vagina and of copulation'.[27]

Are we dealing with ignorance or misrecognition? Freud always thought it was a matter of ignorance, even though everything speaks in favour of a misrecognition and effacement (repression or denial) of the representation of the vagina in childhood. Following Melanie Klein, Ernest Jones maintains more correctly the idea of an unconscious knowledge of the vagina and a disavowal of maternal castration as a defence against the representation of intercourse and penetration. From this point of view the opposition between the clitoris, a masculine organ, and the vagina, a feminine organ, would correspond to a defensive modality characteristic of the phallic phase, with the aim for the little girl of repressing genital pleasure.[28] It is implicit in Freud's formulations that if the little girl's reaction is so animated when she realizes that she does not have a penis like the little boy, this is because it arises in a context where clitoral masturbation has been intensified. The perception of the absence of a penis comes to have meaning in order to repress a genital excitation which, according to an interesting suggestion of Kurt Eissler's, is experienced in a much more traumatic way for girls than boys because of the very possibility of orgasm before puberty.[29] Correspondingly, the abandonment of genital excitation cannot fail to bring about a fear of losing all genital pleasure, which is what Jones noted in relation to the little girl's fear of aphanisis.[30] Experience of actual genital loss made possible by the early narcissistic experience of the loss of the illusion of omnipotence: penis envy as experience of all or nothing anchors itself in these experiences of loss and figures as manifest content, a compromise solution in relation to the identificatory conflict with the mother. From this point of view, penis envy would correspond not so much to a primary envy, as Freud thought, as to a secondary and defensive one with the aim of repressing the little girl's properly feminine desires, characteristic of a primary feminine phase.

As for the boy, the repression of the representation of the vagina does enable him to set aside castration anxiety at the level of the positive Oedipus complex, since he has nothing to envy or fear from his father; but this theory also enables him to set aside all envy in relation to the mother, in both her genital and her procreative role, since he is capable, as is the mother, of satisfying the father and engendering children, because of the vagina–anus equivalence.[31] In relation to Little Hans, Freud correctly observes that in the phobia of the fallen horse both the death of the father and the mother giving birth are involved,[32] but he does not really explain his desire to give birth to children in the same way as his mother, and the role of both this feminine identification and his rivalry with his mother in his misrecognition of the difference of the sexes. A refusal on Freud's part of the maternal transference, as Cosnier stresses, corresponding not so much to a refusal of femininity as to a *refusal of the femininity in his mother* with the 'discovery of the woman in her with all its consequences, hostility and rebellion thenceforth let loose against the mother'.[33] Freud is incapable of analysing in Little Hans what he refuses to see in himself: a blind spot which shows that for boys castration anxiety, as the fear of losing the penis, is also connected to the fear of losing the illusion of bisexual completeness.

A psychosexual destiny whereby boy and girl both find themselves faced with the anxiety of losing a narcissistic state of unlimited possibilities; the castration complex enables it to be worked through in the direction of both differentiation and the setting up of objects. In this process, anatomical and physiological destiny does none the less determine differences in investment of the body. For the girls, bodily experiences and their dimension of invisibility bring about what Cosnier calls 'a perceptual uncertainty as to what the girl sees and touches, reinforcing her dependence on the gaze and the love of the other',[34] as opposed to the boy, who is more capable of relying on the visible penis. It is only at puberty that the girl will be able to rely on visible signs (growth of the breasts, periods) which will come to confirm for her the existence and integrity of a sexed body, to the extent that vision facilitates the realistic representation of the genital organs: whence the girl's greater difficulties during the preceding periods in establishing the meaning of her feminine identity, because of the invisibility of her genital organs.[35] And this is confirmed by the modalities of castration anxiety for little girls during the latency period, which is particularly concerned with the future successful functioning of her genital organs and with doubts about this.

On the other hand, it is probably this dimension of invisibility which can explain the more general and more diffuse erotism which characterizes the female body. First, because of the displacement onto the body in its entirety of the investment in the genital organs, in particular in masturbation, so as to efface all reference to genital excitation and 'the imperfection' of the female genital organs in comparison with the boy's. Also, because of that disposition for mothering to which this invisibility testifies, which, according to Janine Chassguet-Smirgel, could promote in women 'the capacity to "convert" libidinal energy into parts of her body which are not a priori erogenous zones'.[36] It is also this disposition for 'carrying the child inside herself' which, for Evelyne Kestemberg, characterizes the modalities of auto-erotic investment of the female body in a dimension of tender inflection which suits the organization of primary homosexual relationships.[37]

From this point of view, the psychosexual destiny of the girl is easier than the boy's: while for Freud, the girl finds herself in a more difficult situation than the boy because of the need to change erotic zones (from clitoris to vagina) and object (from mother to father), it is precisely her not having to disidentify herself from the maternal body (unlike the boy) which promotes this primary homosexual movement for her and its destiny in the Oedipus complex. As Kestemberg emphasizes, 'this is just what will enable her to love her father, by not completely losing sight of the fact that being like her mother, she can replace her through her disappearance in the murderous oedipal fantasy, without ceasing to love her completely, since within herself, in this identical body, she loves her'.[38] This would probably explain why men are subject to more serious and frequent problems of identity than women, since they have to face up to the danger of identification with the woman, being castrated. It is this differentiating problem in primary homosexuality which allows us to understand why, in another theoretical context, E. Jacobson could correctly note 'that the experience of sexual identity is in no way limited to comparisons between the genital organs of the two sexes'.[39]

Phallic logic is in fact an infantile sexual theory which, in its very reference to the penis as organ and to anatomical destiny, aims at repressing the narcissistic and objectal issues of the Oedipal period: as much individual limits as incestuous and murderous desires. Through its clearly defined oppositions, it also has the advantage of limiting the regressive dangers linked to all that is condensed by what is invisible in the maternal body, as an attraction towards the unknown and the absence of differentiation.

The negative therapeutic reaction, to which Jacqueline Cosnier accords considerable importance in her book, is inscribed in this phallic logic, to the extent that Freud attributed it to a refusal of femininity on the part of both sexes: penis envy for the woman and the revolt against a passive or feminine disposition in relation to another man for the man. With both sexes, the repudiation of femininity corresponds to a refusal after the event of archaic dependence in relation to the mother, who has made the child undergo both her domination, as ambisexed imago, and the distress imposed by her femininity, correlative to her fertility, to which maternal castration refers back. The biological bedrock is in fact a psychological bedrock if, as Cosnier suggests, we link the refusal of femininity to 'unconscious desires for a destructive dispossession of the maternal contents': to desires for sterilizing the mother in her procreative function.[40]

By contrast, genital logic is that which means to surpass *the opposition* of masculine and feminine, figured in particular by the opposition between activity and passivity, and dependent on anatomical destiny (having or not having the penis), to discover the *difference* between masculinity and femininity; this presupposes surpassing the struggle for a third object, for a penis-thing which conceals the real aim of this wish: namely, as Maria Torok emphasizes,[41] the possibility, beyond being and having, of discovering the right *to act* and *to become* — to think and fantasize, adds Cosnier; the possibility of exercising an auto-erotism disengaged from maternal control and correlative with the integration of the procreative dimension of maternal femininity (a surpassing of the vagina/womb split).

This new logic of the unconscious brings with it two consequences. Having the right to act assumes first of all being able to find a freedom in the exercise of activity and passivity, which no longer define masculinity and femininity but reappear in each polarity: at this level, orgasmic experience bears witness to this freedom, in authorizing both loss and reunion with oneself.[42] This also makes it possible to become free from the temptation of the positivism of univocal and systematic thinking, which testifies to the alliance between anal mastery and phallic narcissism, and to authorize the risks of multivocal and polysemic thinking – a logic of difference where one of the terms necessarily refers back to the other, without however leading to an infinite circularity.

The exercise of thinking in fact indicates the integration of psychical bisexuality, in the sense of Christian David's definition of it, as a 'virtual complementarity, potential in relation to the other sexuality, the other psychosexuality ... and by this very virtuality a reminder of incompleteness linked to sexual specifications'.[43] A feminine destiny which is also a masculine one, to the very extent that the possibility of fantasizing and sharing the sexual experience of the other sex 'in a virtual form' does in fact enable there to be a sexual relation.

Jean Laplanche puts forward the hypothesis that genital logic would promote the appearance of an open symbolization, which would introduce a much more ambiguous symbolization than the one Freud initially wanted to see there. Symbolic efficacity, in the sense of the social efficacy of the symbol, would be calculated through the possibility for recognizing and inscribing *two*, equally positive, symbols: for instance, in the circumcision rituals of primitive societies, where the 'symbolic wound' is as much a demasculinization as a defeminization, a taking on of the biological sex and a reminiscence of the 'powers' of the other sex.[44]

But can phallic logic, then, ever be totally surpassed by genital logic? For Jacqueline Cosnier, it would be a matter of letting the two conceptions coexist as the results of two different logics present in us as logics of the unconscious.[45] I would tend to think, as she does, that we are never finished with negotiating the castration anxiety, and that to imagine that a genital logic has been fully reached would assume that the unconscious had been tamed forever. But we know that the recognition of the unconscious is an asymptotic work, which is directed less towards opening it totally than towards re-establishing a circulation between the psychical systems.

Cosnier draws the lessons of this 'bisexual mediation' (in Christian David's phrase) for analytic practice, and tries to identify the figures of femininity and masculinity in the attitudes required for this work: if free-floating attention can be likened to primary maternal preoccupation, it can only be illusory to want to pin down immediate and infra-verbal communication, as opposed to mediated and verbal penetration of the material, to the categories of femininity and masculinity. On the contrary, the analyst's psychical bisexuality assumes, as she stresses, 'a relationship between paternal and maternal identifications, feminine and masculine representations, which privileges their fertility, rather than an opposition in terms of alternatives'.[46] The patient's identification with the function of the analyst is thus an identification with this play between *receptiveness* and *penetration*, where the conditions of analysis (free association and the demands of the frame) echo the conditions of a work of symbolization.

In this light, what connotations for defining masculinity and femininity should be retained? While the criteria and manifestations can vary according to periods and places, we might think that a universal representation reappears in the metaphorization of bodily experience in terms of *desire to penetrate* and *desire to be penetrated*.[47] This difference in no way confirms the oppositions of activity and passivity or sadism and masochism, which, on the contrary, are regressive and fixed modalities of it. The integration of the masculinity/femininity polarity, as source of a free functioning of symbolization and creativity, has as its essential condition for both sexes − and Cosnier has the merit of reminding us of this − the surpassing of the anxieties and terrors inspired by *maternal femininity* in an articulation, and not an opposition, between the visible and the invisible.

Notes

Translated by Rachel Bowlby

1 Sigmund Freud, 'The infantile genital organization' (1923), in SE 19, p. 145.
2 Jacqueline Cosnier, *Destins de la féminité* (Paris: Presses Universitaires de France, 1987), p. 47.
3 Janine Chasseguet-Smirgel, 'Freud et la féminité: quelques taches aveugles sur le continent noir', in *Les deux arbres du jardin* (Paris: Editions des femmes, 1988), p. 56.
4 See Christian David, 'La Bisexualité psychique: Eléments d' une re-évaluation', in *Revue Française de Psychanalyse*, 39 (5−6) (1975), pp. 713−856. ['Maleness' and 'femaleness' are given in English in the text, in parentheses after the words 'virilité' and 'femellité'. The sequence of three oppositions: 'masculin−féminin', 'mâle−femelle', and then the English 'male−female', indicate the lack of

symmetry here between the two languages, which is a constant problem for translation. 'Masculin' and 'féminin' are wider terms than 'masculine' and 'feminine', while 'mâle' and 'femelle' have more directly biological meanings than 'male and 'female' – Translator's note.]

5 Freud, *The Ego and the Id* (1923), in SE 19, p. 31.

6 Cosnier, p. 85.

7 See Denise Braunschweig and Michel Fain, *La Nuit, le jour* (Paris: Presses Universitaires de France, 1975). For Braunschweig and Fain the idea of the censure of the woman lover refers to the function of a receptive and alternative mother who would also be able to become a woman lover open to the wish of the father. This evolution would be accompanied by a censure of the erotic representations shared with the infant, which would thus help the latter organize a positive repression process.

8 Cosnier, p. 53.

9 For Robert Stoller, the constitution of a 'core of gender identity' (in other words, being male or female) depends on three factors: the anatomy and physiology of the genital organs; the attitude of the parents, of brothers and sisters, of peers, to the infant's gender role; and a biological force that can more or less modify the action of the environment (see Robert Stoller, *Sex and Gender: On the Development of Masculinity and Femininity* (London: Hogarth Press, 1968), especially pp. 72–4). The experience of children born with no penis or no vagina and brought up respectively as boys or girls shows that the anatomical factor is not essential, and that parental attitudes, especially the mother's, operate more strongly in connection with the child's sex. This presupposes accepting that there exists from the outset a primary destiny which is different for boys and girls and that the pre-Oedipal phase is not identical for the two sexes.

10 See Freud, 'Some psychical consequences of the anatomical distinction between the sexes' (1925), in SE 19, p. 252, note 2.

11 Freud, 'On the economic problem of masochism' (1924), in SE 19, p. 1.

12 Freud, 'Three essays' (1905), in SE 7, p. 160. The reference to activity and passivity was a 1915 addition, whose final formulation dates from 1924; in other words, the period of 'The economic problem of masochism'.

13 Freud, 'Economic problem', (1924), p. 162.

14 Cosnier, p. 93.

15 If primary identification is organized in the mode of the identical, primary homosexuality enables a first movement in the direction of alterity through its tender inflection, and is thus organized in the mode of resemblance. See further 'Homosexualité et identité', *Les Cahiers du Centre de Psychanalyse et du Psychothérapie*, 8 (1984).

16 See Florence Bégoin-Guignard, 'Le Sourire du chat: Réflexions sur le féminin à partir de la pratique analytique quotidienne', in *Bulletin de la Société Psychanalytique de Paris*, no. 9 (1986), pp. 3–18, and 'A l'aube du

maternel et du féminin: Essai sur deux concepts aussi évidents qu'inconcevables', in *Revue Française de Psychanalyse*, 51 (6) (1987), pp. 1491–503.

17 Freud, 'Femininity' (1933), in SE 22, p. 116.

18 Freud, 'Three essays' (1905), p. 219, note 1.

19 *Ibid., loc. cit.*

20 Freud, 'Femininity', p. 116. Freud maintains an equally critical position on this assimilation of masculine-active and feminine-passive in *Civilisation and its Discontents* (1930), in SE 21, p. 105, note 3.

21 Freud, 'On the sexual theories of children' (1908), in SE 9, pp. 211–12.

22 Freud, 'On transformations of instinct as exemplified in anal eroticism' (1917), in SE 17, p. 128.

23 *Ibid.*, pp. 127–33.

24 See Jean Laplanche, *Castration, symbolisations* (Paris: Presses Universitaires de France, 1980), pp. 56–8.

25 Alain Gibeault, 'Symbolisme inconscient et symbolisme du langage', *Revue Française de Psychanalyse*, 45 (1) (1981), pp. 139–59.

26 Freud, 'Femininity', p. 118.

27 Freud, *Analysis of a Phobia in a Five-year-old Boy* ('Little Hans') (1909), in SE 10, p. 145.

28 Cosnier (*Destins*, p. 43) rightly notes that Freud's insistence on comparing 'the male member and the laughable little clitoris enables a withdrawal of any value or meaning from the difference between the little boy's penis and his father's'. Whence we can see that a masculine scientific theory about woman can refer back to a masculine infantile sexual theory!

29 See Kurt Eissler, 'Comments on penis envy and orgasm in women', in *The Psychoanalytic Study of the Child* 32 (1977), pp. 65–7.

30 Ernest Jones, 'The Early Development of Female Sexuality', in *The International Journal of Psycho-Analysis* (VIII, part 4 (October 1927), pp. 459–72.

31 See Janine Chasseguet-Smirgel, 'Freud et la féminité', note 3 above.

32 Freud, 'Little Hans', p. 128.

33 Cosnier, p. 47.

34 *Ibid.*, p. 211.

35 See Edith Jacobson, *The Self and the Object World* (IUP: New York, 1964).

36 Janine Chasseguet-Smirgel, 'La Féminité du psychanalyste dans l'exercice de son métier', in *Les deux arbres du jardin*, p. 81.

37 Evelyne Kestemberg, '"Astrid", ou homosexualité, identité et adolescence', in *Les Cahiers du Centre de Psychanalyse et de Psychothérapie* 8 (1984), pp. 12–13.

38 Kestemberg, p. 23.

39 Jacobson, E. *The Self and the Object World* (IUP: New York, 1964).

40 Cosnier, p. 210.

41 See Maria Torok, 'La Signification de "l'envie du pénis" chez la femme', in *Recherches psychanalytiques nouvelles sur la sexualité féminine* (Paris: Payot, 1964), pp. 181–219.

42 The opposition between clitoral orgasm and vaginal orgasm, which for Freud again takes up the opposition of masculine and feminine, probably testifies to the dominance of phallic logic and its defensive value. If the vaginal orgasm, in its implied physical and psychical fusion and integration of the clitoral orgasm, can be a goal for the woman's psychosexual development, none the less we know it should not be a criterion for the integration of genital femininity, because it can acquire different values and accompany, for instance, fantasies of castrating the man. The genital sexual function should not, as much for the man as for the woman, be dissociated from invest-ment in an object since, for example, a weak object-investment can promote an adequate genital experience, whereas a more significant object-investment can, on the contrary, inhibit the genital function and make it more vulnerable to feelings of blameworthiness and anxiety. See Kurt Eissler, 'Comments on penis envy and orgasm in women', in *The Psychoanalytic Study of the Child*, 32 (1977), pp. 39–47.

43 Christian David, 'La Bisexualité psychique' (note 4, above), pp. 834–5.

44 Jean Laplanche, *Castration, symbolisations*, p. 84.

45 Cosnier, p. 84.

46 *Ibid.*, p. 168.

47 Kurt Eissler sees in this pair of concepts 'the basic psychobiological entity' enabling an appropriate and adequate definition of masculinity and femininity, without however seeing in them characteristics specific to a single sex. See 'Comments on penis envy', pp. 36–9.

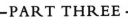

PART THREE

The representation of the body

Introduction

In classical theory, masculinity and femininity refers to the representation of the difference between the sexes centred on the recognition of 'castration'. Femininity is grounded in the representation of a lack. The questioning of phallic monism has lead to a consideration of the role of the girl's body schemata on her psychic apparatus.

In the early 1930s there had already been a recognition of the special role of orality and anality for female sexuality, because of the receptive nature of the oral cavity and because of the proximity of vaginal and anal openings. Helene Deutsch considered orality to be the prototype of genitality. The vagina takes over the role of the mouth. Coitus signifies the restoring of the first relation of unity in which the distinction of subject and object is annulled. Under the stimulus of the penis, the vagina takes over the passive role of the suckling mouth, as was the case in relation to the breast. She distinguishes between a masculine function of the vagina, identified with the penis and active with secretions and contractions like the penis, and 'the truly passive, feminine attitude of the vagina [,] based upon the oral, suckling activity' (Deutsch 1946: 170).

A special place is also given to orality in feminine development by Hans Sachs (1929). He describes oral desires directed towards the father stemming from a 'regression to the oral level, without relinquishment of the Oedipus object'. This tendency to incorporate the father orally 'is a consequence of the vaginal sensations now dimly felt for the first time and displaced to the mouth because they can find no satisfaction in the region of the vagina, which the child has not yet discovered' (p. 45). He suggests that these oral desires are a regular stage in their development through which men do not necessarily pass, and contribute in girls to the formation of the superego through the introjection of the frustrating father.

185

Marjorie Brierley suggests that the female genital impulses which appear during suckling constitute a specific instinctual determinant in feminine development, although she adds that 'what would seem to be specific to women is not any psychic drive as such, but the balance that has to be achieved and maintained in order to produce an integrated feminine personality' (Brierley 1936: 164).

Klein writes that the girl's Oedipus trends are to a far greater extent under the dominance of oral impulses than are those of the boy, and that this greater tendency to take in, to introject will mean that the woman's superego is more severe than the man's. This view is in complete opposition to Freud's, for whom the woman's superego was weaker due to the fact that she did not have to fear castration, put an end to Oedipal strivings and hence identify with a powerful figure. Lampl-de Groot, taking up Freud's view, had even asserted that 'the purely feminine women' have no superego.

Lou Andreas-Salomé was the first to point out the place of anal erotism in femininity, that vaginal pleasure is taken 'on lease' from the cloaca. Freud himself wrote in *New Introductory Lectures* that 'interest in the vagina is also essentially of anal-erotic origin' (1932). Marjorie Brierley made a distinction between anal and urethral sadism, and wrote that 'it is necessary for normal feminine development that the oro-anal system should be stronger than the oro-urethral' (Brierley 1936: 171).

Contemporary work has continued to emphasize the greater connection between genital and anal factors in the girl than in the boy. This is due to their proximity and reciprocal pressures (Kestenberg 1968, Dolto 1965) and to the facility of a displacement from anal erotism to feminine desire and of the representation of an internal sexual organ (Duparc 1986). Oliner also discusses the importance of the anal phase in the girl's development and her problem in integrating anality into genitality (1982). This connection is not necessarily facilitating. I. Bernstein (1983) suggests that the proximity of the genital and rectal-anal area contributes to confusion, uncertainty, and displacement of attitudes about anality to the female genitals with consequent devaluation of the female genitals. D. Bernstein (1990), on the other hand, writes that the anal sphere acquires importance for the female because it is one in which she is able to demonstrate control while she cannot control the vagina. It carries the meaning of power which in boys is distributed between the anal component and the phallic one, a point also made by Klein.

For Helene Deutsch the potential for maternity is central for women and forms part of their sexuality. For Klein too, what is important for the girl is not only having a vagina, but also a uterus and the potential for having a baby. Psychoanalysts more recently have considered the psychological impact of physiological events such as menstruation and maternity (Bibring 1959; Benedek 1960; Breen 1975, 1989a; Pines 1990). This does by no means imply a one-to-one, unmediated relationship between biological events and psychological events, since physiological processes will be lived differently by different women. Dinora Pines also describes the way in which women unconsciously use their body to avoid conflict, through the miscarriage of pregnancy, for instance (1990).

The role of the female anatomy and physiology for ego-functions has also been considered. Erikson was the first to write about the centrality of inner space on females' ego-functions (1964). He observed children at play and discovered that girls and boys used space differently and that certain configurations occurred often in the constructions of one sex and not of the other. Sexual differences in the organization of play space tended to parallel the morphology of genital differentiation. For instance, where girls created house interiors with scenes within that interior, boys built houses with protrusions, towers and exterior scenes. He concluded that 'a profound difference exists between the sexes in the experience of the ground plan of the human body' (Erikson 1964: 273). Donna Bassin (1982) proposes, following Erikson's notion of the female predisposition for the elaboration of inner space, that vaginal sensations and early experiences of inner space contribute to the early constructions of a category of experience, like phallic activity and its representations, which serve as precursors for later cognitive processs. The existence of a bodily schema for productive inner space goes beyond maternal/reproductive functions and, she suggests, we are lacking language categories for the feminine experience outside of woman's biological function, her traditional roles. Doris Bernstein (1990) discusses the role of specific genital anxieties derived from the characteristics of the female genitalia on her psychic development, in the same way that castration anxiety, phallic fantasy is elaborated by boys.

It has been pointed out that Freud's theory relies on the visual experience of sexual difference, but that this is not the only means through which the girl becomes familiar with her genitalia; by the time of the recognition of the anatomical differences, she already is acquainted with her femaleness and female genitalia from proprio-sensory perceptions (Chehrazi 1986; Wilkinson 1991). The special problem afforded the girl in her bodily similarity to the mother which is actualized with puberty has been noted by a number of authors (Breen 1989b). Women struggle with the lifelong task of identification and dis-identification from the internal representation of their mother. A woman has a dual and conflicting task of identifying with her mother's female capacities whilst at the same time emotionally separating from her and taking over responsibility for her own body (Pines 1982).

The two papers in this section emphasize the bodily foundation of masculinity and femininity. Doris Bernstein (1990) considers the role of the representation of the body other than representation of 'lack', of absence of the penis in feminine development. She suggest that the characteristics of the female genitalia give rise to specific modes of mastery and character structures. Mervin Glasser (1985) considers the role of body representation in identificatory processes with the same-sex parent. For Glasser, men's identification with their father has as an essential ingredient the bodily identification with the father, including his penis. He suggests that the fact that the boy's identification with the father is based on bodily aspects while the girl's equally necessary identification with him rests on psychological attributes, will contribute to differences between male and female sexuality.

––––––––––––––– 9 –––––––––––––––

Female genital anxieties, conflicts and typical mastery modes

DORIS BERNSTEIN

In 'Inhibitions, symptoms and anxiety' (1925), an essay that informs all contemporary psychoanalytic thinking, Freud outlined two ways of viewing anxiety. First, he introduced a new theory, signal anxiety; second, he introduced a developmentally based hierarchical conception of anxiety which has the concept of genital anxiety at its apex. Genitality has become a watershed on the path to psychic maturity; the recognition of the differentiation between maleness and femaleness, the attainment of one's own relative wholeness *vis-à-vis* the object and the tolerance for conflict are the rewards of this achievement.

Freud outlined age/phase specific dangers with separation anxiety from the maternal object or figure as the paradigm for subsequent anxieties; he conceptualized phallic phase anxieties differently for boys and girls. For boys, anxiety lay in the threat to their body integrity specifically in castration anxiety (derived from separation from the penis); for girls the danger lay in loss of love of the object (derived from separation from the object). There was no recognition of the role that the girl's own genitals may play in her development or in generating anxiety. Nor does Freud give any recognition to the differences that would follow from such dramatically different formulations: his formulations define the boys' anxieties as much more narcissistically oriented and define the girls' anxieties as much more object-embedded.

One of Freud's most brilliant achievements, and that which differentiates psychoanalysis from other perspectives, is that it unifies psyche and soma. Body and soul, mind and body had in previous psychologies and philosophies been perceived as separated, if not outright antagonistic. Freud achieved a conceptual unity, a comprehensive, complementary interdependence between the body and the psyche; they function as one. Indeed, he elaborated the profound and ongoing impact of the body on

189

the development and functioning of the psyche, on character formation, on critical superego differences (Bernstein 1983) and on relationships with others. Having recognized and included the body's role in psychic development, it is ironic that it should be just one, the male, whose experience has become the model for human psychology, and only the boy's anxieties and developmental crises the model for all human developmental crises.

At no time did Freud consider the impact of the girl's own body on her psychic development. He considered her genital awareness to be limited to her preoccupation with the penis and her body image based on its absence. In describing genital anxiety in 'Inhibitions, symptoms and anxiety', genital is equated with phallus, and the girl's genital is dismissed. 'Where castration has already taken place' (p. 125), anxiety occurs in relation to the object. It is as if she had no genital of her own. Indeed, Freud considered early childhood to be identical for boys and girls until the phallic phase, when the girl's discovery that she lacked the valued penis became the central organizer of her psychic life. He considered her own genitals inert, inactive, unknown, not to be discovered until their maturation in puberty. This position was challenged quite early by analysts. Horney (1924) considered the undiscovered vagina to be a repressed vagina; Mueller (1932), originally a paediatrician, reported girls' early genital interest. Reports of childhood masturbation abound in the literature (see Clower 1976). Kestenberg (1956) has described the ebb and flow of infant girls' genital excitement; Erikson discussed the girl's 'inner space' (1964) as her preoccupation with her inner genital. More recently Stoller (1968) and Money and Ehrhardt (1972) have demonstrated that gender identity is established long before the phallic phase and that there is no evidence to sustain Freud's position that the little girl considers herself '*un homme manqué*'. Despite these observations about little girls' genital awareness and interest, their genital anxiety has always been described as 'castration' anxiety, a legacy of Freud's earlier formulations.

If we do agree that the body is centrally involved in children's psychic development, it seems appropriate that the girl's body, her experiences with it and conflicts about it are as central to her development as the boy's body is to his. As the bodies are different, the nature of the resulting anxieties, the developmental conflicts, the means of resolution and many of the modes of mastery must of necessity be different as well.[1]

These anxieties, conflicts and modes of mastery have a pervasive impact on the resolutions of all childhood developmental tasks, the achievement of separation–individuation, the development of autonomy, the formation of the superego, and the critical identification and resolution of the 'Oedipal crisis' (Bernstein 1983, 1989). A full discussion of these issues is beyond the scope of this paper.

The issues surrounding girls' and womens' reactions to the penis, i.e. penis envy and castration anxiety, are described, documented and elaborated in the psychoanalytic literature. Full discussions abound. Here I will try to separate out the two issues deriving from the role of anatomy in the girl's development. I will attempt to define and explore the impact of her own genitals, assessing their centrality. I will discuss her reactions to the penis only in so far as these reactions affect her integration of her own body image and experience. While several authors (Keiser 1953, 1958; Barnett 1966; Montgrain 1983; Mueller 1932) have addressed female genital anxieties, I am attempting to understand their role in her psychic development, thus viewing her genitals to be as important to her as the boy's genitals are to him. While Roiphe and Galenson (1976) have recently studied toddlers' reactions to the sight of opposite sex genitals, they have viewed their material from the standpoint of a 'genital equals phallic' perspective and have not addressed the issue of integrating the girl's own genitals into her body ego. Their conclusions reaffirm Freud's phallic orientation, although placing the recognition of the differences between the sexes at an earlier age. The timetable is significant since the children studied were between eighteen and twenty-four months old, the same age that Stoller (1968) places for the establishment of core gender identity. Thus, this discovery of genital differences takes place in the traditional anal phase or in the phase of separation–individuation. It is my thesis that the task of integrating one's own genital into one's body image interacts with these other developmental tasks and that some of the anxieties the girl experiences at this time are the result of her struggles with her own body experience. Generally speaking, the female has been described as an open system and the male as a closed system (Kestenberg 1956). In this paper I attempt to explore some of the implications of this formulation.

Access, penetration and diffusivity anxieties

The genital anxieties of girls are not nearly as focused and tidy as boys' anxieties. The boy's penis, with its clearly defined presence, contours, visibility, sensations and vulnerability is quite clear. The girl's genitals differ in every respect. It is my impression, also noted by other observers (Montgrain 1983; Keiser 1953, 1958), that these differences have multiple effects on psychic structuring and forming mental representations that have pervasive influences on female mental functioning.

I do not mean to suggest that 'castration–like' anxieties do not appear in women; these refer to a host of fears and fantasies about lost, damaged or missing parts of the body. I have found these ubiquitous in the analyses of women. However, I have not found that they serve exclusively or even dominantly to describe women's genital anxieties. I am proposing three terms, each of which contains several components and references, a far more complex constellation than 'castration'. Access, penetration and diffusivity seem to describe several clusters of female genital anxieties.

'Access' refers to several different experiences. The girl herself does not have ready access to her genitals; this touches on many levels of experience. She cannot see them as she and the boy can see the boy's genitals. This creates immense difficulty in forming a mental representation of parts of her body in which there are most intense physical sensations. The role of sight in forming mental representations is critical; for example, it has been found that blind children show marked developmental delay in forming body ego/self-images (Kestenberg 1968; Fraiberg 1968).

In addition to the visual difficulty, she does not have complete tactile access to her own genitals; she cannot touch and manipulate them in a desexualized way as can the boy. Hence, she does not acquire tactile, familiar and sensual knowledge of her body that is not forbidden or tied to forbidden fantasies. Moreover, when she does touch her genitals, there is a spread of sensation to other areas; wherever she touches, yet another area is stimulated. Location shifts not only within the genital, from clitoris to vagina, but to pelvis and to urethral and anal sensations as well. This stimulation spread for the girl contrasts with that of the boy, in whom stimulation focuses.

This spread of sensation leads to a second anxiety, that of diffusivity. Development requires the child to define and articulate its body and its world. Touching, seeing, controlling, manipulating and naming (Kleeman 1976) are the equipment with which children build up mental representations of their own bodies, the outer world and their power and control over themselves, people and things. If, indeed, ego is at core a body ego, and body ego is an essential reference to the outer world, the diffuse nature of the girl's genital has a significant impact on the nature of her development. Montgrain (1983) discussed this diffusivity in adult women; he noted a 'general understatement of the overflowing capacity of women's sensuality that escapes the bind of language'. Further, 'the insufficient anchorage is an anatomical reality and has a correlative effect on the symbolic level' (p. 170). Language and imagery are essential for women to build a symbolic world which can be controlled and managed. Under stimulation, the entire apparatus of mind and body is mobilized so that a mind—body interaction that underlies thinking can be reactivated under any stress. It is extraordinary how frequently one hears, in women's analysis, complaints that when they are under stress, particularly intellectual, they cannot 'think straight', their minds blur, they get 'fuzzy', or they experience an incapacity to articulate. One hears equally often that, after an initial 'blank', they are surprised to find how much they really 'know' about a given topic, and how much knowledge they had 'tucked away'. The ordinary senses, sight and touch, are insufficient for girls at this stage of their development. They must rely on additional means, which I will describe fully later as modes of mastery, to articulate and integrate their genitals into their body image.

The third and central cluster of anxieties centres around issues of penetration. The vagina is a body opening over which there is no control over opening or closing as there is with the mouth and anus; girls feel they cannot control access by others or by themselves. The fantasy of the genital as 'hole' is based on the child's experiences with holes in the external world. They are, indeed, passive and inert. Little girls cannot imagine their genitals' functions and co-operation in coital and childbirth experiences: the lubrication and elasticity of her organ is unknown. This contrasts with the boy's awareness of changes in his organ as part of his daily experiences. The penis and testes respond visibly to temperature, tactile and erotic stimulation. Girls experience genital excitement as heat, or an itch or a discomfort, often without awareness of the genesis and often without visible or tactile cause. It is frightening to have an open hole into which things can come and go, and which there is no way to close or open, and no control over access. A derivative appears in a woman, who, angry at her lover, demands the return of her key, so that 'he has no access to me'. Other openings, the mouth and anus, may be drawn into efforts to master the genital.

One implication of the girl's lack of control over access to her genital is awareness that the access can put her into 'penetration' danger. Not only can things go in and come out, but she fears harm from these things. Girls fear damage to their little bodies from the exciting paternal penis. And, very early, they fear damage to their bodies from the babies they long to create.

Girls struggle with definition and boundaries. Boundaries provide definition and immediate access. The imagined penetration carries not only fear of harm but also arouses anxiety about the crossing of the body boundary. Intercourse requires entry to the inside of the body which can threaten newly established or confirmed body integrity.

Two additional anxieties arise during adolescence when the girl is confronted with 'wetness' for which she knows no source (indeed many adult women do not) and menstruation. 'Wetness' necessarily invokes a regressive potential to all the anxieties and conflicts surrounding early bladder and sphincter control, a full discussion of which is beyond the scope of this paper.

It is important to consider the changed timetable for the discovery of anatomical differences and the establishment of gender identity in order fully to appreciate the impact that these anxieties about access, penetration and diffusity have on girls' development and the role that they play in women's psyches.

Stoller has demonstrated rather convincingly that gender identity is established by fifteen to eighteen months of age. Roiphe and Galenson (1976) have noted the recognition and reaction to genital differences at approximately the same time. Hence the discovery and integration of genital differences falls into an already established, though perhaps rudimentary sense of gender identity. These developments take place during the period of development classically considered the anal phase, from Mahler's standpoint, the phase dominated by striving towards separation-individuation. In the realm of cognition, the rapid development of language gives articulated, symbolic form to the developing sense of self and world. In the families of many women with whom I have worked, there is no specific name given to the female genitals (see Silverman 1981; Lerner 1976). Phrases like 'down there', 'boopee', 'hokee' describe the entire genito-urinary anatomy. One woman assures me that in her language (a sophisticated Indian dialect), no word for the female genital exists whereas there is a word for the penis.

The integration of genital differences has an impact on all the developmental tasks and particularly complicates the process of separation-individuation for girls. All the genital anxieties I have just described bring unique problems to phase-specific struggles. The separation–individuation struggle is played out in two directions – in relation to the girl's own body and in relationship to her mother. This interplay affects the girl's efforts at mastery. It is my impression that the achievement and maintenance of separation–individuation is the central development issue for girls.

Female mastery efforts

This variety of specific female anxieties focusing on issues of access, control and definition is central to the developmental task of achieving individuation. There seem to be specific developmental efforts at mastery that are typical in female development. These are different from the mastery efforts in boys and not aberrations of them. Roiphe and Galenson(1976) have noted differences in boys' and girls' reactions to their observations of genital differences. 'The boys reflected the effect of the genital emergence in their choice of those toys and play activities which are usually considered typically masculine, and in the onset of a mild degree of hyperactivity. Furthermore, their masturbation was continued and fairly vigorous from then on.' They describe this as 'low incidence of overt reaction'. By

194

contrast, 'all 35 girls in our research sample showed a definite and important reaction to the discovery ... and eight ... developed extensive castration reactions' (pp. 46–7). First, I think it is incorrect to describe these boys as having a 'low incidence of overt reaction'; it is more correctly characterized as a more uniform and specific reaction. Their concern is clearly with the penis; their reaction is active, stimulating, in control, self-reassuring and perhaps even counterphobic. This *is* their attempt at mastery over anxieties aroused by genital differences. The activity observed was paralleled by an increase in identification with their fathers. Rather than characterize the girls as having important reactions while the boys had none, it would seem more accurate to describe these reactions as quite different.

The girl is confronted with a different task – she must comprehend, integrate and locate what is beyond sight, touch, focus and control. I am suggesting that she mobilizes specific mechanisms to perform this task.

The internal, spreading quality of her sensation quickly and automatically arouses anal and urethral confusion. Roiphe and Galenson report observing oral-regressive behaviour, anal-zone exploration and masturbation. I view these turns to these zones not only as regressive but also as a potential turn to modes of mastery. Manipulation, opening and closing and control of access, holding in are all possible in these body areas.

The following material illustrates the ways in which our usual ways of organizing material can distract us from other essential aspects. The 'phallic equals genital' formulation informs both Parens *et al.*'s (1976) and Roiphe and Galenson's (1976) work, masking the girl's own genital anxiety about being open and her need to feel in control. Parens described this in his report of 2½-year-old Candy (pp. 88–9), who, after exposure to sex differences, became markedly preoccupied with a hole in her sock, troubled, distressed, tried to make the hole go away. When her mother sewed up the hole, Parens described her as seeming relieved and able to leave her preoccupation and join other children in play.

Following this incident, Candy, although previously toilet trained began having accidents, in which she wetted and then suffered much distress and shame. She then reached for and clung to a large doll, and then showed concern about broken things and wanted only whole crackers. She then 'sought the help of her mother and staff to effect a return of her toileting controls' (pp. 88–9). This description was considered by Parens to be 'ample' evidence that Candy was in the phallic phase. What this seems to describe more accurately is that Candy was preoccupied with a hole that she could not close, that this led to regressive wetting that she could not control and anxiety about things being intact. There is not reported in this material a particular fear of loss of something or damage to her body that would warrant the interpretation of phallic anxiety nor does there seem to be any justification for describing this as her genito-urinary concerns, i.e. her *castration complex*. *They are not the same*. After her turn to her mother for help in regaining control, 'ample genital masturbation emerged' (pp. 88–9). Anxiety aroused an array of reactions in Candy; mastery had to precede the pleasure – here a much more complicated route than for the boy, involving *confusion, regression, loss of control, pain, a turn to others* before a resynthesis, including the genitals, permitted the emergence of genital pleasure that was so readily, directly available to boys. Parens' description seems to support the complexity of the girl's task; 'castration' does not do justice to the richness of the girl's experience.

Similar issues are illustrated in the dream of an adult woman during analysis. This woman has particular difficulty in articulating her genital experiences. Raised in a very strict Catholic boarding school, she was trained to dress and undress without looking at or touching her own or other girls' bodies. The prepubescent and adolescent activities of self and mutual exploration, mirror looking, etc., were all suppressed as were the infantile sexual explorations in her repressive home.

She dreamt that *there was a snake in her apartment; she was scared and didn't know where it was, feared that it would 'touch her. There was a woman psychologist in a wheelchair but the patient was not sure she could help since she had some kind of illness or disability*. I interpreted as follows: she was frightened of having her husband 'touch her' sexually and she was worried whether I, a woman whom she saw as a weak, disabled creature, would be able to help her with her fear, which focused on the fact that she didn't know where 'it' was. The patient, who had been quite depressed and listless, came to the next session with the first smile seen in two years of work, and with a twinkle told me of a sudden renewed interest in the stock market, of some trades she had made in the intervening day, of her contemplating buying a seat on a new exchange that was opening that she would *control*, but not necessarily use herself, and earn money by renting the seat to others who wanted to trade. Her movement was clearly to a position in which she did not feel helpless, but could control, manipulate and enjoy; clearly she resurrected an anal position. To have focused on her perception of me as castrated and disabled would have put the two of us together in a helpless heap. She was afraid, not only of her husband's penis, but of sex in her own body. Would I be able to help her with the scary sex that she couldn't see and that could dart out from anywhere?

Like Candy, frightened by the invisible sexuality, she regressed to a mode in which she had already established control (her old interest in the stock market) and turned to an object (the analyst) to help her in establishing not only control but pleasure. For Candy, for my patient, for all little girls, this threatening temporary disorganization must be tolerated by the mother, and the subsequent forward movement towards erotic investment must be welcomed both by mother and father.

Debby, a 24–year-old woman in psychoanalytic therapy, demonstrates a confluence of several of these issues. Unable to have sexual intercourse for five years, following a half-dozen experiences in college that were relatively successful but accompanied by some bleeding, she broke dates, stayed at home and had eating binges. She described her genitals as a 'mystery' and felt that they were damaged, concretized in the memory of a bicycle accident before menarche at the age of 12. She had fallen off her bike into a split with vaginal bleeding. The accident and subsequent medical examination were painful, but there was no medical damage. Nevertheless, the memory came up repeatedly as proof of a damaged state. She became sexually aroused on dates, but then tightened her genitals and felt 'no one can enter me, I am too tight'. Attempts at intercourse were indeed unsuccessful. Her mother had warned Debby against sexual activity until marriage so that she could have control over the man. Her mother also told her not to buy the fur coat she wanted, to wait and let a man buy her one. The therapist began to focus her interventions on Debby's being in control of her pleasures rather than things being done to her or for her. A visit to a gynaecologist for a diaphragm brought associations to worries that her hole is not big enough to have anything go in and a disbelief that her vagina could stretch to accommodate either penis or baby. She watched in the mirror as she practised with the diaphragm, but still was anxious about not seeing her 'insides'. The therapist empathized with her longing to see but encouraged her to define her sensations by feel and touch. Throughout this period (about three months) there was a weight loss of about 8 pounds and a sense of stabilization about food, although neither had come up for manifest work.[2] The therapist interpreted her weight loss in terms of her efforts to control her other opening, her vagina. The therapist worked simultaneously on issues of separation from her mother; Debby recognized her own difficulties in feeling separate from her mother when there was disagreement between them. The confluence occurred when she had successful, pleasurable intercourse, she in a new position, on top (more in control). She longed to run and tell mother but did not act. The focus on her control of her own body, her genital, led her to integrate both sex and food with a sense of mastery and separateness from her mother.

The material I have just described focuses on the efficacy of regression and identification in achieving mastery over the elusive genital and the contribution this can make in developing a sense of mastery. There are other mechanisms girls use for dealing with the internal confusion, some potentially considerably less adaptive. While all the mechanisms I am

197

describing here are also found in boys, it is because they carry an extra burden for the girl in her development that I am emphasizing them in this context.

Renunciation of sexuality (Jacobson 1964) is another mechanism utilized by girls when confronted with sexuality and unsatisfactory pre-genital development to support the new demand. The girl who renounces sexuality often turns into a character type we often meet, who is her boss's right arm, her father's nurse, a woman who has an intense but desexualized relationship to (usually) an older man (Chasseguet-Smirgel 1970).

Another of the mechanisms for mastery of this internal body confusion is *externalization*, elaborated by Kestenberg (1956). Onto the doll, which is already a beloved baby and self, is projected erotic investment. Kestenberg finds that play changes to genital-urethral preoccupation; there is more bathing, wiping, examining in contrast to earlier feeding and cuddling. Girls externalize onto other objects. They develop preoccupation with manipulating and collecting crayons and pens (sometimes father's). While this preoccupation is considered to be a manifestation of a penis envy response to genital differences (Roiphe and Galenson 1976; Kestenberg 1956, 1968), I would emphasize a different interpretation of the search for manipulable objects. I see this behaviour as an extension of the need for concretization, control and mastery of the undefined as demonstrated by the fantasy frequently found clinically: 'I have a penis, one will grow, it is hidden inside.'

Penis envy and fantasy penises can be conceptualized as extremely adaptive fantasies in the girl *at this time*. Confronted with intense sensations in the genital area, to see the boy's penis and think, 'ah, that's what causes these sensations' is a sensible and imaginative fantasy that can bring order to chaos. As with other childhood fantasies, it should be reworked and absorbed in the process of normal development. The presence and use of the fantasy varies. For example, an adult female patient had a dream

I am riding in a car with a man and am growing more and more sexually aroused. I look down at my crotch and see an erect penis. I think to myself, 'how else will he know that I am sexy?'

A pregnant woman, who had just associated to penises said, 'It's just so nice to think something solid that you can imagine is in there. It's always so vague to think about my vagina.' The penis may become an object of covetousness because its fantasied possession is a coherent, cognitive, adaptive explanation for multiple-sensations. In fact, there are times when it seems that 'having a penis' means having sexuality itself — as a concrete, visible, boundaried word concept. Having a concrete image and a word, i.e., language, is an essential part of the ego development that children undergo at this time and the acquisition of language is inherent and intrinsically linked to the child's ability to manipulate images and ideas. The fantasies which should be transient during the early genital and phallic phases can become central and the girl can be unable to absorb them. What should be transient becomes fixed, leading to either manifest or covert phallic feminine organization and to a girl who lacks access to her femininity.

A, an accomplished professional woman, always felt a fraud. Analysis revealed the common unconscious equation of 'brains equals penis'. Intense envy coloured relationships with male colleagues who seemed to her to be able to think and work easily and without conflict, and with great conviction of the value of all their utterances. During a session she described all that she admired and envied in a male colleague — his height, his agility, his strength, his clear thinking, his clear lectures. She complained bitterly how much she envied all these attributes. I pointed out one significant omission that really differentiated them, namely his penis, the lack of which in her experience gave her thoughts and lectures a feeling of inauthenticity. She responded by saying she could never relinquish her 'phallic' brain and her competitiveness; without them, what would motivate her in her work? After a few minutes silence, she reported an image of a baby sitting in a corner of a playpen: I asked her what the baby was doing. Her response was that the baby was biting the wooden bars; her mother often told her she had done that. I responded by saying that I thought she was answering her own question; she didn't need a fantasy penis, she could 'sink her teeth' into a problem, she was not lacking instruments for mastery.

An illustration of a woman's concerns appears in the dreams of a 40-year-old woman in analysis who had been commenting upon her recent and unusual lack of interest in sex, and complaining about her lover's frequent interest.

I have a wound on my hand. I have been bitten – several bites – but it's not bleeding. It becomes like a slash – I can see inside – the tissue, the tendon – there is a skin graft done – two pieces in front, one in back of it – one from me – one brown skin – it all fits beautifully – very clean and tidy – but the two men helping are not being careful to be antiseptic. If they are not careful, there will be infection. The next scene is funny. There is this machine examining the inside of a toilet bowl – I think 'hey, this thing is an X-ray machine' – I can hold up my hand [she holds up the same one she used to illustrate the bite/slash] and you can see the inside – then I put my head in front of it and you can see the inside but what is clear are the lips, which seem very bright red.

199

This is a complex dream; I present it because of the many elements of anxiety expressed. The bite, the dirt, the slash, the men who are not careful, the machine which 'sees' but can be dangerous. As we can gather from 'it's not bleeding', the patient comments that she is menstruating at this time. In addition, in both dream scenes, *one can see inside*; this element repeats in relation to the hand wound, the inside of the toilet bowl, again with the X-ray, the hand and the head. An analysis of all elements is of course necessary. It would be an error to focus only upon the obvious — the patient herself commented, 'I know that the slash is equated with the vagina — that's so classic' with little concern, affect or conviction. My noting how frequently in the dream she was *looking* and could see inside, brought forth more intense feelings. It is of note that this woman, a physician, had recently been expressing worry about not identifying organs correctly during surgery, an anxiety for which there had been no reality base as her familiarity with anatomy is in no way deficient. The patient had begun a menstrual period the prior day, was casual about birth control and somewhat concerned about her fertility. Her dream responds, 'There is no blood, the bites are easily repaired, how clean, how tidy! All is well.' The dream illustrates the confluence of material drawn into genital anxiety and the varied mechanisms attempted to master it; prominent is her wish to see, which must be given equal attention with the more familiar interpretation that she feels her genitals are wounded. This (not incorrect but incomplete) interpretation leaves the female in the helpless condition so often attacked by critics of castration anxiety as central for women. That the very *looking* may be dangerous (the X-ray machine) demonstrates that looking has taken on the familiar dangers of infantile sexuality, to be sure, but again to focus only on the dangers of looking does injustice to her attempt to master her anxiety. Her need to see and know what is inside must be dealt with as positive and adaptive; this woman suffers from feeling insufficiently in control. She often complains (in this session too) that her brain melts and she cannot keep ideas straight. Being able to see and identify is an important element of mastery.

The following week, this same patient presented another dream, this one illustrating the need for control over access:

I had one of my house dreams [these were varied]. There is a big old fashioned kind of Victorian house with windows all around – like a porch – not like Joe's father's – modern and sleek. I am worried about getting locks, it's so open all around. Then I get the locks and somehow you have to put the locks in a fruit, it turns into a puddle, a muddy dirty puddle.

Here the beautiful house is in danger as a result of its lovely, gracious openness. Anxiety over being able to secure entry (the lock) appears (the house is not like the man's). The genital reference is made clear by the fruit, which she describes as very soft and juicy. The fruit turns into the dirty, muddy hole, i.e. the genital is experienced in anal imagery, *but that is where the lock is* in this patient's dream, i.e., where the sphincter has control.

The confusion of anal and genital has long been noted in analytic literature. The vagina is often experienced as dirty, due to the internal location which easily leads to equating the vagina with the rectum. The confusion is reinforced by the diffusion of sensation, amply demonstrated by cloacal theories of childbirth. While all of this is familiar to us, what I wish to introduce as an additional and important factor for the female is that the anal sphere is one in which the female has been able to demonstrate 'control'. It therefore carries meaning of power which, in boys, is distributed between the anal component and the phallic ones.

While girls have long been described as neater, cleaner and more easily toilet-trained, I am proposing that an independent source of this develop-ment derives spontaneously from the girl's need to master and integrate genital anxieties, that the internal nature of the genital connects with anality, and genital excitement redoubles her need to exercise control. This occurs independently from influences of the relationship with her mother.

Inherent conflicts

In the preceding discussion of what I consider to be typically female efforts at mastery of genital anxieties, I did not elaborate the inherent conflicts involved in each attempt at mastery. It is essential to realize that these efforts are not simple, harmonious experiences. One predominant element, the reliance on the mother, is occurring within a relationship fraught with difficulties inherent in the age. A relationship of trust is essential: the girl must rely on her mother's reassurance that her genital is, indeed, inside (Keiser 1953). 'Seeing is believing' gives concrete reality to boys' definition whereas girls must integrate their genital on a sense of faith; she must 'know' it without evidence and must trust her mother's explanation.[3]

The girl's need for her mother to help her master her genital anxieties occurs during the same period in which the natural thrust of develop-ment calls for a turn away from her in the service of the task of separation-individuation. Viewed from a libidinal perspective, this is the period in which children are struggling for 'control' over their own bodies and often are engaged in a power struggle with their mothers. Two of the specific genital anxieties repeat and intensify anxieties already inherent in development conflicts. The turn to mother threatens re-engulfment, requires a 'yes' (I am like you) when autonomous strivings require a 'no'. Hence, the ambivalence and intensity of battles between mother and daughter, the clinging and fighting, are fuelled from multiple sources long before rivalry for father is an issue.

Not only must the little girl turn to her mother in her mastery efforts, she also must, like the little boy with his father, form an identification with her as a female. Kleeman (1976) has pointed out the importance role labelling plays in organizing the child's gender identity, and language begins to play a major role in organizing the world during this same period. This very organizing function, that of being female like mother, important for the integration of genital and gender experiences, threatens the task of individuation, which requires being different from mother. Moreover, every identification is built upon older experiences (Reich 1954), so that the resurrection of the earliest, symbiotic primary identification and diffusivity threatens the ego's struggle for definition. This reverberation between genital anxieties and symbiotic anxieties contributes to the girl's difficulty in articulating boundaries; diffusivity and control issues are pervasive.

The interaction between control of her body and differentiation from the mother is demonstrated by a woman who dreamt

of a building in which she was anxiously trying to secure the doors and window, barring entry.[4]

The associations merited the interpretation that the invasion (her dream word) she feared was genital and that she was trying to secure control over genital entry. Associations to a rape during adolescence confirmed the interpretation and the patient felt relieved of a sullen recalcitrance that had characterized her mood during several sessions. She said she really felt 'understood' and left feeling lightened. She opened the following session with 'I can't give you any credit for my feeling better, you'll make it all yours', a theme often demonstrated in this treatment by chronic complaints that mother always took over her feeling.[5] She again described her inability to have anything good because mother takes it, feeling it more than the patient herself. Associations to the recent illness of her boyfriend reiterated her blurring of boundaries in that his pain became her pain. The whole issue of psychic boundaries flowed from the anxiety about body boundaries.

While there has been a current trend, primarily in academic psychology, sociology and among some psychoanalysts to idealize the mother–daughter tie, it does not reflect accurately the struggles that emerge in the analytic situation, where intense ambivalence seems to predominate. The longing and fear of being one with mother parallel the wish to be like her and both parallel the wish to be different. Whichever way the girl turns at this point, anxiety is generated.

Derivatives of this position seem to present themselves in adult women during pregnancy. A new genital anxiety confronts pregnant women and one hears all the infantile anxieties; women fear damage to their bodies from the forthcoming childbirth, they cannot imagine their body's participation and they fear the pain. They feel an urgency about being close to their mothers but simultaneously push them away. They wish to merge with their forthcoming infants but often structure their lives so as to ensure not becoming immersed in the maternal experiences, as one woman put it, 'being lost in the swamp' of motherhood. As in early childhood, in pregnancy one witnesses all the inner confusion, the regression to other modes of control (sometimes in work, sometimes controlling husband or others by making demands), before some balance of identifications and differentiation from their own mothers is integrated with the physical experience. During pregnancy, fantasies of an internal penis are resurrected as a concretization of the unknown experience. In recent years, several women who have had ultrasound scans during their pregnancies have been delighted about the concretization given by the visual experience of 'seeing' their foetuses. Despite all the explicit educational material available to women, the mysteriousness of what is going on inside their bodies seems to me to reflect that early undefined mysteriousness. One woman enacted the search for concretization by looking closely into the mirror and finding, that if she looked closely, she could 'see' something of her genital. Another revealed the use of a pen for masturbation, describing the need and pleasure in defining her genital experience.

In a case presented to illustrate some of the developing girl's difficulties, Silverman (1981) illustates the confluence of anxieties. Faith demonstrates the symbolic use of the penis as an instrument of control over what can come out of her body. If she had one of those, she could see, touch and, although not manifestly stated, show her 'overalls'. The little girl, Faith, had a boot fetish (worn whenever she left home) and, when excited, wet herself. At 6½ she was insufficiently differentiated from her mother so that she was unable to attend nursery school. Analysis of the fetish revealed two components: Boots was the name of a cat

> whom mother continually threatened to send away because periodically it went round the house spraying the furniture ... living in terror that she herself would be sent away for her own wetting, Faith had contrived to keep Boots with her in one form or other at all times.
> (p. 591)

Recalling her wetting led to the second insight.

She had watched her mother watering the garden and had seen that she *controlled* [italics mine] the stream with something, a nozzle, that very much resembled her brother's penis. If only she had had one of those she told me, she would have been able to *control* [my italics] her urinary stream and would have been able to avoid all her consterna- tion and misery.

(p. 591)

Silverman interprets this material as an example of penis envy and genital confusion. After considerable work in this direction, Silverman made the interpretation to Faith that she wanted what her brother Frank had. Again I quote:

'That's right!' she shouted, and she pounded the table with her fist. 'I want my overalls *outside* like he has. He can *see* his overalls. He can *touch* his overall. I can't see mine. I can't touch mine. I don't *know* myself.' After this the fetish was given up.

(p. 591)

I find this case an extraordinary example of the girl's proccupations. Her needs to have access, to concretize, to control and to retain her object are all expressed in the boots. Here penis envy is clearly metaphor (Grossman and Stewart 1976) for her own concerns over mastery through sensory modes and demonstrates the interaction between body integrity and the developmental task of individuation. While Silverman does not elaborate, we can assume that the relinquishing of the fetish was accom- panied by an increment in psychic individuation and that she became more capable of leaving her own mother as a result. Some resolution of conflicts over mastering her own body diminished anxiety and enabled her to relinquish dependency on an object (Boots/mother/penis), i.e., to effect separation. Her anxiety over genitals that were beyond voluntary sensory control kept her dependently clinging to her mother.

Mastery over the body is a central issue as toddlers attempt individua- tion and autonomy. The issues I have been describing seem to be central for little girls. While the separation–individuation struggle is predominantly an issue between the girl and her mother, fathers play a significant role that has been underestimated. Fathers have not been seen as significant in the first two years of life; they seem to appear as 'knights in shining armour' in the toddler phase and become fully important only during the Oedipal phase.

Recent research finds infants particularly like the father's low voice at 28 weeks; Mohaczy (1968) found a mild stranger reaction only where the fathers were not actively interacting with their infants. Abelin(1971) found precursors of attachments to fathers very early; all but one of the infants studied recognized the father with a happy smile before six months and all were firmly attached to their fathers by nine months. The girls he observed attached themselves earlier and more intensely than boys did.

In Abelin's studies, during the toddler phase, most relevant to this discussion, toddlers' relationships with their fathers were markedly different from those with their mothers. The relationship with fathers were filled with 'wild exuberance'; fathers appeared a 'stable island'; while mothers were ambivalently cathected. Fathers were not experienced as rivals at a time when other children were experienced as rivals for mother's attention. A few weeks following the *rapprochement* crisis, father images were evoked in play, stories and pictures when children were distressed with their mothers. Abelin suggests the resolution of the separation-individuation struggle might be impossible for both mother and child without having father to turn to. Brooks and Lewis's (1979) findings that fifteen-month-olds were able to identify their fathers from a picture, but none was able to identify the mother, stresses the importance of difference in the forming of articulated images.

Chasseguet-Smirgel (1970) has recognized the importance of fathers to girls in their attempts to separate from mothers. Viewing the struggle as saturated with aggression, fathers emerge as those with power over mother. In fantasy, the girl seizes the father's penis to find power against her image of the angry, controlling mother (created by the projection of her own rage), and subsequently the tie to her father is coloured by her guilt towards him for having castrated him. The research on early development I described above suggests the existence of a more benign relationship with her father (the stable island). The father as a reliable resource is as important, if not more so, to girls as he is to boys, since girls must rely more than boys do on others to effect separation. Since her own anatomy cannot help her, the girl's mastery requires a turn to objects for both support and identifications. I will not here elaborate the conflicts inherent in this relationship (see Bernstein 1989); at this early stage it seems to be relatively non-conflictual for children of both genders; I wish to stress the ongoing object embeddedness in the girl's development.

Vignettes from a two-year period of an analysis illustrate the inter-action between mastering female genital anxieties and individuation, and the reliance on others to achieve this. Miss C dreamt

> *she was in her bedroom and there were two heavy doors to give her safety; but high above was a small open transom window she could not lock, leaving her vulnerable.*

This imagery, which I discussed earlier, is always expressive of multiple anxieties including genital ones. In this case the genital anxieties of access and penetration, and relationship issues involving an intrusive mother and domineering powerful men converge in the attempt to achieve individuation. The patient's associations at this time led her to never having privacy or being able to make her own decisions, and to her cultural world in which men indeed had all the power and women were expected peaceably to submit to all their wishes, including sexuality. To interpret solely along the lines of her fear and helplessness about someone entering would not be helpful because the issues involved individuation and autonomy as well. Note that in this dream the patient is quite alone, the only condition in which she has any measure of safety. During the subsequent two years of analytic work, several themes were developed. One of the prominent ones was what I (Bernstein 1979) have called a forbidden identification with the powerful grandfather who lived in and dominated her childhood home. This forbidden identification deprived her of a satisfactory route out of the immersion with her mother and the preparatory familiarity (Glover and Mendell 1982) that would help her into a comfortable relationship with men. Some work on her fear of this unconscious identification led to the transference dream that

> she was driving her doctor's car around, having a wonderful time, although somewhat anxious that she did not have permission to take it.

This anxiety reflects both what I have called a forbidden identification and Chasseguet-Smirgel's description of the guilt-ridden sign of the father's power. The next dream that took place in that same room illustrated her fear of being overwhelmed not only by a man but by her own powerful sexual impulses: she dreamt that

> the ceiling was wide open and everything could come pouring in.

The door, as image, reappeared following some interest in an appropriate man during the analyst's vacation:

> 'A man is trying to get in the door, it is not locked. I turn to this woman in a rage, screaming "Why are you not helping me?"'

A proper rage at her own mother, whose passivity in all things left my patient unaided in her feminine development, was now alive in the transference. As work progressed along these lines of interpretation, the patient dreamt that

> she was trying to get from one floor to another on an elevator, but there was no control panel. She finally found a cleaning woman who helped her.

Association led to a maid who in childhood had washed the patient's hair, and, with further exploration, to memories that she bathed her, including her genitals. My interpretation that she felt she had no control panel but had to rely on others to master her body experiences finally led to the concretization of these anxieties in a dream in which

a bicycle or motorcycle went from between her legs straight at her mother,

with all the overdetermination of that image. These themes in this patient's analysis illustrate several of the issues under discussion: the need to feel in control of her own body sexually as well as in relation to others, her need for a paternal identification to precede sexual involvement and the need for her mother to support her in her sexuality. The wish to control her own body (space) carries both referents of psychic autonomy and body integrity.

There are implications for psychoanalytic and psychotherapeutic technique that have been implicitly suggested in the material that I have presented: here I would like to make them explicit. Viewing female anxieties as unique leads to a variety of issues central to the developing self. The girl's genital anxieties parallel other anxieties characteristic of the early stages of development. One of the most important mechanisms available to her is that of identification, itself a natural mode for both girls and boys in mastering the developmental conflicts of the age. Turning to her mother to help her master anxiety, she is faced with anxiety emanating from the very identification she needs to consolidate. Anxiety arises from conflicts over regression vs. progression; identification vs. differentiation; dependency vs. autonomy; control vs. helplessness. Unlike identifications with father, for both boys and girls, the identifications with mother are dangerous because of the early relationship which is resurrected when the more advanced identifications are being made.

If one interprets the conflicts in these terms, the women will find sources for mastering their anxiety and resolving their conflicts, a far different aim from that of helping them 'accept' a castrated state and settle for substitutes. Female resolution may lead to a wider range of solutions than we are accustomed to seeing in the male; A reached control over anality (money and entry, she will decide who can sit in the seat *she* owns); B will 'sink her teeth' gleefully into many of life's problems and intellectual pursuits without feeling a fraud; D has taken control over her own pleasures, sexual as well as others. All girls must find a way of resolving the anxiety aroused by the necessary identifications with their mother on whom they must rely far more than is necessary for boys. This object embeddedness has long been considered the hallmark of feminine character (Gilligan 1983).

Conclusion

I have tried to illustrate that girls' genital anxieties derive from the characteristics of the female genitalia and to identify some of these anxieties.

Her fears, anxieties and psychic fantasies must be explored in relation to her own body in the same way that castration anxiety, phallic preoccupation and fantasy must be elaborated for boys. As the nature of the genitals and genital anxieties are different, of necessity, the mechanisms for mastering them differ also.

Here, I have identified three interrelated anxieties: access, penetration and diffusivity. I am suggesting that the girl's experience with the unfocused, open, penetrable nature of her genital creates difficulties in forming mental representations of her body that have clear boundaries and sharp definition. Further, I suggest that this unfocused representation of the genitals complicates the formation of ego boundaries and a firm sense of self, and contributes to both the mental and body issues of which women complain; they describe mental 'fuzziness' in trying to think and complain of fluid body images (see Lerner 1976).

Attempts at mastery include externalization, concretization, regression and, unique to the girl, a greater reliance on others than for boys. She must rely on trust, dependency and identification, quite different from the boy's directly sensory modes: visual, tactile, manipulable. This, in turn, contributes to the object embeddedness of the girl's existence, so long an observed female characteristic.

The timetable for integrating gender and the body into the emerging self is complicated because she must turn to her mother at the time that development of autonomy requires a turn away from her. Critical identifications with her father are as important to the girl at this stage as they have always been considered to be for boys. Fathers have a dual role at this point; the girl requires both his affirmation of her femininity and his welcoming identifications with him.

It is not possible here to discuss the girl's Oedipal phase (see Bernstein 1989), only to suggest that the fantasies at this time are an overlay of the earlier ones and the preferred modes of mastery again appear. If the girl has been able to integrate her early genital anxieties, identify with her mother, be at one with her in her femaleness *and* simultaneously, identify with a father who sees her as female but facilitates identification with him securing her difference from her mother, then she is developmentally in a position to enter the fraught rivalrous nature of the Oedipal, bear the fears and disappointments of that phase and arrive at true genitality.

Summary

This paper focuses on the female experience of her own body, the unique anxieties that arise from the nature of the female genitals and the role of the female body in female development. Following Freud's theories of the importance of integrating body experiences in the development

208

of psychic structures, the girl's body and her efforts to integrate it are seen as uniquely feminine.

Three anxieties are described – access, penetration and diffusivity. These represent dangers to body integrity comparable to, but different from, boys' experience of castration anxiety. Not only do different genitals give rise to different anxieties, the different body experiences give rise to different modes of mastery (defence), shaping different character structures.

While males can readily form discrete, concrete mental representations of their genitals, females cannot. While the boy can rely on direct sensory experience, the developing girl must rely on proprioceptive experiences, symbolization, and on other people to aid her in defining her elusive genital experience. This interpretation of the female genital experience provides a psychoanalytic framework for the object embeddedness long observed as part of the feminine character.

Notes

1 I am using the phrase 'modes of mastery' to describe the engagement and integration of developmental tasks. Like crawling, drinking from the cup, walking and acquiring language, integrating the body image, including the genitals, into the psyche is a necessary developmental achievement. 'Defence' is the more usual psychoanalytic term, but always implies danger and conflict. While any developmental task, particularly the integration of the genitals into the self-image, can become conflictual, thereby motivating defence, I do believe there are aspects of each task which are conflict free (Hartmann 1939), simply requiring integration into the ongoing developmental process. 'Mastery' seems to me a more appropriate word to describe aspects of developmental integration than 'defence'.

2 A colleague with whom I have discussed this material has found it useful clinically to interpret the oral disturbance in terms of vaginal control issues.

3 Proprioceptive and vascular sensations occur spontaneously but can be either repressed or integrated: parental support is critical for integration to occur.

4 In my experience, female patients of all ages dream quite frequently of anxiety about entry through doors and windows. Standard interpretation would be about sexual anxiety. I have found that interpretation of the anxiety being over control of the opening to be efficacious in mastery of that anxiety. It makes a big difference whether the patient's fear that she is invadable is confirmed or if her wish for control is confirmed.

5 Such problems are more acute when mothers over–identify with their children as did A's mother or are generally intrusive. Mothers seem to be in this position more frequently with their daughters than with their sons. I think the reflection from the genital to psychic is inherent in girls although it can be made more difficult by particular kinds of mothering.

References

Abelin, E.L. (1971). The role of the father. In *The Separation-Individuation Process*. ed. J.B. McDevitt & C.G. Settlage. New York: Int. Univ. Press. pp. 229–52.

Barnett, M.C. (1966). Vaginal awareness in the infancy and childhood of girls. *J. Amer. Psychoanal Assn.*, 14: 129–41.

Bernstein, D. (1979). Female identity synthesis. In *Career and Motherhood*, ed. A. Roland and B. Harris. New York: Human Sciences Press, pp. 104–23.

—— (1983). The female superego: a different perspective. *Int. J. Psychoanal.*, 64: 187–201.

—— (1989). The female Oedipus complex. In *Personal Myth and Theoretical Streaming*, ed. I. Graham. New York: Int. Univ. Press, in press.

Brooks, G. and Lewis, M. (1979). *Social Cognition and the Acquisition of Self.* New York and London: Plenum Press.

Chasseguet-Smirgel, J. (1970). Feminine guilt and the Oedipus complex. In *Female Sexuality*, ed. J. Chasseguet-Smirgel. Ann Arbor, Mich.: Univ. Michigan Press.

Clower, V.L. (1976). Theoretical implications in current views on masturbation in latency girls. *J. Amer. Psychoanal. Assn.*, 24 (suppl.): 109–25.

Erikson, E. (1964). Reflections on womanhood. *Daedalus*, 2: 582–606.

Fraiberg, S. (1968). Parallel and divergent patterns in blind and sighted infants. *Psychoanal. Study child.* 23: 264–300.

Freud, S. (1924). Dissolution of the Oedipus complex, S.E. 19.

—— (1925). Inhibitions, symptoms and anxiety. S.E. 20.

Gilligan, C. (1983). *In a Different Voice*. Cambridge. Mass.: Harvard Univ. Press.

Glover, L. and Mendell, D. (1982). A suggested developmental sequence for a preoedipal genital phase. In *Early Female Development: Current Psychoanalytic Views*, ed. D. Mendell. New York: Spectrum Publications Inc.

Grossman, W.I. and Stewart, W.A. (1976). Penis envy: from childhood wish to developmental metaphor. *J. Amer. Psychoanal. Assn.*, 24: 193–212.

Harley, M. (1971). Some reflections on identity problems in prepuberty. In *The Separation-Individuation Process*, ed. J.B. McDevitt & C.G. Settlage. New York: Int. Univ. Press.

Hartmann, H. (1939). *Ego Psychology and the Problem of Adaptation*. New York: Int. Univ. Press, 1958.

Horney, K. (1924). On the genesis of the castration-complex in women. *Int. J. Psychoanal.*, 5: 50–65.

Jacobson, E. (1964). *The Self and the Object World*. New York: Int. Univ Press.

Keiser, S. (1953). Body ego during orgasm. *Yearbook of Psychoanal.* 9: 146–57.

—— (1958). Disturbances in abstract thinking and body image formation. *Yearbook of Psychoanal.*, 6: 628–52.

Kestenberg, J. (1956). Vicissitudes of female sexuality. *J. Amer. Psychoanal. Assn.*, 4: 453–76.

—— (1968). Outside and inside, male and female. *J. Amer. Psychoanal. Assn.*, 16: 457–520.

—— (1976). Regression and reintegration in pregnancy. *J. Amer. Psychoanal. Assn.*, 24: 213–50.

Kleeman, J.A. (1976). Freud's early views. *J. Amer. Psychoanal. Assn.*, 24: 3–27.

Lerner, H. (1976). Parental mislabelling of female genitals as a determinant of penis envy and learning inhibitions in women. *J. Amer. Psychoanal. Assn.*, 24: 269–83.

Mahler, M.S., Pine, F. and Bergman, A. (1975). *The Psychological Birth of the Human Infant.* New York: Int. Univ Press.

Mohaczy, I. (1968). Cited by Abelin, E.L. In *The Separation-Individuation Process*, ed. J.B. McDevitt and C.G. Settlage. New York: Int. Univ. Press.

Money, J. and Ehrhardt, A. (1972). *Man and Woman: Boy and Girl.* Baltimore, Md. and London: Johns Hopkins Univ. Press.

Montgrain, N. (1983). On the vicissitudes of female sexuality, the difficult path from 'anatomical destiny' to psychic representation. *Int. J. Psychoanal.*, 64: 169–87.

Mueller, J. (1932). A contribution to the problem of libidinal development of the genital phase in girls. *Int. J. Psychoanal.*, 13: 361–8.

Parens, H. *et al.*, (1976). On the girl's entry into the Oedipus complex. *J. Amer. Psychoanal. Assn.*, 24: 79–107.

Reich, A. (1954). Early identifications as archaic elements in the superego. *J. Amer. Psychoanal. Assn.*, 2: 218–38.

Roiphe H. and Galenson, E. (1976). Some suggested revisions concerning early female development. *J. Amer. Psychoanal. Assn.*, 24 (suppl.): 29–57.

Silverman, M.A. (1981). Cognitive development in female psychology. *J. Amer. Psychoanal. Assn.*, 29: 581–605.

Stoller, R.J. (1968). *Sex and Gender: On the Development of Masculinity and Femininity.* New York: Science House.

—— (1976). Primary femininity. *J. Amer. Psychoanal. Assn.*, 24: 59–78.

211

'The weak spot' – some observations on male sexuality

MERVIN GLASSER

In the first of his 'Three essays on sexuality' (Freud 1905) in which he discusses the sexual aberrations, Freud comes to express his belief that 'the impulses of sexual life are among those which, even normally, are the least controlled by the higher activities of the mind' (p. 149). He continues:

> anyone who is in any way, whether socially or ethically, abnormal mentally is invariably abnormal also in his sexual life. But many people are abnormal in their sexual life who in every other respect approximate to the average, and have, along with the rest, passed through the process of human cultural development, in which sexuality remains the weak spot.

And later in the same essay he states: 'Here again we cannot escape from the fact that people whose behaviour is in other respects normal can, *under the domination of the most unruly of all instincts,* put themselves in the category of sick persons in the single sphere of sexual life' (p. 161, my italics).

One of the themes of this paper will be to challenge this view of sexuality and to demonstrate that far from being 'weak' and 'unruly' man's sexuality is his most powerful and willing servant, or assistant, always ready to aid him in his attempts to find satisfaction and peace. His sexuality is (to choose an appropriate metaphor) his ever-willing genie, able to expand from the confines of a small phial to become an enormous giant, all powerful, capable of conquering time and space, executing miracles – all in the service of bringing about the fulfilment of his master's deepest wishes.

This essential and ubiquitous role of sexuality is nowhere more vividly illustrated than in the perversions: here the observation of the contortions that man's sexuality is willing to undergo in pursuit of its master's well-being cannot fail to convince one of this point. This is acknowledged in one way or another by all those analysts who have worked in the field of the perversions (such as Chasseguet-Smirgel 1978; Gillespie 1956; Glasser 1979; Glover 1933; Khan 1979; Limentani 1976; McDougall 1980; Rosen 1979; Stoller 1975). However, the organizers of this Conference asked me not to centre this talk on the perversions and I must say I welcome this constraint since the points I would like to make would stand the risk of being discredited on the grounds of a bias in my illustrative clinical material.

The patients I shall refer to, then, will be representative of the ordinary patients seen in analytic practice, in so far as this can ever be said to be the case. I have decided mainly to confine my clinical examples to the so-called homosexual aspects of the transference partly because it is so commonly observed, partly to put some limit on what is an endless series of possible discussion points and partly so that the patients mentioned can be compared with one another.

Mr P, a member of one of the helping professions, told me at the start of a session that on the way and while sitting in the waiting-room, he had enjoyed thinking about the meal he was going to prepare for some people he was entertaining that evening. The patient, a bachelor in his early thirties, had a history of the sort of extreme neglect and emotional deprivation which only the children of the very rich can experience. With his father absent at business during the day and generally uninterested in the evenings, with his mother caught up in her daily round of social activities, and with both parents quite often away on holidays abroad, the care of Mr P and his siblings was left to a string of maids, housekeepers, butlers and chauffeurs. One of the ways he had coped with the absence of his mother was by seemingly identifying with the mother he wanted her to be. He thus took great pleasure in playing a benevolent, caring role in his social relationships, being willing to put himself to great trouble for others, giving them financial assistance, and so on. Another way in which he put himself in his mother's place was as the recipient of his father's sadistically-coloured interest, epitomized in masochistic homo-sexual fantasies, which he never acted out.

With a coming long weekend in mind, I considered whether to take up in the transference his feeding-and-entertaining thoughts in terms of a fellatio fantasy (that is, placing the emphasis of my interpretation on his use of sexuality to cope with the pending deprivation) or to concen-trate rather on his identifying with his mother as the person in control of emotional supplies. In the event, after a short silence, he started talking about a meeting he was going to have with the head of a large organiza-tion in the hope of getting an appointment to a post which he very much wanted. With some hesitation, he went on to say that he had to admit that he had had fantasies of this man cuddling him and that these were accompanied by sexual feelings.

This session occurred in the context of his starting at last, after a number of years of the most determined resistance, to acknowledge faults of his defensively idealized mother. As a result of his starting to recognize his rage with her, he had had a number of major quarrels with his mother and he had broken off a long-standing, though rather sterile, relationship with a girlfriend. Although he complained of his general apathy and tiredness, he had not acknowledged his feelings of loss.

We may thus observe him employing his sexuality in a predominantly passive, masochistic, homosexual way to help him deal with the painful affects of loss and insecurity at the pending departure – fundamentally emotional withdrawal – of his mother/analyst. This patient, by the way, had the habit of putting his hand inside his trousers while lying on the couch and holding his penis in a quite unabashed way. He did not obtain an erection, nor did he acknowledge any sexual excitement. It could be said that his penis featured as a comfort, a transitional object,[1] much more than a sexual organ. Yet the sexuality in this act *did* play a part; it could not be denied. It was, after all, not the same as holding any other part of his body, let alone an inanimate object. The 'special' sensation he must have experienced enabled him to experience himself being held, warmed and enlivened by his longed-for mother:[2] because I would not cuddle him in the session, he did it himself, thus again using sexuality to counter feelings of rejection and deprivation.

There were other ingredients in his 'homosexual' relationship to me. We came to see that as much as he longed for his mother he also found it imperative to keep her at a controlled distance from him. This was because he experienced his mother, who was certainly narcissistic and exploitative in her relationship to him, as intrusively possessive or engulfing. A vivid illustration of this in the transference was the occasion when he said that he had the sudden fear as he came into the consulting room that the large leaves of a tree immediately outside would wrap themselves around him and suffocate him. In order to distance himself from such an annihilatory mother he employed his homosexuality. For instance, he became engaged to a girl he felt quite strongly for and they were, for various reasons, separated for a number of months. During this time he talked about how much he longed for her and dwelt on the qualities he admired so much about her or found so desirable in her. At last the time came when he could go to visit her. They rushed to greet each other at the side of a swimming-pool and at the moment that they embraced he found himself looking across the pool at a man he found attractive. This intense longing, counterpointed by a distancing

214

defence, was characteristic of Mr P. In the same session that he expressed his fear of the engulfing leaves, he complained that I left all the work to him and that he was sure the analysis would progress much more rapidly if I gave him a kick up the backside.

As the analysis progressed we came to discern that his seeming homosexual posture also aimed to conceal his sadistic masculinity, that is, to hide both his sadism to avoid guilt and his masculinity to avoid castration. His father had been a frighteningly large and powerful figure in his childhood and he had had no compunction about chastising his children. Mr P's submissiveness was a way of both placating his father and hiding his retaliatory feelings. His Oedipal rivalry was kept well out of the picture by this apparent feminine identification: unlike his brother, for example, who had gone into their father's business, Mr P was in a lowly rated post in a caring profession. But he had learnt, from his family, to be devious so that no one knew of his great ambitions until he spoke of them to me. He had also learnt from his father to be covertly sadistic. For example, Mr P met his father after work one day to learn of the outcome of a meeting his father had attended which was of the utmost importance to Mr P. As they travelled home in the car his father sat in silence with his eyes closed, having said he was very tired, and Mr P had simply to sit and wait to learn what had transpired. This was often repeated with the roles reversed in the treatment situation when he would respond to substantial interpretations with an extended silence, or when he would not tell me of the outcome of some important event which had occurred between the previous and present sessions.

The significance of this patient's 'homosexuality' in the transference may be compared with that of a second patient, Mr Q. He was the married head of an art school, and in his forties. After some time in analysis, he came to talk of matters which pointed to not particularly unusual conflicts in regard to Oedipally centred homosexual interests. He had made some remarks in sessions which obliquely indicated feelings of rivalry with me and he had also talked about rivalrous incidents with colleagues at work. In this context he came to mention his curiosity about some members of his staff whom he knew to be homosexual. This led to his admitting that he occasionally wondered what it would be like to be the passive partner in anal intercourse, an interest which had expressed itself in the transference in various ways – for example, his saying that he had stopped listening to what I was saying because he felt as if my words were being forced painfully into him against his will.

He talked from time to time about how, although he was a fully accepted, liked and respected head of the art school, he always contrived to have an older man on his staff who, while experienced and able to give valuable advice, never challenged his role or status. He felt reassured that he could turn to such a man (and he frequently did so, quite openly) to seek advice on difficult matters of administrative and artistic policy. In this phase of the treatment, he would frequently ask me what I thought a puzzling piece of his behaviour might mean or what I considered to be the interpretation of a dream he had the previous night. He maintained that enquiring in this way was quite sensible on his part since I was the expert and obviously could supply the answer if I wanted to, even though the truth might sometimes be painful.

The significance of his transference fantasy of acquiring my masculine power through submitting to my anal penetration emerged later in his analysis. He had come to recognize his extreme hostility to his mother and how much he had hated her when he was a small boy. He spoke of how she crowded in on him; dominated him with her intense possessivensss and single-mindedness. He had previously spoken of her great love for him and his feeling that in fact he mattered to her more than his siblings. He had also spoken of what a passionate woman she was and recognized, with some discomfort, how sensual she was. At this time he started reporting how he was progressing, especially professionally: he found himself preferring to take more independent action in his work and he was no longer being so accommodating to his dominating wife. Although he gave impressive examples, I felt rather doubtful about his progress: I wondered if this was not an example of how a patient 'borrows' his analyst's masculinity and therefore appears to be functioning with a new-found confidence, assertiveness and effectiveness. At the same time, I thought he could be experiencing me as his dominating, obliterative mother and was therefore making a sort of 'flight into health'.

In his early years, Mr Q's father was absent for most of the time. He was involved in an international organization and was therefore away from home for extended periods. In the clinical material, his father's visits initially featured as unwelcome intrusions into the contented snugness of his seemingly exclusive relationship with his mother – his siblings being some years older were away at boarding-school for a lot of the time. But with the persistent analysis of the patient's seductiveness with me, and of his anger with me for not supplying the answers or giving directives and, above all, from his reactions to my absences, we came to see that his anger with his father was not so much because of his presence but more because of his *absence*. We came to see how much he wanted his analyst-father to be his ally, give him support and advise him on how to withstand the possessive dominance of his analyst-mother. His homosexuality, then, was predominantly an attempt to find a way of internalizing his father as an inner ally against his acquisitive internalized mother. I shall be considering these matters more extensively shortly but now I would like to emphasize how Mr Q was being aided by his sexuality in seeking to establish an inner bulwark to withstand being over-whelmed by his mother.

It will be seen that with both Mr P and Mr Q, I have focused my attention on how the heterosexual ingredient of the transference carries anxieties reflecting a fear of annihilation by the mother and the homosexual component carries the aim of averting this by turning to the father. It is my view that this is a reflection of processes in normal development and I would now like to elaborate what I have in mind. From my clinical study of patients with perversions I came to identify a dynamic organization which I referred to as the 'Core Complex', and I subsequently came to regard this complex as a normal phase through which the infant has to pass (Glasser 1979). It seemed to me that different clinical conditions reflected different outcomes of the core complex – a point that this paper will illustrate incidentally.

The ingredients of the core complex are intimately interrelated so that each is strongly coloured by the others. The first of these which I shall consider is the infant's intense longing for a condition of satiety and security achieved through fusion with the mother, a state which is expressed by the adult as a longing for 'union', 'merging', 'at-one-ness' and other such phrases. However, based probably on a combination of the projection of the infant's own all-consuming needs and its 'knowledge' of the incorporative desires of the mother, such a concept of fusion carries with it the attribute of an inevitable complete possession by the mother and thus total annihilation. This was well-expressed by Mr R, a patient I shall be considering later, when he said it was 'like sugar dissolving in a cup of coffee'.

One of the reactions to this threat of annihilation is 'flight', that is, essentially a narcissistic withdrawal. However, this brings with it a situation of total isolation with its attendant feelings of complete deprivation and abandonment. Furthermore, the only focus for the aggression initially directed towards the object (which I shall consider in a moment) is the self, often the body. The intense anxieties of abandonment and the pain of deprivation prompt longings for complete and indissoluble union with the object and we can thus observe that this aspect of the core complex has the quality of a vicious circle.

A second fundamental reaction to the threat of annihilation by the possessing mother is aggression. I must digress briefly at this point to state my understanding of aggression and distinguish it from sadism, because these are basic concepts to my discussion. In keeping with the outlook of contemporary biology (Coxon 1983) and a viewpoint expounded by Freud (1915) in his 'Instincts and their vicissitudes', my view is that aggression is provoked by any threat to the physical or psychological homeostasis of the individual, that is, ultimately, his survival. Aggression

217

is thus always self-preservative and aims at totally obliterating, *negating*, the threat. In this sense it is essentially adaptive and not object-related. Sadism, on the other hand, is entirely object-related. In the sadistic act, the effect on the object is essential: the specific aim is to cause the object to suffer physically or mentally. Domination and control are obviously critical features common to both aggression and sadism: in the former they are sought only to promote the aim of negating the danger: while in sadism they play an essential role in engaging the object but at 'a safe distance', as I shall elaborate shortly.

To return now to the core complex: since the mother is considered to be annihilatory she will provoke an aggressive reaction which is aimed at totally destroying her. But she is, after all, the (only) object which can gratify all the infant's needs. Thus the infant is confronted by an irreconcilable conflict of opposites. The pervert shows us that one of the attempted solutions to this is the employing of *sexualization* which converts aggression into sadism: the intention to destroy is converted to the wish to hurt and control. In this way the mother is preserved and the viability of the relationship to her is ensured albeit henceforth in sadomasochistic terms.

The threat of total deprivation and the turning of the aggression on to the self resulting from the withdrawl component of the core complex is also dealt with by sexualization, the aggression thus being converted into *masochism* and the mother being retrieved by what we may call 'the masochistic invitation' of the infant.

Clinical observation shows us that both sadism and masochism have the characteristic of engaging the object in an intense relationship but intimacy and union are never present, the object and the self are very carefully kept 'at a safe distance' from each other.

In my view, these ingredients and processes of the core complex are passed through in the course of normal development and how they are dealt with plays an important part in the individual's future make-up. In the case of the pervert, he remains fixated at this stage for reasons I need not go into. But this is not, of course, the only possible outcome. I have not studied psychotics in sufficient number or depth to generalize, but the kind of 'solution' they 'chose' may be exemplified by the patient who believed himself to be in his own abdomen. He would conduct a dialogue with himself in his own abdomen. Every now and then he would emit a weird, intensely violent exhaling sound, opening his mouth as wide as it could go and sticking his tongue out as far as he could. This could be understood as an intense attack on his mother-self (the aggressive, self-preservative reaction) as well as expelling his infant-self (the withdrawal reaction) and then returning to what we may fancifully call the intra-uterine symbiotic state of fusion.

In the ordinary family set-up, what offers a different solution from those found by the pervert and the psychotic is, as indicated by the clinical material I have provided, the presence of the father. With the father present, the infant can seek a solution to the core complex's 'irreconcilable conflict of opposites' by turning to the father as an alternative object, and this step then has a number of variable outcomes. The turning to the father is essentially an *internalizing* step for it is in the internal world that the self is in danger of being taken over by the mother and it is in the internal world that the father must act in two ways: firstly he must serve as the wall of the fortress that keeps the mother out (an image frequently encountered in patients' dreams and metaphors) and secondly, he must be an alternative object or the infant's libidinal feelings and need for caring. In this way he can decrease the intensity of the need for the mother and allay anxieties of insecurity. For such a step to become stable and permanent, the internalization must proceed to identification.[3]

The differences in these particular processes of internalization make a substantial contribution to the future differences between male and female sexuality. In the boy's identification to the father, he can assert his separateness from his mother by the *bodily* ingredients of the identification which he emphasizes. The girl, on the other hand, identifies more with the *psychological* attributes of the father and it is to these she particularly turns in her heterosexual needs to separate herself from her mother.[4] I consider these influences contribute to the tendency in males to approach their sexual relationships with physical features playing a more important role than is the case with females, who tend to be more affected by psychological factors. I also believe this is one of the psychological factors which combine with the anatomical determinants to make men experience intercourse as 'outside' themselves while women experience it as taking place 'inside' themselves. I believe it is in this context that we should place Lichtenstein's (1961) argument that non-procreative sexuality', as he calls it, serves the establishment of the primary identity theme in man.

If we return to Mr Q we can now appreciate that he was, in his homosexual transference relationship, trying to achieve the resolution of his core complex attachment to his mother by aiming to internalize the analyst in order to reinforce his tenuous identification with his father. I remind you of how he felt his mother to be powerful and possessive to the point of being annihilatory and how the presence of a father-figure enabled him to be assertive and expressive of his own personality. The sexual ingredient in the transference expresses the fantasy of an incorporation which promotes independence, an *assimilation*, to use Freud's (1900) word which results in a sense of freedom and self-expression rather than simply a transfer of subjugators. The doubts I expressed about

219

Mr Q's progress could now be restated as my not being able to tell whether his improvement was simply a result of *imitation* (Gaddini 1969) or whether identificatory processes were taking place. Later, I could observe that Mr Q came to experience great pleasure in his paternal role in his family, paying attention to his hitherto neglected sons and comfortably assuming the responsibilities of the man of the house, i.e., the development was a full and permanent one established by identification.[5]

Like Mr Q, Mr P (the first patient I discussed), attempted to make use of homosexuality to establish a pathway to identification with his father's masculinity as a means of withstanding his mother's possession of him. But we see that in this he is only partly successful and the clinical picture is a mixed one. Core complex anxieties play a prominent part. You will remember his fear of the engulfing leaves and his fiancée's embrace: these can now be understood as expressions of the ever-present, pervasive annihilatory anxiety. It was difficult to observe the other basic anxiety of the core complex – abandonment anxiety – in the transference, because of his extensive repression of affects. Holidays or weekends, for example, were met with evident equanimity and it was only after some time that these feelings could be reached by pursuing the relationship of his masturbation to loss.

I referred earlier to Mr P's *seeming* identification with his mother. Perhaps I should have used the word *partial*, because to the extent that his internal dynamics are governed by the primitive anxieties of the core complex, we would *expect* identification to be prevented since it would carry the meaning of possession by the internal mother. In fact this could be *experienced* clinically by sensing at times the sort of inconsistent and rather shallow quality of the identification. And it could be *observed* in many areas of his clinical material: it was most impressive, for example, to watch over a period of time how the recipients of his good work and benevolence disappeared out of his life without the slightest evidence of his experiencing any sense of loss. I initially understood such clinical material to be the result of a massive repression of his affects but, although, as I've said, this was extensive, I came to understand that to a substantial degree his core complex anxieties made identification with his primary objects only partially possible; to a large extent his internalization could go no further than *imitation*. *Some* degree of identification could be seen to have taken place not only with his mother but also with his father, the latter serving rather like Mr Q, as a protection from his mother's engulfment. (I remind you of the scene at the swimming-pool.) But because of the heavy imprint of the core complex and because of his father's remoteness and sadism, the nature of Mr P's masculine way of relating is closer to that of the pervert where, as I've discussed, full, intimate engagement is avoided and sadomasochism keeps the object engaged but at a controlled distance. I illustrated this when I described how he used his silences in the sessions. The limited extent to which identification took place can be seen in the fact that he was greatly restricted in his use of sexuality with both men and women, emotionally and physically. One of the ways this showed clinically was in the quality and relative infrequency of his castration anxiety.

This leads me to assert at this point that in my view to refer to a person's 'castration anxiety' is nowadays much too crude and gross a description. We have come to see the great extent of individual variation that exists within this form of anxiety, in terms of its antecedents, the precise quality of the affect experienced, the nature of the objects who threaten castration, the role of sexuality in the individual's dynamics (as this paper discusses) and other such considerations.

The differences in the nature of castration anxiety, and the influence which the core complex may exert on it, is well illustrated by comparing Mr P and Mr Q with a third patient, Mr R, who also assumed a submissive, homosexual attitude in the transference. He was a young business-man who came for treatment complaining of depression and occasional impotence. He expressed intensely narcissistic, grand ambitions such as hoping to be president of British Leyland and having his photograph on the front page of *The Times*. Of course he wanted to be an outstanding patient and provide me with whatever clinical material he thought was impressive. There was, evident from the start, a certain false quality to his expression of substantial insight and to his promotion of the therapeutic process. And his analysis was characterized by episodes of what appeared to be negative therapeutic reactions.

From time to time he would leave a session which we would both have felt to have been very productive and he might have commented that he believed he had made great progress in understanding himself. However, in the next two or three hours he would somehow set about demolishing this good feeling and in fact end up feeling just the reverse, that is, insecure, uncertain and lacking in any positive self-confidence.

There seemed to be an Oedipal significance to this as was highlighted by his reaction to a strongly competitive situation at his place of work: when the anxieties of the situation became particularly intense, he expressed his feelings of wanting to lie back, open his legs and let his rivals 'screw' him. He would feel tense, apprehensive and bite his nails. He even went so far as to sprain his ankle badly, an act which, on the basis of other material, had a definite self-castrating significance. At other periods of his analysis, often in relation to substantial success, he would report feeling extremely anxious about his apparent shortcomings. He would find this or that to doubt about himself and even condemn himself, usually in contradiction to the observable facts. He would describe how he felt his feet sweating and his penis shrinking. He would experience the same sort of reaction directly to me in the transference.

Nevertheless he had, over the course of his analysis, progressed impressively in his business career, moving to another firm and building himself up so well that he became something of a wonder in his commercial circles; and when he moved to a third job he could command a substantial salary and status as a managing director. Between moving from the second to the third job he went on holiday with his girlfriend, Sandra.

He returned from this holiday looking healthy and cheerful. He started the session by speaking enthusiastically about what a wonderful time he had had. He spoke glowingly about Sandra. She was such a wonderful person – straightforward, un-neurotic, good-humoured. She was so loving to him and, in contrast to his mother, was content to let him just be himself. And she was so beautiful! And their time in bed together was so wonderful! He really, really appreciated her and loved her. It was the first time in his life that he had been able to have a real, loving relationship. He went on to say that although he was telling me this just to let me know how his holiday had gone, he also wanted to express his gratitude to me because all this was undoubtedly the result of his analysis, and he wanted to let me have the pleasure of seeing the results of my therapeutic good work.

He then went on to tell me that at the same time as he was having such a wonderful time with Sandra in the day, he was having a terrible time at night having awful dreams about failure. As an example, he quoted a dream

in which he had joined his new company, the head of which turned out to be a great fool – something the head of the previous firm somehow knew, with the result that he could mock Mr R and triumph over him for having left his firm for a new one.

All the dreams were characterized by his being humiliatingly castrated through his being a failure.

Rather than taking up the evident Oedipal rivalry meanings of this, I chose to point out that just as I was invited to look at his daytime achievements as evidence of my success, so I would have to see his dreams as evidence of my failure. I related this to what we had worked at extensively, namely, his intensely mixed relationship to his mother. She had very much seen him as the vehicle for the achievement of her dreams and ideals. She had devoted herself to bringing him up to be the very best. Although they had come from a farming family in the North, she had taught him to speak English without a provincial accent, to read and write well ahead of his years, to have perfect manners, to have the right taste in his dress, to be charming and so on. Once she had said: 'You are my Ming vase.' She would boost his self-esteem but always convey-ing how pleased she was that he was coming up to *her* ideals and expectations. In short, she related to him in an extremely narcissistic way, making little or no allowance for his individual needs and qualities.

Particularly relevant to my discussion is the way the clinical material showed how he was used by her to deal with his penis envy feelings. On the one hand, he was meant to give her the vicarious fulfilment of her longings by being exceptionally successful in the male field and in this way, because it was all fundamentally her doing, to be her magnifi-cent, universally admired, triumphant phallus. On the other hand, her envy expressed itself in a strong condemnation of sexual man. She con-veyed her contempt for his father and expressed her disgust with his male ways. She insisted that her son bathed regularly so that he would never emanate what she called 'man-smell'. Male sexuality was, in short, denigrated to being something anal and greedy and she would never countenance that sort of thing in her son.

Mr R had always wanted to earn his mother's love by fulfilling her narcissistic needs. For example, when writing to his parents while on holiday he felt a sense of shame that Sandra was not anyone socially special. What his mother would want was that Sandra was 'Lady-Princess So-and-So, who had written books on cooking and things like that, and was a friend of the Queen'. But at the same time he felt that any of his achievements or successes would not serve as any affirmation of *him*: it would be evidence of how capable his mother had been in the way *she* had brought him up and moulded him. In becoming a Ming vase his own form and colour was lost in the interests of demonstrating how good a potter she was.

If success carried the meaning of annihilation of his own individuality, the only way of self-affirmation open to him was, paradoxically, failure. In this he could be sure he was being something of *his* choice, something to which his mother would certainly never lay claim. Thus, while on the surface he was being the successful young man, inwardly he could give himself concrete reassurance through his experiencing his bodily symptoms of anxiety and his near-delusional belief that his penis had shrunk, that he was withstanding his mother's annihilatory possession.[6]

I made the point when discussing Mr P that, because of the core complex anxieties, his capacity to internalize was substantially restricted to *imitation*. This was even more the case with Mr R who can best be regarded as having a *false self* system (Winnicott 1960). It seems to me that imitation is the essential mechanism of the false self personality. His being the exceptional patient, the successful business-man and so on were all the result of his use of imitation − an imitation, it should be noted, not so much of real individuals in his past or present environment,

223

but rather of ideal fantasy figures held up to him by his own or his mother's narcissism. But the inner, secret 'castrated' self was also a contrivance and we may thus think of a false self within a false self. Somewhere, even more deeply hidden, was a true self of which he had little or no knowledge. (See also Limentani 1979.)

The skill and subtlety of his evasive imitations aimed at protecting his true self could often be observed in the way he reacted to interpretations. He would endorse what I had just said in a way which conveyed that he fully recognized in himself what I was pointing out and that he could see with some enthusiasm the benefit of his altered perspective. Then, as if to develop the point, using a phrase like 'and also' he would expound a new line of thought which, though not exactly irrelevant and even, perhaps, quite worthy in its own right, completely took his attention away from the point I had made. In this way he totally divested himself of my influence while seeming to be just what he believed I wanted him to be.

It might seem contradictory to his great need for failure that he did so well in his career and that the personality he manifested generally was always substantially masculine. I found this puzzling, particularly since his father featured as a weak figure who had failed in his life (a fact which his mother did not hesitate to emphasize) so that he did not appear to be an appropriate identificatory figure. But we know that a false self personality can be extraordinarily successful in public life: it is a success driven by intense narcissistic needs (brought about by the isolation into which his true self has been driven), needs which make him particularly adept at imitating (identification not being available to him) the ideal male figure of the fantasy held up to him by his mother.

It will be appreciated that the core complex occurs within an essentially narcissistic context, and among the consequences of the individual being fixated at this point is that his sexuality cannot be employed to help him in his development and in establishing object relationships. I could observe evidence of Mr R making attempts to establish real relationships via hints at polymorph-perverse fantasies (paedophilia, bestiality, etc.) and via sadistic fantasies involving women, such as Sandra, but these always fell away, like the sea sweeping up the beach but always receding. It was not that Mr R's sexuality was his 'weak spot', it was its unemployability which left him vulnerable.

If we compare the three patients I have considered, we can see that there is a complex relationship between the core complex dynamics, the processes of internalization, the use of sexuality and castration anxiety, or to put it another way, the particular significance of the penis. For normal male development, an essential ingredient is the boy's bodily identification with his father, including, particularly, his penis. In the case of

Mr R, his father's penis hardly seems to feature. Much greater prominence is given to his mother's phallus and her narcissistic involvement with it, and his castration anxiety takes place predominantly in these terms. With Mr Q, in contrast, his turning to his father to acquire his penis, that is, to carry out an identificatory process, implies a recognition and a valuing of it by the mother, despite the father's physical absence for a substantial portion of time. While with Mr P, the situation in these respects is a mixed one in which we can observe a mixture of identification and imitation and the penis he has at his disposal, so to speak, is a mixture of his mother's phallus and his father's sadistic (i.e., perverse) penis. The nature of each of these men's sexuality and their castration anxiety is thus substantially different.

I have limited my discussion to a confined area of male sexuality in the transference in order to make such a discussion manageable. When first considering this paper I found myself becoming more and more perplexed by the extent of the subject and by my attempt to characterize male, as distinct from female, sexuality. I saw that, whatever animal or endocrinological studies might tell us (Limentani 1979), human sexuality was so capable of transformation and adaptation according to the internal and external circumstances of the individual — family configurations, cultural attitudes, traumata, identificatory processes and so on — that a simple characterization of the fundamental, or original, nature of male sexuality could be no more than a distortion. Even 'bisexuality' seemed to me to underestimate the multipotential qualities of human sexuality. In this paper I have tried to demonstrate by discussion and clinical illustration that, with its capacity to bind and its extraordinary pliability, male sexuality (and, of course, female sexuality), far from being a 'weak spot' plays a major role in the protection of psychological survival and in the promotion of psychic growth of the individual.

Summary

Male sexuality plays an essential role in the protection of psychological survival and in the promotion of psychic development. This proposition is explored in the 'homosexual' transference of three male patients and their differing uses of sexuality is compared. The concept of the core complex is briefly elaborated. The interrelations between the core complex, processes of internalization and castration anxiety, and the role played by sexuality in these contexts are considered.

Notes

This paper was presented at the London Weekend Conference for English Speaking Members of European Societies. 12–14 October 1984.

1 I am grateful to Prof.ssa Renata Gaddini de Benedetti for pointing out, in the discussion following the presentation of this paper, that this should more appropriately be referred to as a *precursor* of a transitional object, as the object involved is part of the individual's body.
2 I arrived at this understanding of this behaviour of Mr P after hearing M. Eglé Laufer's (1982) paper on 'Female masturbation'.
3 I am grateful to Mr Donald Campbell who, after I had discussed Mr Q with him in these terms, drew my attention to Greenson's (1968) paper, 'Dis-identifying from the mother', which follows a rather similar line of thinking.
4 This adds an additional ingredient to the meaning of penis envy. I would add in passing that these considerations make us appreciate that the girl can only properly identify with her mother if she has the protection of an identification with her father.
5 I'm inclined to believe that, to put this more precisely, the process which takes place is that existing paternal identifications are released and reinforced, rather than features of the analyst himself being utilized.
6 In my experience similar considerations can play an important role in suicide attempts and other self-destructive pathology.

References

Coxon, A. (1983). Organic aspects of violence. Unpublished.

Chasseguet-Smirgel, J. (1978). Reflexions on the connexions between perversions and sadism. *Int. J. Psychoanal.*, 59: 27–35.

Freud, S. (1900). The interpretation of dreams. S.E. 4–5.

—— (1905). Three essays on the theory of sexuality. S.E. 7.

—— (1915). Instincts and their vicissitudes. S.E. 14.

Gaddini, E. (1969). On imitation. *Int. J. Psychoanal.,* 50: 475–84.

Gillespie, W.H. (1956). The general theory of sexual perversion. *Int. J. Psychoanal.*, 37: 396–403.

Glasser, M. (1979). Some aspects of the role of aggression in the perversions. In *Sexual Deviation*, ed. I. Rosen. London: Oxford Univ. Press, pp. 278–305.

Glover, E. (1933). The relation of perversion formation to the development of reality sense. *Int. J. Psychoanal.*, 14: 486–504.

Greenson, R.R. (1968). Dis-identifying from mother: its special importance for the boy. *Int. J. Psychoanal.*, 49: 370–4.

Khan, M.M.R. (1979). *Alienation in Perversions*. London: Hogarth Press.

Laufer, M.E. (1982). Female masturbation in adolesence and the development of the relationship to the body. *Int. J. Psychoanal.*, 63: 295–302.

Lichtenstein, H. (1961). Sexuality and identity. *J. Amer. Psychoanal. Assn.*, 9: 179–260.

Limentani, A. (1976). Object choice and actual bisexuality. *Int. J. Psychoanal. Psychother.*, 5: 205–19.

—— (1979). The significance of transsexualism in relation to some basic psychoanalytic concepts. *Int. Rev. Psychanal.*, 6: 139–54.

McDougall, J. (1980). *Plea for a Measure of Abnormality*. New York: Int. Univ. Press.

Money, J. and Tucker, P. (1975). *Sexual Signatures*. London: George G. Harrap.

Rosen, I. (1979). Perversion as regulator of self-esteem. In *Sexual Deviation*, ed. I. Rosen. London: Oxford Univ. Press, pp. 65–78.

Stoller, R. (1975). *Perversion: the Erotic Form of Hatred*. London: Harvester Press.

Winnicott, D.W. (1960). Ego distortion in terms of true and false self. In *The Maturational Processes and the Facilitating Environment*. London: Hogarth Press, 1965, pp. 140–52.

PART FOUR

Bisexuality

Introduction

Bisexuality brings to the foreground again the question of the relationship of body and mind, of biological bisexuality and psychological bisexuality. As with femininity, Freud felt that, although fundamental, the concept of bisexuality was impregnated with obscurity.

Bisexuality is originally for Freud a clinical concept: 'without taking bisexuality into account I think it would scarcely be possible to arrive at an understanding of the sexual manifestations that are actually to be observed in men and women' (Freud 1905: 22). This concept reflects the duality inherent in Freud's work. It is used at times to express the biological predisposition of the human individual, while at other times Freud uses it to refer to the balance of object relationships. Sometimes it is seen as a given from which there is a necessary involution as development proceeds in order to achieve a sexual identity; at other times it is seen as a state necessary for psychic and sexual integration. This does not necessarily imply object choice but refers to mental functioning and mental characteristics and identifications. The latter meaning has been given increasing importance in contemporary writings with the identification to each parent being seen as serving important functions.

Neither model helps to *explain* or describe the differential account Freud gives of masculine and feminine development, but the second one – that of a psychological bisexual functioning essential to sexual integration – describes an ongoing dynamic within each development which gives it its complexity. In that sense his theory of bisexuality runs somewhat in parallel to that of psychosexuality. The concept of the Oedipus complex became widened to incorporate the notion of bisexuality since it came to represent both positive and negative versions and simply refer to the child's position in the triangle, while at the same time, the concept of

231

the Oedipus complex was still retained to give meaning to masculine or to feminine development.

In the case of female sexuality, bisexuality took on an added meaning in that Freud describes two discrete phases of development, first masculine, then feminine. For this reason he believed that women were more bisexual than men, and he recognized 'masculinity' in women more than 'femininity' in men.

While Freud thought that women were more bisexual than men because of the early 'homosexual' attachment to the mother, more recent writings stress the importance of the feminine component in men due to the early identification with the mother. This feminine identification is now understood as being not just a threat to masculinity but, more importantly, as potentially positive for intrapsychic and interrelational balance.

Clinically, bisexuality is a concept which has been used extensively implicitly or explicitly, though writings on the topic are surprisingly few. This section comprises papers which have made clinical use of the idea of psychic bisexuality.

McDougall (1989) discusses the importance of identifications with both parents and their role in the structuring of sexual identity. Greenson (1968), Aisenstein (1984) and Limentani (1989) all, in different ways, consider the large part played by femininity in men.

The dead father: on early psychic trauma and its relation to disturbance in sexual identity and in creative activity

JOYCE MCDOUGALL

Psychoanalysis has as yet no comprehensive theory of core gender and sexual identity (in the sense in which Stoller (1968) defines these terms). As a psychic construction, gender and sexual identity have both biological and acquired origins and are thus at the research crossroads of several scientific disciplines. Nevertheless psychoanalysis has a specific contribution to make to the study of aberrations in core gender identity and in the established sense of one's sexual role, in so far as these have their roots in the experiences of early childhood and the unconscious problems of parents.

The origins of sexual knowledge

It is well known that the genital organs, from the time that they form a manifest mental representation in the mind of the small child, have a special relationship with the visual discovery of the difference between the sexes. The toddler's eye, avid to acquire new knowledge, seizes very early, usually between the twelfth and the eighteenth month of life, this striking visible difference in the observable bodies of other children, bodies which from this time onward are for ever identified sexually. Children of both sexes display manifest anxiety about this surprising discovery and this in turn brings about a reorganization of both their relationship to and interest in their own bodies as well as in their play activities (Roiphe and Galenson 1981). Until this disquieting revelation, every child has an intuitive knowledge of its own sexual body, based on the mother's touch and the overall bodily contact with both parents, as well as the coexcitation aroused by affective experiences, both pleasurable and unpleasurable. But following the discovery of anatomical difference, the

233

genital suddenly becomes an object that can be pointed out and named, and that marks you as belonging ineluctably to one clan only and excluded for ever from the other. It is evident that this knowledge will not be acquired without conflict, for the narcissistic and megalomanic child inevitably wishes to possess both sexes as well as the powers and privileges attributed to the personalities and genital organs of each parent (McDougall 1986a). Much psychic work is required in order to carry out the task of mourning that will eventually allow the child to accept the narcissistically unacceptable difference and assume its monosexual destiny.

In this respect I recall the analytic session of a 5-year-old on return from a summer vacation, who rushed into the consulting room in a state of evident excitement to announce an unusual event: 'During the holidays we were in a camp where all the kids bathed together, *naked*!' 'You mean boys and girls together?' Looking startled, he shouted: 'Don't be stupid! How could I tell? I've already told you, they didn't have their *clothes* on!'

Faced with the scandalous evidence of humanity's monosexual status and its anxiety-arousing consequences, children are not the only ones to maintain a split between knowing and not-knowing – the phenomenon that Bion (1963) named 'minus-K'. Certain adults also disavow and render meaningless their biological sex – as witnessed in the extreme remedies to which transsexuals of both sexes are willing to submit. Others again, while accepting their biological sex as inescapable reality, refuse the sexual role that society attributes to masculine or feminine identity. This is the homosexual response to an internal conflict regarding sexual role and object choice. The reasons for this deviation in gender identity are various and highly complex. In part, the so-called homosexual choice can be understood, in the light of psychoanalytic experience, as a construction that is founded on what the child during its formative years has interpreted of the parental discourse concerning the significance to be attached to the mysterious difference, as well as the model of a sexual couple that the parents unwittingly offer to the child's alert eye (McDougall 1978, 1982, 1986b). Thus the psychic representation of the parental couple, as well as their words, may either help or hinder the child in its attempt to give up universal wishes of both a bisexual and an incestuous nature, and may indeed favour a deviant representation of the small individual's developing sense of core gender and sexual identity role.

With the help of a clinical illustration, I hope to throw some light on certain fundamental factors that contribute to sexual identity formation and its inversions, in particular the importance of the different identifications with *both* parents that essentially structure the sense of sexual identity for all children. Here several psychic dramas intertwine: the one to receive most attention in our psychoanalytic literature is the heterosexual Oedipal crisis which involves, among other important factors, the wish to possess in the most literal sense of the word the parent of the opposite sex while wishing death upon the same-sex parent. But there is also the homosexual Oedipal drama which also implies a double aim, that of *having* exclusive possession of the same-sex parent and that of *being* the parent of the opposite sex. This twofold dilemma has been explored elsewhere (McDougall 1986a).

The lost father

The vignette that I am about to present raises a number of questions of both a clinical and a theoretical order with regard to disturbance in sexual identity, but before formulating these I should like to introduce my patient and give a glimpse into our first meeting.

Benedicte grew up in a large city in the south of France where all her close relatives also lived. A writer by profession, she sought help because of an almost total blockage in her work. She felt unable to terminate a novel she was working on in spite of considerable talent and the fact that she had already gained a certain reputation for her writing. I opened my waiting-room door to discover a woman who appeared to be in her middle thirties: her face, framed by short curly hair, bore not a trace of make-up; her tight blue jeans and well-cut cashmere sweater revealed an attractive feminine silhouette. She nodded gravely and walked into my consulting-room in a hesitant manner. With extreme caution she lowered herself into the chair facing mine, watching me all the while like a sleuth-hound seeking to surprise in the eyes of the other some secret knowledge. After a long moment's silence she began to speak haltingly, almost stammering, in a voice so soft that I had difficulty in hearing her. She would stop abruptly in the middle of a sentence, as though unwilling to allow her words to reach me, or as though each phrase had to be checked before being uttered.

BENEDICTE: I don't ... er ... don't know if analysis can help ... er ... me. Also I don't ... er ... have confidence in it. But I read something ... er ... written by ... er ... you. My writing ... something's wrong ... I can no longer ... er ... create ... I don't like that word ... you might be able ... er ... to help me.

I asked her what kind of help she had in mind.

B: Perhaps you could collaborate with ... er ... me ... that is ... er ... I don't think it's a real analysis that ... er ... I need ... but someone like ... er ... you ... who writes as well.
J: But I'm an analyst rather than a writer.

B: I'm completely blocked ...

J: Perhaps we might discover what is blocking you.

B: I've accomplished nothing in my life. I'm ashamed ... er ... to be still alive ... to have done so little. (*Long pause*) I shall be ... er ... forty next week. (*Another long pause*) My ... er ... father died ... at forty.

Benedicte stared intently at me for some minutes in anguished silence. In order to break it I made a meaningless comment.

J: So you have reached the age at which your father died.

B: Yes ... but ... I never knew him. I was only about fifteen months old at the time. (*A further long tense silence*)

J: Perhaps people talked to you about him?

B: Yes ... and ... no. No one told me he was dead.

Benedicte stopped abruptly and appeared this time to sink into an interminable silence. I began to feel ill at ease and to wonder if she were suffering from some form of thought disorder. However, her expression was most communicative, a desperate expression as though no words could hope to transmit what she was feeling. In an attempt to re-establish communication I remarked that it must be difficult to talk of a father who one had the impression one had never known.

B: It's just that my ... er ... mother hid his death from me. She always said when I asked about him 'He's in the hospital'. She made everyone in the family lie to me also. I was more than 5 ... when a neighbour ... er ... told me the ... the truth.

Benedicte did not believe that this discovery had upset her unduly. (No doubt because she already knew the truth, for it seems unlikely that a child of five would not have suspected that there was some mystery about her supposedly alive but invisible father.) I thought to myself that possibly the mother had invented the fiction of the eternally ill father because she herself could not deal with her bereavement and thus, to the little girl, the father's death might have been experienced as forbidden knowledge. Benedicte went on to say that when she confronted her mother with the neighbour's news her mother burst into tears causing Benedicte to feel upset at having made her suffer. She added that her mother never spoke to this neighbour again. Benedicte's thoughts now turned to a fictitious aspect of her mother's personality.

B: My mother's an unreal person. Everything about her is false ... even her nose that she had remade. Whenever I was worried about anything she'd say: 'Don't frown! You'll get wrinkles on your forehead.' My worries didn't interest her, only my appearance ... er ... that is, only what the 'others' would think if they ... er ... saw me.

Benedicte frowned at me as though seeking to reasssure herself that I would be more interested in her anxiety than her wrinkles.

B: She never understood why I didn't want to be what she called ... er ... feminine. We have nothing in common, my mother and I. She ... er ... she can keep it ... her ... er ... femininity! It's totally inauthentic. Only what she thinks the others think you're supposed to be like. Her infallible system for getting through life. (*Long silence*)

J: So you resisted her system?

B: I only like ... er ... authentic women.

There followed another extremely long mute interval before Benedicte could continue.

B: To resemble her would have been ... er ... to stop existing ... to be ... nothing.

Although Benedicte spoke slowly and softly, every word and every bodily movement revealed an inexpressible tension. After much hesitation she said she felt she had some difficult life-situations to face and to resolve. She then asked if she might see me from time to time. Sensing her extreme anxiety I proposed a second consultation for the following week – the day of her fortieth birthday. She smiled and replied gravely: 'Thank you. I shall stay alive until then.'

At our second meeting Benedicte talked of her love-relationships, the difficult 'life-situations' at which she had hinted the previous week.

B: There is a woman who has meant a great deal to me. Fredrika and I have been lovers for many years – ever since the ... er ... death of her husband. Her presence was always ... vitally important to me. But now ... I've lost interest in the ... er ... passionate side of our relationship. We're still very close friends, and see each other every day ... but I can't bear the pain that I'm causing her. And yet I can't go back either ...

Benedicte went on to describe a love relationship of the past three years with Marie-Christine. She hid all knowledge of this friendship from Fredrika, adding it was the first time she had ever deceived or lied to her. Outwardly there appeared to be some similarity between Benedicte's two lovers. In each case it was the other woman who initiated the love relationship. Both women were mothers and both were widowed. Perhaps Benedicte read in my expression the thought that a dead man always appeared on the scene in her life-story. In any case she continued with a statement that could have been a negation of my unspoken thought.

B: Neither of these two ... er ... important women in my life has the slightest resemblance to my ... er ... mother.

Benedicte threw me a wary glance as though fearing I might not be in agreement. A few weeks later, before regular sessions had begun, she believed she had the proof of this. She had just bought a book on female sexuality to which I had contributed a chapter entitled 'On homosexuality in women' (McDougall 1964). Benedicte mentioned this as soon as she arrived saying, with much stumbling and circumlocution, that she disagreed with what I had written. I encouraged her to express her criticism. (I might add that today I am no longer in agreement myself with many of the ideas expressed in this article written some twenty years ago. However, I still feel the importance I attributed to the role of the father in the girl's inner universe is pertinent.

B: You say that the . . . er homosexual girl has an idealized image of her . . . er . . . mother as an unattainable model and therefore gives up all hope of rivalry with her. I loathed my mother. No rivalry with her! As for my . . . er . . . father, since I never knew him it's improbable that he could have been a model for me, beneficial or otherwise.

Indeed, in view of the parental imagos that Benedicte had brought to our initial interviews (and of which I have given the salient features) she appeared to be something of a psychic orphan. Her internal world, as she presented it, was inhabited only by an 'unreal' mother regarded as a mannequin and a dead father experienced as never having existed.

Although she was reticent about engaging in a 'real analysis' Benedicte asked if she could come to see me regularly since she now had a clearer vision of what she was seeking to discover about herself. Eventually the analysis began on a four-times weekly basis and continued for eight or nine years.

The notes of my first sessions with Benedicte and the questions they aroused in my mind may be summarized under three major headings:

1 Would this psychoanalytic adventure be dedicated to the search for the lost father? Early parent loss is almost inevitably traumatic. A fifteen-month-old-child has little capacity to carry out the work of mourning. Where, in a small child's psyche, might we hope to find the buried trace of a dead father?

2 How would a little girl of this age construct her image of her core gender and sexual identity under the circumstances described by Benedicte: a father presented to the growing child as alive but invisible and a mother whose behaviour was interpreted by the daughter to mean that she was little more than a mere narcissistic extension of her mother?

3 What might Benedicte be able to teach me about the creative process and its vicissitudes? When these give rise to work inhibitions, there ensues a complicated inner drama that has interested me for a number of years.

238

What constitutes psychic trauma?

The first question, of both clinical and technical interest, brings up the issue of early psychic trauma and a traumatic event that is frequently revealed in analytic practice. The number of patients in psychoanalytic therapy whose fathers (whether due to abandonment or death) disappeared during childhood appears to be greater than that found in the population at large. Should this potentially traumatic disappearance occur in early childhood it tends to be compensated by defensive structures that are different from those constructed by the already verbal child.

Early psychic trauma of this kind plays an evident role in the life of any child. It must nevertheless be emphasized that the long-range traumatic impact of a catastrophic event depends to a large degree on the *parental reactions* to the trauma in question. An event can be judged traumatic (that is to say as having left lasting psychological scars) only to the extent that the child's psychic reality has been reorganized in such a way as to prevent the return of the helpless state experienced at the time of the traumatizing event. The way in which the potential trauma is handled by the environment is therefore a crucial factor in determining the extent to which the child will suffer future pathological consequences (McDougall 1986c).

The fact that Benedicte's father died unexpectedly when she was fifteen months old, although it certainly contributed to her disturbed sense of sexual identity, could not be considered as a sufficient explanation. With regard to early parent loss it should also be emphasized that a father who is dead may be carried within the child's mind as a very alive figure, depending on the mother's way of talking about the father, and on the nature of his own former relationship to the child. Concomitantly, a father who is physically present might nevertheless be lived as symbolically lost, absent or dead in the child's inner world depending once again on the father's own personality and on the way the mother invests and speaks of him to the child. In this respect it seemed evident that Benedicte's mother had not handled the father's death in such a way as to mitigate its traumatic potential for her daughter.

It should be added that the earlier a child is exposed to traumatic loss of any kind the greater will be the tendency to over-invest the external and the visible world, in the search for reassuring points of identification to shore up a feeling of uncertainty with regard either to subjective or sexual identity feeling. Thus, early psychic trauma stemming from the parents' unconscious problems, whether exacerbated or not by external catastrophes, will frequently favour deviant sexuality in an attempt not only to preserve the right to sexual and love relations in adult life but also to stem a rising tide of panic at any threat to the feeling of subjective identity. The individual concerned will sometimes feel compelled to seek his or her own image in the mirror provided by another of the same sex. The importance of the narcissistic dimension in homosexual relationships is self-evident.

On the origins of sexual identity

Question two, of a theoretical order, concerns the infantile roots of sexual identity-feeling. What are the leading elements that contribute to structure an individual's representation of his or her own gender identity and sexual role? These psychic acquisitions, as Freud was the first to point out, cannot be taken for granted. They have to be created by the growing child, using information received from the parents. A quarter of a century in psychoanalytic practice, including the analysis of a number of homosexual patients, has led me to give considerable weight to the importance of the mother's unconscious projections upon her infant in the first year of life. These influence her ways of handling and talking to her baby and her future wishes for this baby. Of crucial importance is the place given to the baby's father in the mother's mind. From birth, babies of both sexes begin to create intense sensuous and libidinal ties to both parents. Every infant experiences in its mother's arms the earliest schema of sexual and love relationships to come and thus the beginnings of a sense of sexual identity. The attitude of the tiny infant's father is equally vital to the transmission of early erotic investments. If the father's personality and sexuality are devalued or play little role in the mother's life, and if in addition the father himself is uninterested in his small offspring and accepts being excluded, then there is a strong risk that he may be leaving the infant to fulfil a role arising from the mother's unconscious problems. A mother who regards her baby as a narcissistic extension of herself, or who puts her children in the place of their father as her libidinal complement, may be laying the groundwork for future deviant sexual development. If on the other hand children see their parents as a loving couple who desire and respect each other, they will tend to follow the parental model in their own adult sexual and love lives. Even a mother who brings her children up alone will not necessarily incur the risk of pathological maturation provided she does not regard her children as a substitute for adult love relationships.

After the first year of life the endogenous perceptions of sexual awareness become highly significant following the discernible difference between boys and girls. Most authors who have dealt with the establishment of gender identity (Stoller 1968; Roiphe and Galenson 1981) agree that the most critical period for the establishment of gender identity occurs in the second half of the second year.

From this point of view my patient suffered the loss of her father at a highly important period in the development of her sense of identity.

Creativity and the integration of bisexual wishes

My third question arises from observations made over a number of years with creative analysands (in artistic, scientific and other fields requiring the capacity for original thought and imagination) whose work had become sterile. Homosexual libido once deflected from its original twofold aim (namely, to *have* the same-sex parent for oneself in a world in which all members of the opposite sex are excluded, and to *be* the opposite-sex parent with this parent's genitals and supposed powers) finds many paths of integration in the adult personality. It enriches not only each individual's narcissistic self-image but also the heterosexual love-relationship through identification with the pleasure of one's partner. Reflection has led me to the conviction that the creative process also depends to a considerable extent on the integration of bisexual drives and fantasies. Our intellectual and artistic creations are, so to speak, parthenogenetically created children. A breakdown in the capacity to work creatively frequently involves an interdiction concerning unconscious homosexual identification, as well as unresolved conflicts attached to the significant inner objects involved (McDougall 1986a).

One further point, the necessity for a writer to be able to identify profoundly with characters of both sexes, has been immortalized by Flaubert who, when questioned about the source of his inspiration in writing *Madame Bovary*, replied: 'Madame Bovary, c'est moi!' An unconscious refusal to become aware of and explore one's capacity for ambisexual identifications may well involve the risk of producing writer's block.

The beginning of the analytic adventure

Before quoting a few fragments from Benedicte's analysis to illustrate the above themes, I shall give an over-all impression of our first two years' work together.

Benedicte became rapidly and intensely involved in her psychoanalytic adventure, bringing dreams, day-dreams, thoughts and feelings with an unusual richness of metaphor. At the same time her verbal expression was laborious, stumbling and often inaudible or interspersed with long periods of silence. Every gesture, every word was retained and carefully checked before being released. In the early months of our work I did not interpret the possible significance of this inaudibility, convinced as

I was that Benedicte could not communicate otherwise without doing violence to her own way of relating to another human being. There were glimpses also of a fantasy that any *rapprochement* between us was potentially dangerous. Benedicte kept an avid eye on me as though drinking in my surroundings, but at the same time like a thirsty wanderer searching the desert for fear that the oasis would become a mirage. Thus she would suddenly break off her staring as she did her words. In a painfully halting manner she would comment on the slightest modification in the haphazard arrangement of a pile of reviews, or the displacement of a lamp or an art object. The same close scrutiny was applied to my appearance or the exact position of my chair in relation to the couch. These infinitely small changes, of which I was rarely aware, gave rise to timid but insistent questioning on Benedicte's part. Faced with my silence she constructed highly improbable theories to explain the insignificant changes, usually leading to the conviction that 'her presence bothered me since I preferred to be with someone else or engaged in some other occupation'. In other words, she constantly sought some sign that would confirm the contrary, namely, that would dispel her uncertainty as to whether her existence counted for me.

This incessant search for meaning, which, once found, resembled a child's reasoning, was of course intimately connected with her attempts in the past to make sense out of her mother's fabulations and incoherent communications. Benedicte seemed to believe, much as psychotic children tend to do, that she must discover the truth alone or otherwise invent her version of the truth. This concerned not only her father's death but also her mother's frequent absences, for once widowed, Benedicte's mother conducted a feverish search for a new mate. Transposed on to the psychoanalytic stage, these preoccupations added their weight to my patient's difficulty in talking without having to chop her phrases or muffle the sound of her voice.

Quite apart from the fantasy of danger attached to communication with others, Benedicte was frightened of words in themselves. She handled them like concrete objects capable of turning into dangerous instruments. Her way of using language also created confusion as though the interpenetration of primary and secondary process thinking that leaves its mark on the free-associative analytic discourse was, in Benedicte's case, closer to dream-work.

The following notes, taken from two consecutive sessions in the third year of our work together, give a glimpse into the relationship that my patient maintained with a constraining and implosive representation of her mother. At the same time, this vignette illustrates some of the reasons for which all interchange with others, verbal or otherwise, filled Benedicte with anxiety.

B: *I dreamed that I was getting on a city bus. I had t* ... *er* ... *stamp a one-hundred franc note that was for* ... *er* ... *you. But the machine was blocked. Something was missing on the note. Someone behind me said 'Go on! It'll work'* and I ... *er* ... *woke up.*

Benedicte's associations, announced in a low stifled voice, led her to think of her friend Fredrika and of the pleasure she felt in giving her money for herself and her children, in spite of the fact that Benedicte had little money for her own needs.

B: I ... er ... suppose I'd like to be the father of your family too ... instead all I can give you is money. But there's something ... er ... missing. I dare not imagine I could give you something more valuable.

J: This sounds like a certain image of your mother; you said it was impossible to know what she really wanted from you.

B: Oh! She wanted me not to exist — outside of herself! *The machine is in my dream* ... *it made a crunching noise as though it were chewing off a bit of the note.* 'Oblitérer votre billet' (cancel your ticket) — that's what you have to do as you get in the bus. I have trouble pronouncing that word because it's so violent. 'Oblitérer' only means stamp your ticket, but it's like stamping out, obliterating a person. Total destruction. That machine is ... my mother. The infernal, maternal machine.

Benedicte had easy access to her hatred of her mother as a dangerous and destructive introject, but this got in the way of her recognizing her own primitive wishes of a violent and destructive kind, for she too is the 'blocked machine', as well as myself for whom the note is intended. I therefore redirected her associations to the transference situation.

J: But in the dream the destructive exchange took place between *us*.

B: That idea displeases me. Billet ... billet-doux ... I can recognize tender feelings for you. But violence, even in words, hurts me.

Benedicte then goes on in a dream-like way to examine other words and play on words associated with the dream images in which violent, then erotic thoughts occurred in rapid succession. I interpreted her fear that destructive and erotic desires might become confused.

B: My mother made everything seem dirty. That's why I couldn't even pronounce some of the words that came to mind just now. They had to do with excrement.

Benedicte's struggle with words

Benedicte's chain of anal-erotic and anal-sadistic signifiers revealed classic fantasies underlying infantile sexual theories. However, I did not interpret these since her dominant anxiety at this point centred around *symbolic equivalents* (Segal 1957) in which word and thing became confused. (We see here certain factors that underlie speech defects. Although Benedicte did not suffer from stammering, a casual meeting with her might have given this impression.) I pointed out to Benedicte her fear of words.

B: You're right. I'm as terrified of words as children are of ghosts.

At that moment I felt as though I too were meeting a ghost on Benedicte's psychoanalytic voyage. The strange silence that surrounded her father, his never-mentioned illness and his zombie-like existence that the mother's fabulations had created in the little girl's mind continued on the analytic stage. I invited Benedicte to tell me more about 'ghost stories' that children might fear.

B: Stories of people returning from the tomb always fascinated me for some reason . . . especially those about ghosts with visible wounds that still continued to bleed.

J: Do you have any particular ghost in mind?

B: Oh! You mean . . . *him*? yes . . . I think I waited for . . . him to come back.

Thus Benedicte was able to tell me at last, after three years of silence, the cause of her father's death. The word as well as its referent had seemed until then literally unspeakable. Benedicte's father died at the age of 40 of a rectal cancer.

By the following session, Benedicte's metaphors and the fantasies they evoked in me were still vivid in my mind: an excited-and-terrified little girl awaiting the return of her father from beyond the tomb: the father's death in terms of anal implosion; fantasies of the primal scene in anal-sadistic terms; the conflictual dream-images in which traces of an archaic primal scene may be detected in the meeting between the machine and the hundred-franc note, a phallic-anal signifier in Benedicte's associations, and destined to be 'obliterated' while at the same time representing a love-gift, the 'billet-doux'. The session brought some confirmation of these hypotheses as well as giving a glimpse into new elements.

Benedicte began with an association concerning her distrust of verbal communication and her urgent need to 'close herself up' against eventual invasion from others.

B: My mother never took her eye off me. She believed she had the right to know everything I did and everything I thought.

At this stage of our work together Benedicte could not accept that I too might be experienced as an anally implosive and controlling mother who watched her every gesture and her every word. When this aspect of the transference became interpretable, and recognizable to Benedicte herself, along with the exploration of the fantasies of mutual destruction, she began for the first time to speak easily and audibly, not only in the session but also with her friends who commented on the fact that she no longer 'mumbled'. (Fredrika had always accused Benedicte of 'swallowing her words'.)

B: As an adolescent I never dared open my mouth ... as though my mother might fly into it. And I could never close a door. She would surge after me and throw it open. Even now, on my rare visits back home she listens in to all my telephone conversations.

Underlying fantasies of oral as well as anal-sadistic penetration became transparent. The little girl of the past had believed that it was forbidden to close either the doors of her body or her mind against the invasive representation of her mother. (A year later fantasies of her mother killing the father in primitive oral and anal terms were able to be reconstructed.)

B: My mother constantly tidied up after me. My papers, my notes, my cigarettes were all put away the moment my back was turned. I would no sooner get out of a chair than she rushed forward to smooth away the trace of my body on the cushions. I was not to leave the slightest sign of my presence.

The unwelcome trace

This question of the 'trace' and its effacement was destined to become a leitmotif rich with significance.

B: Then I had to look at her too. She would put on a sort of erotic spectacle for me, dressing and undressing in front of me, and asking which of her clothes I found the most seductive and so on. This was part of her ritual for catching a new husband. She would insist that 'we' must look nice, that 'we' must dress to impress eventual suitors. Violence was the only way out. I closed myself off in stony silence. She complained for years that I wouldn't talk to her.

I asked Benedicte to tell me more about the fantasies of violence in the face of her mother's demands. Her associations led her to recount hesitantly, and for the first time, some of her erotic fantasies.

B: This is the most exciting scene I can imagine ... I'm a young man and I'm having a violent sodomic relationship with a much older man.

My own associations went as follows: the fantasy of the father killed through anal penetration is transformed into a scene in which the father becomes a live and phallic representation while anal penetration becomes erotically exciting and no longer mortally dangerous. The scene implies a literal fantasy of incorporating the father's penis and phallic strength, much as small children may imagine the narcissistic and libidinal possession of their parents could take place. I then thought of the predicament of a little girl of fifteen months whose father is suddenly missing when she needs him. At this age most children turn to their fathers in an attempt to detach themselves from their wish-for-and-fear-of fusional dependence upon their mothers (Roiphe and Galenson 1981). Thus, they strengthen not only their sense of subjective but also of sexual identity. Where did Benedicte turn to accomplish this task?

J: You say the only response to your mother's seductive attitude was violence. Could the violent sodomy also be a way of protecting yourself against her?

B: That reminds me. I had to hide all my childhood games from her ... Superman, Batman and the others were my constant companions. I was always a boy amongst men. She would never have allowed that.

J: You had to hide your wish to be a boy as well as your wish to have a man as a friend?

B: Yes ... I'm beginning to see ... this was the only way to have a secret relationship with my father ... in spite of her! If she'd found out she'd have taken him away from me again. I used to spend hours dreaming and writing stories about these powerful men who were my friends. Oh, I'd forgotten ... when I was adolescent I wrote what I called an 'opera'. Months of work. Then one day the book disappeared from my room. I never found it again. She destroyed it. It was something that took me away from her.

The theme of Benedicte's 'opera' was revealing. The whole action takes place in a subway station. An all-male cast, the central characters were a little boy, a gang of bad boys and a villainous old man. The little boy is betrayed by the old man and, broken-hearted, at the end of the opera he throws himself under a train! Benedicte linked the intriguing idea of calling her play an opera to 'operation' fantasies of her father 'in the hospital'. She must surely have felt betrayed by the absent father who, imprisoned in her mother's words, gave her no sign of recognition or remembrance. Did she have a little girl's fantasy that her father, in abandoning her, had castrated her? That he had left her to the mercy of her mother so that she was driven to keep him alive in fantasy, in games and, later, in her written stories? And was she able thus to maintain her own feeling of integrity and identity?

The writer's relation to words

I should like to emphasize at this point the extent to which words began to reveal themselves in Benedicte's analysis as the embodiment of paternal power and presence.

In a sense this unconscious significance is true for everyone in that it is through words that bodily perceptions and fantasies become organized as verbal constructs, aiding the child to maintain a clear representation of the difference between its own and its mother's body. This becomes a protection against the *voice* of the siren (rather than her words) since her voice and presence awaken fantasies of the wish for fusion with the consequent loss of both subjective and sexual identity. It seems evident that the transitional objects of infancy (Winnicott 1951) give way to language as an important internal possession, capable eventually of replacing the need for the external object with thoughts about the object.

Thus, words always leave in the shadow not only the 'thing' presentation for which they are the symbol, but also half of the meaning that they are purporting to transmit. In this sense they are doubly symbolic. Over and beyond the essential importance of the role of language in structuring the human psyche, for someone who is a writer, words may come to play a specifically privileged role due to their link with unconscious bisexual fantasies.

In Benedicte's case, the paralysis of her creative possibilities represented, among other aspects, an imaginary way of renouncing her secret link with her father through language and story-building, a link that was forbidden by her mother. In destroying her 'opera', Benedicte's mother may well have sensed in a confused way that this work incorporated a serious rival and that her only child was escaping her. On the psychoanalytic stage, as the image of the internal father slowly came alive, mobilizing dynamic thoughts and fantasies in its wake, Benedicte began to write again. Her first book published after the beginning of her analysis led to her being invited to participate in a national television programme devoted to present-day authors whose work attracts attention. During this broadcast a member of the panel asked Benedicte a question concerning the sophisticated and somewhat impalpable impression conveyed by the novel. Benedicte replied: 'It's because ... this is a book written by a child.'

The father, loved and hated

However, the search for the lost father did not proceed easily, for there was in Benedicte, as in every child, an internal father to be eliminated as a stumbling-block to the illusory hope of taking full possession of the mother. In addition, the apparent determination of Benedicte's mother to create in her child's mind an illusory family where only females counted suggests that Oedipal interdictions were transmitted at an unduly young age, perhaps before the age at which the sense of sexual identity is normally well established. Thus, the mother's unconscious fears and wishes coincided with that part of the little Benedicte who wanted an exclusive relationship with her mother. It was not surprising that dreams and day-dreams came to light in which Benedicte herself was responsible for the death of her father. A dream-theme that had persisted for many years depicted her being pursued for a crime she had committed.

One day when Benedicte was struggling in a confused way with these various internal fathers and mothers, I decided to interpret the different 'I's' seeking to express themselves in her associations.

J: There are several Benedictes talking at the same time. First of all there's the little boy trying to keep alive an absent father, then the young man who is protecting himself 'violently' from his omnipresent mother. And then there's the woman in you who seeks to repair another woman with her love, as well as trying to be different in every way from her own mother. But you seem to be having difficulty with the *little girl* who longed for both her parents so that she might know her place in the family — who she was, and for whom. You're still struggling with the incoherent images of your parents as a couple.

The latter statement aroused a massive reaction.

B: It's absurd to hear you say 'your parents'. No child ever wished for two parents . . . In that way at least I was lucky. That little girl had no father!

Benedicte's anger over my interpretation continued for many weeks during which time she accused me of being the victim of social bunkum, of second-hand ideas and of sentimentality over the death of an unknown father.

The first 'trace' of mourning

An unforeseen incident provided us with the opportunity of crystallizing the first trace of the dead father and the undoubtedly catastrophic conse-quences of his sudden disappearance. One day, a sound from the office next to my consulting-room alerted me to the fact that I had forgotten to switch on my answering machine. For the first time in some four years of analytic work with Benedicte, I got up in the middle of the session and left the room.

B: While you were out I dreamed up an amusing scene. I had an impulse to leave the room myself and began to imagine what you would think on coming back and finding the room empty.

J: What was I going to think?

B: Well first of all you wouldn't be sure if I'd really been there or not before you left the room. But then, just as I imagined myself running away, I remembered that I'd left so quickly I'd forgotten my jacket on the chair! So the whole scene was ruined.

Thinking of Benedicte's mother who 'could not tolerate the slightest trace' of Benedicte's bodily presence, plus the sudden disappearance of her father, I answered without reflecting.

J: You would have left a trace behind?

B: The jacket. His jackets! He must have left his jackets. My cousins told me it was a lightning illness. No one expected him to die. The jackets . . . I remember the smell of them. Not my father's . . . my uncle's. When I was six or seven, after we went back to live with my grandmother, I would spend hours playing in his wardrobe, smelling and touching his jackets. It was one of my favourite games, but I was very careful to hide it from my mother.

Later Benedicte came to tell me how, in her early adolescence, she played for some years a game in which she imagined that it was her job to select and buy men's clothes for an important enterprise. She would spend hours in clothing stores, examining the cut, the quality and so on of the suits and jackets. When her adolescent girl-friends pretended they were adult women picking out the clothes they would buy for themselves, Benedicte would say that she was a married woman and had to choose her husband's clothes. She was well aware that she did not dream of a future husband but was totally unaware that she sought to keep alive a link with her lost father.

Thus we found the first signs of the work of mourning, instituted by a small girl who sought some trace of her father through his clothes, in the way that many children create their first transitional objects, demanding to sleep with a handkerchief or piece of clothing belonging to their mothers.

B: All my childhood games . . . I've never thought of their meaning nor why they were different from other children's games. I only knew that my mother would disapprove. I had to play her games, not mine!

A recurring screen memory acquired additional poignancy around this time.

B: Those two dolls that someone gave me when I was nearly three, a boy and a girl ... I only ever played with the boy, talking to him, dressing and undressing him ... then one day my mother said they needed repairing. When they came back, both were girls. The boy ... my mother killed him! I still recognized him by a tiny little trace, but I never touched the dolls again.

Shortly after the session in which Benedicte announced the assassination of the boy–doll, a new version of her repetitive crime-dream came forth in which she was merely the witness.

Benedicte dreamed that she watched a scene in which a man was killed in a neighbour's kitchen.

Her associations led her to think of the film *La Grande Bouffe* in which a dead man is laid out amidst the food that has been prepared for the funeral celebration. The principal characters were men but Benedicte sought to remember the role of the woman in this film. Her various associations to the dream and the film led me to suggest that as a little child she had perhaps believed that her mother had killed her father by devouring him.

This interpretation created a shock-effect and led Benedicte to bring forth a stream of memories ... of mother eating more than her share of Benedicte's ice-creams, or displaying lengthily her constant digestive and eliminatory problems.

The following day Benedicte brought another dream in which heterosexual desire and love would lead to death. For some time she had talked of her strong attraction to and admiration for a young man who was a clarinet-player. Although the attraction appeared to be shared, Benedicte forbade herself any realization of her desire on the grounds of her friend's age and the fact that she had known his mother in the past which she felt made him something like a son. In other words she lived the relationship as an incestuous one. Here is the dream.

B: *I was admiring a rare and beautiful bird ... it was enclosed in a clarinet. I watched it with fascination. Then I turned to tell you about it and saw on your face a look of absolute horror, because the bird was being crushed inside the musical instrument. His blood was flowing through all the holes and his body was being torn to pieces. I realized suddenly that he was going to die and ... I woke up.*

A chain of associations formed in my own mind while listening to Benedicte's account of her dream: the bird whose body was being crushed while it lost its blood through the holes seemed to point to fantasies of the father's rectal cancer and death, and was confirmed in a sense by the incest taboo associated in Benedicte's mind with the young clarinet-player. The instrument then became a dream representation of Benedicte's own sex as an organ that would be dangerous for any man she desired. Once again there is a glimpse into a strange and terrifying primal scene, as imagined by a child. My role in the dream is to reveal its horror to Benedicte. Her associations took this as their starting-point.

B: My first thought ... I want you to shock me, perhaps batter my mind, with your interpretations. Like yesterday ... about my mother having killed my father by eating him.

Thus Benedicte now invites me to commit violence; through my words I am to embody the castrative and murderous image that the small Benedicte of the past attributed to her mother. While examining her transference feelings, Benedicte began to think of her own violence and fierce jealousy of my other patients, as well as her anger at having discovered my husband's name on a letter-box at the entrance to my building.

B: In fact I want to be not only your sole patient but the only person in your life.
J: To devour me?
B: Yes ... to crush the life out of you. I'm ... exactly like my mother!

We see here that the phallic castration represented in the dream hides a prototypic castration-fantasy in which life itself is endangered.

B: Under the mask of love my mother sucked the blood from my veins ... and I'm shocked to discover that there's a part of myself that wants to do exactly that with the people I love. But there's something different. In love I refined my body through the body of another woman, provided she herself loves her body and takes pleasure in love-making. Then there's no murderous exchange. That's one thing my mother did not manage to crush and obliterate.

Benedicte remained silent as she reflected over the changing images in the dream and the thoughts that followed. Just before the end of the session she posed, for the first time, the following question.

B: But whose body do I live in?

Her father's? Her mother's? Which is hers? Here my patient touched upon her confusion since childhood as to her sexual identity and even her identity as a separate individual. A final fragment from her analysis may serve to illustrate the theme of sexual identity as it relates to a small child's identification to both parents. In Benedicte's case, the task was rendered more difficult due to the specific circumstances in which the sudden loss of her father had constituted an early psychic trauma that could not be elaborated mentally because Benedicte's mother herself was unable to deal with it. The following sessions were noted in the fifth year of our work together.

Benedicte's transformation

B: I study you attentively ... your way of holding yourself ... the way you walk and sit ... your clothes, your hair style, your make-up ...

I asked her what she sought to learn from this careful study.

B: I want to know how you see yourself as a woman ... and what it feels like to be a woman. I don't know what a woman is ... nor a man either. This weekend I tried, for the first time in five years, to imagine your body under your clothes.

There followed a heavy silence as though Benedicte were afraid to continue. I also was struck by her emphasis on the 'five years', thinking of the secret calendar we all carry in our preconscious minds, and of the fact that Benedicte was 5 years old when the truth of her father's death could no longer be denied.

B: But I could not go any further with the thought of your body, as though ... I were afraid you would ... disapprove.
J: What would I disapprove of?
B: The idea comes to me that you might have something to hide. (*A long silence*)
J: And what am I hiding?
B: Something like ... a mutilation ... or a shameful deformity.

The fact that on several occasions we had already discussed the fantasy of woman as a castrated man led me to feel that the present associations had to do with something more primitive, or more specific to Benedicte, than the quasi-universal fantasy of feminine 'castration'. I invited her therefore to try to imagine further the nature of my deformity.

B: It'll be difficult to tell all my thoughts since last Friday ... things I have carefully avoided telling from the very beginning of my analysis.

Benedicte then went on to recount that her friend Marie-Christine had once told her, many years ago, that Benedicte's pubic hair was distributed in a masculine way. Her lover claimed she found it attractive, but it evoked in Benedicte a feeling of explosive rage and hatred towards her. She had suffered all her life from an impression that her body was monstrous and, as she put it, 'ambiguous' and that it had become more so as she advanced into adulthood. Marie-Christine's words suddenly confirmed this fantasy.

B:That's the reason I always wear tight-fitting jeans and clinging sweaters . . . if anything is floating around my body it might give the impression I have something to hide . . . as though my female shape might not be evident or as though I might be afflicted with a man's sex . . . even if I may have wished this as a child, it's certainly not true today. But the sudden appearance of these secondary sexual characteristics is just as terrifying to me. I've not worn shorts or a bathing suit for over ten years and I've given up swimming and sunbathing altogether.

In reply to a question on my part concerning the 'sudden' appearance of this masculine pubic hair Benedicte explained in detail that as far as she could make out it had occurred shortly after the death of Fredrika's husband. For a number of years before his (quite unexpected) death Benedicte, knowing Fredrika was very unhappy with her husband, desired ardently to take his place, and had frequently imagined ways of killing him. She had often wondered since then whether the shock of his actual death may have produced this hormonal change. Just before the end of this session I pointed out to Benedicte that she had talked of her own feeling of being mutilated but had not been able to explore further her fantasy of my shameful deformity. The thought that our bodies were both feminine and could be compared apparently gave Benedicte the feeling, after the session, that she had a right to study her own body in more detail, perhaps in the manner of a little girl seeking to gleam knowledge about her feminine self from her mother's body and way of being.

B: Last night I tried to imagine your body and to grasp what was so forbidden about this thought. This allowed me to stand in front of the mirror and for the first time in ten years look at myself in the nude. Would you believe it – there's nothing at all wrong with my pubic hair. Absolutely nothing! It isn't the neat and pretty triangle it could be, but there's no hint of anything masculine. And to think of all those years I have hidden my monstrosity from everybody!

We then spent some time examining Benedicte's conflictual feelings following the death of Fredrika's husband. On the one hand, a husband had to die before she could feel sure of her place in the world; in her imagination this would allow her to possess her own femininity through the femininity of the other woman. At the same time, a deeply unconscious fantasy prompted her to seek any possible trace of a living father-figure that she could keep as a vital part of herself. In her total illusory 'hormonal change', she had carried out a fantasy of *incorporating* the dead husband of her lover. As a very small child she would seem to have believed that she had *become her lost father by a similar process of primitive internalization*. In seeking to possess the mental representation of two parents capable of conferring upon her the status of subjective and of sexual identity, it appeared that the price to be paid was her own castration – the loss of her femininity.

B: You were the first person ever to tell me that I had had two parents. I now see that I had kept traces of my father alive everywhere, both outside and inside myself.

Indeed this seemed to me to be profoundly true, for Benedicte's professional life as well as her love-life were both living monuments to her dead father.

B: And I also thought that you, or any woman, should be wary of me ... because I do not possess my own female body. It's only through the body of another woman that I regain mine.

J: In order to possess your own body, in order to be a woman, you have to dispossess me? There cannot be two women?

I thought to myself that unconscious identifications are something like one's liberty. The latter cannot be handed out with permission; one has, at some time, to reach out and assume it for oneself. It requires the sexual representation of two parents in order to acquire a firm sense of one's own sexual identity, but the confusing and traumatic circumstances that surrounded Benedicte's understanding of what constituted her own sexual identity had left her with only partial identifications concerning her gender and sexual role.

B: Yes! it's as though I have to take something away from you but I don't know why. Also I still can't imagine what your deformity might be ... but I had an important thought about that. I said to myself that I love you and that no matter what monstrosity or what bodily deformity you might hide, it would make absolutely no difference to my feelings for you.

J: In other words you have never been sure that this is also true for you ... that you too could be loved no matter what body, no matter what sex, you have?

There followed an astonished silence before Benedicte was able to reply and when she did her voice trembled through her tears.

B: How strange ... I never believed I could be loved, with my body, with my sex ... just as I am ... just because I am ... me.

I shall leave the story of Benedicte's analysis at this point, simply adding that, among other changes, her analysis permitted her to refind and truly liberate her creative potential. Within a relatively short span of time Benedicte produced several intense and fascinating works and I feel confident that this creative source will not dry up again in the future. She also found the courage to ask her mother to give her more details of her father and her relationship with him before his death. The mother replied that it could not possibly have any meaning for Benedicte because children of that age are unaware of their fathers! She did however add, in the face of Benedicte's insistence that her father had been the one who principally cared for her when she was teething or restless in her sleep. He also frequently helped with her bodily care, since he did not suffer, as did her mother, from any repugnance about soiled diapers. 'There you were, so excited, jumping up and down at the sight of him, with your diaper full of shit, and he would grab you up and hold you in his arms as though it didn't matter. You see, he wasn't a classical father.'

Concluding remarks

In this paper my primary object has been to trace, with the aid of a pertinent clinical example, the early elements that contribute to the origins of one's sense of sexual identity and the factors that may hinder the psychic process essential to the establishment of a secure sense of core gender and sexual role. These include identifications to both parents and therefore require the capacity to resolve the universal bisexual and incestuous wishes of childhood as well as institute the mourning processes needed to assume one's monosexuality without neurotic, characterological or sexual distortions. The integration of the bisexual longings of childhood enriches the personality in many ways, strengthening one's narcissistic self-image and sense of sexual identity, as well as contributing to the capacity to be creative in intellectual, scientific or artistic fields. In the clinical illustration to these themes, the role of early psychic trauma played an essential role for Benedicte who lost her father at the age of fifteen months and was thus left a prey to her mother's internal confusions and inability herself to face the traumatic loss of her husband. Her attempt to deny that the father had ever truly existed for her daughter had forced the latter to accomplish a magical mourning for her lost father by, in a sense, becoming him.

It is my hope that I have been able to communicate something of the struggle that a little girl, in traumatizing circumstances, felt obliged to maintain, in order to protect her feeling of identity and her sexuality.

Perhaps this analytic vignette might at the same time throw some light upon the struggle of every little girl in her attempt to safeguard her sense of integrity and the conviction of her personal and sexual value.

Summary

This paper explores the origins of two clinical phenomena which are frequently related in analytic practice, namely sexual deviancy and inhibition in creative or intellectual work. The analysands in question seek psychoanalytic help not for their sexual acts and object–choices but because of blockage in their professional activities.

In the author's opinion the roots of both sexual deviancy and creativity may often be traced back to early psychic trauma. The sexual 'solution' and the creative activity both represent ways of attempting to overcome the traumatic situation of infancy.

These propositions are illustrated by the case of an author who sought help because her writing was completely blocked and because her homosexual love relations caused tension and concern. The sudden death of her father when she was fifteen months old and her mother's disturbed way of handling the tragic situation were decisive factors in both the patient's sexual and professional life.

References

Bion, W. (1963). *Elements of Psychoanalysis.* London: Heinemann.

McDougall, J. (1964). Homosexuality in women. In *Female Sexuality: New Psycho-analytic views*, ed. J. Chasseguet-Smirgel. Ann Arbor: Michigan Univ. Press. 1970.

—— (1978). *Plea for a Measure of Abnormality.* New York: Int. Univ. Press, 1982.

—— (1982). *Theatres of the Mind.* New York: Basic Books, 1985.

—— (1986a). Eve's reflection: on the homosexual components of female sexuality. In *Between Analyst and Patient*, ed. H. Meyers. New York: Analytic Press.

—— (1986b). Identifications, neoneeds and neo–sexualities. *Int. J. Psychoanal.*, 67: 19–31.

—— (1986c) Parent loss. In *The Reconstruction of Trauma*, ed. A. Rothstein. New York: Int. Univ. Press.

Roiphe, H. and Galenson, E. (1981). *Infantile Origins of Sexual Identity*. New York: Int. Univ. Press.

Segal, H. (1957). Notes on symbol formation. *Int. J. Psychoanal.*, 38: 391–7.

Stoller, R. (1968). *Sex and Gender*. New York: Jason Aronson.

Winnicott, D.W. (1951). Transitional objects and transitional phenomena. In *Collected Papers*. New York: Basic Books, 1958.

———————————— 12 ————————————

Dis-identifying from mother: its special importance for the boy

RALPH R. GREENSON

The early psychoanalytic literature stressed the special problems the little girl has to overcome in order to achieve a satisfactory sex life and the capacity to love. The female child must work through two important conflictual areas from which the male is spared. She must shift her major erogenous zone from the clitoris to the vagina and must renounce the mother as her primary love object and turn to the father and men (Freud 1925, 1931, 1933, 1940). The purpose of this presentation is to focus attention on a special vicissitude in the normal psychological development of the boy which occurs in the pre-Oedipal years. I am referring to the fact that the male child, in order to attain a healthy sense of maleness, must replace the primary object of his identification, the mother, and must identify instead with the father. I believe it is the difficulties inherent in this additional step of development, from which girls are exempt, which are responsible for certain special problems in the man's gender identity, his sense of belonging to the male sex.

The girl too must dis-identify from mother if she is to develop her own unique identity, but her identification with mother *helps* her establish her femininity. It is my contention that men are far more uncertain about their maleness than women are about their femaleness. I believe women's certainty about their gender identity and men's insecurity about theirs are rooted in early identification with the mother.

I am using the term 'dis-identify' in order to sharpen my discussion about the complex and interrelated processes which occur in the child's struggle to free himself from the early symbiotic fusion with mother. It plays a part in the development of his capacity for separation-individuation, to use Mahler's terminology (Mahler 1963, 1965; Mahler and La Perriere 1965). The male child's ability to dis-identify will determine the success or failure of his later identification with his father. These two phenomena,

258

dis-identifying from mother and counter-identifying with father, are interdependent and form a complementary series. The personality and behaviour of mother and father also play an important and circular role in the outcome of these developments (Mahler and La Perriere 1965). The mother may promote or hinder the dis-identifying and the father does the same for counter-identification.

I became alerted to the possibility of some special difficulty in the development of the male's gender identity from a variety of clinical experiences. I have been working for five years in a research project at the University of California at Los Angeles studying transsexuals, people who wish to undergo surgery in order to change their anatomical sex.[1] These patients are normal biologically, and are not psychotic; but they are convinced that they belong mentally and emotionally to the opposite sex. (Incidentally, they abhor homosexuality.) On the basis of the prevalence of women's penis envy and men's contempt of women in our society, I had expected that most of the transsexual patients would be women wanting to become men. Instead, the study of a hundred cases over a nine-year period revealed that between two-thirds and three-quarters were men hoping to become women (Stoller 1964). Similar studies by others indicate an even higher ratio (Pauly 1965; Benjamin 1966).

These patients are a very select and small group and perhaps not a reliable indicator of the male's greater discontent with his gender identity. The fact that transvestitism is almost exclusively a male disease and more widespread than commonly believed, is a more impressive testimonial for man's dissatisfaction with maleness and his wish to be a female. Furthermore, my own clinical experience with relatively healthy neurotics in psychoanalysis also points in the same direction. It is true that my female patients envy men in a variety of ways, particularly their possession of a penis, as well as their greater social, economic and political advantages. However, I am impressed by the fact that on an earlier, more deeply unconscious level, my male patients harbour an intense envy of the female, particularly the mother. Each sex is envious of the opposite sex; but the male's more covert envy underneath his external façade of contempt, seems to be particularly destructive in regard to his gender identity (Bettelheim 1954; Greenson 1966b).

I can illustratre this point by the following material: my men patients frequently reveal a history of putting on some female undergarment in their masturbatory activities as a sign of their fantasy of being a woman. I do not recall any female patient describing anything analogous. This may well be related to the fact that fetishism is also almost 100 per cent a male disease. Even neurotic women who imagine they are enacting male, phallic activities in the sexual act, usually visualize themselves as women with a penis, not as men. (The overt 'butch' homosexual is a special problem and beyond the limits of this paper.)

It is my clinical impression that the dread of homosexuality in the neurotic, which is at bottom the fear of losing one's gender identity, is stronger and more persistent in men than in women (Greenson 1964). Observations of the current social scene also demonstrate that men are far more uncertain about their masculinity than women are of their femininity (Mead 1949). Women may doubt their attractiveness but they are quite sure of their femaleness. Women feel at their most feminine in the company of the opposite sex, whereas men feel at their most masculine in the presence of men. Furthermore, as women have become sexually more assertive and demand equal orgasms along with their other equal rights, men seem to have become sexually more apathetic and lethargic (Greenson 1966b).

Let me return to the problem of the male's envy of woman. I believe that envy is one of the main driving forces in man's wish to be a woman and originates in the early envy all children feel towards the mother. The Kleinians have attempted to explain this on the basis of the infant's envy of the mother's joy — and security — giving the breast (Klein 1957). Although I do not deny this explanation, it nonetheless neglects other important factors which seem to explain better the *difference* in the envy of men and women.

The general clinical findings sketched above were the starting point for my deliberations about the role of the boy's early identification with the mother and the importance of his ability to dis-identify from her. In my work with a 'transsexual-transvestite' 5½-year-old boy, Lance, I had an opportunity to observe the problem of dis-identifying at first hand (Greenson 1966a).

This lively, intelligent, well-orientated boy was highly disturbed in two major interrelated areas of his development. In the first place, he had not made that step in the maturational process which enables one to distinguish loving someone from identifying with someone. As a consequence, he was consumed by the wish to be a female: he acted and dressed as a girl. This was not an obsession or compulsion but an all-consuming wish that approached a conviction, a delusion. If Lance had not been treated, I believe he would have become either a full-fledged transsexual or a transvestite, in order to fulfil this conscious wish. (In *homosexuals* this wish is *unconscious*.)

In the presentation of this case at Amsterdam Congress, I described how Lance dressed up his 'Barbie' doll as a princess and went to a ball with her and how he danced her around the ballroom very joyously. When I followed the princess and told her how beautiful she was, how much I wanted to hold her and dance with her, and that I loved her, etc., Lance finally said to me, 'Go ahead, you can be the princess.' I replied, 'I don't want to *be* the princess, I want to dance with her.' Lance was baffled. I repeated this several times until the boy permitted me to dance with the princess. He watched this, puzzled and upset. Finally he asked me if I dance with my wife, love my wife, etc. I said 'Yes, I do.' The boy left the session deep in thought.

Shortly after this episode, Lance no longer referred to the Barbie doll as 'I' or 'we' but only as 'she'. Soon after that he rarely played with Barbie and when he did there was a sexual element in the play which had not been present before. From this time onward he developed a strong identification with me and then with his father. For the first time Lance manifested behaviour which indicated he was unmistakably in the phallic Oedipal phase.

I believe that Lance's central problem was his inability to complete his separation–individuation from his mother. Lance's mother was extremely possessive and gratified him excessively in terms of tactile and visual contact. In addition, the mother hated and disrespected her husband and men in general. I was an exception. The father was afraid of his wife and a failure in his work. He was absent from the home a great deal and had little if any pleasurable contacts with the boy. In my opinion, although Lance was able to develop a self-representation as distinct from object representation, this failed when it came to establishing a realistic gender identity.

It is precisely in this area that I believe the boy's capacity to dis–identify himself from his mother is of paramount importance. The girl can acquire feminine characteristics by means of her identification with the mother. Her femaleness is practically assured if she is raised by a female mothering person. The boy has a more difficult and far less certain path to pursue. He must dis–identify from mother and identify with a male figure if he is to develop a male gender identity. Greenacre (1958: 618) hints at this point when she states that women seem to show more frequent but *less gross disturbances* in this area. Jacobson (1964) also raises the question of why women do not develop more identity problems than men. I believe that both authors are touching on the same issues I am trying to delineate – the boy's special problem of dis-identifying from mother and forming a counter-identification with father.

I would like to pursue this last point in a little more detail, although the limitations of space will only permit an outline of the subject. I believe that we would all agree that in early infancy both girls and boys form a primitive symbiotic-identification with the mothering person on the basis of the fusion of early visual and tactile perception, motor activity, introjection and imitation (Freud 1914, 1921, 1923, 1925; Fenichel 1945; Jacobson 1964). This results in the formation of a symbiotic relationship to the mother (Mahler 1963). The next step in the development of ego-functions and object relations is the differentiation of self-representation from object representations. Mahler (1957), Greenacre (1958), Jacobson (1964) and others have elucidated how different forms of identification play a central role in this transition as maturation makes it possible to progress from total incorporation to selective identifications. The capacity to differentiate between similarities and contrasts eventuates in the capacity to discriminate between inside and outside and ultimately the self and the non-self. In this process, the child learns he is a distinct entity, different from mother, dog, table, etc. However, he also gradually learns by identification to behave and perform certain activities like the mothering person, such as speaking, walking, eating with a spoon, etc. These activities are not duplications, but are modified in accordance with the child's constitution and his mental and physical endowment. The style of his behaviour and activities are further changed by his later identifications with others in the environment. What we call identity seems to be the result of the synthesis and integration of different isolated self-representations (Jacobson 1964; Spiegel 1959).

I would now like to focus on one aspect of these developments – the development of the gender identity. The formation of one's gender identity is still relatively nebulous. In a previous presentation (Greenson 1964), I suggested three factors which play a role in this process: (a) awareness of the anatomical and physiological structures in oneself, according to Greenacre (1958), primarily the face and the genitals; (b) the assignment to a specific gender, done by the parents and other important social figures, in accordance with the overt sexual structures: (c) a biological force which seems to be present at birth. To verify these points, I can state that in our Gender Identity Clinic, I have seen boys who behaved completely boyishly despite the fact that they were born without a penis and no visible testes. They were treated like boys by their parents and this seemed to be decisive. We have seen many pseudo-hermaphrodites in this clinic who live their life in a biologically false gender role without any manifest doubts about their identity. Yet we also know that in some children there seems to be a biological force which is strong enough to counteract their overt anatomy and the parent's assignment of sex (Stoller 1964). This is rare and does not represent a typical outcome. Clinically, all three factors interact to establish one's sense of gender.

I believe that a fourth factor must be added, in the boy, to those already mentioned. I am referring to the dis-identifying from mother and his developing a new identification with the father. This is a special problem because the boy must attempt to renounce the pleasure and security-giving closeness that identification with the mothering person affords, and he must form an identification with the less accessible father. The outcome will be determined by several elements. The mother must be

262

willing to allow the boy to identify with the father figure. She can facilitate this by genuinely enjoying and admiring the boy's boyish features and skills and must look forward to his further development along this line (A. Freud 1965).

The other vital component in this switch of identification in the boy consists of the motives the father offers for identifying with him. Lance (Greenson 1966a) did not identify with his father because his father was a frightened, joyless man. There was little motive for identifying with him. The essential therapeutic part of his work with me was his eagerness to identify with me because I seemed to him to enjoy life and to be unafraid. Later on, when his father improved from his own psychotherapy, Lance did identify with the father. I should add that part of the motivation to identify with the father stems from the mother's love and respect for the father. Identification based on other grounds seem to be less reliable (A. Freud 1965).

The questions which now arise are the following: What happens to the original identification with mother, after the boy has identified with father? Does the identification with mother disappear, its place taken by the new identification? Does it remain but become latent because it is superseded in importance by the identification with father? How much of the boy's identification with the father is a counter-identification, actually a 'contra'-identification, a means of counteracting the earlier identification? Is it not in this area where we can find an answer to why so many men are uncertain about their maleness? Perhaps it is the shaky basis of their identification with the father, their contra-identification, which makes them so reactively contemptuous of women and so envious, unconsciously. Perhaps the mothers of fifty years ago who dressed and combed their boys as girls intuitively recognized that one had to gratify each phase of the child's development in order to ensure his future maturation. By satisfying the boy's early need to identify with mother, he was better able to make the later step of identifying with father.

I realize I have raised more questions than I have answered, but I hope future work and discussion will bring greater clarification to this important area.

Notes

Presented at the 25th International Psycho-Analytical Congress, Copenhagen, July 1967. The author is Clinical Professor of Psychiatry, UCLA School of Medicine, Los Angeles, California; Scientific Director, Foundation for Research in Psychoanalysis, Beverly Hills, California.

1 Gender Identity Research Project, Robert Stoller, M.D., Director, UCLA School of Medicine, Los Angeles, California.

References

Benjamin, H. (1966). *The Transsexual Phenomenon*. (New York: Julian Press.)

Bettelheim, B. (1954). *Symbolic Wounds*. (Illinois: The Free Press.)

Fenichel, O. (1945). *The Psychoanalytic Theory of Neurosis*. (New York: Norton.)

Freud, A. (1965). *Normality and Pathology in Childhood*. (New York: Int. Univ. Press.)

Freud, S. (1914). 'On narcissism: an introduction.' S.E., 14.

—— (1921). *Group Psychology and the Analysis of the Ego*. S.E. 18.

—— (1923). *The Ego and the Id*. S.E., 19, 3

—— (1925). 'Negation.' S.E., 19.

—— (1931). 'Female sexuality.' S.E. 23.

—— (1933). *New Introductory Lectures on Psycho-Analysis*. S.E., 22.

—— (1940). *An Outline of Psycho-Analysis*. S.E. 23.

Greenacre, P. (1958). 'Early physical determinants in the development of the sense of identity.' *J. Amer. Psychoanal. Assoc.*, 6.

Greenson, R. (1964). 'On homosexuality and gender identity.' *Int. J. Psycho-Anal.*, 45.

—— (1966a). 'A transvestite boy and a hypothesis.' *Int. J. Psycho-Anal.*, 47.

—— (1966b). 'The enigma of modern woman.' *Bull. Philadelphia Assoc. Psychoanal.*, 16.

Jacobson, E. (1964). *The Self and the Object World*. (New York: Int. Univ. Press.)

Klein, M. (1957). *Envy and Gratitude*. (London: Tavistock.)

Mahler, M. (1957). 'On two crucial phases of integration concerning problems of identity: separation-individuation and bisexual identity.' Abstracted in Panel on Problems of Identity, reported by Rubinfine. *J. Amer. Psychoanal. Assoc.*, 6.

—— (1963). 'Thoughts about development and individuation.' *Psychoanal. Study Child*, 18.

—— (1965). 'On the significance of the normal separation-individuation phase.' In: *Drives, Affects, Behavior*, Vol. 2, ed. Schur. (New York: Int. Univ. Press.)

Mahler, M., and La Perriere, K. (1965). 'Mother-child interaction during separation-individuation.' *Psychoanal. Quart.*, 24.

Mead, M. (1949). *Male and Female*. (New York: Morrow.)

Pauly, I. (1965). 'Male psychosexual inversion: transsexualism.' *Arch. Gen. Psychiatr.*, 13.

Spiegel, L. (1959). 'The self, the sense of self, and perception'. *Psychoanal. Study Child*, 14.

Stoller, R. (1964a). 'A contribution to the study of gender identity.' *Int. J. Psycho-Anal.*, 45.

—— (1964b). 'Female (vs. male) transvestism.' Unpublished paper presented before the American Psychoanalytic Association, May 1964.

Clinical notes on the identification with the little girl

MARILIA AISENSTEIN

Beguiling and bewitching, the little girl appears throughout Freud's writing. She has a special place in it: is it not the vision of her which leads to the discovery of castration? She lays down forever the roots of primal fantasy.

In literature, from Perrault to Nabokov by way of Grimm and Andersen, small girls elicit complex feelings. Out of a dream or fantasy arises all the ambiguity and the overdetermination of the seductive image. The 'Rat Man' has a day–dream which stages a little girl cutting the link between the two partners of the same sex.[1]

The patient from whom I take my material came to analysis because he had become the father of a little girl. In the course of three sessions, I thought I could read a particular destiny in his identification with the small girl: it grants him a reunion in the transference with an as yet undifferentiated object relation, under cover of which he will be able to tackle a homosexuality that had been put in second place and intolerable up till then.[2]

This man is extremely virile in appearance, and does not have the back-up of a homosexual pragmatism, nor even that of a 'phobia, or at least of a fear of being homosexual, constituted and felt as such. Yet homosexuality, in its most diverse modes, infiltrates his entire neurotic organization, including some costly failures such as moments of violence or acts of delinquency.

His childhood was an odd one. His family constellation is strangely similar to the one Freud describes in 'A childhood memory of Leonardo da Vinci':

> Leonardo's childhood was remarkable in precisely the same way as this picture. He had had two mothers: first, his true mother Caterina, from whom he was torn away when he was between three and five,

and then a young and tender stepmother, his father's wife, Donna Albeira. By his combining this fact about his childhood with the one mentioned above (the presence of his mother and grandmother) and by his condensing them into a composite unity, the design of 'St Anne with Two Others' took shape for him.[3]

I will give my patient the name Leonard, not only because of this similarity and the interest of this text from 1910 for a psychoanalytical understanding of homosexuality, but also following some different associative voices, of which one is his constitution in analysis of a sublimation.

To illustrate the avatars of his feminine identification, it does not much matter, I think, that my patient is not homosexual, for perverse activity often constitutes an escape outside the physical field which masks[4] — more than it illuminates — the identificatory levels constituted around Oedipal structuring and the two moments of castration.

The sequence presented here takes place around the beginning of the third year of treatment. Leonard committed himself to his analysis enthusiastically. It was the end of a long journey, for there is nothing in his background or his history which could lead him there. His demand, both imperious and touching, had left me puzzled: 'I want an analysis because I can't speak,' he had said to me, hammering away at his arm-chair. He no longer wanted to be violent. He had just become a father, he had a little girl: 'I want to be a real father.' What I understood at the time was: 'and not beat her or seduce her'; nowadays I would add: 'and not feel like a little girl'.

He had himself been violently treated by a brutal and unfair father whose inverted Oedipus complex at the homosexual level was revealed to be fairly virulent. This same father knew how to be gentle with the sisters, while they were little. He seduced the young women servants. Coming from the fallen and impoverished lower aristocracy of Britanny, the family led the life of deprived peasants, in a huge, dilapidated residence. The mother, a foreigner by birth, was relegated to one wing of the house with her children. She was pregnant, expecting Leonard, when she got herself married. In the first years of his life, Leonard moved around between the two wings. At the time of his adolescence, he was defini-tively installed in the one occupied by his paternal grandmother, his father and his young beautiful mistress, Aurélie, a former servant who had been seduced by the father when she was fifteen. Unlike the others, she had not left the house. She had made sure of her reign by taking in hand what was left of the estate, and she helped to bring about an unexpected material improvement. Leonard's father also moved around between the two wings. After Leonard he had had five daughters, and also continued his short-lived affairs.

Leonard describes a childhood during which the quantities of excitation to which he was subjected seem intolerable. He remembers a passive, overwhelming mother, who would endlessly fuss over him, and a step-mother too close to him in age who used to draw him into ambiguous, exciting games, and an authoritarian grandmother. Stick in hand, she got obedience from everyone. Leonard was a bad pupil. Beaten and badly treated by a father who could not bear any closeness with his son, or any investigative activity on his part, he attracted blows and punishments from masters and teachers. Very early on he got into running away. He became involved with gangs of 'thugs'. Together they made trouble, caused havoc, created panic at village dances and attacked girls on their own.

The violence, which was going to make him so afraid later on, always appears in situations of homosexual closeness. In the army, in a moment of blind anger, he had broken everything in sight and beaten up an officer. Instead of military service, he was made to do fifteen months in a psychiatric hospital. He came out of it very depressed, equipped with a 'prescription' decreed by a smart colonel–doctor: 'In civil life, you will marry and then you will forget all about that.'

For a time this was true. Leonard had broken off with his family. He came to Paris with no education and no money at all. He married the first girl he came across in a bar. He knew that up till then she had lived from prostitution, but he loved her none the less for that. He was very happy for two years with his first wife. This was always the way he spoke of her, without revealing her first name. One day, she disappeared. He was never to see her again. From this point he was to go through a number of years veiled in obscurity, which he does not much speak of. He committed thefts, 'jobs'. The day the others suggested an armed robbery, he put a brutal stop to his delinquent activity. 'You don't come back from that.'

I don't want to go on too long about Leonard's childhood, but we must return briefly to the episode of the first wife, who was also to reappear at times in the transference. The break–up of his marriage condenses some complex elements. It seems that Leonard was able to live through a period of tranquillity, protected by the presence of this woman who was highly attractive, lively and not passive like his mother, very much a woman and not adolescent like the Aurélie of his childhood. In the course of analysis, there would be revealed the very specific point[5] in their relationship, where he could not stop himself identifying with her, penetrated and prostituted. This movement was all the more unbearable to the extent that it was obviously opaque to him. He became violent, beat her several times to the point of sending her to hospital. He got back into dubious friendships. He had the idea of putting his wife out on the street so as to cease working for her. In short, he scared her enough for her to run away without leaving any traces. Leonard experienced this departure and his descent once more into delinquency as a repetition of fate, a repetition which had come about solely from the relentlessness of his feminine identification, against which he never ceases to struggle (among men, he sees himself in danger of being a woman, and with a women he tries to find a mode of investment emptied of any identification. So he is seeking the impossible and is thus always sent back to what he refuses).

At the time when he came to ask for analysis, he was living with a woman, very different from the first one, authoritarian and determined: a militant. The birth of his little girl was a challenge to this precarious situation. He had to be a father, and in order to do this he sought a father for himself beneath the exterior of a woman analyst. Against all appearances, it was the stability of the superego, much more than his remarkable insights,[6] which convinced me of Leonard's capacities for benefiting from a classical analysis. He knew how to make a novel out of his dreadful childhood, half Balzac, half Zola, and his text, more than his history, guaranteed that his functioning was predominantly neurotic.

To make the account clear, I should say that during the six months that preceded the first session, after the preliminary interviews, Leonard bought a small wood. He went there on Sundays, and often in the evenings after the session; he cleared space, cut down wood and chopped it ardently. This wood linked to the analysis (a way of managing his violence, his wood is also the place where he can be on his own) is the subject, like it, of quarrels between him and his wife. What is more, two years later he decided to acquire a professional qualification. He passed an entrance examination and completed a long training period under conditions which he considered very close to those of the army. He derived considerable benefit from this and has just taken the examination certifying the end of the training.

In the session following the exams – he had been absent while they were going on – he talks about the completed training. He is sorry it has ended, he had felt good 'between men'. He remembers his military service: at the time he had not been capable of profiting from it. The theory orals that he had been afraid of have gone very well. He was sure of himself and even calm. But the next day he almost 'had an attack'. The test consisted of creating a technical model, he was proud of it. The examiner passes behind him and 'fiddles with [*tripote*]' his model. Leonard is very upset, he wants to punch out. He restrains himself, but hears himself shouting while he is replying to the questions. He shouts during the session, getting angry with the examiner, with me, with himself. He remembers the army, and also his childhood investigations around a bicycle which he apparently 'fiddled with' to see how it worked. For this he got a tremendous thrashing from his father. Why did this panic overwhelm him one more time? What made him frightened [*mouiller*]? ['Mouiller in French means 'to wet'. By extension and in slang it means to be frightened. In the sexual vocabulary it means the feminine vaginal lubrication. Hence the patient could be heard saying 'I am excited like a woman' – Editor's note.] I simply stress this word. When he leaves me he is in a fury.

The next day he had a dream: he was making love with a little girl. The little girl is me, the analyst, he declares. He has already told me that I am like his first wife's little sister. He thinks of his father's Don Juan behaviour, of Aurélie, of his young sisters, and relates an old memory that has been gone over numerous times. He saw himself masturbating in a dress of his mother's with red spots, then the scene changed: he was slipping the dress on and masturbating in front of the mirror.

He is very pleased with this dream, he says, but still, when I link it back to the material from the day before, he says it is unbearable: 'everything is mixed up'.

Leaving this session, he does not go home; he takes himself to his wood where he prunes some trees with his saw and falls asleep. He is awoken by a nightmare: 'two men have penetrated into his wood'. He assures himself that it is a dream, but continues to be afraid. He imagines he needs an alarm, then understands the absurdity of his idea because the wood is isolated. He remains awake, realizing angrily that for the first time in his life he is afraid of being alone in his wood at night.

The movement of these three sessions is linear. Confronted with paternal seduction through the examiner who aroused him – fiddler – Leonard in vain attempts an identificatory reversal of the sadism; but faced with castration, of whose existence he wishes to be ignorant – even though his castration anxiety is strong – he finishes with his feminine identification in the heart of the Oedipus complex, which is the identification with the little girl. In other words, he discovers in his predicament the dual layering of castration. The classic problematic of castration–feminine identification is all the more poignant for not resulting in homosexuality, whether active or fantasized. His mother is not an Oedipal rival. Having set off to affirm himself woodcutter-wolf-rapist, poor Leonard finds himself forced to go and play at experiencing in reality the feeling of *Little Red Riding Hoods when they are alone in the woods*.

The appearance of the identification with the little girl, an ambiguous and overdetermined image, is always a fruitful but difficult moment during men's analyses, whether or not they are homosexual. Moreover, the affective charge is so great that Leonard breaks an associative chain by acting out:[7] going into the woods in the evening. It is an acting out in the analysis, taken back to the field of mentalization by way of a dream, so very different from the classic regressive moments that were habitual for him.

Leonard is the son of a Don Juan who, because of the 'negation of Oedipal failure'[8] cannot take on the role of the father of a son. I discern in my patient an early failure of homosexuality as something looking after intellectual acquisitions (the bad pupil), at the same time as a non-completion of resexualizing erotogenic masochism. His moments of blind violence don't seem to me to guarantee an identification with paternal sadism. They signify an attempt at dramatic escape outside the Oedipal conflict, less organized than homosexual activity would have been. They go back to a homosexuality repressed below the point of being figurable.

In spite of all these difficulties, Leonard requests an analysis because he has been unable to recognize and differentiate the father's gentle attitude towards his little girls. How could he be gentle with the little girls who are his rivals (in terms of siblings, he had five sisters)? And when he had always been fighting the little girl in himself? So it is with this capacity of his father's that he wants to identify.[9] He seeks to organize a basic gentle tendency in himself, both to make possible homosexual or heterosexual regressive movements, and in order to constitute sublimatory movements. To do this, he sets up a paternal transference onto a woman analyst, supported by a rigid and reassuring analytic framework. He seeks an unexciting father completely removed from the father he had loved. I would say that my being a woman was 'a guarantee', at the beginning of his treatment, of both the continuity of transferential movements and the narcissistic integrity of the analyst. If it is possible to be a man in the guise of a woman, the opposite is eminently dangerous.

The detail of the first two sessions, highly condensed, is interesting: Leonard says that he was able to feel alright in what Michael Fain has called 'the homosexual mass of brothers'. Moreover, he was able to be calm when confronted with non-fiddling examiners (the theory orals; we should remember that he also came to analysis to be able to speak). When faced with the seduction on the part of the examiner-fiddler, he risks becoming murderous and falls back on the feminine identification. He understands my intervention as 'You are a little girl'. The next day he responds with the dream of a small girl where it is no longer clear who is who. He declares that the little girl is me,[10] the analyst. He is doubly referred back to the paternal excitation.

Every time I represented the first wife in the transference, that brought in the first wife's little sister. Now it's certainly that which drives him crazy. If I am also a little girl, he no longer knows on whom to rely for support, and everything gets mixed up. Therein, it seems to me, lies the meaning of the screen-memory reworked in the transference.

First version: he is masturbating *in* his mother's dress = receptacle.

Second version: he is masturbating *disguised in* his mother's dress = he identifies with his mother who is archaic, pre-Oedipal, not sexually differentiated. In this situation he is defended against castration, but also he confirms in the mirror that he is himself a man in the mother's clothing. Which enables him to rediscover the hidden indestructible penis under a woman's skirts.

Protected by the maternal imago, he can approach, and it isn't simple, his feminine identification at the heart of the Oedipus complex. Nothing is yet decided.

But it is also here that all the ambiguity of the identification with the little girl emerges. In the 'Rat Man' case history, Freud had stressed the complexity of the appearance of a little girl (his own, indeed) in dreams. The theme of the identification with the little sister had been treated at length in the 'Wolf Man'. In the Schreber case and 'A seventeenth-century demonological neurosis', the question comes up of desires for castration engendered in the man by his feminine desires.[11] Yet the little girl herself has nothing to lose; she is the most confirmed in her narcissistic integrity. When Leonard goes into the depths of the woods in the evening, it is to establish the little girl's experience from the inside, but he also perhaps knows that in fairy tales, Little Red Riding Hoods come out again unharmed even when they have been eaten.

A stage or a turning-point in the hollow of the feminine identification, the image of the little girl is still there. In the course of any analysis, in the same way as with painting a picture, we have to rediscover the 'mixed unity' of little girl–venal woman- (the analyst or the patient, the classic fantasy sometimes being the reversal into the opposite)[12] mother.

Notes

Translated by Rachel Bowlby

1. Freud, 'Notes upon a case of obsessional neurosis' (1909), in SE 10, pp. 155–249.
2. I would like to say here how much use I have made of Evelyne Kestemberg's two very fine seminars, 'Homosexualité primaire' and 'Homosexualité masculine, homosexualité féminine' (Centre de Psychanalyse et de Psychothérapie, 1981 and 1981–2). But it is impossible for me to mention them every time I am alluding to them, since they provided me with the framework for this piece of work.

3 Freud, 'Leonardo da Vinci and a memory of his childhood' (1910), in SE 11, p. 113.

4 In the sense that anything done, even when it has a direct link with the fantasy on which it is based, may obliterate its meaning by a play of reversals.

5 She had asked him for sodomy, and taught him it.

6 'Insights' is in English in the original — RB.

7 In English in the original — RB.

8 Cf. Michel Fain, 'Réflexions à partir de certains aspects de la sexualité masculine', in Denise Braunschweig and Michel Fain, *Eros et Anteros* (Paris: Payot, 1971). (I have referred below to the theory of the double and of the role of siblings as the support of an early homosexuality.)

9 And not with the Don Juan figure, in whom he senses the inadequacies of the superego.

10 Cf. children's games during which they chant: 'It's the one who says it who is it.'

11 See Freud, 'Notes upon a case of obsessional neurosis' (note 1, above); 'From the history of an infantile neurosis' (1918), in SE 17, pp. 7–122; 'Psychoanaltyic notes on an autobiographical account of a case of paranoia' (Dementia Paranoides)' (1911) in SE 12, pp. 9–79; 'A seventeenth-century demonological neurosis' (1923) in SE 19, pp. 73–105.

12 Having put himself in a materially difficult situation, and after a highly elaborate dream of castration, Leonard has momentarily (so he says) ended his analysis. He would like to live 'an artist's life and not work for me any more'.

To the limits of male heterosexuality: the vagina-man

ADAM LIMENTANI

The men I describe in this paper may go through life without acknowledging any difficulty with their heterosexuality. They are intelligent, gifted and usually untroubled by the variations of their sexual drives, or the occasional fleeting interest in people of their own sex. Their femininity, only faintly noticeable to others, is as a rule well integrated and often put to good use in their professional lives. On the debit side, although they are capable of fairly lasting and deeply satisfying relationships with women, we find a high divorce rate and frequent changes of partners. Some of them can be exceptionally promiscuous, exploiting their capacity to attract women in a wholly effortless manner. Their promiscuity has a striking oral quality, in so far as they give the impression of being sexually insatiable, thus confirming the psychoanalytic observation of the equation penis = mouth. Many of them are little affected by an orgasmic incompetence which is hidden by a reasonable sexual performance. All these men are incapable of a full homosexual contact, though some have experimented with boys in childhood or early adolescence, but never intensely.

Brief reference should be made to their partners, who are mostly said to be strikingly beautiful, rather masculine, and intellectually powerful women. Whilst this description fits into the popular or psychoanalytic definition of the phallic woman, no notable features are reported about the partners of the promiscuous males, except for a willingness to engage in frequent, casual sexual intercourse.

Life stresses, physical illness and especially a breakdown in the relationship with a partner, make these people aware of the areas of darkness in their heterosexuality. Should they seek help, the added stress of the therapeutic situation highlights anxieties about their femininity and threatened homosexuality. Their early life invariably shows the presence of some traumatic experiences, but the picture of early object relations that emerges within the transference is in no way suggestive of true homosexuality. There is, for instance, no evidence that the latent homosexuality, if present, is being used as a defence against paranoid anxieties; there is no suggestion of seductive behaviour on the part of mother; there are no allegations of a very weak, or alternatively terrifying, father figure. On the other hand, and this may seem a contradiction, there is a great deal of evidence that mother was somewhat masculine, if not a phallic type of woman, who also treated her child as a phallus. My observations may also suggest that these mothers are possessive but capable of temperamental withdrawals and sudden rejections.

In the course of psychoanalytic treatment, the extent of the disturbance is brought to light, notably on account of a secret wish to be a woman, associated with a profound envy of everything female. In some instances the desire to be a woman is accompanied by an even more jealously guarded secret of possessing a fantasy vagina, when not only the anus and the mouth, but also the eye, the ear and the urethral orifice are endowed with receptive qualities similar to those of the vagina. It should be noted that in the majority of cases this fantasy has been subjected to repression. In some cases this part-object identification is implicit but well concealed by the whole-object identification.

If my notion of a vagina-man, the counterpart of the phallic woman, proves acceptable, we shall have to consider the reasons for the fact that the fantasy of having a vagina has not received the attention which it deserves. I can only offer some tentative explanations. In the first instance it is possible that the overwhelming orality displayed by these men in their analyses, coupled with our enslavement to conventional and generally accepted beliefs, has contributed to the neglect. On the other hand, the refinement of psychoanalytic techniques with a better understanding of the implications of protective and introjective identification has contributed to the clarification of the symptomology described in this paper.

Furthermore, the greater freedom enjoyed by men and women in expressing their desire to cross the boundaries of sexual genders, has encouraged the bringing into consciousness of fantasies which were until now subjected to denial, suppression and repression. The lesson to be learnt from the studies of transsexualism has not yet been absorbed by psychoanalysts. Is it not to be expected that many men could prefer to indulge in perverse fantasies of belonging to the other sex, avoiding fear of castration, and worst of all, the mutilation of their bodies?

Clinical illustrations

(1) Alan was thirty years old when he began a psychoanalysis on account of difficulty in sustaining relationships with women and work inhibitions. His heterosexuality was not questioned until the third year of analysis when it became apparent that his sexual experiences, though they could not be criticized in any way, were not accompanied by much satisfaction. It turned out that during intercourse his almost exclusive interest was focused on what the partner felt. The fact that he had no male friends and that in the transference he experienced ill-concealed anxiety towards the analyst as a man, naturally led to a careful investigation of latent homosexuality. This lack of male friends seemed to make little or no difference to his capacity to be in male company. Alan was in every way a male in physical appearance and deportment; yet he felt that his feminity was immediately noticeable to anyone who met him. That his girl friends did not share his view was of no reassurance to him. There had been, in fact, a succession of affairs, lasting long spells, with allegedly very beautiful women who without exception were remarkably intelligent, masculine and career-orientated. None of them had any interest in having children, which suited him well.

Alan's passivity and pervasive orality had been carefully and relentlessly analysed. Again there had been little change but, in view of many other improvements, as we reached the ninth year of the analysis, we decided to give ourselves one year's notice of termination. Alan was now under severe pressure and not only because he feared that he might be incapable of mourning me, just as at one time he had not been able to cope with his mother's death. He was worried because, having lived with a girl for three years, he had to decide whether he should marry her. He had no wish to interfere with her career, but he thought they should have a family. He feared ending up staying at home looking after the baby and hated the prospect of giving up his work. There were also other problems, as his professional success had brought him more responsibility, which he felt he should accept as a real man, but he still felt unequal to the task. His rapidly increasing passivity was reflected in the analysis, when he would lie motionless on the couch with his legs wide apart, demanding to be given interpretations whilst attempting to get inside my mind by urging me to express opinions on all sorts of problems. Alan bitterly complained that as a result of the analysis he was in the unpleasant position of having to give all the time, when all he wanted to do was to be at the receiving end. This material was at first understood in the light of the impending separation, still a long way off, but the situation remained unchanged. On the other hand, the emphasis began to shift towards a renewed intensity of his anxieties about his femininity. I made some very incomplete notes at the time, concentrating on what was relevant for me to some work I was doing on transsexuals.

275

Alan announced at the start of the session that he had some big things to talk about but promptly took up other matters in an attempt to divert attention from himself. I allowed him to get back on course, on his own, as in the counter-transference I was getting a feeling that I was being forced into a role of a powerful, controlling female, the dominating figure in his infancy and love life. He then said he had seen Shaw's *Man and Superman* and had been deeply impressed because the woman in the play knew how to choose her man, someone who was charming, talked easily and freely to people. True, the man was feminine, but he handled his femininity very well. He wished he could be like that. I commented that as usual he was trying to deal with his problem by referring to someone else, as if we had not become sufficiently familiar with his anxiety. I ended up with a clumsy remark that for him to be feminine meant to be homosexual and that was the issue he wanted to avoid with me. As usual Alan readily agreed, but this time he did not proceed to attack and destroy what I had given him, as he was clearly preoccupied with other thoughts. As he got immersed into explaining his views on feminine women, it occurred to me that he was equating femininity with passivity, a common enough notion, and not with homosexuality. Alan received this modest enlightenment with a furious outburst, complaining that I had never given him such an important explanation before. At the time it did not occur to either of us that none of his women friends had been in the least passive, either in their personal lives or sexually. His current partner, however, had caused him considerable alarm because she was forcing him into a more active position by never taking the initiative about sexual matters.

This session seemed to give Alan a sense of freedom about talking of his desire to be a woman and some time later he said: 'I feel I have been a vacuum cleaner . . . that is my idea of having a huge, bottomless vagina. But I want to know, where is everything I have taken in. When I watch my girl friend and you [the analyst], it looks as if you have everything in your minds . . . it grows and grows. . . .' Alan was at long last getting affectively in touch with his envy of the genital woman, mother who had the paternal phallus and all the babies.

There is nothing particularly unusual about this material, which was meant to show how ten years had gone by before the patient felt he could talk about his fantasy of having a vagina. It was not clear to me how long the fantasy had been conscious and I have no recollection of it having appeared in any dream, although the patient dreamt profusely. I should point out that the fantasy occupied a great deal of space in the analysis but for not more than a few sessions. After that it seemed if it was of no particular importance, and for that reason I failed to make any further notes. Several months later, however, I made a note, commenting on how 'There are times when I lose contact with Alan, usually after a *good* interpretation. He seems to become absorbed by his own thoughts, due to his desire to discover how I have reached a certain conclusion. It strikes me as if he is reliving his relationship with women.' It was indeed through the comprehension and the accurate analysis of the projective and introjective identifications, in the transference, that the true nature of the patient's relationships was revealed and understood. From the beginning of the analysis Alan wished to impress me with his associations, dreams, and his behaviour in the session, and in due course with his capacity to give himself some interpretations. He often readily admitted that he wished to be as exciting as possible 'for the good of the work that we are doing', he would say. On such occasions a good response from me was felt by him to be similar to a woman's orgasm. This kind of experience would make him feel well satisfied with his session. In the counter-transference I often felt that the patient wished to force me into a feminine and passive position, making me hope that I would receive something from him that would get us out of a stagnating situation. Whilst he was able to get rid of some of his passivity in the manner I have just described, he was less successful about his femininity. Apart from all this, the patient at times impressed me as behaving as something like an analytic phallus, thus reliving his very special relationship with his mother.

Alan and his mother had, in fact, been very attached to one another, in the first two years of his life, but he had felt rejected when she had a second child. Through the transference, it had been possible to reconstruct that his mother had treated him as her phallus.

This patient falls within my notion of the vagina–man, the male who relies on his heterosexual inclinations, supported by an identification with the woman (the primal object) in order to escape from threats of homosexuality. Alan was a charming man who, according to his own admission when he was a little more honest and spontaneous, could be very popular with both men and women, yet I doubt he would ever succeed in being really friendly with a man. His need to equate femininity with passivity was absolutely essential as part of a defensive manoeuvre against homosexuality. This defence was also very effective in containing his castration anxiety, which was little in evidence in his analysis. I believe this was the reason for the conscious appearance of the fantasy of his identification with the partial object (the maternal vagina), at a time when he felt very exposed within the transference and his life situations. I have already alluded to and have tried to show in this brief account of the analysis of this patient, how an excessive preoccupation with homosexuality and the pressure to interpret it within the transference, can lead us astray. In the case of my patient, I was quite certain that his psychopathology was not typical of a homosexual. I shall add that there was nothing whatever that had occurred to him during the first years of his life, to make me even remotely consider the possibility that I was dealing with a person who was close to the pathology of transsexualism.

(2) John was a highly intelligent young man, an intellectual with a remarkable capacity for absorbing knowledge. He was curious and inquisitive about things and people and was most sensitive to changes and sounds. In his childhood he had undergone abdominal surgery and it seemed fair to assume that this had mobilized severe castration fears. Yet his sexual development had, in general, been normal and since adolescence he had enjoyed a very active sexual life. His home background was regarded as having been good, but from the beginning of the analysis it was clear that he had been the object of much ambivalent attention on the part of his mother.

Questioning thoughts about his heterosexuality had appeared early in the analysis. The following sessions are meant to show how the patient had been fighting a defensive battle against castration fears and threats from a powerful mother, from whom he had difficulty in separating. The unknown quantity of a gentle but firm father added to his problems.

Session 1: The patient dreams of being with a woman who has the face of a girl (*sic*) with lots of freckles. She was delightful and acted very sexually, rubbing her body against his. He could feel her wetness. He associated the woman in the dream with a girl with whom he had had a similar experience. Recalling that the only flaw in his sexual development was a complete absence of nocturnal pollutions, I began an interpretation on these lines, but the patient interrupted me, saying: 'You are curious about that, aren't you? All that is in your mind, not mine.' I said he was quite satisfied that it should be the woman who was wet and not himself, and it seemed as if he wished me to go on being as confused as he was about it.

Session 2: Next day John expressed disappointment that I had failed to show my appreciation for his self-control, to the point of stopping himself from having an orgasm. He claimed he could do the same with all his partners, waiting for a signal from them.

Session 3: A few days later, after being silent for a while, John said, 'I had a dream once, when I was in therapy. I had a vagina and I was giving birth to a baby. The baby spoke with a very cultured accent and started telling me some riddles that I could not solve.' In his associations, the patient remembered that he had the dream at a time when he was very involved with a male friend at university. They probably were very much in love with each other and he could not understand why they had not had an affair. As he hesitated, I took the opportunity of drawing his attention to the fact that at the time he seemed to have a fantasy of being a woman and having a baby. Perhaps he could not easily think of having sex with a man. John responded: 'Funny you should say that, as I remember standing in front of a mirror at the time, thinking, "Look at that body, I could make love to it."' He suddenly felt embarrassed and fell silent. I interpreted that it was not clear to me whether the image in the dream wished to make love to him, or the other way around, not that it mattered much but I also thought he felt there was something of that nature developing between us.

I should note here that the incident reported in this session is the only occasion when the patient had felt close to becoming involved in a homosexual act.

Session 4: Next day the patient started by praising the analysis because he felt free to be what he wanted on the couch. 'If I want to be a woman, so be it, it does not matter', he said. A dream of the previous night came to his mind. He was in a garden. In a corner there was a birds' bath with lots of penises in it. He tells himself he does not want them.

Session 5: The session began with the report of a dream which the patient had shortly after hearing a radio broadcast about a British ship being turned away from a port because it was carrying nuclear weapons. 'I was on a beach', he said, 'and there was a pretty pussy cat, jumping about. It was loaded with nuclear bombs or a microchip. It could have gone off any moment. There was a most beautiful, small object that could be made to fly; it was made of silver. Later, it was put inside a phantom jet.' He associated the silver object with a nickname his mother had for him. 'Pretty phallic, don't you think?' He now reminded me that in the past we had discovered how a cat stood for his femininity which got out of control now and again. He then started laughing, saying: 'I had not thought of it until now but can't you see that the phantom jet is my phantom vagina, with that small, beautiful silver thing shooting out of it . . .'

The sessions reported were important for several reasons. They provided some direct evidence that the patient's mother had treated him as her phallus in his early life (see the association to the small object in session 5). In the counter-transference I had often felt that some of his heterosexual exploits were intended to fill me with admiration and vicarious satisfaction. The father was constantly being kept out of the picture, but he seemed to return now and again under the guise of the phallus hidden in mother's body. The threat from the paternal phallus and all the anxieties related to it are met with a revival of an identification with the whole or the part object (the vagina).

279

The patient's attitude was summed up some months later when, quite spontaneously, he said that the only way he found really safe and satisfactory to deal with powerful masculine women, was to 'feel like a woman, or better still, to become like a woman'. Nothing else would do with them, or indeed with the analyst, who would admirably fit into the image of a combined male and female figure. Hence his need to impress me with his pleasure in being a woman on the couch, if he so wished (see end of session 4).

Several months later, I had the opportunity of showing to the patient that he wished me to know that he was still seeking phallic women as a good match for his fantasy vagina. The patient replied, pointing out that he could not follow what I was saying. Had I confused him with someone else, he asked. After a silence, he began vaguely to remember mentioning such a fantasy *ages ago*, but he still could not remember what made me say that so firmly. I then found it necesssary to remind him of his dream about the phantom jet, etc., and this was followed by immediate recognition, making it unnecessary for me to give further details.

It would seem, therefore, that the fantasy I am describing in this paper is liable to be suppressed or disavowed, or even re-repressed, but that it can reappear into consciousness equally suddenly.

(3) Francis was a middle-aged man who had spent the last twenty years of his life chasing a great many women, very successfully. On entering analysis his problem was one of vacillation, in so far as he never had less than a masculine and feminine woman to choose a partner from. This had enabled him to remain a bachelor, indulging his sado-masochistic tendencies at the same time. In the analysis he was soon to discover that his psychic femininity was not only his secret, but also a stumbling block to his capacity to relate to men and women. His unhappy home life as a child was still haunting him. His father, who had publicly admitted to having been a homosexual until his marriage, treated his mother abominably. Francis was convinced that his father expected him, and indeed wanted him, to be a homosexual, but he hated the idea. Throughout his adolescence he was troubled by his attraction for boys of his own age and still experienced embarrassing feelings with some men. It was not long before a strong resistance developed in the analysis, easily traced to a florid homosexual transference. Nevertheless, this was helpful in recapturing some early screen memories. For instance, as a child of three, the patient often played a game which consisted of putting father's penis to his ear pretending it was a telephone. He also remembered how rubbing his back against that of his mother would be 'extraordinarily soothing', especially if he had been frightened (no detail of the source

of the fear was given). This is the history that is often given by practising homosexuals, but Francis was able to avoid this outcome by allowing free rein to his fantasy of being a man, besides acting it out in his relationships with his partners, through projective and introjective identification. In the transference the soothing interpretations were highly sexualized experiences when the analyst's voice would reach him through his ear (which he often *equated* with the female genital), whereas the more unpleasant interpretations were experienced as unwelcome anal attacks.

(4)   This clinical illustration will demonstrate how the vagina–man can at times reach the very extreme limit of heterosexuality, bringing him dangerously close to homosexuality. In these instances, the desire to be a woman is not associated with a fantasy of having a vagina, but is more directly experienced as a conscious, passive desire for penetration by another man. It is perhaps the threat of castration anxiety coming from members of both sexes that leads them away from fulfilling the desire.

Oscar had become impotent with his wife and other women, following a surgical operation on the genital–urinary system. This had occurred during a long analysis which had been stagnating for some time, owing to the patient's sexualization of the relationship with the analyst, which was experienced as reciprocal sodomization. He frequently achieved orgasm without an erection, simply by stimulating his anus. He would succeed in having an erection if his wife inserted a finger in his anus, but still could not achieve penetration. He regarded his wife, a career-orientated woman, as being 'absolutely phallic', not at all interested in having children, which did not displease him. Oscar was a charming, middle-aged man. He was brilliant, sensitive, and professionally successful, but plagued by guilt which prevented him from enjoying his achievements. He read voraciously and absorbed all in his environment with his mind and eyes that missed little. He had managed to keep his masculine aggressiveness under control by exploiting his femininity to the point of making himself utterly passive and dominated by large numbers of people. His early object relations were disastrous. The father was an effeminate, ineffectual man, intellectually brilliant and highly respected within his own professional circle. He represented the maternal side of the parental couple, whilst mother was the decision-maker and the active partner. Oscar was deeply confused, as he always had been from the age of five when an older boy had handled his penis, to show him what sex was like. In late adolescence he got involved in some work with a homosexual and he recalls how fascinated he was by the stories this man recounted of his sexual encounters with large numbers of men. The operation had left him a feeling of having had a bad pregnancy, and as he said this, he would feel his abdomen. The insertion of a catheter was just what he had imagined it would be like to be penetrated anally.

I have described in some detail this man's desires and fears about homosexuality, as it seemed in direct contrast with his earlier life which had been one of remarkably active heterosexual pursuits. As he was only seen in consultation, it was not possible to have a clear picture of his early sexual development, although he insisted that in spite of his sexual confusion, he had never experienced any particular difficulties, certainly nothing like what had happened to him since the operation had deeply affected him.

Discussion

The men described in the clinical illustrations share a sufficient number of qualities and characteristics to allow me to put forward the hypothesis of a vagina-man who is, to some extent, to be considered the counterpart of the classical concept of the phallic woman. It is well known that the latter is mainly a pre-Oedipal fantasy, that the woman (mother) is endowed with a phallus (external or internal). In later life, it is met in men who feel masochistic and submissive towards women. There is, however, also the woman who considers herself, or is considered by others, to be endowed with phallic attributes, consciously or unconsciously. In my view an analogous situation occurs in those men who consider themselves to be endowed with very strong feminine attributes, a belief which can at times be shared by others. But that is where the analogy with the phallic woman ends, in so far as in this latter case we are dealing with a much more primitive kind of fantasy.

The vagina-man is basically narcissistic, intelligent, charming and friendly. He is easily affected by contacts with people, when he becomes engulfing or engulfed. Some of his character traits could be regarded as oral: he reads voraciously; he looks at things with unfailing avidity; he insatiably seeks the company of others especially that of women, in or outside a sexual context. He is feminine, but his femininity is almost entirely psychic; yet he is vulnerable in so far as he fears it is noticeable to others. Only occasionally do women remark on his femininity. The vagina-man is attentive to women and as a result of it, his sexual performance is in general better than average, but his own pleasure is somewhat diminished by the envy of what the partner is experiencing, coupled with a desire to know exactly what that experience is.

His partner is usually a masculine woman, who has a distinct preference for the more feminine male. It is interesting that both John and Francis had championed the cause of feminism to the delight of their lady friends.

An outstanding feature of the personality of the vagina-man is his passivity. This is in no way a problem in relation to the more phallic type of woman because of the opportunity to be feminine without having to compete whilst offering himself as the presumably desired phallus. On the other hand, the passivity is an unwelcome character trait when relating to men, especially those in authority. The anxiety is mainly one of being controlled rather than of homosexual submission. At one time Alan was less afraid of ending up as a homosexual than of being controlled by men in his professional life; on the whole, he would always feel reassured by his heterosexuality.

As I have already indicated throughout this paper, I believe that projective and introjective identifications play a dominant role in negotiating all that is needed in establishing and maintaining the counter-phobic measures so necessary to the vagina-man's survivial. In some instances it will be the control or anxiety which is defended against as it implies a disintegration and loss of identity. On the other hand many other cases will show the main source of anxiety to be the inability to give up the primal object. I should stress that the analysis of men with this symptomatology, without exception, reveals the presence of at times severe narcissistic disturbance. They cannot, however, be regarded as suffering from narcissistic personality disorders, at least as I understand Kohut's definition of this nosological category. Neither do they come close to Joyce McDougall's description of 'some narcissistic perturbation, which results from perpetual oscillation between the two poles of libidinal investment, the constant swing from narcissistic libido to object libido'. The patients described by this writer have a 'sexuality which is secretive and obscure, or marked by indifference' (McDougall 1982: 381).

The reader could well be wondering whether the individuals I have described should be regarded as bisexual. The fact that all human beings have a number of psychic characteristics belonging to both sexes continues to receive attention from psychoanalysts and the general public. More often than not this generalization leads to preconceived ideas about the social roles of males and females, thus tending to confuse the issue. Any behaviour which is passive, intuitive, submissive or masochistic is feminine, whilst active, sadistic, intellectual and penetrative behaviour is typical of masculine attributes. These attributes, however, also vary from one society to another. In any case, the concept of bisexuality is something that Freud may well have come to regret after he introduced it at the instigation of his friend Fliess, as he never seems to be quite at home with it. This could have been due to the incomplete state of knowledge of embryology, biology and physiology at the time he was writing the *Three Essays*. In a footnote to the differentiation between men and women, he states 'in human beings pure masculinity or femininity is not to be found either in a psychological or a biological sense' (Freud 1905a: p. 220). But in 1930 he writes:

> The theory of bisexuality is still surrounded by many obscurities and we cannot but feel it is as a serious impediment in psychoanalysis that it has not yet found any link with the theory of the instinct. However this may be, if we assume it as a fact that each individual seeks to satisfy both male and female wishes in his sexual life, we are prepared for the possibility that those [two sets of] demands are not fulfilled by the same object.
>
> (Freud 1930: 106)

The notion of the vagina-man shows that some individuals are capable of satisfying their needs in one object, and in some ways it lends support to the somewhat unsatisfactory concept of bisexuality which, given its prevalence in psychoanalytic thinking, would seem to be almost indispensable.

In my view, our understanding of bisexuality can be improved by the adoption of a concept which covers a constellation of symptoms, behaviour patterns and personality traits to be found in men who manage to exist at the limits of heterosexuality. My conclusions are based on observations of a very large number of individuals I have met in psychoanalysis and psychotherapy during the past thirty years that could not be included as clinical illustrations. The fantasy of having a vagina is not wholly necessary to the hypothesis and in any case, even if it is part of their psychic life, it may never come into consciousness. I am in no way advocating the neglect of analysing latent homosexuality or homosexual impulses as they may appear in the transference relationship. I nevertheless hope that the acceptance of this concept could lead us to review some of our stereotyped ideas about homosexuality, or of many cases of promiscuity. Its acceptance also means that we do not need to take a romantic view of Don Juan as someone who was hoping to find the ideal woman (the primal object), to the last; neither do we need to accuse him of being a latent homosexual. Perhaps Don Juan is nothing more than a man who has found a way of avoiding the outbreak of some primitive anxiety which threatens to destroy him, by turning to the pursuit of a chimera.

Note

This paper was first published in 1984 in the *Journal of Analytic Psychotherapy and Psychopathology* 2: 115–29.

References

Freud, S. (1905a) *Three Essays on the Theory of Sexuality, Standard Edition of the Complete Psychological Works of Sigmund Freud* (SE), London: Hogarth Press (1950–74), SE 7.

—— (1930) *Civilization and its Discontents*, SE 21.

McDougall, J. (1982) 'The narcissistic economy and its relation to primitive sexuality', *Contemporary Psychoanalysis*, 18: 373–96.

Bibliography

Abelin, E.L. (1971) 'The role of the father in the separation–individuation process', in J. McDevitt and C. Settlage (eds), *Separation-Individuation: Essays in Honor of Margaret S. Mahler*, New York: International Universities Press, pp. 229–52.

—— (1975) 'Some further observations and comments on the earliest role of the father', *International Journal of Psycho-Analysis*, 56: 293–302.

Abraham, K. (1920) 'Manifestations of the female castration complex', *International Journal of Psycho-Analysis*, 3: 1–29.

—— (1922) 'Manifestations of the female castration complex', in *Selected Papers on Psycho-Analysis*, London: Hogarth (1927).

Aisenstein, M. (1984) 'Notes cliniques sur une identification à la petite fille', *Les Cahiers du Centre de Psychanalyse et de Psychothérapie*, 8.

Alexander, F. (1922) 'The castration complex in the formation of character', *International Journal of Psycho-Analysis*, 4 (1923): 11–42.

Andreas-Salomé, L. (1972) *Sigmund Freud and Lou Andreas-Salomé: Letters*, London: Hogarth Press.

Arden, M. (1987) 'A concept of femininity: Sylvia Payne's 1935 paper reassessed', *International Journal of Psycho-Analysis*, 14, part 2.

Baker, H.J. and Stoller, R.J. (1968) 'Can a biological force contribute to gender identity?' *American Journal of Psychiatry* 124 (12): 1653–8.

Balint, E. (1973) 'Technical problems found in the analysis of women by a woman analyst: a contribution to the question "What does a woman want?"' *International Journal of Psycho-Analysis*, 54: 195–201.

Barglow P. and Schaefer, M. (1976) 'A new female psychology?' *Journal of the American Psychoanalytic Association*, 24 (5): 305–50.

Barnett, M. (1968) '"I can't" versus "he won't"; further considerations of the psychical consequences of the anatomic and physiological difference

286

between the sexes. *Journal of the American Psychoanalytic Association*, 16: 588–600.

Barnett, M.C. (1966) 'Vaginal awareness in the infancy and childhood of girls', *Journal of the American Psychoanalytic Association*, 14: 129–42.

Bassin, D. (1982) 'Woman's images of inner space', *International Review of Psycho-Analysis*, 9, part 2: 191–205.

Begoin-Guignard, F. (1987) 'A l'aube du maternel et du feminin', *Revue Française de Psychanalyse*, 6: 1491–1503.

Benedek, T. (1956) 'Psychobiological aspects of mothering', *American Journal of Orthopsychiatry*, 26: 272.

—— (1960) 'The organisation of the reproductive drive', *International Journal of Psycho-Analysis*, 51 (1): 1–15.

—— (1968) 'Discussion of Sherfey's paper on female sexuality', *Journal of the American Psychoanalytic Association*, 16: 424–48.

Benvenuto, B. and Kennedy, R. (1986) *The Work of Jacques Lacan: An Introduction*, London: Free Association Books.

Bergler, E. (1969) 'Differential diagnosis between spurious homosexuality and perversion homosexuality', in *Selected Papers 1933-61*, pp. 614–23, New York: Grune & Stratton.

Bernstein, D. (1990) 'Female genital anxieties, conflicts and typical mastery modes', *International Journal of Psycho-Analysis*, 71, part 1: 151–67.

Bernstein, I. (1983) 'Masochistic pathology and feminine development', *Journal of the American Psychoanalytic Association*, 31 (2): 467–87.

Bettelheim, B. (1955a) *Truants from Life: the Rehabilitation of Emotionally Disturbed Children*, New York: The Free Press.

—— (1955b) *Symbolic Wounds: Puberty Rites and the Envious Male*, London: Thames & Hudson.

Bibring, G. (1959) 'Some considerations of the psychological processes in pregnancy', *Psychoanalytic Study of the Child*, 14: 113–21.

Bigras, E. (1983) 'Le refus de n'être qu'un: une étude sur les origines de la séxualité', *Topique: Revue Freudienne*, 13 (32): 61–78.

Blanck, G. (1984) 'The complete Oedipus complex', *International Journal of Psycho-Analysis*, 65: 331–41.

Blanck de Cereijido, F. (1983) 'A study on feminine sexuality', *International Journal of Psycho-Analysis*, 64: 93–105.

Blos, P. (1984) 'Son and father: before and beyond the Oedipus complex', *Journal of the American Psychoanalytic Association*, 32: 301–24.

Blum, H.P. (1976) 'Masochism, the ego ideal, and the psychology of women', *Journal of the American Psychoanalytic Association*, 24 (5): 157–93.

Boehm, F. (1930) 'The femininity complex in men', *International Journal of Psycho-Analysis*, 11.

Bonaparte, M. (1935) 'Passivity, masochism and femininity', *International Journal of Psycho-Analysis*, 16 (3): 325–33.

——— (1953) *Female Sexuality*, New York: International Universities Press.

Braidotti, R. (1989) 'The politics of ontological difference', in Teresa Brennan (ed.), *Between Feminism and Psychoanalysis*, London: Routledge.

Braunschweig, D. and Fain, M. (1971) *Eros et Anteros*, Paris: Payot.

Breen, D. (1975) *The Birth of a First Child*, London: Tavistock Publications.

——— (1988) 'Another look at female homosexuality', unpublished, Oslo.

——— (1989a) *Talking with Mothers*, London: Free Associations.

——— (1989b) 'Working with an anorexic patient', *International Journal of Psycho-Analysis*, 70: 29–40.

Brenman Pick, I. (1985) 'Male sexuality: a clinical study of forces that impede development', *International Journal of Psycho-Analysis*, 13: 415.

Brierley, M. (1932) 'Some problems of integration in women', *International Journal of Psycho-Analysis*, 13: 446.

——— (1936) 'Specific determinants in feminine development', *International Journal of Psycho-Analysis*, 17: 163–80.

Britton, R. (1989) 'The missing link: parental sexuality in the Oedipus complex', in (J. Steiner (ed.)), *The Oedipus Complex Today*, London: Karnac.

Burgner, M. and Edgcumbe, R. (1975) 'The phallic–narcissistic phase', *Psychoanalytic Study of the Child*, 30: 161–80.

Calogeras, R.C. and Schupper, F.X. (1972) 'Origins and early formulations of the Oedipus complex', *Journal of the American Psychoanalytic Association*, 20: 751–5.

Castoriadis-Aulagnier, P. (1967) 'Remarques sur la féminité et ses avatars', in *Le Désir et la Perversion*, Paris: Editions du Seuil, pp. 53–90.

Chasseguet-Smirgel, J. (1964) *Female Sexuality*, London: Virago (1981).

——— (1964) 'Feminine guilt and the Oedipus complex', in *Female Sexuality*, London: Virago (1981).

——— (1976) 'Freud and female sexuality', *International Journal of Psycho-Analysis*, 57: 275–87.

——— (1981) *Female Sexuality*, London: Virago.

Chehrazi, S. (1986) 'Female psychology: a review', *Journal of the American Psychoanalytic Association*, 34: 141–62.

Chodorow, N. (1978) *The Reproduction of Mothering: Psychoanalysis and the Sociology of Gender*, Berkeley: University of California Press.

——— (1989) *Feminism and Psychoanalytic Theory*, Cambridge: Polity Press.

Cixous, H. (1975) '"Sorties" and "The laugh of the Medusa"' in E. Marks and I. de Courtivon (eds), *New French Feminisms*, Sussex: Harvester Press (1981).

Cosnier, J. (1987) *Destins de la Féminité*, Paris: Presses Universitaires de France.

Cramer, B. (1979) 'Sur quelques Présupposés de l'observation directe de l'enfant', *Nouvelle Revue de Psychanalyse*, 19.

David, C. (1964) 'A masculine mythology of femininity', in J. Chasseguet-Smirgel (ed.) *Female Sexuality*, London: Virago (1981).

——— (1973) 'Les belles différences', *Nouvelle Revue de Psychanalyse*, 7: 231–50.

——— (1975) 'La Bisexualité psychique: éléments d'une réévaluation', *Revue Française de Psychanalyse*, 39 (5/6): 713–856.

Dejours, C. (1986) *Le Corps entre biologie et psychanalyse*, Paris: Payot.

Delaisi de Parseval, G. (1985) *Les Sexes de l'homme*, Paris: Editions du Seuil.

Denis, P. (1982) 'Homosexualité primaire: base de contradiction', *Revue Française de Psychanalyse*, 46(1).

Deutsch, H. (1946) *The Psychology of Women: Psychoanalytic Interpretation*: vol. 1, *Girlhood*; vol. 2, *Motherhood*, London: Research Books Ltd.

Diatkine, R. (1979) 'La Psychanalyse de l'enfant', *Nouvelle Revue de Psychanalyse*, 19: 49–64.

Dinnerstein, D. (1976) *The Mermaid and the Minotaur*, New York: Harper & Row.

Dolto, F. (1965) 'La Libido et son destin feminin', in *La Psychanalyse VII*, Paris: Presses Universitaires de France.

Duparc, F. (1986) 'La Peur des sirènes', *Revue Française de Psychanalyse*, 50: 697–725.

Edgcumbe, R., Lundberg, S., Markowitz, R. and Salo, F. (1976) 'Some comments on the concept of the negative Oedipal phase in girls', *The Psychoanalytic Study of the Child*, 31: 35–62.

Edgcumbe, R. and Burgner, M. (1975) 'The phallic narcissistic phase', *The Psychoanalytic Study of the Child*, 30: 161–80.

Enriquez, M. (1974) 'Fantasmes paranoiaques: différences des sexes, homosexualité et loi du père', in *Topique*, 13: 23–58.

Erikson, E. (1964) 'Womanhood and inner space', in *Identity, Youth and Crisis*, New York: Norton (1968), pp. 261–94.

Fast, I. (1979) 'Developments in gender identity: gender differentiation in girls', *International Journal of Psycho-Analysis*, 60: 443–55.

Feldstein, R. and Sussman, H. (1990) *Psychoanalysis and . . .*, London: Routledge.

Ferenczi, S. (1936) 'Male and female: psychoanalytic reflections on the "theory of genitality" and on secondary and tertiary sex differences', *The Psychoanalytic Quarterly*, 5: 249.

Fine, R. (1986) 'Understanding the male psyche', *Current Issues in Psychoanalysis*, 3 (2–4): 1–368.

Fliegel, Z. (1973) 'Feminine psychosexual development in Freudian theory: a historical reconstruction', *The Psychoanalytic Quarterly*, 42: 364–84.

Fliess, W. (1973) 'Masculin et féminin', *Nouvelle Revue de Psychanalyse*, 7: 167–78.

Formanek, R. (1982) 'On the origins of gender identity', in D. Mendell (ed.), *Early Female Development*, London: MIT Press Ltd.

Frejaville, A. (1982) 'De la scène primitive à l'homosexualité primaire et à la paranoia', *Revue Française de Psychanalyse*, 35(1).

—— (1984) 'L'homosexualité primaire', *Les Cahiers du Centre de Psychanalyse et de Psychothérapie*, 8.

Freud, S. (1899) 'Complete letters of Sigmund Freud to Wilhelm Fleiss 1887–1904', *Standard Edition of the Complete Psychological Works of Sigmund Freud*, SE 1.

—— (1900) *The Interpretation of Dreams*, SE 4.

—— (1905) *Three Essays on the Theory of Sexuality*, SE 7.

—— (1910) *Leonardo da Vinci and a memory of his childhood*, SE 11.

—— (1920) 'The psychogenesis of a case of homosexuality in a woman', SE 18.

—— (1923) *The Ego and the Id*, SE 19.

—— (1925) 'Some psychical consequences of the anatomical distinction between the sexes', SE 19.

—— (1930) *Civilization and its Discontents*, SE 21.

—— (1931) 'Female sexuality', SE 21.

—— (1933) *New Introductory Lectures*, SE 22.

Galenson, E. (1976) 'Panel report on the psychology of women', *Journal of the American Psychoanalytic Association*, 24: 141.

Galenson, E. and Roiphe, H. (1976) 'Some suggested revisions concerning early female development', *Journal of the American Psychoanalytic Association*, 24 (5): 29–59.

—— (1980) 'The pre-oedipal development of the boy', *Journal of the American Psychoanalytic Association*, 28: 805–27.

Gallop, J. (1981) 'Phallus/penis: same difference', in Janet Todd (ed.) *Men by Women*, New York: Homes & Meier, pp. 243–51.

—— (1983) 'Quand nos lèvres s'écrivent: Irigaray's body politics', *Romanic Review*, 74: 78–9.

Gantheret, F. (1971) 'Remarques sur la place et le statut du corps en psychanalyse', *Nouvelle Revue de Psychanalyse*, 3: 137–46.

Gardiner, M. (1955) 'Feminine masochism and passivity', *Bulletin of the Philadelphia Association*, 5: 74–9.

Garner, S. N., Kahane, C. and Sprengnether, M. (eds) (1985) *The M(other) Tongue: Essays in Feminist Psychoanalytic Interpretation*, Ithaca, NY, and London: Cornell University Press.

Gibeault, A. (1988) 'Du Féminin et du masculin', *Cahiers du Centre de Psychanalyse et de Psychothérapie*, 16–17: 107–27.

Gillespie, W.H. (1969) 'Concepts of vaginal orgasm', *International Journal of Psycho-Analysis*, 50: 495–7.

Gilligan, C. (1983) *In a Different Voice*, Cambridge, MA: Harvard University Press.

Gitelson, M. (1952) 'Re-evaluation of the role of the Oedipus complex', *International Journal of Psycho-Analysis*, 33: 351–5.

Glasser, M. (1985) '"The weak spot" – some observations on male sexuality', *International Journal of Psycho-Analysis*, 66: 405–14.

Glenn, J. and Kaplan, H. (1968) 'Types of orgasm in women: a critical review and redefinition', *Journal of the American Psychoanalytic Association*, 16: 549–64.

Gray, P. (1967) 'Activity-passivity, a panel report', *Journal of the American Psychoanalytic Association*, 15 (3): 709–28.

Gray, S.H. (1976) 'The Resolution of the Oedipus complex in women', *Journal of the Philadelphia Association for Psychoanalysis*, 3: 103–11.

Green, A. (1973) 'Le genre neutre', *Nouvelle Revue de Psychanalyse*, 7: 251–62.

—— (1979) 'L'Enfant modèle', *Nouvelle Revue de Psychanalyse*, 19: 27–49.

—— (1986) *On Private Madness*, London: Hogarth Press.

Greenacre, P. (1948) 'Special problems of early female sexual development', *The Psychoanalytic Study of the Child*, 5: 122–38.

—— (1950) 'Special problems of early female sexual development', in *Trauma, Growth and Personality*, New York: International Universities Press (1969), pp. 220–40.

—— (1953a) *Affective Disorders: Psychoanalytic Contributions to their Study*, New York: International Universities Press.

—— (1953b) *Trauma, Growth and Personality*, London: Hogarth Press.

—— (1953c) 'Certain relationships between fetishism and faulty development of the body image', *The Psychoanalytic Study of the Child*, 8: 79–98.

—— (1953d) 'Psychoanalysis and the cycles of life', *Bulletin of the New York Academy of Medicine*, 29 (10): 796–810.

—— (1953e) 'Penis awe and its relation to penis envy', in *Drives, Affects, Behaviour*, L.F. Lowenstein (ed.)

—— (1958) 'Early physical determinants in the development of the sense of identity', in *Emotional Growth*, New York: International Universities Press (1971), pp. 113–27.

Greenson, R.R. (1954) 'The struggle against identification', *Journal of the American Psychoanalytic Association*, 2: 200–17.

—— (1968) 'Dis-identifying from mother: its special importance for the boy', *International Journal of Psycho-Analysis*, 49: 370–4.

Groddeck, G.W. (1923) *The Book of the It*, New York: Funk & Wagnalls (1950).

Grossman, W. (1976) 'Discussion of Freud and female sexuality', *International Journal of Psycho-Analysis*, 57: 301–5.

Grossman, W.I. and Stewart, W.A. (1976) 'Penis envy: from childhood wish to developmental metaphor', *Journal of the American Psychoanalytic Association*, 24 (5): 193–212.

Grunberger, B. (1964) 'Outline for a study of narcissism in female sexuality, in J. Chasseguet-Smirgel (ed.) *Female Sexuality*, Virago (1981).

Gutton, P. (1983) 'Le Commencement d'une femme dans la fin d'un enfant', *Adolescence*, 1(2): 201–16.

Heimann, P. (1962) 'Notes on the anal stage', *International Journal of Psycho-Analysis*, 43: 406–14.

—— (1968a) 'Discussion of Sherfey's paper on female sexuality', *Journal of the American Psychoanalytic Association*, 16: 406–16.

—— (1968b) 'Female sexuality: introduction', *Journal of the American Psychoanalytic Association*, 16 (3): 565—8.

Herman, I. (1935) 'The use of the term "active" in the definition of masculinity', *International Journal of Psycho-Analysis*, 16: 219.

Hoffen, W. (1950) 'Development of the body ego', *The Psychoanalytic Study of the Child*, 5: 18—24.

Horney, K. (1926) 'The flight from womanhood', in K. Horney (ed.) *Feminine Psychology*, London: Routledge & Kegan Paul (1967).

—— (1932) 'The Dread of Women', in K. Horney (ed.) *Feminine Psychology*, London: Routledge & Kegan Paul (1967).

—— (1967) *Feminine Psychology*, London: Routledge & Kegan Paul.

Irigaray, L. (1985) *The speculum of the Other Woman*, B.C. Till (trans), Ithaca, NY: Cornell University Press.

—— (1988) *Women Analyze Women*, in E.H. Baruch and L.J. Serrano, New York University Press.

—— (1989) 'The gesture in psychoanalysis', in T. Brennan (ed.) *Between Feminism and Psychoanalysis*, London; Routledge.

Jacobson, E. (1950) 'Development of the wish for a child in boys', *The Psychoanalytic Study of the Child*, 5: 139.

Jaffe, D. (1968) 'The masculine envy of woman's procreative function', *Journal of the American Psychoanalytic Association*, 16 (3): 521—48.

Jones, E. (1927) 'The early development of female sexuality', *International Journal of Psycho-Analysis*, 8: 459—72.

—— (1933) 'The phallic phase', *International Journal of Psycho-Analysis*, 14: 1—33.

—— (1935) 'Early female sexuality', *International Journal of Psycho-Analysis*, 16: 263—73.

—— (1938) *Papers on Psycho-Analysis*, (4th edn), London: Baillière, Tindall & Cox.

Keiser, S. (1956) 'Female sexuality', *Journal of the American Psychoanalytic Association*, 4: 563—74.

—— (1968) 'Discussion of Sherfey's paper on female sexuality', *Journal of the American Psychoanalytic Association*, 16: 449—56.

Kestemberg, E. (1984) '"Astrid" ou homosexualité, identité, adolescence: quelques propositions hypothétiques', *Les Cahiers du Centre de Psychanalyse et de Psychothérapie*, 8.

Kestenberg, J.S. (1968) 'Discussion of Sherfey's paper on female sexuality', *Journal of the American Psychoanalytic Association*, 16: 417—23.

—— (1976) 'Regression and reintegration in pregnancy', *Journal of the American Psychoanalytic Association*, 24 (5): 213—51.

—— (1980) 'The three faces of femininity', *Psychoanalytic Review*, 67: 313—36.

Kleeman, J. (1976) 'Freud's views on early female sexuality in the light of direct child observation', *Journal of the American Psychoanalytic Association*, 24: 3—29.

Klein, M. (1932a) 'The effects of the early anxiety-situations on the sexual development of the girl', in M. Klein, *The Psycho-analysis of Children*, London: Hogarth Press (1980).

—— (1932b) 'The effects of the early anxiety-situations on the sexual development of the boy', in M. Klein, *The Psycho-analysis of Children*, London: Hogarth
Press (1980).

—— (1945) 'The Oedipus complex in the light of early anxieties in *Love, Guilt
and Reparation*', London: Hogarth Press (1975).

Kramer, S. (1978) 'Panel report on the role of the father in the pre-Oedipal
years', *Journal of the American Psychoanalytic Association*, 26: 143–62.

Kubie, L. (1974) 'The drive to become both sexes', *The Psychoanalytic Quarterly*,
43: 349–426.

Lacan, J. (1966) *Ecrits*, Paris: Editions du Seuil.

Lampl-de Groot, J. (1927) 'The evolution of the Oedipus complex in women',
in *Man and Mind: Collected Papers*, New York: International Universities Press
(1985), pp. 1–11.

—— (1933) 'Problems of femininity', in *Man and Mind: Collected Papers*, New
York: International Universities Press (1985).

—— (1946) 'The pre-Oedipal phase in the development of the male child',
in *Man and Mind: Collected Papers*, New York: International Universities Press
(1985).

—— (1985) *Collected Papers*, New York: International Universities Press.

Laplanche, J. (1970) *Vie et Mort en Psychanalyse*, Paris: Flammarion.

Laplanche, J. and Pontalis, J.B. (1973) *The Language of Psycho-analysis*, London:
Hogarth Press.

Laufer, M.E. (1982) 'Female masturbation in adolescence and the development
of the relationship to the body', *International Journal of Psycho-Analysis*, 63:
295–302.

—— (1984) 'The Oedipus complex: female development', *The British Psycho-
analytical Society Bulletin*, 6: 11–24.

—— (1986) 'The female Oedipus complex and the relationship to the body',
The Psychoanalytic Study of the Child, 41: 259–77.

Le Guen, A. (1984) 'L'Envie du bébé et la connaissance du vagin', *Adolescence*,
2 (2): 253–60.

Lerner, H.E. (1976) 'Parental mislabelling of female genitals as a determinant
of penis envy and learning inhibitions in women', *Journal of the American
Psychoanalytic Association*, 24 (5): 269–85.

Lichtenstein, H. (1961) 'Identity and sexuality', *Journal of the American Psychoanalytic
Association*, 9.

Limentani, A. (1989) 'To the limits of male heterosexuality: the vagina-man',
in *Between Freud and Klein*, London: Free Association Books.

—— (1989) *Betweeen Freud and Klein*, London: Free Association Books.

—— (1991) 'Neglected fathers in the aetiology and treatment of sexual devia-
tions', *Bulletin of the British Psycho-Analytical Society*, 27 (1).

Loewald, H.W. (1951) 'Ego and Reality', *International Journal of Psycho-Analysis*,
32: 10–18.

—— (1979) 'The waning of the Oedipus complex', *Journal of the American Psychoanalytic Association*, 27: 751–76.

Luquet, P. (1984) 'A propos de l'identification', *Revue Française de Psychanalyse*, 48(2).

Luquet-Parat, C. (1964) 'The change of object', in J. Chasseguet-Smirgel (ed.), *Female Sexuality*, London: Virago (1981).

Mahler, M. (1971) 'A study of the separation-individuation process and its possible application to borderline phenomena in the psychoanalytic situation', *The Psychoanalytic Study of the Child*, 26.

—— (1975) *The Psychological Birth of the Human Infant*, London: Hutchinson.

McDougall, J. (1964) 'Homosexuality in women', in J. Chasseguet-Smirgel (ed.) *Female Sexuality*, London: Virago (1981).

—— (1989) 'The dead father: on early psychic trauma and its relation to disturbance in sexual identity and in creative activity', *International Journal of Psycho-Analysis*, 70.

Mack Brunswick, R. (1940) 'The pre-Oedipal phase of the libido development', *The Psychoanalytic Quarterly*, 9: 293.

Masson, J. (ed. and trans.) (1985) *Complete Letters of Sigmund Freud to W. Fliess, 1887–1904*, Cambridge, MA: Belknap Press, p. 364.

Masters, W. and Johnson, V. (1966) *Human Sexual Response*, Boston: Little, Brown.

Meltzer, D. (1973) *Sexual States of Mind*, Scotland: Clunie Trust.

Mendell, D. (1982) *Early Female Development*, Lancaster: MTP Press.

Metcalfe, A. and Humphries, M. (eds) (1985) *The Sexuality of Men*, London: Pluto Press.

Mijolla, A. de (1973) 'Femininity laid bare by the bachelors: Freud and Jones', *Revue Française de Psychanalyse*, 37 (1–2): 195–224.

Miller, J. (ed.) (1973) *Psychoanalysis and Women: Contributions to New Theory and Therapy*, New York: Brunner/Mazel.

Miller, J.B. (1976) *Towards a New Psychology of Women*, Boston: Beacon Press.

Mischel, W. (1966) 'A social-learning view of sex differences in behaviour', E. Maccoby (ed.), *The Development of Sex Differences*, Stanford, CA: Stanford University Press, pp. 57–81.

Mitchell, J. (1974) *Psychoanalysis and Feminism*, London: Allen Lane.

Mitchell, J. and Rose, J. (1982) *Feminine Sexuality*, London: Macmillan Press.

Money, J., Hampson, J.G. and Hampson, J.L. (1955) 'An examination of some basic sexual concepts: the evidence of human hermaphroditism', *Bulletin of Johns Hopkins Hospital*, 97: 301–99.

Montgrain, N. (1983) 'On the vicissitudes of female sexuality: the difficult path from "anatomical destiny" to psychic representation', *International Journal of Psycho-Analysis*, 64 (2): 169–86.

Montrelay, M. (1970) *Recherches sur la Féminité*, Critique translated in P. Adams and E. Cowie (eds), *The Woman in Question M/F*, Boston: MIT Press (1990).

Moore, B. (1968) 'Physiological studies of female orgasm', *Journal of the American Psychoanalytic Association*, 16: 569–87.

—— (1976) 'Freud and female sexuality: a current view', *International Journal of Psycho-Analysis*, 57: 287–300.

Morgenthaler, F. (1970) 'Panel on disturbances of male and female identity as met in psychoanalytic practice', *International Journal of Psycho-Analysis*, 51 (2): 251–4.

Muller, J. (1932) 'A contribution to the problem of libidinal development of the genital phase in girls', *International Journal of Psycho-Analysis*, 13: 361–8.

Nagera, H. (1975) *Female Sexuality and the Oedipus Complex*, New York: Aronson.

Needles, W. (1966) 'The defilement complex: a contribution to the psychic consequences of the anatomical distinction between the sexes', *Journal of the American Psychoanalytic Association*, 14 (4): 700–10.

Ogden, T.H. (1987) 'The transitional Oedipal relationship in female development', *International Journal of Psycho-Analysis*, 68: 485–99.

Oliner, M. (1982) 'The anal phase', in D. Mendell (ed.), *Early Female Development*, Scotland: MTP Press.

O'Shaughnessy, E. (1976) 'On the concept of the anal organization of instincts', *Bulletin of the British Psycho-Analytical Society*, 2: 9–15.

Parens, H., Pollock, L., Stern, J. and Kramer, S. (1976) 'On the girl's entry into the Oedipus complex', *Journal of the American Psychoanalytic Association*, 24: 79–109.

Parker, A. (1986) 'Mom', *Oxford Literary Review*, 8: 96–104.

Payne, S.(1936) 'A conception of femininity', *British Journal Medical Psychology*, 15–16: 18–33.

Person, E. (1974) 'Some new observations on the origins of femininity', in J. Strouse (ed.) *Women and Analysis*, New York: Grossman, pp. 250–61.

Person, E.S. (1986) 'Male sexuality and power', *Psychoanalytic Enquiry*, 6 (1): 3–25.

Pfeiffer, E. (ed.) (1972) *Sigmund Freud and Lou Andreas-Salomé Letters*, London: Hogarth Press.

Pines, D. (1982) 'The relevance of early psychic development to pregnancy and abortion', *International Journal of Psycho-Analysis*, 63: 311.

—— (1984) 'Review of "Early female development"', K. Mendell (ed.), *International Journal of Psycho-Analysis*, 65: 234–8.

—— (1989) 'Emotional aspects of infertility and its remedies', *International Journal of Psycho-Analysis*, 71: 561–9.

—— (1990) 'Pregnancy, miscarriage and abortion', *International Journal of Psycho-Analysis*, 71.

—— 'A woman's unconscious use of her body: a psycho-analytical perspective', unpublished.

Pontalis, J-B. (1979) 'La Chambre des enfants', *Nouvelle Revue de Psychanalyse*, 19: 5–13.

Quinodez, J-M. (1984) 'Homosexualité féminine, féminité et transfert', *Revue Française de Psychanalyse*, 48: pp. 751–69.

Rangell, L. (1991) 'Castration', *American Journal of Psychoanalysis*, 39 (1).

Rank, O. (1924) *The Trauma of Birth*, London: Kegan Paul, Trench & Treber (1929).

Rees, K. '"I want to be a daddy": Meanings of masculine identification in girls', *The Psychoanalytic Quarterly*, 56 (3): 497–522.

Rey, J.M. (1974) 'Parcours de Freud', in *De la Bisexualité*, Paris: Edition Galilée.

Riviere, J. (1929) 'Womanliness as masquerade', *International Journal of Psycho-Analysis*, 10.

Roiphe, H. and Galenson, E. (1981) *Infantile origins of Sexual Identity*, New York: International Universities Press.

Ross, J.M. (1975) 'The development of paternal identity: a critical review of the literature on nurturance and generativity in boys and men', *Journal of the American Psychoanalytic Association*, 23: 783–818.

Rustin, M. (1989) in L. Miller *et al.* (eds), *Closely Observed Infants*, London: Duckworth.

Sachs, H. (1929) 'One of the motive factors in the formation of the super-ego in women', *International Journal of Psycho-Analysis*, 10.

Safouan, M. (1976) *La Sexualité féminine dans la doctrine Freudienne*, Paris: Editions du Seuil.

Sarlin, C. (1963) 'Feminine identity', *Journal of the American Psychoanalytic Association*, 11: 790–816.

Sayers, J. (1982) *Biological Politics*, London: Tavistock Publications.

Schafer, R. (1974) 'Problems in Freud's psychology of women', *Journal of the American Psychoanalytic Association*, 22: 459–87.

Segal, H. (1990) Hanna Segal interviewed by Jackie Rose in *Women*, (2).

Sherfey, M.J. (1966) 'The evolution and nature of female sexuality in relation to psychoanalytic theory', *Journal of the American Psychoanalytic Association*, 14: 28–128.

Silverstein, B. (1985) 'Freud's psychology and its organic foundation: sexuality and mind–body interactionism', *Psychoanalytic Review*, 72 (2): 203–28.

Schneider, M. (1988) interviewed in E.H. Baruch and L.J. Serrano (eds) *Women Analyze Women*, New York: New York University Press.

Sophocles, *Oedipus Tyranus*, L. Berkowitz and T.F. Brunner (trans. and eds) (1970). A Norton Critical Edition, New York: Norton & Co.

Starcke, A. (1921) 'The castration complex', *International Journal of Psycho-Analysis*, 11: 179–201.

Stein, C. (1961) 'La castration comme negation de la femininité', *Revue Française de Psychanalyse*, 25: 221–42.

Stoller, R.J. (1965) 'The sense of maleness', *The Psychoanalytic Quarterly*, 34: 207–18.

—— (1972) 'The bedrock of masculinity and femininity', *Archives of General Psychiatry*, 26: 207–12.

—— (1976) 'Primary femininity', *Journal of the American Psychoanalytic Association*, 24 (5): 59–79.

—— (1986a) 'The sense of femaleness', *The Psychoanalytic Quarterly* 37: 42-55.

—— (1986b) *Sex and Gender*, New York: Science House.

Sullivan, S. and Weil-Halpern, F. (1984) 'L'ombre blanche: homosexualité féminine, homosexualité primaire', *Les Cahiers du Centre de Psychanalyse et de Psychothérapie*, 8.

Thompson, C. (1942) 'Cultural pressures in the psychology of women', *Psychiatry*, 5: 331–9.

Ticho, G. (1976) 'Female autonomy and the young adult woman', *Journal of the American Psychoanalytic Association*, 24 (5): 139–56.

Torok, M. (1964) 'The significance of penis envy in women', in J. Chasseguet-Smirgel (ed.), *Female Sexuality*, London: Virago (1981).

Turkle, S. (1978) *Psychoanalytic Politics: Freud's French Revolution*, London: Burnett Basic Books.

Tyson, P. (1982) 'A developmental line of gender identity, gender role and choice of love object', *Journal of the American Psychoanalytic Association*, 30: 61–86.

—— (1986) 'Male gender identity, early developmental roots', in R.M. Friedman and L. Lerner, (eds), *Towards a New Psychology of Men: Psychoanalytic and Social Perspectives*, Hove, E. Sussex: Guildford Press.

—— (1989) 'Infantile sexuality, gender identity, and obstacles to Oedipal progression', *International Journal of Psycho-Analysis*, 37: 1049–68.

Van der Leeuw, P.J. (1958) 'The pre-Oedipal phase of the male', *The Psychoanalytic Study of the Child*, 13: 352–74.

Van Ophuijsen, H.W. (1924) 'Contributions to the masculinity complex in women', *International Journal of Psychoanalysis*, 5: 39–49.

Wilkinson, S.M. (1991) 'Penis envy: libidinal metaphor and experimental metonym', *International Journal of Psycho-Analysis*, 72: 335–46.

Winnicott, D. (1971) *Playing and Reality*, London: Tavistock Publications.

Wittels, F. (1935) 'The psychological content of "masculine" and "feminine"', *International Journal of Psycho-Analysis*, 16 (4): 487.

Wolheim, R. (1975) 'The cabinet of Dr Lacan', *The New York Review* (25 Jan.)

Zanardi, C. (1990) *Essential Papers on the Psychology of Women*, New York: New York University Press.

Name index

Abelin, E.L. 30, 56, 59, 204–5
Aeschylus 119–21
Aisenstein, M. 265–71
Alan (case study) 275–8, 283
Alexander, F. 32
Andreas-Salomé, L. 186
Artaud, A. 145

Bachofen, J.J. 119–20, 122
Balint, E. 9
Barnett, M.C. 102, 191
Bassin, D. 187
Begoin-Guignard, F. 171
Benedek, T. 13, 22, 187
Benedicte (case study) 235–8, 239, 241–55
Benjamin, H. 259
Benvenuto, B. 19
Bergler, E. 35
Bernstein, D. 186, 187–8, 189–209
Bernstein, I. 186
Bettelheim, B. 26, 259
Bibring, G. 22, 62, 187
Bion, W.R. 86, 87, 234
Blanck, G. 45
Blanck de Cereijido, F. 46
Blos, P. 47, 48, 49–65
Blum, H.P. 9, 14, 15
Boehm, F. 26
Bonaparte, M. 6, 7
Braunschweig, D. 23, 37, 102, 103, 121, 130–44, 179n

Breen, D. 22, 187
Brenman Pick, I. 31
Brierley, M. 7, 186
Britton, R. 30, 47, 48, 82–94
Brooks, G. 205
Burgner, M. 9, 46

Candy (case study) 195–6
Chasseguet-Smirgel, J. 9, 10, 15, 30, 67, 102, 105–23, 146–8, 167, 175, 198, 205, 206, 213
Chehrazi, S. 187
Chodorow, N. 8
Clower, V.L. 190
Cosnier, J. 103, 166–78 passim
Coxon, A. 217

David, C. 32, 34, 35, 39n, 177
de Mijolla, A. 19
de Saussure, F. 10, 11
Debby (case study) 197
Denis, P. 35, 47
Deutsch, H. 6, 7, 71, 155, 185, 186
Diatkine, R. 18, 141
Dinnerstein, D. 8
Dolto, F. 22, 153, 186
Dora (case study) 49
Duparc, F. 32, 102, 186
Duras, M. 156

Edgcumbe, R. 9, 46
Ehrhardt, A. 190

Subject index

abandonment anxiety 220
access anxiety 192, 193
activity–passivity polarity 25, 166, 171, 172, 173, 178
adolescence, male 52–65
adult ego ideal 62, 63
'after revision' 19
aggression 217–18
ambisexuality 34, 169
anal ego ideal 134
anal eroticism 141, 186
anal phase 194
anal primacy 31
anal sadism 186
anal sexual intercourse 112
anal-genital confusion 201
anality 133–6, 185, 186
anatomical destiny 3–4, 21, 175, 176
anatomy and female ego-functions 187
annihilatory anxiety 217, 220
anorexia 155
anxiety/anxieties 148; core complex 220; see also castration anxiety; genital anxieties
après coup 19
auto-eroticism 133, 136, 170, 171, 176–7

babies: 'transgression beyond sex' of 139

baby wish 101; see also maternal instinct
biology: and femininity 4–7; and sexuality 37
bisexuality 33–5, 36–7, 105, 169, 172, 231–84; biological 231; Freudian notion of 5, 34, 231–2; psychological 231

castration: feminine 157–8; representation of 149–51
castration anxiety 27, 31, 32, 33, 43, 44, 99, 102, 104n, 149–57, 175, 177, 189, 221, 224, 225
castration complex 2–3, 15, 19–20, 21, 28, 31–3, 71–8, 102, 103, 112, 173
castration threat 138, 141
castration wish 75
clitoral excitation 13, 106, 126–8, 129
clitoral orgasm 12, 128, 181n
clitoral-vaginal transfer theory 12, 126–7
clitoris 17, 114, 140, 141; and pre-Oedipal sexuality 14
concentricity of feminine sexuality 147, 148
conscious representation of castration 149–50
'container and contained' 86
core complex 217–21, 224

301